1600.io SAT® Math

Volume I

A DIFFICULT SUM.

HARRY is pulling his hair, as if that would help him out of the difficulty. The figures won't come right, do what he will, and he has worked at it an hour. Many little boys would give it up; but Harry is persevering, and intends to go over the sum until he finds out his mistake.

My Pretty Present. (New York: Thomas Nelson & Sons, 1789)

SAT® MATH

VOLUME I

Every SAT Math Topic, Patiently Explained

J. Ernest Gotta, Daniel Kirchheimer, and
George Rimakis

First paperback edition February 2021
Manuscript revision 1.17.3

Book design by J. Ernest Gotta, Daniel Kirchheimer, and George Rimakis

ISBN 9798708609786 (*paperback*)

Published by 1600.io Press
www.1600.io

Joe, you made this possible, and your unwavering loyalty and commitment cannot be forgotten. Megan, the only reason I've done anything is for you. John and Paige, I couldn't wish for more fun and intelligent kids. Mom and Dad, you inspire me to be a good person, a good father, and a good teacher. Nettie, Billy, Steffie, Keith, Danny, Jared, Matt, Sean, and Brandon, you shaped the humor needed to survive writing a book this long. Mustafa, Radhika, Mahoney, Timo, Elijah, Carolina, Arun, Lenny, Corbett, Will, McKayla, Sarah, Annesha, Selena, Lana, and Tanay, I'm honored to have worked alongside you. Prof. Goloubeva and Mr. Speidel, you showed me what it was to be a math educator. My former students, you inspired many of the weirdos found in the problems.

J. Ernest

My contributions to this book are dedicated to my amazing parents, who celebrated learning every day and who made me believe that I could do anything; to my beautiful, patient, and indulgent wife Jill and my brilliant son Matthew, who both endured a ceaseless barrage of terrible dad jokes (but I repeat myself) while I worked on this text; and to my extraordinary daughter Danielle, the world's best 3rd-grade teacher, who knew long before I did what a joy it is to help educate young people.

Dan

This project is dedicated to all the students reading this book right now who dare to become smarter. You've made it this far: remember that the pursuit of knowledge, with its ups and downs, is always a worthy adventure. I would also like to dedicate this book to my parents, who have supported me in everything I have ever done; to my sister Katherine, who shared her love of math with me at an early age; and to all of the teachers and professors I have had the good fortune to learn from. Without their support and inspiration, I don't think that this book would have been possible.

George

We could use up two Eternities in learning all that is to be learned about our own world and the thousands of nations that have arisen and flourished and vanished from it. Mathematics alone would occupy me eight million years.

–Mark Twain

Table of Contents

Appendix

Preface

Why did we decide to write an SAT math book? Amazon is groaning under the weight of such works. Does the world really need another? Our answer was an emphatic "yes." We felt that existing books either relied too much on tricks and tactics for trying to game the test, or the topics they taught weren't well-aligned with the current style of SAT, or the instruction was cursory, confusing, and scattershot, and these realizations crystallized our shared determination to wade into this crowded field and craft a contribution based on our collective wisdom.

Though the notion of creating a math book had been bandied about among us for some time, credit for initiating the project goes to Joe Zirkel, founder of Clarion Prep, who pushed the boat away from shore. Using our amazing math skills, we computed that it would take no more than six months to complete, and we only missed that estimate by a factor of four, which is close enough for jazz. Despite (or, perhaps, because of) the intensity and length of this process, the three authors forged an extraordinary working relationship that exceeded our expectations, and though the hours (and days, and months) have been long, the gratification we received along the way has been immense, and we could not be prouder of each other's efforts, contributions, willingness to accept constructive criticism, and good humor along the way. We set out to create the finest SAT math book possible, and we hope the reader finds that we have indeed succeeded.

Finally, a word about us. Collectively, we've helped thousands of students of all abilities, backgrounds, and educational levels prepare for the SAT. We operate under the conceit that we see things that others don't, and with the humility that drives us to believe there are always better ways to teach. This book, in its structure, tone, and approach, is a distillation of everything we've observed, learned, and implemented over the years with great success, and we think it's the best SAT math book ever written.

Acknowledgements

We must offer our profound thanks to the thousands of wonderful students who contributed to this book through their innumerable interactions with us as we helped them educate themselves. This encompasses the legions of people who have entrusted to us a part of their futures whether through our years of private tutoring, as members of 1600.io, as participants in our rich and diverse Discord server, via their posts and comments on Reddit, in the form of participation in our live classes, through their thousands of constructive comments on our explanatory videos, via countless DM conversations, and in their emails. This book is, in many ways, a distillation of everything we've learned from all those interactions, and our gratitude is deep and heartfelt. We couldn't have done it without you.

Introduction

This is not an SAT book.

That is, it's not a traditional "test prep" book that discourages students from actually becoming better-educated but instead touts a "secret method" or an array of "tricks" that are purported to help the student "game the test." We think that's insulting and fundamentally counter to the central reason students take the SAT, which is to further their education by gaining admission to the best possible college, and the reason students want to go to college is to become better-educated still. Education isn't merely an annoying chore; education is the point, the larger goal, and a good SAT score helps students along the path to a great education.

One underlying assumption that appears to be built into many books and test-prep programs, and that pervades the thoughts and discussions among students studying for the test, is that the SAT is like a complicated safe, and if you can just figure out the combination, you can unlock it and ace the test—that even though the SAT purports to assess students' skills, if you know the "secrets," you don't have to actually *have* those skills in order to score well.

This is complete nonsense. It's insulting and demeaning to students, and it serves to unjustifiably undermine their self-image with respect to their intelligence and potential. The reality is that the SAT is an exquisitely well-crafted test, and it does an extremely good job of assessing exactly what it tries to assess. And what it tries to assess is a thoughtfully chosen and appropriately broad set of basic academic skills. Therefore, the best way to have your score indicate that you have mastery of all those skills is *to actually have those skills*. And it sends a terrible message that without tricks and a gaming-the-test approach, you can't get a good score, because it tells you that you can't *really* learn; you have to resort to clever tactics in hopes you can dupe the test into indicating you're smart when you're really not.

We think better of you. We know for a certainty that given the right guidance, you can be a great reader, you can learn all the grammatical and writing structure principles necessary, and, most relevantly for this work, you can really learn the math—all of it. You're not dumb, you're not un-educable, and you're not so desperate that you'll grasp for any cultish trick to try to avoid actually learning what's being tested. We believe in you, and we don't want you to accept the message that all these side-door methods subtly send you—that you're just not smart enough to learn the material, so you have to find some way to fool the test (and colleges) about your abilities. Don't be lured into the "tricks" and "secrets" cult; think more of yourself. You're better than that.

Our philosophy is radically different from that of most test preparation resources. As alluded to earlier, we view the SAT not as a *goal*, but rather as a *tool* that provides colleges with an assessment of students' level of proficiency in three core academic areas. It follows that what students should be focused on isn't getting any particular score on the test, but rather on becoming as well-educated as possible in the areas the SAT assesses. The test will then do its job and reflect that level of achievement as a natural consequence. This, in our view, is by far the best way to approach the test: go right through it rather than attempting to sneak around it. The test is far too good; it can't be tricked into reporting that you're better at math, reading, or writing than you really are, and any plan to "beat the test" is doomed, as well as being a cop-out, a surrender, an acceptance of defeat. If, instead, you acquire the skills assessed by the test, you can free yourself of all the confusing static about strategies and tricks, and you can be confident that if you put in a smart, honest effort, the test will reward you with a fair result.

Lest the reader think that we've conjured up our philosophy merely to be contrarian, we'd like to make it clear that we, too, once believed that it was a winning mindset to view the test as a challenge that could be gamed through a set of strategies, but our long experience has proven that to be a fool's errand. We now know that we were not seeing the deeper truth about the test, and it is absolutely clear to us that the approach we are now preaching, as embodied in this work, is without question the better one.

The Essence of the SAT

Many students have a core misconception about the SAT, due no doubt to their scholastic experiences with tests. It is essential to understand that the SAT in general, and the math section in particular, is not a test of *facts*; it's a test of *processes and principles*. This distinguishes it from many of the exams students take in school: it doesn't demand *memorization of information*; it requires mental muscle memory gained through *performing processes*. It's about *doing* things, not *knowing* things. It's not a history test that demands the recitation of names and dates; it's not an English test that relies on remembering the hidden meanings in an assigned work of literature; it's not a vocabulary test that's susceptible to memorizing word lists; and it's not a math or science formula regurgitation exam. Many students don't realize these essential facts about the test, and their studying proceeds along all sorts of tangents and detours that don't make any sense. In short, you should not feel tormented by the fear of forgetting something when you open the test booklet; just focus on *doing*, and the rest will take care of itself.

The math section of the SAT does have a certain format, and the problems that appear tend to fit into certain general templates, so familiarity with the format and templates is valuable. This is not at all a trick or a secret; the College Board™ itself specifically encourages students to learn their way around the test by taking practice exams and by using Khan Academy for practice. But, importantly, there aren't any very difficult math problems on the SAT (the reading section is another story!). That's right: There are no problems that take ten minutes and dozens of steps to solve, that require some weird math skill you've never been taught (if you use this text, of course), or that demand some special "math smarts" insight that either you have or you don't. Indeed, the problems that seem to be the hardest often turn out to have very simple solutions; don't mistake a failure to recognize how to solve a particular problem for an assessment that the problem is therefore extremely difficult.

We're going to repeat this, because it's so important: *There are no very hard math problems on the SAT*. The difficulty is *intentionally* capped, and the complete set of skills needed to solve *any problem that has ever appeared on an administered SAT* is well-defined by the College Board itself in a public document. So, you might not know how to approach a specific problem; you may be completely baffled by it. You might be flummoxed by several problems, or by nearly *all* the problems, if you're just starting your studying and you've had terrible math teachers. But you must understand that this does not mean that the problems are inherently *difficult*; it just means you don't *yet* know how to solve them. That's all. And you *can* learn how to do them—all of them. We will teach you everything you need to know.

What's in This Text, and Why

The structure and content of this work is unlike that of any other math text or SAT prep book you've ever seen. On the one hand, it's not a collection of "tricks," intended to add a few points here and there while avoiding the matter of actually educating you. On the other, it's not just a general-purpose math textbook, though it covers every one of the topics that are at the core of the American high school mathematics curriculum.

Instead, this text teaches every math skill that has appeared on the SAT, and it is intimately linked to that test. We've been guided by the College Board's official specifications for the math section of the SAT and we've exhaustively analyzed every single released test problem—well over a thousand of them—to ensure that the skills needed to solve them are thoroughly explained herein, and we've crafted over 900 example and practice problems that exercise those skills. That means that students can have the confidence that they are learning *all the skills needed* to solve the problems they're likely to see on future tests.

The size of this work might be intimidating, and that's understandable. However, it is crucial for the reader to know that the reason this text is so hefty is because it is complete, thorough, and provides multi-level instruction throughout. It doesn't just cover some of the topics on the SAT; it covers every single one of them. It has hundreds of example problems so that students aren't just thrown into practice sets after an explanation; these examples are very carefully worked through with detailed comments along the way (and, often, with alternative solutions, too). There are a dozen tests' worth of practice problems, each carefully crafted to maximize their value. Every concept is explained in great detail, complete with illustrative diagrams, summary boxes to highlight essential principles, and a concise but complete topic summary that concludes each chapter. So, the size of this text is a *good* thing, because it means that no corners have been cut and no compromises have been made, but there are multiple levels of summarization available, too, so if you want the shorter version, or are looking for a quick refresher, we've got that covered. Once you dive in, we think you'll realize that the heft of this tome is a consequence of the depth and quality of the instruction we've provided.

As noted, this isn't an SAT strategy guide. More specifically, we don't engage in digressions about test-taking tactics or time management. This text is intended to teach you the skills you need to do the math, so we've focused our attention on clear, in-depth explanations and extensive, high-quality example and practice questions. However, we decided that while having a wealth of examples and practice problems is necessary, it's not enough. Most math problems on the SAT center around one topic—finding the solutions to a quadratic equation, for example—but they necessarily also require the use of several constituent skills. Furthermore, just as math expressions are like molecules assembled from atoms such as numbers and variables (a parallel we draw herein), many SAT math topics are also like molecules; they're composed of elemental skills (the "atoms" of the topic) that are combined to form the higher-level skill. This means that trying to solve complete SAT-style problems before mastering the underlying atomic skills can be frustrating and inefficient.

In response to this realization, we invented the SkillDrill™. SkillDrills are sets of micro-problems that focus on just one atomic skill, such as finding the two numbers that sum to the b coefficient and that multiply to the c coefficient in a quadratic expression, which is an essential atomic skill for the larger skill of factoring (which itself is a component of solving a quadratic). Another such SkillDrill just requires the student to decompose an improper fraction into a mixed number; this is never tested on its own, but it's an atomic skill essential for solving certain exponent problems. By working through these highly-specific drills, students engage in the essential repetitive practice needed to become comfortable with the "atomic toolkit" that serves as the foundation for proficiency with the larger topic—solving quadratics, manipulating exponential expressions, and so on. That this approach is highly effective is not mere speculation: we've tested it extensively, and the results confirm the value of this methodology. As with so much of education, a firm and complete foundation provides the solid support needed for building upon.

Every topic here not only has SAT-style example and practice problems and SkillDrills; we've also provided curated lists at the end of each topic section of *every SAT problem related to that topic that has ever appeared on a released test*, and we've marked the particularly challenging problems we've inducted into the 1600.io Hall of Fame with a special indicator. This provides the student with an additional resource—real test problems—for practicing the skills they just learned.

The linkage between the text and the real tests doesn't only go in one direction. To close the loop, we've provided an appendix that allows a student to look up any math problem from any released SAT and to find the topic or topics in this work that relate to that problem. This means that after a student takes a practice test, they can look up our detailed, patient, thorough, and empathetic guide for acquiring the mathematics techniques needed to solve the questions they struggled with without having to hunt through the text for relevant information.

Driving all of the ideas detailed above is a simple set of principles that we hold and that we kept foremost in our minds as we were crafting this text:

- We want you to understand concepts and techniques no one was ever able to explain to you before
- We want you to realize that math topics you thought were really hard are actually easy
- We want you to truly understand aspects of math that you had blindly accepted on faith

These principles have a common root: the goal of instilling in students the confidence that mastery of a subject produces, because mastery plus confidence equals 800.

A final word about the structure of the text: There is an expectation that students have a foundation in elementary algebra and that they are familiar with the various symbols that are used at the level of high school mathematics, and there are a few questions on each test that probe those elementary skills. In support of that, we start off the instruction with what we came to call "Chapter 0," now named Foundations, and it is a concise collection of the most basic math skills that are necessary for all the more-focused topics that follow. It is *essential* that students feel comfortable with these building-block skills before moving into the topic instruction, so give the Foundations chapter a read-through to be sure you're on solid footing before proceeding further.

How to Use This Text

There are many ways to leverage the instruction in this work. Here are a few of the primary scenarios we anticipate, though we expect that nearly all students will end up using a hybrid approach:

1. **Read and work through the text cover-to-cover:**

   If your math skills are particularly shaky or you never even learned the high school math topics assessed by the SAT, or you just want to be absolutely sure you've covered all the bases, you can simply go through the entire text, reading all the instructional material, doing all the SkillDrills, and solving all the practice problems. Practically speaking, most students will end up skipping or skimming portions of many topics when they realize they are already knowledgable in the subject being discussed, but there are explanations for every aspect of every topic in case you need help.

2. **Use the summaries as a refresher:**

   If you have a reasonably solid foundation but are rusty, you can focus on the condensed topic and subtopic explanations that are broken out in the boxed text and chapter recaps, referring to the full explanations as needed, and then you can work the practice problems to check your skills.

3. **Focus on your weaknesses:**

   Students can identify the major topics in which they are less proficient and then work through just the chapters that cover those areas.

4. **Use the text as an instructional reference:**

   Some students prefer to take practice tests or to use other resources for working problems; they can use the text as a reference tool when they discover a topic or a concept with which they are unfamiliar. This work makes that mode of use easy, because we've thoughtfully provided an appendix that maps every released tests' problems to the location in the text that explains the relevant topics, so when you're confused by a practice problem, you can get right to the explanation of the associated math principles.

5. **Work the problems for practice:**

   If you feel that your concept knowledge is basically sound, but you need more practice, you can use the hundreds of practice problems to solidify your skills. You can concentrate on the topics that need the most work, and any needed instructional support is available right where the practice problems are presented; additionally, individual video explanations are available at our website **1600.io** for every practice problem in this work.

6. **As a sleep aid:**

   See scenario 1.

Beyond the Book

As thorough as it is, this text does not stand alone; it's part of the 1600.io ecosystem of educational resources. We have extensive expertise in video-based standardized test instruction, and we put that experience to use by offering explanatory videos for *every practice problem and SkillDrill* for those who want to supplement their self-studying with a familiar video resource wherein George walks you through solving each problem. Other supporting resources will also be available at our website 1600.io, providing a rich set of tools that support students' efforts to master the math section of the SAT.

Wait, What's a "Wormhole?"

At the start of some of the example problem solutions, you'll see this curious symbol:

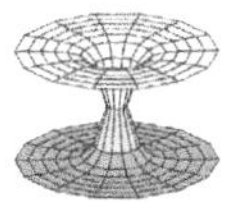

Sprinkled throughout the SAT, hiding in plain sight, are members of a class of math problems that have a non-obvious, accelerated solution that we've dubbed a **wormhole**. A real wormhole is a warp in the fabric of space that brings two distant locations close together; the wormhole allows travel from one such location to the other very quickly, as the normal distance between the points does not have to be traversed. So it is too with wormhole solutions: they let the student go from the question to the answer with just a few easy steps, rather than requiring them to travel through the usual lengthier solving procedures for that general type of problem.

Importantly, **nearly all wormhole problems can also be solved with more generalized methods**. What this means is that wormhole problems are really like several little tests, all packed into one. Though from a scoring standpoint, a right answer is a right answer, no matter how you get there, the solving procedure that takes advantage of a wormhole will proceed much more rapidly (and with a smaller probability of error due to the simpler procedure) than will the longer, more generalized procedure. That rewards the student with more than just the points for the answer; in effect, it grants the student a bit of bonus time that can be used on some other problems, or the time can be used for double-checking answers once the first pass through the section is done. Also, as alluded to earlier, the simpler procedure is less susceptible to error; the more steps there are in a process, the greater the likelihood an error will creep in. Wormhole problems are thus very powerful in sifting the test-takers by ability, because one problem can classify students into those who spot the wormhole, those who don't but who nonetheless solve the problem correctly with a generalized method, and those who fail to solve the problem.

Taking advantage of wormholes is not a test-taking trick. It doesn't attempt to evade the test's purpose in assessing the student's ability to efficiently solve math problems—quite the contrary, in fact: one of the test's many facets is that it allows students who have the aptitude and mental acuity to see things that others might not to demonstrate that ability and to have it pay off in their score.

Because this underappreciated aspect of the test is important, we've got a chapter dedicated to it, where example problems that are inspired by real SAT problems are presented and explained. Don't overlook it; a few precious seconds saved, or errors avoided, could be the difference between a good score and a great one. Also, it (rightly) makes you feel clever, and that builds confidence, which can fuel your efforts throughout the test.

A Few Words of Advice

While this text is not going to delve into test-taking tactics, we do have a few words of advice (and caution) that students should heed.

Calculators: Tools of the Devil

We strongly discourage the use of calculators while learning the math skills assessed by the SAT for anything other than time-consuming arithmetic. We're fond of declaring that calculators are tools of the devil because they produce a reliance on the device that causes math skills to atrophy (if they ever developed at all).

The skillful student will have no difficulty completing the math sections on the test without resorting to the use of a calculator for solving or graphing, and there is hardly a worse feeling than finding out during the test that your calculator won't turn on, and you're so reliant on it that you can't solve some problems without it. Don't be that person.

When studying, if you find yourself tempted to turn to your calculator to do something you don't know how to do—or don't *want* to do—just say no. You'll be far better off.

Plugging-in Is Surrender

There is an alarmingly widespread belief that the best way to solve certain types of problems is to pick some value and substitute it for the variable in the provided expression or equation to see if a unique match with an answer choice is obtained. This is a terrible solving method, because it's nondeterministic (it's not guaranteed to produce the answer) and it's a cop-out—a way of avoiding actually learning and understanding the math needed to simply solve the problem directly. We strongly urge the reader not to resort to this technique. Note, importantly, that we are *not* referring to the practice of testing the provided answer choices to see which one(s) produce a valid equation; in some cases, that is a perfectly appropriate method for solving a multiple-choice math problem. We are instead directing our scorn at the very different procedure whereby the student cooks up some value—0, 1, 2, for example—and plugs it in. Please think better of yourself than to employ this method.

Writing Out Your Work Is Smart; Mental Math Is Dumb

One of the chief score killers in the math section of the SAT is sloppy arithmetic mistakes: dropping a sign, adding instead of subtracting, failure to distribute across all terms in an equation, and so on. One of the leading causes of these errors is students' unhealthy tendency to use mental math to compress solving steps rather than taking the effort to carefully (and legibly) write out their work as they go. Students perceive it as some sort of show of prowess to be able to do math in their heads rather than write it out, and, on the other side, they view it as some sort of failing to rely on written-out steps when doing a math problem that they feel they could probably handle without that process. This is dumb, and you don't want to do dumb things. **The best way to eliminate sloppy mistakes is to write out your work.**

A Note about Student-Produced Responses ("Grid-ins")

Many of the practice problems in this text and on the test require the student to write their answer rather than select it from a set of choices. Keep in mind the constraints on these grid-in answers; they must be enterable into an answer form like this:

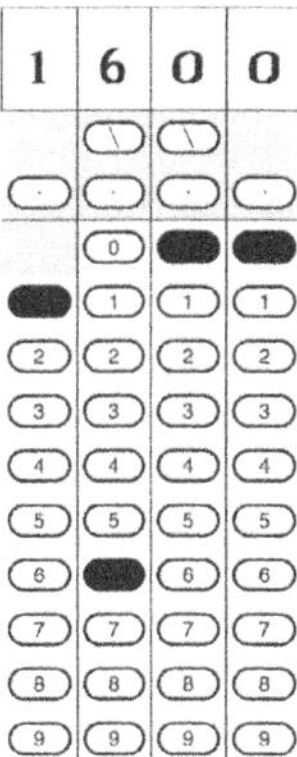

Here are the restrictions that apply:

- You cannot enter a negative number (so if you get a negative answer, you made a mistake!)
- You cannot enter a zero in the first column (that is, as the first digit in a four-character answer); you are *never* required to enter a leading zero, so this should never cause any confusion
- You have a maximum of four character positions including a decimal point or a fraction slash
- Unless the problem specifies otherwise, you can either round or truncate decimal answers that don't fit into the grid, so $\frac{5}{3}$ could be entered as 5/3, 1.66, or 1.67, but you must use all four character positions for such values
- You cannot enter a mixed number such as $2\frac{1}{2}$; you must either enter the decimal equivalent (2.5) or an improper fraction (5/2)
- It doesn't matter in which position you start entering your answer as long as you enter the complete value (unless it's a value with more decimal digits than would fit into the four positions, in which case you must start with the first position)

Help Us Help You

We've made this work as good as we can make it, but all the same, we know it can be made better. If you have ideas, suggestions, criticisms, or if you spot errors, we very much would like to hear what you have to say. Email us at **MathBook@1600.io**, use the contact form at our website 1600.io, chat with us through our site, or DM us in our Discord server or through Reddit. This text could not have been written without your input, and that feedback is also essential to improving it. To ensure that all readers get the benefit of any corrections as soon as they are recognized, we will maintain an Errata page on our website 1600.io to log these changes.

Get Started!

You're holding this book in your hands. Take the next step forward: get a sharp pencil and some scrap paper, get focused, and turn the page. You're about to get smarter.

Foundations 0

This chapter covers the foundational arithmetic and algebraic knowledge that is required in order to get the most out of this book. The instruction in this text progresses in a methodical manner, working its way from writing simple expressions all the way through most of Algebra II and covering the necessary topics in statistics and geometry. However, you need to be proficient with skills such as manipulating fractions, simple factoring, and isolating variables in order to get started. Some skills in this chapter will be covered in more depth in later chapters when necessary, but others are going to be assumed at all points going forward. Even if you consider yourself reasonably well-grounded in basic techniques, look over this chapter to be sure you're well-equipped to move ahead.

0.1 Definitions and Fundamentals

First, we need to differentiate between **expressions** and **equations**. **Expressions**, strictly speaking, consist only of numerical and variable terms being added, subtracted, multiplied, and so on. For example, $40 + 2x$ is an expression. When we set this value equal to another expression, we can make an equation. **Equations** consist of two expressions that are set equal to each other using an equals sign (=). For example, $40 + 2x = 80 - 4x$ is an equation.

The expressions on both sides of the equals sign are exactly equivalent to each other (that's what equals means), even if they don't *look* exactly the same. Therefore, the expressions can switch sides of the equals sign; the equation $40 + 2x = 80 - 4x$ could also be written as $80 - 4x = 40 + 2x$.

One of the most essential foundational principles of mathematics is that **because the expressions on both sides of an equation are equivalent, we can perform the same operation on both of those expressions and the resulting equation will still be valid**. This can be analogized to a scale that has an assortment of weights on each side that produce a perfect balance; if we then add the same amount of weight to each side of the scale, the balance will be maintained. It is *absolutely crucial* that you understand and accept this principle so that you to have confidence in all that follows.

Obviously, you need to be familiar with how to add, subtract, multiply, and divide numbers (positive and negative) in order to solve any of the problems on this test.

A few basic arithmetic terms that will be used frequently herein:

Integers are all of the **natural numbers** (positive counting numbers), the negatives of these numbers, and zero, e.g. $\ldots -4, -3, -2, -1, 0, 1, 2, 3, 4, \ldots$.

Non-negative numbers are all positive numbers (not just integers) and 0.

Non-positive numbers are all negative numbers (not just integers) and 0.

The result of an addition is called the **sum**. The result of a subtraction is called the **difference**. The result of a multiplication is called the **product**. The result of a division is called the **quotient**.

Important Symbols

The following table shows some of the symbols you will encounter on this test and in this text, some of which are discussed in greater detail in chapters in the book when needed. Consider this a quick primer on what to expect.

Name	Symbol	Usage
Equals	$=$	This symbol is used in equations to show that two values or expressions are equal. The equation $a = b$ is read as "a equals b" or "a is equal to b"
Not Equals	$\neq$	This symbol is used to show that two values or expressions are NOT equal. For example, $3 \neq 5$ because 3 is not equal to 5.
Approximately Equals	$\approx$	Used to show that a value is approximate. For example, $a \approx 3.14$ means that a is approximately—but not exactly—3.14.
Infinity	∞	An indefinitely large number.
Less Than	$<$	The value on the left (on the smaller side of the symbol) is less than the value on the right (on the larger side of the symbol). Mathematical statements involving less-than signs (and the next three symbols as well) are called **inequalities**. The inequality $x < 5$ means that x can be any value from $-\infty$ up to, but **not** including, 5.
Less Than Or Equal To	$\leq$	The value on the left is less than or equal to (no more than) the value on the right. For example, $x \leq 5$, means that x can be any value from $-\infty$ up to 5, including 5 itself.
Greater Than	$>$	The value on the left (on the larger side of the symbol) is greater than the value on the right (on the smaller side of the symbol). The inequality $x > 5$ means that x can be any value greater than 5 up to ∞.
Greater Than Or Equal To	$\geq$	The value on the left is greater than or equal to (no less than) the value on the right. For example, $x \geq 5$ means that x can be any value from 5 (including 5 itself) up to ∞.
Absolute Value	$\|a\|$	Produces a non-negative value indicating how far a number is from 0. ($\|-5\| = 5$)
Root	$\sqrt[n]{x}$	Indicates the n-th root of the operand x; when n is absent, its implied value is 2, so $\sqrt{x}$ indicates the second or square root of x. (See Chapter 6.)
Braces	$\{m, n, \ldots\}$	Braces indicate that elements m, n, etc. belong to a set.
Plus-Minus	$\pm$	Indicates that both the positive and negative values should be considered.
Ratio	$a : b$	Shows the relative value of a compared to b. (See Chapter 12.)
Percent	%	A relative measure expressed in hundredths of some reference value. (See Chapter 13.)
Line Segment	$\overline{AB}$	Used to refer to a line segment between points A and B.
Parallel	$\ell \parallel k$	Used to show that lines ℓ and k are parallel to each other (spaced a constant distance apart).
Perpendicular	$\ell \perp k$	Used to show that lines ℓ and k are perpendicular to each other (intersecting at a right angle).
Angle	$\angle A$ or $\angle ABC$	Used to refer to an angle in a figure, such as a triangle.
Pi	π	This Greek letter is used to represent the ratio of a circle's circumference to its diameter. $\pi \approx 3.14$ (See Chapter 20)
Theta	θ	This Greek letter is often used to represent the measurement of an angle.
Arc	$\widehat{AB}$ or $\widehat{ACB}$	Used to denote an arc on a circle.

What You Should Already Know About Fractions

The **numerator** is the expression on the top of a fraction. The **denominator** is the expression on the bottom of a fraction.

$$\frac{\text{numerator}}{\text{denominator}}$$

Any number can be represented as a fraction where the numerator is the number itself and the denominator is 1 because any number divided by 1 is equal to itself. For example, 2 can be written as $\frac{2}{1}$.

Fractions can be **reduced** if the numerator and denominator share a common divisor (factor) other than 1. For example, the fraction $\frac{4}{6}$ can be reduced to $\frac{2}{3}$ because the numerator, 4, and the denominator, 6, share a common factor of 2. Dividing both the numerator and denominator by 2 produces the reduced fraction. Other examples are $\frac{3}{9} = \frac{1}{3}$ and $\frac{7}{7} = \frac{1}{1} = 1$.

When a fraction cannot be reduced any further, it is said to be **in lowest terms**. Note that reducing is **not** the same as simplifying, which refers to making expressions simpler (a somewhat subjective concept); try to use the correct terms for these totally different procedures.

To multiply a fraction by a single value, **multiply just the numerator** of the fraction by the value. For example, $6\left(\frac{4}{5}\right) = \frac{6(4)}{5} = \frac{24}{5}$. Note that this is equivalent to multiplying $\frac{6}{1}$ and $\frac{4}{5}$ (see the next principle).

To multiply two fractions, multiply the numerators to form the numerator of the product and multiply the denominators to form the denominator of the product. For example, $\frac{1}{4}\left(\frac{3}{5}\right) = \frac{1(3)}{4(5)} = \frac{3}{20}$.

Dividing by a fraction is the same as multiplying by the **reciprocal** of the fraction (formed by "flipping" the fraction, swapping the positions of the numerator and denominator).

$$\frac{6}{\frac{1}{2}} = 6\left(\frac{2}{1}\right) = \frac{12}{1} = 12$$

When dividing one fraction by another, the same principle applies; multiply the fraction in the numerator by the reciprocal of the fraction in the denominator.

$$\frac{\frac{2}{3}}{\frac{1}{2}} = \frac{2}{3}\left(\frac{2}{1}\right) = \frac{4}{3}$$

You can **add or subtract fractions *only* when they have the same denominator**. When doing so, the addition or subtraction operation is applied to the numerators, while the denominator stays the same. For example, $\frac{1}{5} + \frac{2}{5} = \frac{1+2}{5} = \frac{3}{5}$.

When the denominators are *not* the same, you can make a **common denominator** (make the denominators match) in order to then be able to add or subtract the fractions. To create the common denominator, you have to multiply both the numerator and denominator of one or both fractions by values that will make the denominators of both fractions equal; that is, you will multiply one or both fractions by 1 expressed as a fraction (such as $\frac{2}{2}$) so the original fractions' *values* don't change, but the way they're *written* does. The simplest case arises when the denominator of one fraction is a multiple of the denominator of the other fraction as in the example below.

$$\frac{2}{3} + \frac{1}{6} = \frac{2}{3}\left(\frac{2}{2}\right) + \frac{1}{6} = \frac{4}{6} + \frac{1}{6} = \frac{5}{6}$$

If neither denominator is a multiple of the other, then you can try to make the common denominator of the fractions the **lowest (or least) common multiple** of the two denominators. Often the lowest common multiple is just the product of the two denominators. For example, in the example below, the denominators are 3 and 4, whose lowest common multiple is 12, which is equal to 3 times 4.

$$\frac{1}{3}-\frac{1}{4}=\frac{1}{3}\left(\frac{4}{4}\right)-\frac{1}{4}\left(\frac{3}{3}\right)=\frac{4}{12}-\frac{3}{12}=\frac{1}{12}$$

In the following example, the denominators, 8 and 12, share a lowest common multiple of 24 because both can go into 24 evenly (finding this value will result in smaller numbers than would using the product of 8 and 12, which is 96, as the common denominator).

$$\frac{3}{8}+\frac{5}{12}=\frac{3}{8}\left(\frac{3}{3}\right)+\frac{5}{12}\left(\frac{2}{2}\right)=\frac{9}{24}+\frac{10}{24}=\frac{19}{24}$$

When fractions appear in an equation rather than just in a lone expression, you can avoid making common denominators by eliminating fractions entirely (multiplying both sides of the equation by the denominators of any fractions so the denominators all get canceled).

Mixed numbers consist of a whole number part and a fraction part. For example, "two and a half" can be represented by the mixed number $2\frac{1}{2}$; however, mixed numbers are confusing when working in a mathematical context, and you can't fill them in as answers on the test anyway, so avoid them except in certain situations involving exponents as explained in Chapter 6.

If you are presented with a mixed number, you should immediately convert it into a fraction; because the absolute value of the fraction will be greater than or equal to 1 due to the presence of the whole number in the original mixed number, this represents a particular type of fraction called an **improper fraction** (a fraction in which the numerator has a larger absolute value than does the denominator). Do so by converting the whole number part into a fraction that shares a common denominator with the fraction part of the mixed number and then adding the two parts together.

$$3\frac{1}{4}=3+\frac{1}{4}=3\left(\frac{4}{4}\right)+\frac{1}{4}=\frac{12}{4}+\frac{1}{4}=\frac{13}{4}$$

0.2 Solving Equations/Isolating Variables

When we want to solve equations for a variable, symbolic constant, or expression, such as x, we need to isolate the term or expression whose value we want to find. To do so, we simply need to undo any mathematical operations that are being performed on the term we want to isolate. To undo an operation, we perform the inverse operation; addition and subtraction are inverse operations, and multiplication and division are inverse operations. Exponentiation and taking a root are also inverse operations, but there are some special considerations when performing those operations as explained in Chapter 9.

Let's start with the very basic equation $2x = 8$ and solve for x. The variable x is being multiplied by the **coefficient** 2, so we should perform the inverse operation to that multiplication and divide both sides of the equation by 2 to determine that $x = 4$.

Let's go one step further and solve the equation $-2x - 3 = 7$. We need to "peel away" the other parts of the expression on the left side of the equation to isolate x. The coefficient of -2 is most closely grouped with the x term, so we will come to that last. The outermost operation is the subtraction between the two terms, so first, we need to add 3 to both sides of the equation in order to cancel the -3. The equation becomes $-2x = 10$, and then we can divide both sides of the equation by -2 to get $x = -5$.

$$-2x - 3 = 7$$
$$-2x - 3 + \mathbf{3} = 7 + \mathbf{3}$$
$$-2x \cancel{-3} \cancel{+3} = 10$$
$$-2x = 10$$
$$\frac{-2x}{\mathbf{-2}} = \frac{10}{\mathbf{-2}}$$
$$\frac{\cancel{-2}x}{\cancel{-2}} = \frac{10}{-2}$$
$$x = -5$$

Example 0.2-1

1 0.2

What value of x satisfies the equation $4x + 4 = 24$?

A) 4

B) 5

C) 7

D) 24

Solution

1. Subtract 4 from both sides of the equation to cancel the +4, which is the outermost operation.

$$4x + 4 = 24$$
$$4x + 4 - \mathbf{4} = 24 - \mathbf{4}$$
$$4x = 20$$

2. Divide both sides of the equation by 4 to cancel the multiplication of x by 4 in order to solve for x.

$$4x = 20$$
$$\frac{4x}{\mathbf{4}} = \frac{20}{\mathbf{4}}$$
$$x = 5$$

3. The answer is B.

If the **coefficient** of the variable (the constant that is multiplying the variable) you need to isolate is in the form of a fraction, you can first multiply both sides of the equation by the coefficient's denominator and then divide both sides of the equation by the numerator. However, the best approach is to multiply both sides of the equation by the **reciprocal** of the fraction, which isolates the variable in one step, as it combines the multiplication and division operations. Note that this procedure is equivalent to dividing both sides of the equation by the fraction; division by a fraction can be implemented as multiplication by the reciprocal of the fraction.

Example 0.2-2

2 1600.io 0.2

$$\frac{3}{5}t = \frac{7}{3}$$

What value of t is the solution of the equation above?

Solution 1

1. To solve for t, we want to divide both sides of the equation by the coefficient of t, which is $\frac{3}{5}$. We can accomplish this by multiplying both sides by the reciprocal of $\frac{3}{5}$, which is $\frac{5}{3}$.

$$\frac{3}{5}t = \frac{7}{3}$$

$$\mathbf{\frac{5}{3}}\left(\frac{3}{5}\right)t = \mathbf{\frac{5}{3}}\left(\frac{7}{3}\right)$$

$$\frac{\cancel{15}}{\cancel{15}}t = \frac{35}{9}$$

$$t = \frac{35}{9}$$

2. The answer is $\frac{35}{9}$.

Solution 2

1. Multiply both sides of the equation by 5, the denominator of the fraction on the left side of the equation.

$$\frac{3}{5}t = \frac{7}{3}$$

$$\cancel{\mathbf{5}}\left(\frac{3}{\cancel{5}}\right)t = \mathbf{5}\left(\frac{7}{3}\right)$$

$$3t = \frac{35}{3}$$

2. Divide both sides of the equation by 3 (or multiply by $\frac{1}{3}$) to isolate and solve for t.

$$3t = \frac{35}{3}$$

$$\frac{\mathbf{1}}{\cancel{\mathbf{3}}}(\cancel{3}t) = \frac{\mathbf{1}}{\mathbf{3}}\left(\frac{35}{3}\right)$$

$$t = \frac{35}{9}$$

3. The answer is $\frac{35}{9}$.

View related real-test problems at 1600.io/p/smtex?topic=0.2

0.3 Substitution

If you are given the value of a constant or a particular value of a variable, you can replace that constant or variable with the given value. For example, if we are given the equation $3x + a = 13$ and told that $a = 1$, we can **substitute** 1 for a to make the equation $3x + 1 = 13$. From there, we can solve for x by subtracting 1 from both sides of the equation to get $3x = 12$ and then dividing both sides by 3 to arrive at $x = 4$.

Example 0.3-1

 0.3

If $\frac{x-2}{4} = k$ and $k = 3$, what is the value of x ?

A) 3

B) 7

C) 12

D) 14

Solution

1. Substitute 3 for k.

$$\frac{x-2}{4} = k$$
$$\frac{x-2}{4} = 3$$

2. Multiply both sides of the equation by 4.

$$\frac{x-2}{4} = 3$$
$$\cancel{\mathbf{4}}\left(\frac{x-2}{\cancel{4}}\right) = \mathbf{4}(3)$$
$$x - 2 = 12$$

3. Add 2 to both sides of the equation to solve for x.

$$x - 2 = 12$$
$$x \cancel{-2} \cancel{+\mathbf{2}} = 12 + \mathbf{2}$$
$$x = 14$$

4. The answer is D.

View related real-test problems at 1600.io/p/smtex?topic=0.3

0.4 Solving for Expressions; Distributing and Factoring

Many questions on the test ask you to solve for an expression rather than for a lone variable, and usually this is a clue that you might be able to take a more direct route to the answer if you are thoughtful. However, in this section we are just interested in solving for the lone variables and substituting their values into the solve-for expression (we'll discuss the optimizations in later chapters). Most importantly, don't solve for a variable and assume that is the answer; **always double check what the problem is asking you for**.

Example 0.4-1

1  0.4

If $3x + 5 = 7$, what is the value of $6x + 8$?

A) 2

B) 5

C) 12

D) 14

Solution

1. Subtract 5 from both sides of the equation.

$$3x + 5 = 7$$
$$3x \cancel{+5} \cancel{-\mathbf{5}} = 7 - \mathbf{5}$$
$$3x = 2$$

2. Divide both sides of the equation by 3 to solve for x, whose value needs to be substituted into the solve-for expression.

$$3x = 2$$
$$\frac{\cancel{3}x}{\cancel{\mathbf{3}}} = \frac{2}{\mathbf{3}}$$
$$x = \frac{2}{3}$$

3. Now that we have the value of x, we can substitute $\frac{2}{3}$ for x in the solve-for expression, which is $6x + 8$.

$$6x + 8 = 6\left(\frac{2}{3}\right) + 8$$
$$6x + 8 = \frac{12}{3} + 8$$
$$6x + 8 = 4 + 8$$
$$6x + 8 = 12$$

4. The answer is C.

In the following example, we must first translate a sentence into an equation and then solve for the desired expression. When translating a sentence, handle one phrase at a time. Place the equals sign immediately when you see a phrase like "is equal to" or "the result is," and anything that comes after that phrase should go on the other side of the equals sign.

Example 0.4-2

2 0.4

When 6 times the number x is added to 8, the result is 2. What number results when 3 times x is added to 4 ?

A) -1

B) 1

C) 2

D) 7

Solution

1. The phrase "6 times the number x" translates to $6x$, and that is added to 8, so the first expression we should write is $8+6x$ (note that because you can perform addition in any order—it's **commutative**—this could also be written as $6x+8$, which you might find more natural).

2. The phrase "the result is 2" means that we should set the first expression we wrote equal to 2.

$$8 + 6x = 2$$

3. Subtract 8 from both sides of the equation.

$$\begin{aligned} 8 + 6x &= 2 \\ \cancel{8} + 6x - \cancel{\mathbf{8}} &= 2 - \mathbf{8} \\ 6x &= -6 \end{aligned}$$

4. Divide both sides of the equation by 6 to solve for x.

$$\begin{aligned} 6x &= -6 \\ \frac{\cancel{6}x}{\cancel{\mathbf{6}}} &= \frac{-6}{\mathbf{6}} \\ x &= -1 \end{aligned}$$

5. Don't forget that we need to construct the solve-for expression, which is specified in the second sentence of the question. Based on the phrase "3 times x is added to 4," the solve-for expression is $4 + 3x$ (you could also write this as $3x + 4$).

6. Substitute -1 for x in the solve-for expression.

$$\begin{aligned} 4 + 3x &= 4 + 3(-1) \\ 4 + 3x &= 4 - 3 \\ 4 + 3x &= 1 \end{aligned}$$

7. The answer is B.

In the following example, the equation contains two unknown quantities represented by letters, so we cannot solve for the value of either one by itself. Instead, we must take advantage of an existing grouping and isolate the grouped expression to solve.

Example 0.4-3

3 1600.io 0.4

If $5(a+b)=7$, what is the value of $a+b$?

A) $\frac{5}{7}$

B) $\frac{7}{5}$

C) 5

D) 7

Solution

1. The solve-for expression consists of two unknown terms added to each other. Because we have only one equation, but two unknown values, a and b, we cannot find the value of either one individually. However, because the solve-for expression $a+b$ appears in the original equation, we can isolate the solve-for expression by simply dividing both sides of the equation by 5.

$$5(a+b)=7$$

$$\frac{\cancel{5}(a+b)}{\cancel{5}}=\frac{7}{5}$$

$$a+b=\frac{7}{5}$$

2. The answer is B.

Distributing and Factoring Constants

When an expression involving addition or subtraction is multiplied by a constant (the expression is often enclosed in parentheses as in the previous example) or when an expression is divided by a constant (which is the same as multiplying by a fraction), to perform the multiplication or division the constant must be **distributed** to all the terms in the expression, meaning every term in the expression must be multiplied by the constant, and then all those products (results of multiplication) must be added together. For example, given the expression $3(x+2)$, we can distribute the 3 to both terms in the parenthetical expression (multiply both x and 2 by 3) to rewrite the expression as $3x+3(2)=3x+6$.

If you have to distribute a negative number, just **make sure the negative part is also distributed** (using extra parentheses around negative terms helps reinforce this). For example, $-2(x-4)=-2x-2(-4)=-2x+8$; notice how we placed -4 in parentheses to remind us to be careful about multiplying two negative numbers.

Example 0.4-4

4 0.4

Which of the following is equivalent to $4(x+3)-8$?

A) $4x-5$

B) $4x-4$

C) $4x+4$

D) $12x-8$

Solution

1. Distribute the 4 to both terms in the parentheses, then combine the numerical constants.

$$4(x+3)-8$$
$$4x+4(3)-8$$
$$4x+12-8$$
$$4x+4$$

2. The answer is C.

Distribution also occurs if we divide an expression by a constant: all the terms in the expression must be divided by the constant. For example, if we want to divide the expression $8x+4$ by 4, we simply have to divide both of the terms in the expression by 4 (split the numerator into two fractions to visualize this).

$$\frac{8x+4}{4}=\frac{8x}{4}+\frac{4}{4}=2x+1$$

Alternatively, you can think about this as multiplying the expression in the numerator by $\frac{1}{4}$ (the reciprocal of 4) and then distributing the multiplication.

$$\frac{8x+4}{4}=\frac{1}{4}(8x+4)=\frac{1}{4}(8x)+\frac{1}{4}(4)=\frac{8x}{4}+\frac{4}{4}=2x+1$$

Another way to think about and handle the operation is to realize that since both terms in the expression $8x+4$ include multiples of 4, we can **factor** 4 out of both terms.

$$8x+4=4(2x)+4(1)=4(2x+1)$$

Note, importantly, that **factoring is the inverse operation of distributing**:

Factoring (→)

$$8x+4=4(2x+1)$$

Distributing (←)

Factoring constants out and then dividing by the factor to isolate the remaining expression is often used to produced wormhole-like shortcut solutions to problems like the following example (see the Wormholes chapter for a thorough definition of that term and an in-depth discussion of this principle). Realizing that we can factor as the first step leads to an optimization that helps us find the solve-for expression immediately. These processes are covered in later chapters, but the clue that factoring is the best approach is the need to make the coefficient of the variable term in the given equation match the coefficient of the variable term in the solve-for expression (this can be used as a mini optimization on some of the real-test problems that are suggested in the previous section but is more applicable to the ones suggested in this section). Note that the following problem has two unknown values, so we cannot solve for the individual values but must instead solve directly for an expression containing both of those unknowns.

Example 0.4-5

5 1600.io 0.4

$$6ax - 3 = 30$$

Based on the equation above, what is the value of $2ax - 1$?

A) 5

B) 6

C) 10

D) 15

Solution 1

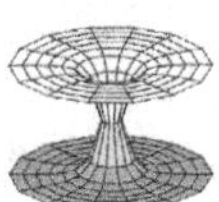

1. We can factor 3 out of both terms on the left side of the equation, which will produce the solve-for expression as the other factor.

$$6ax - 3 = 30$$
$$3(2ax - 1) = 30$$

2. Divide both sides of the equation by 3 to isolate and solve for the solve-for expression.

$$3(2ax - 1) = 30$$
$$\frac{\cancel{3}(2ax - 1)}{\cancel{3}} = \frac{30}{3}$$
$$2ax - 1 = 10$$

3. The answer is C.

Solution 2

1. Add 3 to both sides of the equation.

$$6ax - 3 = 30$$
$$6ax = 33$$

2. Divide both sides of the equation by 6 to solve for ax (we cannot solve for either unknown value individually, but the term ax appears in the solve-for expression, so solving for ax is sufficient) and reduce the resulting fraction.

$$6ax = 33$$
$$\frac{\cancel{6}ax}{\cancel{6}} = \frac{33}{6}$$
$$ax = \frac{11}{2}$$

3. Substitute $\frac{11}{2}$ for ax in the solve-for expression.

$$2ax - 1 = 2\left(\frac{11}{2}\right) - 1$$
$$2ax - 1 = 11 - 1$$
$$2ax - 1 = 10$$

4. The answer is C.

Section 0.4 Suggested Problems from Real Tests

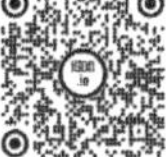

View related real-test problems at 1600.io/p/smtex?topic=0.4

0.5 Combining Like Terms

We already know that numbers can be combined with addition or subtraction, but the same goes for variable terms as well as constants and expressions. For example, $x + x = 2x$ because all we've done is add two x terms together. Similarly, we can add $2x$ and $3x$ to make $5x$, and we can subtract $6x$ from $4x$: $4x - 6x = -2x$. Constants can be treated the same way, so $4a + 3a = 7a$, and like expressions can also be combined: $9(x + 4) - 7(x + 4) = 2(x + 4)$.

Note that **two different variables, constants, or expressions cannot be combined in any way like this**. For example, $2x + 5y \neq 7xy$ (or any other nonsense way people can think of to combine two incompatible things).

Example 0.5-1

1 1600.io 0.5

If $3x + 5 = 2x - 3$, what is the value of $x + 9$?

A) -8

B) -1

C) 1

D) 8

Solution

1. Subtract 5 from both sides of the equation in order to eliminate constants on the left side of the equation. Combine constants on the right side of the equation.

$$3x + 5 = 2x - 3$$
$$3x \cancel{+5} \cancel{\mathbf{-5}} = 2x - 3 - \mathbf{5}$$
$$3x = 2x - 8$$

2. Subtract $2x$ from both sides of the equation in order to combine the x-terms on the left side of the equation.

$$3x = 2x - 8$$
$$3x - \mathbf{2x} = \cancel{2x} - 8 \cancel{\mathbf{-2x}}$$
$$x = -8$$

3. Substitute -8 for x in the solve-for expression.

$$x + 9 = -8 + 9$$
$$x + 9 = 1$$

4. The answer is C.

In the following example, in order to combine the variable terms, we also have to either make use of common denominators or multiply both sides of the equation by a value that will eliminate the fractions entirely.

Example 0.5-2

2 0.5

$$\frac{1}{2}x - 1 = 2 - x$$

What value of x satisfies the equation above?

A) $\frac{1}{2}$

B) 2

C) 3

D) $\frac{9}{2}$

Solution 1

1. Multiply both sides of the equation by 2 in order to eliminate any fractions, and then distribute.

$$\frac{1}{2}x - 1 = 2 - x$$
$$\mathbf{2}\left(\frac{1}{2}x - 1\right) = \mathbf{2}(2 - x)$$
$$\cancel{2}\left(\frac{1}{\cancel{2}}x\right) - 2(1) = 2(2) - 2(x)$$
$$x - 2 = 4 - 2x$$

2. Add 2 to both sides of the equation in order to eliminate constants on the left side of the equation. Combine constants on the right side of the equation.

$$x - 2 = 4 - 2x$$
$$x \cancel{-2} \cancel{+\mathbf{2}} = 4 - 2x + \mathbf{2}$$
$$x = 6 - 2x$$

3. Add $2x$ to both sides of the equation in order to combine x-terms on the left side of the equation.

$$x = 6 - 2x$$
$$x + \mathbf{2x} = 6 \cancel{-2x} \cancel{+\mathbf{2x}}$$
$$3x = 6$$

4. Divide both sides of the equation by 3 in order to solve for x.

$$3x = 6$$
$$\frac{\cancel{3}x}{\cancel{\mathbf{3}}} = \frac{6}{\mathbf{3}}$$
$$x = 2$$

5. The answer is B.

Solution 2

1. Add 1 to both sides of the equation in order to eliminate constants on the left side of the equation. Combine constant terms on the right side of the equation.

$$\frac{1}{2}x - 1 = 2 - x$$

$$\frac{1}{2}x \cancel{-1} \cancel{+\mathbf{1}} = 2 - x + \mathbf{1}$$

$$\frac{1}{2}x = 3 - x$$

2. Add x to both sides of the equation in order to combine the x-terms on the left side of the equation. Make a common denominator (write the second x-term's implied coefficient of 1 as $\frac{2}{2}$) in order to allow the adding of the coefficients.

$$\frac{1}{2}x = 3 - x$$

$$\frac{1}{2}x + \mathbf{x} = 3 \cancel{-x} \cancel{+\mathbf{x}}$$

$$\frac{1}{2}x + \frac{\mathbf{2}}{\mathbf{2}}x = 3$$

$$\frac{1+2}{2}x = 3$$

$$\frac{3}{2}x = 3$$

3. To solve for x, divide both sides of the equation by $\frac{3}{2}$; this is accomplished by multiplying by the reciprocal of $\frac{3}{2}$, which is $\frac{2}{3}$ (this method is much neater than writing out division by a fraction).

$$\frac{3}{2}x = 3$$

$$\frac{\cancel{\mathbf{2}}}{\cancel{\mathbf{3}}}\left(\frac{\cancel{3}}{\cancel{2}}\right)x = \frac{\mathbf{2}}{\cancel{\mathbf{3}}}(\cancel{3})$$

$$x = 2$$

4. The answer is B.

The next problem has us combining many like terms, which follows exactly the same principles as are used in the simpler examples above. For example, $x + 2x + 3x + 4x = 10x$ because the coefficients add to 10 $(1 + 2 + 3 + 4 = 10)$.

Example 0.5-3

3 1600.io 0.5

$$5(p+1) + 9(p-1) = 11p$$

What value of p is the solution of the equation above?

Solution

1. Distribute the constants 5 and 9 through their respective parenthetical expressions on the left side of the equation. Combine like terms on the left side of the equation.

$$\begin{aligned} 5(p+1)+9(p-1) &= 11p \\ 5p+5+9p-9 &= 11p \\ 14p-4 &= 11p \end{aligned}$$

2. Add 4 to both sides of the equation in order to eliminate constants on the left side of the equation (f you wanted to, you could instead subtract $14p$ from both sides of the equation in order to combine p-terms on the right side of the equation, but it is good practice to maintain a positive coefficient for the variable that you want to solve for, and following the steps shown below will allow us to do that).

$$\begin{aligned} 14p-4 &= 11p \\ 14p\cancel{-4}\cancel{+\mathbf{4}} &= 11p+\mathbf{4} \\ 14p &= 11p+4 \end{aligned}$$

3. Subtract $11p$ from both sides of the equation in order to combine p-terms on the left side of the equation.

$$\begin{aligned} 14p &= 11p+4 \\ 14p-\mathbf{11p} &= \cancel{11p}+4\cancel{-\mathbf{11p}} \\ 3p &= 4 \end{aligned}$$

4. Divide both sides of the equation by 3 in order to solve for p.

$$\begin{aligned} 3p &= 4 \\ \frac{\cancel{3}p}{\cancel{\mathbf{3}}} &= \frac{4}{\mathbf{3}} \\ p &= \frac{4}{3} \end{aligned}$$

5. The answer is $\frac{4}{3}$.

Section 0.5 Suggested Problems from Real Tests

- Test 3-NC-17
- Test 5-NC-17
- Test 5-C-33
- Test 6-C-32
- Test 8-NC-1
- Test 10-NC-1
- Test 10-C-27
- Apr 2017-C-1
- May 2017-NC-18
- May 2017-C-24
- Mar 2018-NC-6
- May 2018-NC-14
- Mar 2019-NC-4
- Mar 2019-NC-16
- Mar 2019-C-3
- Apr 2019-NC-6
- May 2019 (Int)-NC-18
- May 2019 (Int)-C-4
- Oct 2019-C-22
- Mar 2020-C-1
- Oct 2020-NC-17
- Mar 2021-NC-3
- May 2021 (US)-NC-4
- May 2021 (Int)-NC-17
- May 2021 (Int)-C-9

View related real-test problems at 1600.io/p/smtex?topic=0.5

0.6 Unknown Values in Denominators

If an unknown value is in the denominator of a fraction, you should eliminate the fraction by multiplying both sides of the equation by the denominator (just as you would when numbers are in the denominator). For example, if you are given the equation $\frac{8}{x} = 160$ and are asked to solve for x, simply multiply both sides of the equation by x to get $8 = 160x$, and then divide both sides of the equation by 160 to solve for x: $x = \frac{8}{160} = \frac{1}{20}$.

Note that sometimes, having an unknown in the denominator can lead to extraneous solutions (which are covered in Chapter 9) because the denominator might end up being equal to 0, but those problems are easily spotted on the test, and none of those are included in the scope of this section. Therefore, in the cases covered here, simply multiplying by the denominator to eliminate the fractions works well.

When an expression appears in the denominator, we cannot simply split the fraction into parts as we could when the numerator is an expression and the denominator is just a number. For example, $\frac{2x+2}{2} = \frac{2x}{2} + \frac{2}{2} = x + 1$, but $\frac{2}{x+2} \neq \frac{2}{x} + \frac{2}{2}$, so be careful not to make that mistake moving forward.

In the following example, the unknown value appears in the denominator of two fractions (and the denominators aren't the same so we can't just combine the fractions). Instead of making a common denominator, we just need to multiply both sides of the equation by *both* of those denominators to eliminate both fractions.

Example 0.6-1

1 1600.io 0.6

$$\frac{1}{x} + \frac{2}{x-2} = 0$$

What value of x satisfies the equation above?

Solution

1. Our first goal is to eliminate fractions, so first multiply both sides of the equation by x, which is the denominator of the first fraction.

$$\frac{1}{x} + \frac{2}{x-2} = 0$$

$$\boldsymbol{x}\left(\frac{1}{x} + \frac{2}{x-2}\right) = \boldsymbol{x}(0)$$

$$\cancel{x}\left(\frac{1}{\cancel{x}}\right) + x\left(\frac{2}{x-2}\right) = 0$$

$$1 + \frac{2x}{x-2} = 0$$

2. Multiply both sides of the equation by $x - 2$, which is the denominator of the remaining fraction. Combine like terms.

$$1 + \frac{2x}{x-2} = 0$$

$$(\mathbf{x - 2})\left(1 + \frac{2x}{x-2}\right) = (\mathbf{x - 2})(0)$$

$$(x-2)(1) + \cancel{(x-2)}\left(\frac{2x}{\cancel{x-2}}\right) = 0$$

$$x - 2 + 2x = 0$$

$$3x - 2 = 0$$

3. Add 2 to both sides of the equation in order to isolate the x-term.

$$3x - 2 = 0$$

$$3x \cancel{-2} \cancel{+\mathbf{2}} = 0 + \mathbf{2}$$

$$3x = 2$$

4. Divide both sides of the equation by 3 to solve for x.

$$3x = 2$$

$$\frac{\cancel{3}x}{\cancel{\mathbf{3}}} = \frac{2}{\mathbf{3}}$$

$$x = \frac{2}{3}$$

5. The answer is $\frac{2}{3}$.

Occasionally, you will see a fraction in which both the numerator and denominator are unknown. If you know the value of a fraction $\frac{x}{y}$, then the value of the reciprocal, $\frac{y}{x}$, is equal to the reciprocal of the original value (this should come as no surprise). For example, if $\frac{x}{y} = \frac{2}{3}$, then $\frac{y}{x} = \frac{3}{2}$; we've just taken the reciprocal of both sides of an equation. Looked at another way (literally), if you stand on your head, the equation is still true.

In the following example, we cannot find the individual values of a and b, but we can solve for an expression that is useful to us by taking advantage of the reciprocal.

Example 0.6-2

2 0.6

If $\frac{3a}{b} = \frac{1}{3}$, what is the value of $\frac{b}{a}$?

A) $\frac{1}{9}$

B) 1

C) 3

D) 9

Solution 1

1. Multiply both sides of the equation by $\frac{1}{3}$ (this is the same as dividing by 3) in order to isolate the expression $\frac{a}{b}$, which is the reciprocal of the solve-for expression.

$$\frac{3a}{b} = \frac{1}{3}$$

$$\frac{1}{\cancel{3}}\left(\frac{\cancel{3}a}{b}\right) = \frac{1}{3}\left(\frac{1}{3}\right)$$

$$\frac{a}{b} = \frac{1}{9}$$

2. Since $\frac{a}{b} = \frac{1}{9}$, then the reciprocals of both sides are also equal.

$$\frac{b}{a} = \frac{9}{1} = 9$$

3. The answer is D.

Solution 2

1. Multiply both sides of the equation by b to eliminate the fraction on the left side of the equation.

$$\frac{3a}{b} = \frac{1}{3}$$

$$\cancel{b}\left(\frac{3a}{\cancel{b}}\right) = b\left(\frac{1}{3}\right)$$

$$3a = \frac{b}{3}$$

2. Multiply both sides of the equation by 3 to eliminate the fraction on the right side of the equation.

$$3a = \frac{b}{3}$$

$$3(3a) = \cancel{3}\left(\frac{b}{\cancel{3}}\right)$$

$$9a = b$$

3. Divide both sides of the equation by a to create and solve for the solve-for expression.

$$9a = b$$

$$\frac{9\cancel{a}}{\cancel{a}} = \frac{b}{a}$$

$$9 = \frac{b}{a}$$

4. The answer is D.

Section 0.6 Suggested Problems from Real Tests

- Test 1-NC-8
- Test 3-NC-5
- Test 4-NC-10
- Test 8-NC-12

View related real-test problems at 1600.io/p/smtex?topic=0.6

Linear Relationships 1

1.1 Demystifying Linear Relationships

You might believe that you don't understand some of the math concepts on the SAT, but if I had a dollar for every student who wrongly thought they didn't understand linear relationships...

Let's say it's been a thousand students; then, you'd probably be able to figure out pretty quickly that I would have $1,000. If it had been twice as many students, I'd have twice as much money. If this makes sense, then you already get the essence of **linear relationships**. We often encounter real-life situations in which two quantities are related in such a way that a change in one of them results in a corresponding change in the other. If you get paid hourly, then working twice as many hours will double your pay. If your new school is only half as far away as your old one, it will take you half as long to get there if you travel at the same speed.

The phrase "linear relationships" doesn't necessarily make sense as a result of this knowledge because the phrase comes from the shapes of the graphs of these relationships, and we will get to those eventually. To get started though, we just need to be able to model these relationships by writing mathematical expressions that allow us to calculate values without simply listing a long series of numbers. You don't have to understand lines in an abstract way in order to express these relationships. Before we get into an algebraic understanding of lines, we can use common sense to work our way through some questions based on this type of relationship.

For example, Mindy lives within walking distance of three buffet restaurants that have different price structures.

The first buffet charges $20 to enter and dine, no matter how much food she eats. Whether Mindy eats 4 plates of food or 20 plates of food, she will pay a fixed amount of $20 to eat there.

$$\text{Total Cost} = \text{Entrance Charge}$$

The second buffet only charges by the plate (there is no entrance fee). Each plate of food Mindy eats costs $4. Here, Mindy will pay $4 times the number of plates of food she eats. If she eats one plate of food, her bill will be $4; if she eats 4 plates, her bill will be $\$4 \times 4 = \$16$. If she eats p plates of food, her bill will be $4p$ dollars.

$$\text{Total Cost} = \text{Price Per Plate} \times \text{Number of Plates}$$

The third buffet combines the approaches of both of the other buffets. This third buffet imposes a smaller entrance charge than does the first buffet: entrance to the third buffet only costs $5. The third buffet also charges less per plate than does the second buffet: each plate of food costs $2. Here, Mindy will pay $5 plus $2 per plate of food. In order to enter the restaurant, she pays $5; if she has a heart attack while waiting in line and gets 0 plates of food, the whole trip will still cost her only $5 (aside from medical bills). If she eats one plate of food, the trip will cost $2 for the one plate of food ($2 times 1 plate) plus the $5 entrance fee (a total of $7). If she eats two plates of food, the cost will be $4 for the two plates of food ($2 times 2 plates) plus the $5 entrance charge for a total of $9. If she eats p plates of food, her bill will be $2p$ ($2 times p plates) plus the $5 entrance charge for a total of $2p + 5$ dollars.

$$\text{Total Cost} = (\text{Price Per Plate} \times \text{Number of Plates}) + \text{Entrance Charge}$$

The different styles of buffet demonstrate different facets of linear relationships. In the simplest case, there can just be a constant amount that never changes (the entrance charge). More commonly, the value produced can be changed by some amount (here, the price per plate) every time a variable (the number of plates) is changed. And finally, in the most general situation, there can be a combination of both of these attributes.

1.2 Writing Linear Expressions

On the test, you will be responsible for writing mathematical expressions to represent linear relationships.

Example 1.2-1

1 1600.io 1.2

One pound of peanuts costs \$3. At this price, how much will p pounds of peanuts cost?

A) $3p$

B) $3+p$

C) $\frac{3}{p}$

D) $\frac{p}{3}$

Solution

1. Since each pound costs \$3, multiply 3 by the number of pounds, p, to find the total cost, which is $3p$.
2. The answer is A.

Notes

If you need to verify that this works, just list out a few values to see that this is true.

Pounds of Peanuts	Cost	Pattern Representation
1	\$3	3(1)
2	\$6	3(2)
3	\$9	3(3)

Notice in each row that the value in the Cost column is three times the value in the Pounds of Peanuts column. If p is the number of pounds of peanuts, then three times p, or $3p$, is the cost of those p pounds of peanuts.

Now suppose that George starts a pen collection with 20 pens that were gifted to him by his grandfather. He plans on buying 3 new pens every month to add to his collection. How could we write an expression to show the total number of pens he would have after m months?

The number of new pens George would have after m months follows the same pattern we have already talked about. If he adds 3 pens a month for m months, he would have $3m$ *new* pens. All we have to do is add the original 20 pens to find out the total number of pens he has after m months: $3m + 20$.

Let's look at this situation as represented by a table to see how this expression makes sense as a way of representing the pattern of how his collection grows.

Number of Months	Total Number of Pens	Pattern Representation
0	20	$20 + 3(0)$
1	23	$20 + 3(1)$
2	26	$20 + 3(2)$
m	$20 + 3m$	$20 + 3(m)$

Example 1.2-2

2 1.2

One of the requirements for becoming a journalist was the ability to write notes at a rate of 100 words per minute. Lewis was able to write only 40 words per minute when he started reporting, but through practice, he was able to increase his speed by 2 words per minute each week. Which of the following represents the number of words per minute that Lewis could write after w weeks of practice?

A) $2 + 40w$

B) $40 + 2w$

C) $100 + 2w$

D) $100 - 2w$

Solution

1. Since Lewis's speed increases by 2 words per minute every week, the amount his speed increases is equal to 2 times the number of weeks, w. His speed increases by $2w$ overall.
2. Since Lewis started at a speed of 40 words per minute, to find his overall speed, we need to add his speed increase to his original starting speed. Lewis's overall speed after w weeks of practice is $40 + 2w$.
3. The answer is B.

Notes

You may have noticed that in this example, the constant term (40) appears before the variable term ($2w$), but it's important to understand that the ordering of the terms does not matter: $40 + 2w$ is equivalent to $2w + 40$. Linear expressions on the test can appear in either arrangement. By convention, variable terms appear first when writing expressions, but the ordering has no mathematical consequences.

Note that in this problem, you're given some information that you do not need: the requirement that a journalist be able to write at 100 words per minute. This happens occasionally on word problems (though very rarely on strictly mathematical problems).

You should understand that just because you don't use a given quantity or other piece of information, that does not mean that you are not properly solving the problem.

SkillDrill 1.2-1

Directions: Based on the situation described, write a mathematical expression that can be used to answer the question.

1. Emily earns \$12 for every pizza she sells. How much money will she have if she sells p pizzas?

2. The Tooth Fairy gains one tooth for every house she visits. How many teeth will she have after visiting h houses?

3. Brandon started the day with \$50 in his wallet, and he will get another \$20 from each of his aunts. How much money will he have after he visits a of his aunts?

4. Charlie has 84 baseball cards and he buys 3 more every weekend. How many cards will he have after w weekends?

5. Priscilla has to eat 20 hamburgers to win a prize. It takes her 3 minutes to eat each hamburger. If she has already eaten h hamburgers, how much *longer* will it take her to eat the remaining hamburgers?

View related real-test problems at 1600.io/p/smtex?topic=1.2

Section 1.2 Practice Problems

1 1600.io 1.2

Saquon spent a total of \$450 on his hotel room during his vacation. Each day of his vacation, he bought a dinner at a restaurant for \$28. If Saquon bought d dinners, how much money, in dollars, did Saquon spend during his vacation on his hotel room and dinners?

A) $450 + 56d$

B) $450 + 28d$

C) $450 + 14d$

D) $28d$

2 1600.io 1.2

An artisan is crafting a custom chess set by carving each of the 32 pieces in the set by hand. It takes the artisan 40 minutes to carve each piece. If p of the pieces are already carved, which of the following represents the number of additional minutes needed to finish carving the set of chess pieces?

A) $32(40 - p)$

B) $32(p - 40)$

C) $40(32 - p)$

D) $40(p - 32)$

1.3 Writing and Solving Linear Equations

We have seen a few problems in which we wrote mathematical expressions that represent a certain type of simple pattern or relationship. **Expressions**, strictly speaking, consist only of numerical and variable terms being added, subtracted, multiplied, etc. For example, $40 + 2w$ is an expression. When we set this value equal to another expression, we can make an equation. **Equations** consist of two expressions that are set equal to each other using an equals sign (=). For example, if we wanted to make an equation to represent Lewis's writing speed, we could set s, the speed that Lewis can write words, equal to the expression $40 + 2w$, which tells us Lewis's writing speed after w weeks of practice. In equation form, the relationship is written $s = 40 + 2w$. Note that the linear expression could appear on either side of the equals sign; the equation $s = 40 + 2w$ could also be written as $40 + 2w = s$.

Choose Variable Letters that Make Sense

When writing your own equations, you should always choose letters that tell you what a variable stands for. For example, in the case of Lewis's writing speed, we used s to represent the *speed* that he writes (we were told to use w for the number of weeks).

Avoid always using x and y when writing your own equations for real world word problems, because—although x and y are usually the most familiar variable letters to most students—it is very easy to forget what each letter represents (unless you're working with xylophones and yodelers).

In the case of Lewis, if we write $y = 40 + 2x$ it is not apparent what x and y represent, but when we write $s = 40 + 2w$ it is much easier to see that s represents the speed and w represents the number of weeks he practiced.

To take the next step into writing linear *equations*, all we need to do is set the kinds of *expressions* we have been building equal to some other quantity or variable that represents the total.

Example 1.3-1

1 1.3

A drone, initially hovering 80 feet above the ground, begins to lose altitude at a rate of 3 feet per second. Which of the following equations represents the drone's altitude above the ground a, in feet, t seconds after the drone begins to lose altitude?

A) $a = 80 - 3$

B) $a = 80 + 3t$

C) $a = 80 - 3t$

D) $a = 80t - 3$

Solution

1. The altitude, or height, goes down by 3 feet every second (that is, the change in height is −3 feet every second), so to find the total change in the height, we have to multiply −3 by the number of seconds, t. The change in height after t seconds is $-3t$.

2. Since the drone's altitude started at 80 feet and *decreased* by $3t$ feet after t seconds, we start with 80 and *subtract* $3t$, then set it equal to a, the altitude of the drone after t seconds. The final equation used to find the height after t seconds is $a = 80 - 3t$.

3. The answer is C.

Notes

This is the first time we've seen a negative change in the value in a linear relationship. If you are unsure whether the change should be added or subtracted in this example, think about the way the height changes. A negative change in the height should be reflected in the equation by subtracting the change in height from the initial height.

Here, we have an ordinary linear relationship written as a constant first, then a variable term: $a = 80 - 3t$. You might already be familiar with Slope-Intercept Form for a linear equation, which, by convention, places the variable term first, followed by the constant (the "y-intercept", which we will explain thoroughly a bit later); here, that would be $a = -3t + 80$. Note, importantly, that this has *no effect whatsoever on the relationship*; it's just a matter of writing the terms in a different order which happens to make sense for the situation in the problem.

Having equations to represent this type of situation is useful for when we need to calculate values that we would not easily be able to count to. For example, it's easy to add the cost of a single item two or three times, but when we are buying hundreds or thousands of items, we can use the equations to easily find particular values in a way that involves no repetition.

Example 1.3-2

2 1600.io 1.3

A partially filled aquarium contains 20 gallons of water. A hose is turned on, and water flows into the tank at a rate of 4 gallons per minute. How many gallons of water will be in the aquarium after 30 minutes?

Solution

1. We have to start by writing the equation to represent the situation. Let w be the total amount of water in the aquarium after being filled for m minutes. The amount of water starts at 20 gallons and then increases by 4 gallons every minute, so the equation that represents the situation is $w = 4m + 20$ (again, note that we could have written this as $20 + 4m$, which you might feel matches the real-world situation more naturally; it makes no difference).

2. We want to know how much water there will be in the aquarium after 30 minutes, so we should replace m with 30 and find the value of w.

$$w = 4m + 20$$
$$w = 4(30) + 20$$
$$w = 120 + 20$$
$$w = 140$$

3. The answer is 140.

We now know how to find final values for situations where we know what to substitute into the equations: we can find the cost of a buffet when we know how many plates of food are eaten, and we can find the number of gallons of water in an aquarium after filling it for a certain amount of time. But what if we were told the total amount Mindy spent at a buffet, and we were then asked to figure out how many plates of food she ate? What if we were told how much water was in the aquarium after a certain amount of time, and we were then asked how many minutes the hose must have been filling the aquarium in order for there to be that much water? Essentially, we are being asked to substitute a different value for a different variable in an equation that models a linear relationship. The following example illustrates this concept.

Example 1.3-3

3 1.3

The monthly membership fee for a food delivery service is \$22.50. The cost of dinners is included in the membership fee, but there is an additional fee of \$2.50 for each dessert. In April, Gus's membership and dessert fees were \$32.50. How many desserts did Gus have delivered that month?

A) 2

B) 3

C) 4

D) 5

Solution

1. We have to start by writing the equation that represents the total cost. Let's use t for the total amount of money Gus pays each month and d for the number of desserts. There is a constant charge of \$22.50, and the cost goes up by \$2.50 for every dessert Gus orders that month, so the equation is $t = 2.50d + 22.50$.

2. We know that his total charge in April was \$32.50, so we should replace t with 32.50.

$$t = 2.50d + 22.50$$
$$32.50 = 2.50d + 22.50$$

3. Now that we have substituted the total cost for April in the correct place, we can solve for d, the number of desserts Gus ordered that month.

$$32.50 = 2.50d + 22.50$$
$$10 = 2.50d$$
$$\frac{10}{2.50} = d$$
$$4 = d$$

4. The answer is C.

Notes

A problem like this could appear on either the Calculator or No Calculator section of the test. Don't panic when you see decimals and fractions. You know how many times \$2.50 goes into 10 dollars, just like you know how many times 25 cents goes into \$1.

When we're working with a linear equation of the form $y = mx + b$, we can be given any three of the four components (the value of x, the value of y, the coefficient m of x, and the value of the constant b) that comprise these equations and use them to determine the value of the remaining component. As long as you understand what type of information is represented by each component, you can easily work through problems that involve these types of relationships regardless of which values are given and which are unknown. If you write a nice equation, with well-chosen letters, it should be easy to substitute values for the information that you know in order to solve for the variable whose value you would like to find.

SkillDrill 1.3-1

Directions: Based on the situation described, write a mathematical equation that can be used to answer the question. If you have to choose your own variable, make sure to choose a letter that makes sense. Solve the equation to find the unknown value.

1. Emily earns \$12 for every pizza she sells. How much money, in dollars, will she have if she sells 5 pizzas?

2. The Tooth Fairy gains one tooth for every house she visits. How many teeth will she have after visiting 31 houses?

3. Brandon started the day with \$50 in his wallet, and he received another \$20 from each of his aunts during the day. If he has \$110 at the end of the day, how many aunts did he visit?

4. Charlie has 84 baseball cards and he buys 3 more every weekend. How many cards will he have after 2 weekends?

5. Priscilla has to eat 20 hamburgers to win a prize. It takes her 3 minutes to eat each hamburger. If she has been eating for 15 minutes, how many more hamburgers does she still have to eat?

Section 1.3 Suggested Problems from Real Tests

View related real-test problems at 1600.io/p/smtex?topic=1.3

Section 1.3 Practice Problems

1 1.3

The Finer Things Club (FTC) in a certain high school plans to increase its membership by a total of n members per year. There were m members in the FTC at the beginning of this year. Which function best models the total number of members, y, the FTC plans to have as members x years from now?

A) $y = nx + m$

B) $y = nx - m$

C) $y = mx + n$

D) $y = mx - n$

2 1.3

A home security company charges homeowners a onetime setup fee of \$220 plus d dollars for each month of home monitoring. If a homeowner paid \$640 for the first 12 months, including the setup fee, what is the value of d ?

A) 25

B) 35

C) 40

D) 50

3 1.3

An eagle takes off from a perch that is 10 feet above the ground. If the eagle rises at a constant rate of 23 feet per second, which of the following equations gives the height, h, in feet, of the eagle s seconds after it starts flying upwards?

A) $h = 10s + 23$

B) $h = 10s + \frac{23}{10}$

C) $h = 23s + 10$

D) $h = 23s + \frac{23}{10}$

4 1.3

Charles is planning to ride his bike 200 miles to prove something to himself. If he plans to ride 15 miles per hour, which of the following represents the remaining distance d, in miles, that Charles will have to ride his bike to achieve his goal after riding for n hours?

A) $d = 200 + 15n$

B) $d = 200n - 15$

C) $d = 15n - 200$

D) $d = 200 - 15n$

1.4 Function Notation/Inputs and Outputs

Let's look at an alternative way of writing equations that uses a different notation to represent the total amount. We call equations written in this new form **functions**. With functions, an input value is plugged into the function, some operations are performed on the input value, and then an output value is produced. We can represent the relationships we have talked about in this chapter using function notation, so let's write an equation as a function to see what functions look like.

For example, if 30 cubic feet of water is being pumped into a pool every minute, we could use v to represent the volume of water and t to represent the amount of time the pool is being filled. We could say that the volume of water in the pool is a **function** of time, t, because the volume of water is dependent only on the amount of time that has passed. Instead of just using v to represent the volume, we can use the notation $v(t)$ (pronounced "v of t") to show that v is a function of time. The equation representing this relationship could be written as $v(t) = 30t$ (the volume of water in the pool is 30 gallons per minute times the number of minutes the water flows into the pool).

The t in the parentheses is a placeholder for an input value just as variables are always placeholders. If we wanted to know how much water there would be after 3 minutes, we would use 3 for the value of the function's input variable t. Using function notation, we may be asked to find the value of $v(3)$ (pronounced "v of 3"), which means the value of v when t is 3. Whatever value replaces the variable in the parentheses gets substituted in for the variable everywhere it appears in the expression that defines the function, so in this case we replace each instance of t with 3.

$$v(t) = 30t$$
$$v(3) = 30(3)$$
$$v(3) = 90$$

Realize that **the function notation $v(3)$ does not mean "v times 3."** Many students get this confused because this is the first time they have seen parentheses used for a purpose other than multiplication. The test will let you know that v is a function by using the word "function" in the question. Even if the word "function" is not explicitly stated, it is more likely that $v(3)$ is function notation because v times 3 (or 3 times v) would normally be written as $3v$.

If a function called $f(x)$ is defined by the equation $f(x) = 3x + 2$, we can find $f(4)$, the output value when the input value is 4, by substituting 4 for x regardless of whether the function represents some real-world situation or it's a purely abstract mathematical construct; we simply substitute the input value and evaluate the expression to get the output value.

SkillDrill 1.4-1

Directions: Given the three functions below, $f(x)$, $g(x)$, and $h(x)$, find the value you are asked to find.

$$f(x) = 2x + 1 \qquad g(x) = -3x + 4 \qquad h(x) = \frac{1}{2}x - 2$$

Note that answers here can be negative, which is not the case with the test's Student Produced Response ("grid-in") questions.

1. $f(1)$ **2.** $g(0)$ **3.** $h(4)$ **4.** $f(-2)$

5. $g(4)$ **6.** $h(5)$ **7.** $f(10)$ **8.** $g(-2)$

9. $h(2)$ **10.** $f(0)$ **11.** $g(-3)$ **12.** $h(12)$

Directions: Using the same three functions listed above, find the input value x that will result in the given output value of the function.

13. $f(x) = 5$ **14.** $g(x) = 10$ **15.** $h(x) = 4$ **16.** $f(x) = 14$

17. $g(x) = -20$ **18.** $h(x) = -31$ **19.** $f(x) = 0$ **20.** $g(x) = 4$

21. $h(x) = -4$ **22.** $f(x) = 11$ **23.** $g(x) = 1$ **24.** $h(x) = \frac{1}{2}$

Example 1.4-1

1 1.4

$$f(x) = 4x + 1$$

The function f is defined above. What is the value of $f(-2)$?

A) -8

B) -7

C) 7

D) 9

Solution

1. Replace each x with -2.

$$f(x) = 4x + 1$$
$$f(-2) = 4(-2) + 1$$
$$f(-2) = -8 + 1$$
$$f(-2) = -7$$

2. The answer is B.

If you are told the value of a function for a particular x-value, you should substitute the x-value, but also replace the $f(x)$ term with the value of the function.

Example 1.4-2

2 1.4

$$f(x) = \frac{1}{2}x + b$$

In the function above, b is a constant. If $f(4) = 5$, what is the value of $f(-4)$?

A) -5

B) -2

C) 1

D) 3

Solution

1. When we are told that $f(4) = 5$, we know that the value of the function is 5 when x is 4. Replace each x with 4.

$$f(x) = \frac{1}{2}x + b$$

$$f(4) = \frac{1}{2}(4) + b$$

$$f(4) = 2 + b$$

2. Since we know that $f(4) = 5$, we can replace $f(4)$ with 5. Remember that $f(4) = 5$ does NOT mean "f times 4 equals 5," but instead tells us that the value of the function is 5 when x is 4. Making this replacement enables us to solve for b.

$$f(4) = 2 + b$$
$$5 = 2 + b$$
$$3 = b$$

3. Now that we have the value of b, we can replace b with 3 in the given function.

$$f(x) = \frac{1}{2}x + b$$

$$f(x) = \frac{1}{2}x + 3$$

4. Since we want to find $f(-4)$, which denotes the value of the function when x is -4, we should replace each instance of x with -4.

$$f(x) = \frac{1}{2}x + 3$$

$$f(-4) = \frac{1}{2}(-4) + 3$$

$$f(-4) = -2 + 3$$

$$f(-4) = 1$$

5. The answer is C.

Function notation is used in a variety of problem types on the test, so it's essential that you become familiar and comfortable with it. In general, when dealing with the graphs of functions in the xy-plane (which begins in the next chapter), the expression $f(x)$ refers to the y-value for a given x-value. For example, $f(4)$ is the y-value of the function when the x-value is 4 (this may be a hint that plugging in 4 for x is a useful step in that hypothetical problem).

Section 1.4 Suggested Problems from Real Tests

View related real-test problems at 1600.io/p/smtex?topic=1.4

Section 1.4 Practice Problems

1 1.4

$$f(x) = 3(x - 4) + 1$$

For the function f defined above, what is the value of $f(4)$?

A) -2

B) 0

C) 1

D) 4

2 1.4

A tank initially contains 4,678 cubic inches of orange juice. A pump begins emptying the orange juice at a constant rate of 63 cubic inches per minute. Which of the following functions best approximates the volume $v(t)$, in cubic inches, of orange juice in the tank t minutes after pumping begins, for $0 \leq t \leq 74$?

A) $v(t) = 4{,}678 - 63t$

B) $v(t) = 4{,}678 - 74t$

C) $v(t) = 4{,}678 + 63t$

D) $v(t) = 4{,}678 + 74t$

3 1.4

$$b(t) = \frac{3(6t - 10k)}{2} - 120$$

The number of people who bike on a public trail can be modeled by the function b above, where k is a constant and t is the air temperature in degrees Fahrenheit (°F) for $70 < t < 100$. If 480 people are predicted to bike on the trail when the temperature is 80°F, what is the value of k ?

A) 8

B) 10

C) 28

D) 30

4 1.4

$$f(x) = bx + 4$$

In the function above, b is a constant. If $f(1) = 3$, what is the value of $f(-3)$?

A) -3

B) -1

C) 1

D) 7

CHAPTER 1 RECAP

- Total Amount = (Amount per Thing × Number of Things) + Starting Amount
- **Expressions** consist only of numerical and variable terms being added, subtracted, multiplied, etc. For example, $40+2w$ is an expression. When we set this value equal to another expression, we can make an equation. **Equations** consist of two expressions that are set equal to each other using an equals sign (=).
- When writing your own expressions and equations, use letters that make sense for the variables so that you don't mistake what the letters stand for.
- The four components of a linear equation in the form $y = mx + b$ are the y-value (also called an output value when an equation is represented as a function), the x-value (the input value when working with function notation), the coefficient m of the x-term, and the constant b. We can solve for any one of these when we know the other three. Make sure you substitute given values for the the correct component.
- Functions are a type of equation for which an input value, often x, is plugged into an equation, producing an output value $f(x)$, which is read as "f of x."

  Note that $f(x)$ means the output value of a function when x is plugged into the function. It *does not* mean "f times x." For example, $f(3)$ means the value of the function when 3 is substituted for x.
- Whatever goes into the parentheses in a function is the input value. Replace all instances of the input variable with whatever is in the parentheses in order to find the function's value.

  If you are given the value of $f(x)$ and you're asked to find the corresponding value of x, you should replace the expression $f(x)$ with that value and then solve for the x-value that produced that output.

Additional Problems

1 1.4

$$f(x) = \frac{(x+8)}{5}$$

For the function f defined above, what is the value of $f(7) - f(-3)$?

A) 3

B) $\frac{12}{5}$

C) 2

D) $\frac{4}{5}$

2 1.3

A magazine debuted with 1,329 subscribers. The magazine's growth plan assumes that 270 new subscribers will be added each quarter (every 3 months) for the first 10 years. If an equation is written in the form $y = ax + b$ to represent the number of subscribers, y, subscribed to the magazine x quarters after the magazine debuted, what is the value of b?

3 1.2

John earns \$14.70 per hour at his part-time job. When he works z hours, he earns $14.70z$ dollars. Which of the following expressions gives the amount, in dollars, John will earn if he works $5z$ hours?

A) $5 + 14.70z$

B) $14.70(z + 5)$

C) $5z + 14.70z$

D) $5(14.70z)$

4 1.3

Cranjis rented a motorcycle for one day from a company that charges \$100 per day plus \$0.35 per mile driven. If she was charged a total of \$149 for the rental and mileage, for how many miles of driving was Cranjis charged? (Assume there is no tax.)

A) 35

B) 140

C) 285

D) 425

5 1.3

The acceleration due to gravity, in feet per second per second (ft/s^2), on Jupiter is 7 ft/s^2 less than 3 times the acceleration due to gravity on Venus. If the acceleration due to gravity on Jupiter is 80 ft/s^2, what is the acceleration due to gravity, in ft/s^2, on Venus?

6 1600.io 1.3

The equation $y = 0.2x$ models the relationship between the number of different exercises a certain fitness model performs, y, during an x-minute workout session. How many exercises did the fitness model perform if the session lasted 40 minutes?

A) 2

B) 5

C) 8

D) 20

7 1600.io 1.3

$$p = 17f - (6f + t)$$

The profit, p, in dollars, from producing and selling f frisbees is given by the equation above, where t is a constant. If 300 frisbees are produced and sold for a profit of \$2,150, what is the value of t?

8 1600.io 1.4

$$c(x) = mx + 360$$

A company's total cost $c(x)$, in euros (€), to produce x pantaloons is given by the function above, where m is a constant and $x > 0$. The total cost to produce 50 pantaloons is €660. What is the total cost, in euros, to produce 500 pantaloons? (Disregard the € sign when writing your answer.)

9 1600.io 1.4

$$f(x) = \frac{x+2}{3}$$

For the function f defined above, what is the value of $f(-2)$?

A) $-\frac{2}{3}$

B) 0

C) $\frac{1}{3}$

D) 1

10 1600.io 1.3

$$T = 2{,}000 + 20a$$

In the equation above, T represents Penny's total points in a video game, where a represents the number of apples she has caught in the game and 2,000 represents a starting bonus for choosing to play on a harder difficulty. If Penny scored a total of 4,400 points, how many apples did she catch in the game?

A) 100

B) 120

C) 220

D) 440

11 1.2

The top floor of a trapezoidal building has 4 rooms. There are 45 floors in total. If each floor has 3 more rooms than the floor above it, which expression gives the total number of rooms on the bottom floor?

A) $4 + 3(45 - 1)$

B) $4 + 3(45)$

C) $45(4 + 3)$

D) $4 + 3^{45}$

12 1.3

Paige was 37 inches tall the day she turned 4 years old, and she was 41 inches tall the day she turned 5 years old. If Paige's height increases by the same amount each year between the ages of 4 and 9, how many inches tall will she be the day she turns 8 years old?

Questions 13 and 14 refer to the following information.

Species of tree	Growth factor
Hackberry	3.1
Cottonwood	1.6
Silver maple	2.0
Norway maple	3.0
Blue spruce	2.1
Ponderosa pine	2.3
Crabapple	2.6
Honeylocust	2.7

One method of calculating the approximate age, in years, of a tree of a particular species is to multiply the diameter of the tree, in inches, by a constant called the growth factor for that species. The table above gives the growth factors for eight species of trees.

13 1.3

According to the information in the table, what is the approximate age of a Norway maple tree with a diameter of 18 inches?

A) 36 years

B) 42 years

C) 54 years

D) 58 years

14 1.3

If a ponderosa pine tree and a hackberry tree each now have a diameter of 10 inches, which of the following will be closest to the difference, in inches, of their diameters 10 years from now?

A) 1.0

B) 1.1

C) 1.2

D) 1.3

15 1600.io 1.3

A water company charges Franklin \$0.04 per gallon of water he uses in his house. If Franklin was charged \$40 by the water company, how many gallons of water did Franklin use?

A) 0.01

B) 100

C) 160

D) 1,000

16 1600.io 1.4

The function g is defined as $g(x) = \frac{4x}{5} + 4$. What is the value of $g(-50)$?

A) −46

B) −44

C) −36

D) −6

17 1600.io 1.3

On its opening day, a bicycle shop had an inventory of 42 bikes. During the first 3 months, 21 additional bikes were purchased by the shop each week, and the sales team sold an average of 14 bikes per week. During the first three months, which of the following equations best models the bike inventory, b, at the shop t weeks after opening?

A) $b = -7t + 42$

B) $b = \frac{2}{3}t + 42$

C) $b = 7t + 42$

D) $b = 14t + 42$

18 1600.io 1.3

A company that makes plastic toys purchases a 3D printer for \$4,360. The printer depreciates in value at a constant rate for 8 years, after which it is considered to have no monetary value. How much is the printer worth 2 years after it is purchased?

A) \$1,090

B) \$2,180

C) \$3,270

D) \$3,815

Answer Key

SkillDrill 1.2-1

1. $12p$
2. h
3. $50 + 20a$
4. $84 + 3w$
5. $3(20 - h)$ or $60 - 3h$

Section 1.2 Practice Problems

1. B
2. C

SkillDrill 1.3-1

1. 60
2. 31
3. 3
4. 90
5. 15

Section 1.3 Practice Problems

1. A
2. B
3. C
4. D

SkillDrill 1.4-1

1. 3
2. 4
3. 0
4. -3
5. -8
6. $\frac{1}{2}$
7. 21
8. 10
9. -1
10. 1
11. 13
12. 4
13. 2
14. -2
15. 12
16. $\frac{13}{2}$ or 6.5
17. 8
18. -58
19. $\frac{-1}{2}$ or -0.5
20. 0
21. -4
22. 5
23. 1
24. 5

Section 1.4 Practice Problems

1. C
2. A
3. A
4. D

Additional Problems

1. C
2. 1329
3. D
4. B
5. 29
6. C
7. 1150
8. 3360
9. B
10. B
11. A
12. 53
13. C
14. B
15. D
16. C
17. C
18. C

Slope-Intercept Form 2

2.1 Why They're Called Linear Relationships

Now it's time to see where linear relationships get their name. To start, you need to be familiar with the ***xy*-plane**.

The xy-plane consists of two lines called **axes**. The ***x*-axis** goes from left to right (horizontal). The ***y*-axis** goes from bottom to top (vertical).

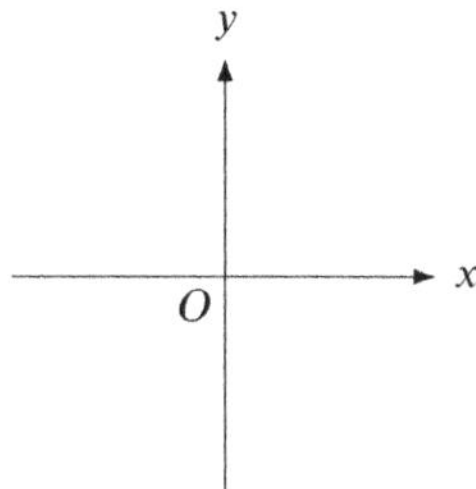

Typically, the point where the two axes cross is called the **origin** (usually marked with an O), and it is the point where both the x-value and y-value are equal to 0. When working with graphs of mathematical functions, the x- and y-axes will comply with this arrangement, but it's important to note that data sets represented as scatter plots, lines of best fit, and other statistical information are sometimes shown on graphs where the axes do **not** cross at their 0 values, and you must be alert for this situation, as it comes up often on the test.

There are often additional vertical and horizontal lines drawn on the plane that form a grid; these are evenly spaced lines that mark successive x- or y-values.

Because the y-axis goes straight up through the origin, which has an x-value of 0, all the points on the y-axis also have an x-value of 0. To the right of the y-axis are positive values of x, and to the left of the y-axis are negative values of x. The other vertical gridlines are usually (but not always!) used to denote the successive whole number values of x: 1, 2, 3, etc. To find the x-value of a point from a graph in that common arrangement, just count how many gridlines there are to the left or right of the y-axis.

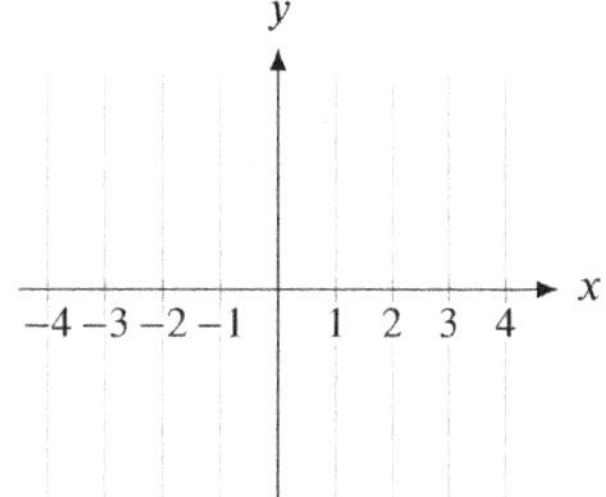

The x-axis goes straight through the origin from left to right, and because the origin has a y-value of 0, all the points on the x-axis also have a y-value of 0. Above the x-axis are positive values of y, and below the x-axis are negative values of y. The other horizontal gridlines are usually (but not always!) used to denote the successive whole number values of y: 1, 2, 3, etc. To find the y-value of a point from a graph like that, count how many gridlines there are above or below the x-axis.

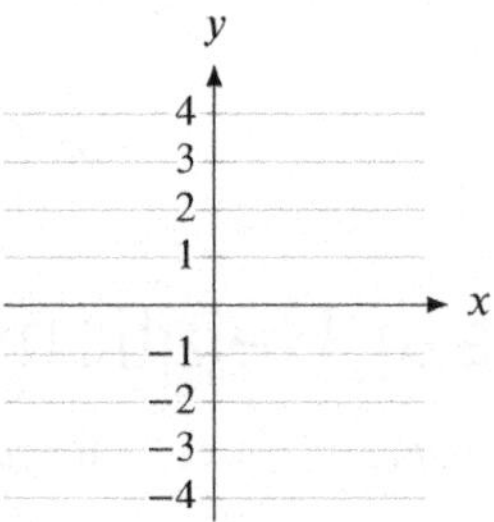

Points on this xy-plane will often be provided using the notation (x, y) where the first number tells us the x-value, and the second number tells us the corresponding y-value. For example, the point $(4, 2)$ is 4 lines to the right of the y-axis because the x-value is 4, and it's 2 lines above the x-axis because the y-value is 2. Because the *order* in which the two elements appear is important—the first value is the x-value, and the second, the y-value—this notation represents what is called an **ordered pair**. The ordered pair that represents the origin is $(0, 0)$ because both the x-and y-values are 0.

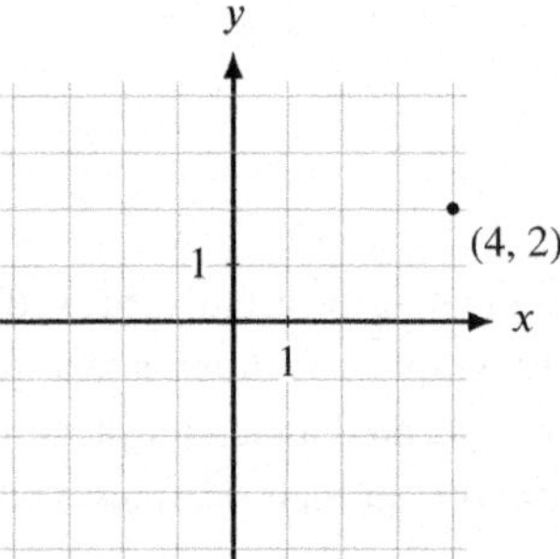

Another way you may be given the coordinates of points is based on function notation. For example, if you are told that $f(4) = 2$, then you know that $(4, 2)$ is a point on the graph of the function because the function's y-value is equal to 2 when the x-value is equal to 4. In other words, when plotting a function f on the xy-plane, $y = f(x)$.

The x- and y-axes divide the xy-plane into four **quadrants** that are numbered with Roman numerals starting in the upper right hand corner and going counter-clockwise.

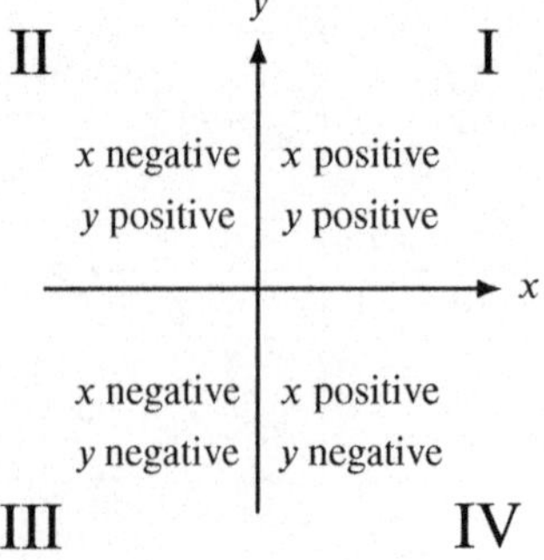

SkillDrill 2.1-1

Directions: Write the ordered pair of x- and y-coordinates for each labeled point in the figure below.

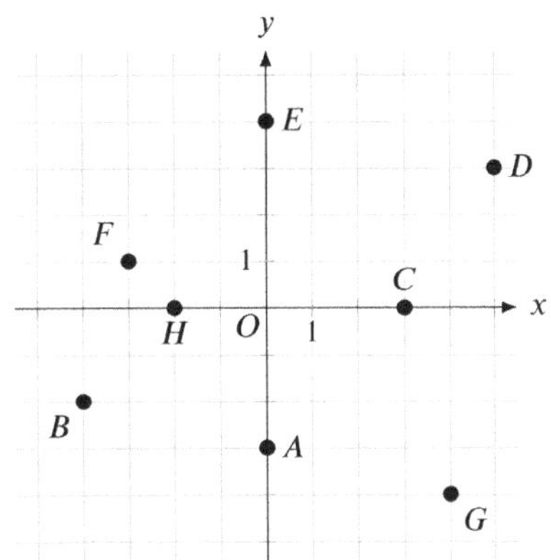

1. Point A

2. Point B

3. Point C

4. Point D

5. Point E

6. Point F

7. Point G

8. Point H

Slopes

Now that we know about how points are represented on the xy-plane, let's relate this idea to a real world situation. We will plot some data points based on a scenario and see how they form a **line**, and linear relationships, when graphed in the xy-plane, produce **lines**—that's precisely why these relationships are "linear" (line-ar).

Molly is taking a ride on a cable car to the top of a tall building in a big city. The boarding platform is at ground level, and the building, which is located 500 feet away from the boarding dock, is 1,000 feet tall.

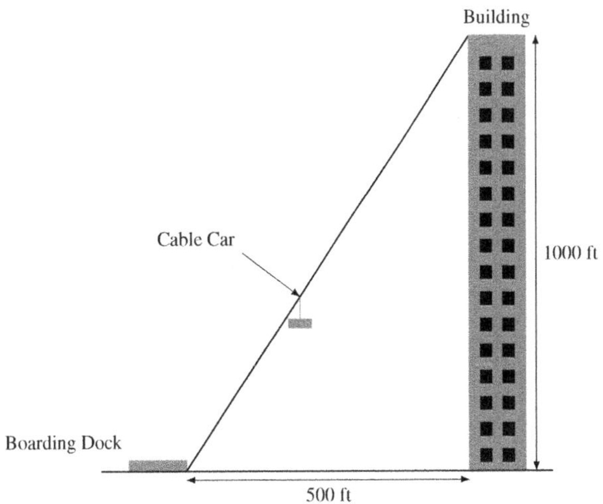

If Molly wanted to get to the top of the building without riding the cable car, she would have to walk horizontally 500 ft along the ground and then ride an elevator vertically 1,000 ft. The cable car, on the other hand, travels a straight line path from the dock to the top of the building that covers both the horizontal distance and vertical distance at the same time.

We can represent the cable on the xy-plane and use it to find the equation of the linear relationship between the height of the cable car and its horizontal distance from the boarding dock. If we use x to represent Molly's horizontal distance from the dock and y to represent her height above the ground, then when Molly is first starting her ride, we can say that 0 is an x-value and 0 is the corresponding y-value (she is at the boarding dock). Therefore, if we were to graph this point, we would graph the point $(0, 0)$, which is the origin.

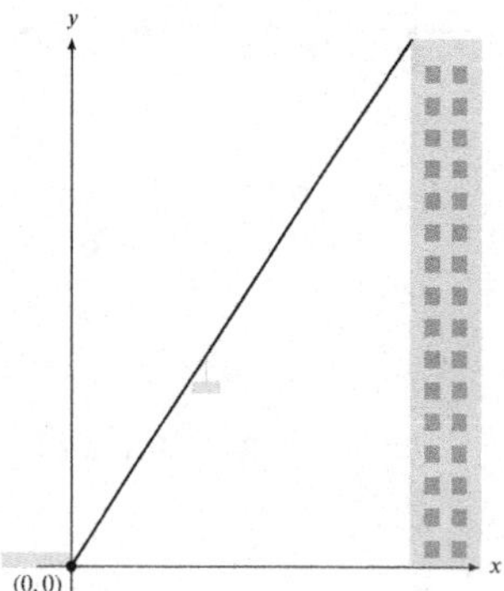

In order to define a specific line on a graph, we need at least two points so we can draw a line through both of them. When Molly is at the top of the building, she is 500 feet away horizontally (the x-value is 500) from the boarding dock, and she is 1,000 ft above the boarding dock (the y-value is 1000), so another point on the graph is (500, 1000). When we graph this point and draw a line connecting the two points we have labelled, we can see a representation of the vertical distance from the boarding dock as a function of the horizontal distance from the boarding dock.

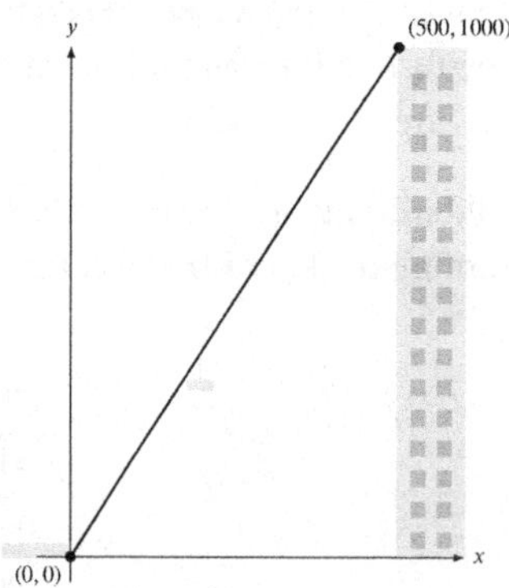

If the boarding dock were built closer to the base of the building, this would affect how slanted the line graph would be. The cable car would have to cover the same vertical distance in a smaller horizontal space. For example, if the boarding dock were only 250 ft away from the building, the tow line would be twice as steep.

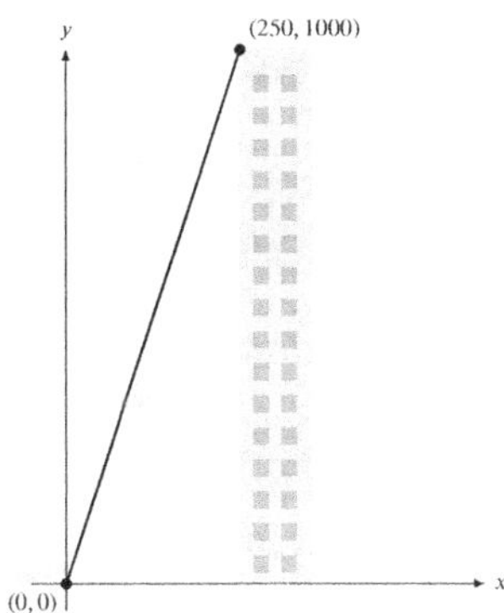

We can write an equation to represent Molly's height as a function of the distance from the boarding dock based on the new, steeper configuration. Her starting height is 0, but we also need to find the amount that her height changes as she moves away from the boarding dock. When we look at any two points on the line, we can find how much Molly moves upward for every foot she moves forward. Let's use the points $(0, 0)$ and $(250, 1000)$.

We can draw two arrows that show how far away the end point at the top of the building lies from the starting point horizontally (in the x-direction) and vertically (in the y-direction). How far across we go represents the *change* in x-value; we can use the Greek letter delta (Δ) to mean "change in," so we write the change in x-value as Δx, pronounced "delta x." Similarly, how far up or down we go (that is, the movement parallel to the y-axis) represents the *change* in y-value; we write that change in y-value as Δy, pronounced "delta y."

Between the two points in our picture, $(0, 0)$ and $(250, 1000)$, we can draw in two arrows (the over-and-up arrows) showing the change in the x- and y-values.

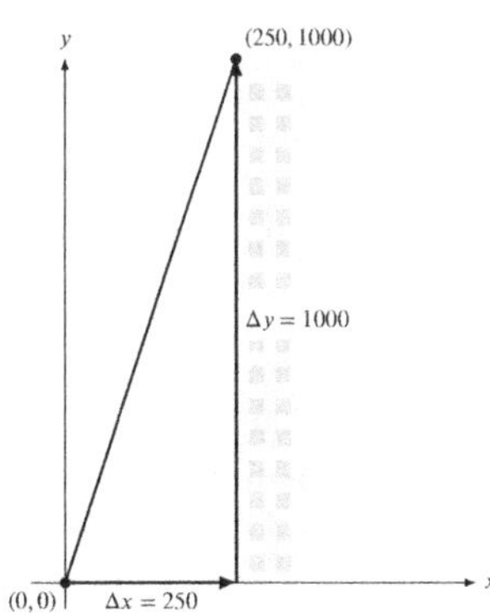

The y-value goes up by 1,000, so $\Delta y = 1000$. The x-value increases by 250, so $\Delta x = 250$. The word that we use to describe the steepness of such a graphed line is **slope**, and we define slope as the amount y changes relative to a change in x, so slope is calculated simply by dividing Δy (the change in y) by Δx (the change in x). For this line, the slope is therefore $\frac{1000}{250}$ or 4.

Slope

Slope is a quantity that shows the "steepness" of a line. It is commonly denoted by the variable m, and it is calculated using the following formula, where Δy is the change in y-values and Δx is the change in x-values.

$$m = \frac{\Delta y}{\Delta x}$$

Alternatively, the change in y-values can be more formally written as $y_2 - y_1$, where y_1 is the y-value of the first point and y_2 is the y-value of the second point. The change in x-values can be written as $x_2 - x_1$, where x_1 is the x-value of the first point and x_2 is the x-value of the second point. This equation is referred to as the **Slope Formula**.

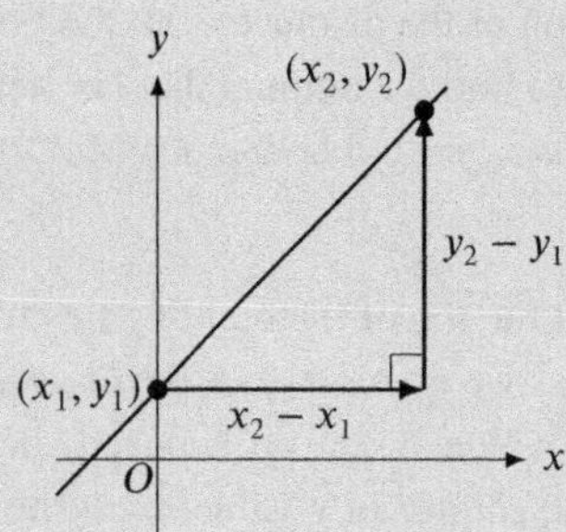

$$m = \frac{y_2 - y_1}{x_2 - x_1}$$

While this second form of the equation is not incorrect and is sometimes useful, in general, a quicker and less error-prone method of finding the slope is by traveling from one point to the other by drawing the over-and-up arrows (as in the example above) and determining their lengths to find Δy and Δx based on the graph alone. It is very easy to mess up signs and values when substituting the coordinates of two points into the Slope Formula. However, if the points are far apart, it could be very time-consuming to do all the incremental counting required using the traveling method, and errors can creep in, so in these circumstances, the Slope Formula is the better choice.

When given points on a line, you should always start by finding the slope whenever possible. It is very rare that the slope is not important to solving a problem involving lines.

For completeness, we will demonstrate using the Slope Formula to find the same information, though we recommend drawing the over-and-up arrows on the graph to find the slope directly. The first point we will choose is $(0, 0)$, which means that $x_1 = 0$ and $y_1 = 0$. The second point is $(250, 1000)$, which means that $x_2 = 250$ and $y_2 = 1000$. Plug these values into the slope formula and be careful that you are consistent about which point is (x_1, y_1) and which point is (x_2, y_2).

$$m = \frac{y_2 - y_1}{x_2 - x_1}$$

$$m = \frac{1000 - 0}{250 - 0}$$

$$m = \frac{1000}{250}$$

$$m = 4$$

The slope of a particular line will be the same no matter which two points are chosen or which point is (x_1, y_1) and which point is (x_2, y_2). What if, instead of $(0, 0)$ and $(250, 1000)$, we chose the points $(250, 1000)$ and $(125, 500)$ (this is the midpoint of the tow line because it is half of the total x distance and half of the total y-distance between the boarding dock and the top of the building)? Note also that it doesn't matter whether we draw the over-and-up arrows above or below the line in question, as long as we make sure to go from left to right (it is not wrong to go from right to left, but you have to be careful to take negative signs into account because Δx would be negative if we go from right to left).

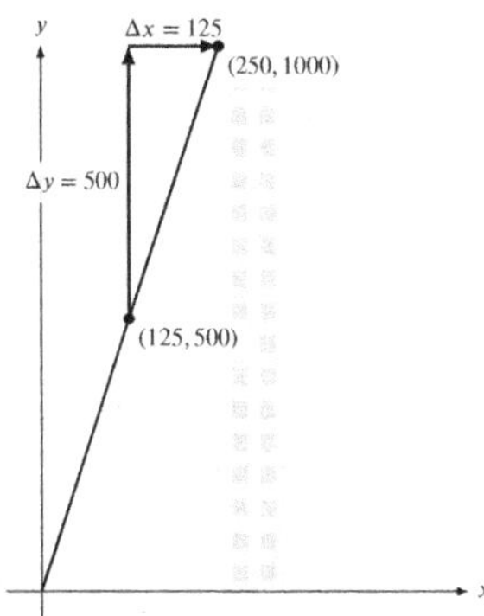

The y-value goes up by 500, so Δy is 500. The x-value goes up by 125, so Δx is 125. The slope is $\frac{500}{125}$, which still simplifies to 4.

SkillDrill 2.1-2

Directions: Find the slope of the line containing the two points found in the figure below.

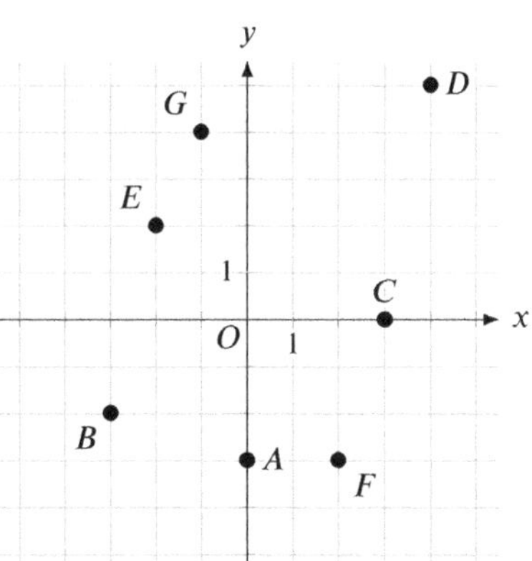

1. Points A and C
2. Points A and D
3. Points C and D
4. Points B and E
5. Points C and F
6. Points D and F
7. Points B and D
8. Points B and G

Slope-Intercept Form

The next thing to determine when you are trying to find the equation of a line based on a graph is the points where the line crosses the axes. These crossing points are called **intercepts**.

Specifically, we are interested in the point where the line crosses the y-axis. For any linear graph, the point where the line crosses the y-axis is called the ***y*-intercept**.

y-intercept

The *y*-intercept is the point where a line crosses the *y*-axis. Another way of thinking about the y-intercept is that it's **the value of *y* when the *x*-value is 0** (the y-intercept is the value of $f(0)$). This quantity is often represented by the variable b.

In the graph below, the y-intercept is 2 because the line passes through the point $(0, 2)$, which is on the y-axis.

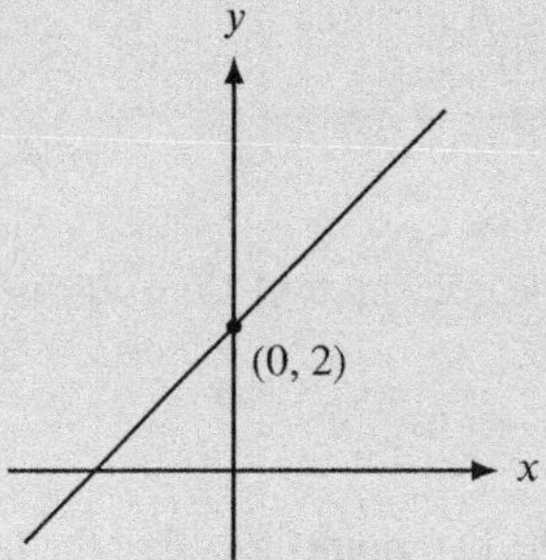

In real world problems, the y-intercept represents a starting or base amount when the x-value is 0. For example, if your cell phone plan charges you a fixed fee for the line each month plus an additional amount depending on how much data you use, the y-intercept of the function representing this linear relationship will be that base fee for the line; that's what you'd pay even if you use 0 gigabytes of data in a given month. As another example, in the last chapter, we talked about George's numerous pens, and the number of pens he started his collection with is 20, so 20 is the y-intercept.

When you need to solve for the *y*-intercept of the graph of an equation or function, substitute 0 for *x* and solve for *y*.

x-intercept

The *x*-intercept is the point where a line crosses the *x*-axis, and it can also be thought of as the value of *x* when the *y*-value is 0.

In the graph below, the x-intercept is -2 because the line passes through the point $(-2, 0)$, which is on the x-axis.

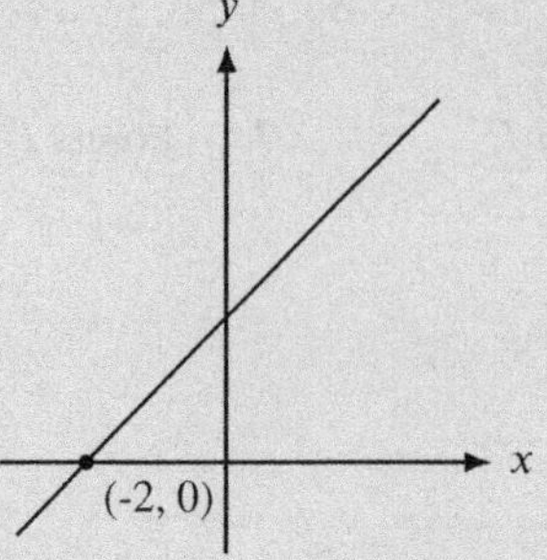

When you need to solve for the *x*-intercept of the graph of an equation or function, substitute 0 for *y* and solve for *x*.

All we have done is given new names to concepts we were already familiar with. The starting amount is the y-intercept, and the amount the values change is the slope. We can use this information to define a general linear equation that can be used even when we don't have a real world context to work from. It's called the **Slope-Intercept Form** of a line, and it's one of the most useful representations of lines on this test.

Slope-Intercept Form

For a line with slope m and y-intercept b, the Slope-Intercept Form of linear equations is the following:

$$y = mx + b$$

Note that any of the letters in the Slope-Intercept Form can change; the letters used above are the ones most commonly used by convention, but sometimes different letters that are more meaningful in the context of a specific problem are used instead for clarity. The arrangement and meaning of the terms are what really matter.

In the case of Molly on the cable car, we can find the equation that represents the linear relationship between her height above the ground and her distance (horizontally) from the boarding dock based on just two points on the line. We used the points $(0, 0)$ and $(250, 1000)$ to find that the slope of the line is 4. Also, we know the y-intercept of the line because the cable passes through the point $(0, 0)$; since the x-value of the point is 0, this point is the y-intercept of the line. Since we know the slope is 4 and the y-intercept is 0, the equation that represents the linear relationship in this example is $y = 4x + 0$, or just $y = 4x$.

SkillDrill 2.1-3

Directions: Given a linear equation in Slope-Intercept Form, identify the value of the slope, m, and the y-intercept, b.

1. $y = 2x + 1$ **2.** $y = 3x + 6$ **3.** $y = x - 7$ **4.** $y = 5x$

Directions: Write the equation of the line in Slope-Intercept Form given the value of the slope, m, and the y-intercept, b.

5. $m = 5, b = -4$ **6.** $m = 8, b = 1$ **7.** $m = 1, b = 0$ **8.** $m = 2, b = -2$

Let's walk through an example problem that requires us to write the equation of the line without any real world context. To do so, we will need to pull points from the graph in order to find the equation of the line. Sometimes points on a line are marked by black dots that are labelled with the x- and y-value of the point. Often, however, you will have to determine points on a line by using the gridlines to read the x- and y-values of the point. **Make sure to use points where the line crosses through the intersection of two gridlines whenever possible so that you know the exact coordinates of the point on the line**.

Example 2.1-1

1 1600.io 2.1

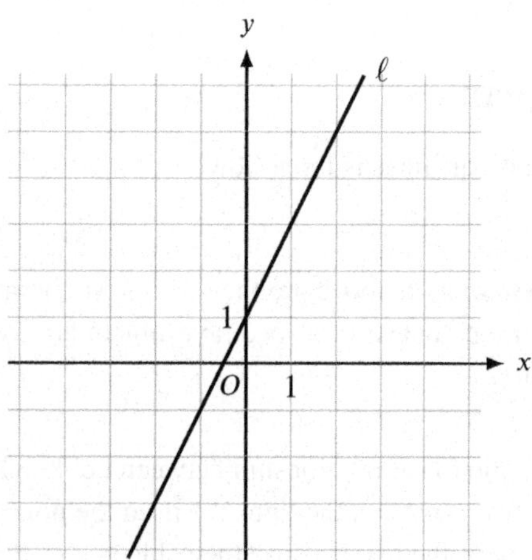

Which of the following is an equation of line ℓ in the xy-plane above?

A) $x = 2$

B) $y = 1$

C) $y = x + 2$

D) $y = 2x + 1$

Solution

1. We know the equation of a line is of the form $y = mx + b$, and we need to find m, which represents the slope, and b, which represents the y-intercept (you can find them in any order depending on which is easier).

2. It is clear that the line passes through the point $(0, 1)$, which tells us that the y-intercept of the line is 1. We can replace b in the general Slope-Intercept Form with 1.

$$y = mx + b$$

$$y = mx + 1$$

3. We can find the slope by picking any two points on the line and finding the changes in x- and y-values between those points. Make sure to pick points that are located at the crossing of two gridlines. The best one to start with is the point $(0, 1)$ because this is the y-intercept and this tells us that the y-intercept is 1. We can pick any other point on the line that is also where two grid lines meet. Let's use $(2, 5)$ (the point $(1, 3)$ is also a good choice).

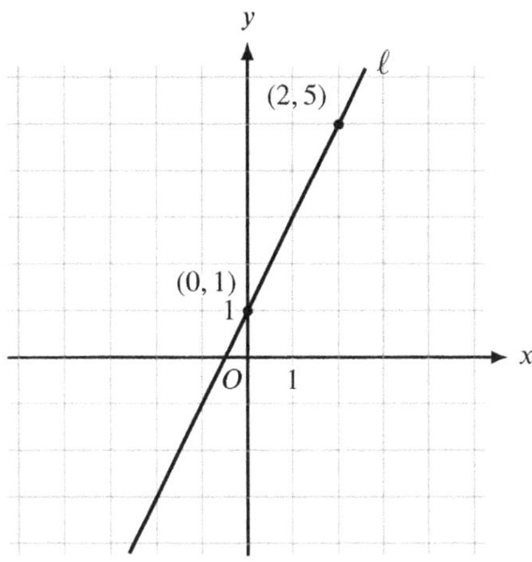

4. Draw the over-and-up arrows to find Δy and Δx.

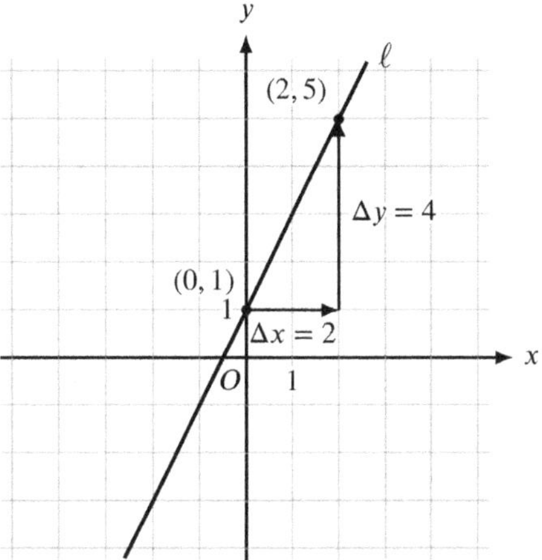

5. The y-value increases by 4, so $\Delta y = 4$, and the x-value increases by 2, so $\Delta x = 2$. Therefore, the slope, which is equal to $\frac{\Delta y}{\Delta x}$, is $\frac{4}{2}$ or 2.
6. Replace m with 2 in the general Slope-Intercept Form to find the equation of the line.

$$y = 2x + 1$$

7. The answer is D.

Notes

You can also use the Slope Formula to find the slope of the line, but usually drawing the over-and-up arrows is the preferred method, especially when the picture is already halfway drawn for you.

Slopes Aren't Always Positive Integers

The slopes of lines are not always positive; they can be positive, negative, or zero. Also, a slope does not need to be an integer.

David owns an adventure course with a zipline on which the rider starts 20 ft in the air, and the zipline is sloped such that the height drops by 1 ft for every 4 ft that a rider travels horizontally.

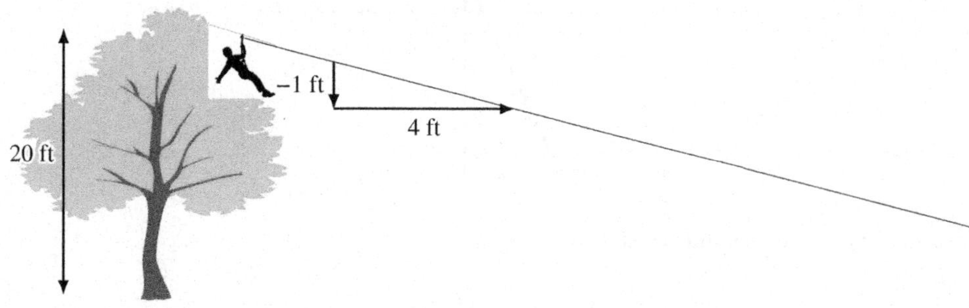

In this example, we can say that the y-intercept is 20 because the zipliner starts at a height of 20 feet off the ground when he has moved 0 ft away from the tree. The slope is $\frac{-1}{4}$ because the rider's height goes down by 1 ft (that is, it changes by -1 ft) for every 4 ft he moves away from the tree. The equation of the line is $y = \frac{-1}{4}x + 20$.

Note that a negative fractional slope might be written in the form $\frac{-1}{4}$ or $-\frac{1}{4}$, but the value is the same; in the example below, the second form is used, so don't let that confuse you. Also note that when we draw the over-and-down arrows, we are still working from left to right so that Δx (the "over") will always be positive and Δy can be positive or negative depending on how the y-values change between the two points.

Example 2.1-2

2 1600.io 2.1

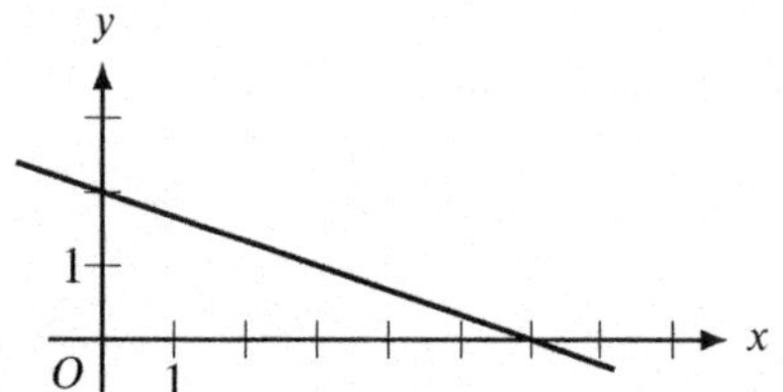

Which of the following could be an equation for the graph shown in the xy-plane above?

A) $y = -\frac{1}{3}x + 6$

B) $y = -3x + 2$

C) $y = -\frac{1}{3}x + 2$

D) $y = -3x + 6$

Solution

1. We need to pick points to find the equation of the line. In this case, since there are no gridlines, the only points we can use are the y-intercept, which is the point $(0, 2)$, and the x-intercept, which is the point $(6, 0)$. Since we know from the graph that the y-intercept is 2, we can eliminate choices A and D, which show 6 as the y-intercept.

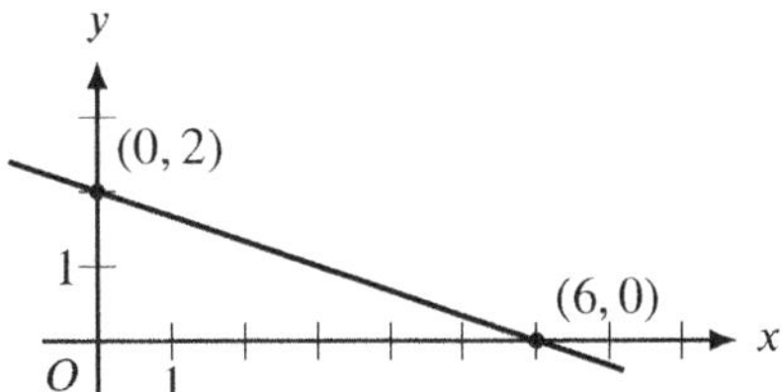

2. Draw the over-and-down arrows to show the change in the y-values and the change in the x-values.

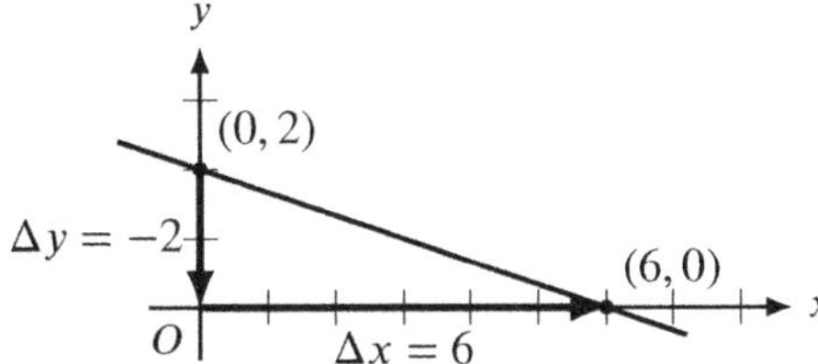

   The y-value decreases by 2, so $\Delta y = -2$. The x-value increases by 6, so $\Delta x = 6$. Therefore, the slope is $\frac{-2}{6}$, or $\frac{-1}{3}$ when we reduce the fraction.

3. Since the slope is $\frac{-1}{3}$ and the y-intercept is 2, the equation of the line is $y = \frac{-1}{3}x + 2$.

4. The answer is C.

Notes

You could have used the Slope Formula to find the slope; we'll use $(0, 2)$ as point 1 and $(6, 0)$ as point 2, but you could have chosen the reverse assignment, as it has no effect on the result.

$$m = \frac{y_2 - y_1}{x_2 - x_1}$$

$$m = \frac{0 - 2}{6 - 0}$$

$$m = \frac{-2}{6}$$

$$m = \frac{-1}{3}$$

Once again, this method is not incorrect, but it is easy to mess up. If you are going to choose to use the Slope Formula, make sure your work is neatly written out, with all steps shown.

As you can see, it's possible to encounter linear relationships that do not have positive integer slopes, but finding the slope of these lines is just as easy when you are given a graph on which to find the slope. If you are given a real world situation in which the y-variable decreases as the x-variable increases, you do not necessarily need to graph the points to find the slope or equation of the line. For example, if the average temperature in a certain country drops by 1°C every 10 days during the winter, then in a linear equation representing the average temperature in this country during winter, we can say that the slope must be $\frac{-1}{10}$ because the temperature decreases by 1 when the number of days increases by 10.

Vertical and Horizontal Lines

One last topic that is related to slopes of lines is the slopes of vertical and horizontal lines.

Vertical Lines

Vertical lines are lines where the x-value never changes. They have equations like $x = 5$, which tells us that the x-value is always 5 and the y-value does not depend on the x-value at all.

The slope of these lines is undefined, and looking at the Slope Formula will tell us why. Since the x-value does not change, $\Delta x = 0$. When we substitute 0 for Δx in the Slope Formula, we have a problem because it is impossible to divide by 0.

$$m = \frac{\Delta y}{0} = \text{undefined}$$

From this, it should be clear that vertical lines have equations written in the form $x = c$, where c is a constant value. Note, importantly, that this equation is not in Slope-Intercept form, because that form cannot represent a vertical line. For any point on vertical lines, the x-value is fixed, but each point will have a different y-value.

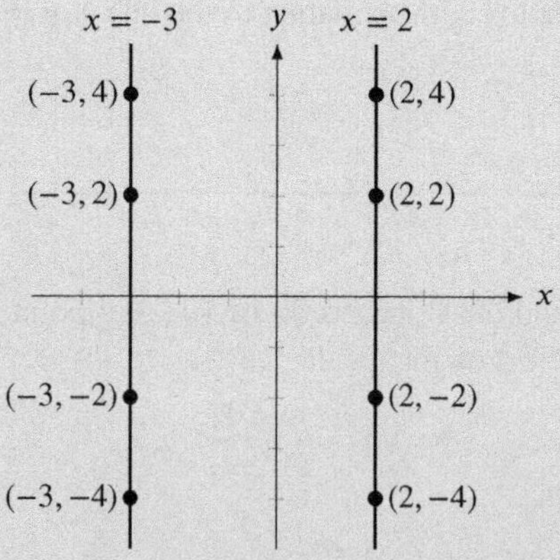

We can use the Slope Formula to verify that the slope between any two of these points is undefined. From the line $x = 2$, let's use $(2,4)$ as (x_1, y_1) and $(2,2)$ as (x_2, y_2).

$$m = \frac{y_2 - y_1}{x_2 - x_1} = \frac{2-4}{2-2} = \frac{-2}{0} = \text{undefined}$$

Horizontal Lines

Horizontal lines are lines where the y-value never changes. They have equations like $y = -2$, which tells us that the y-value is always -2 no matter what the x-value is.

The slope of these lines is 0. Since the y-value does not change, $\Delta y = 0$. When we substitute 0 for Δy in the Slope Formula, the numerator is 0, and 0 divided by a number is still 0.

$$m = \frac{0}{\Delta x}$$

From this, it should be clear that horizontal lines have equations written in the form $y = c$, where c is a constant value. Note that, unlike the equation for a vertical line, the horizontal line equation is in Slope-Intercept form, as it is equivalent to $y = 0x + c$.

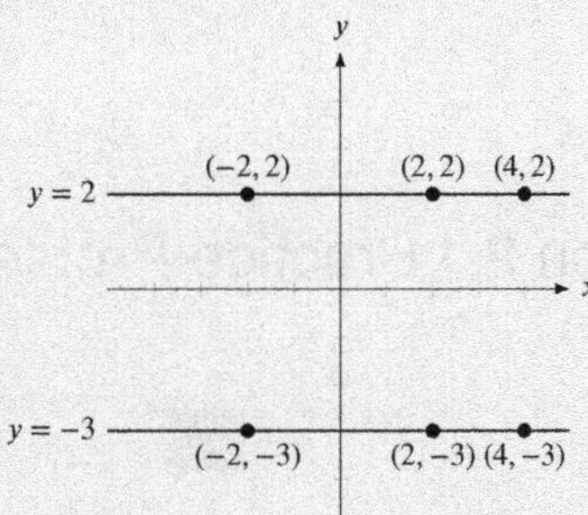

We can use the Slope Formula to verify that the slope between any two of these points is equal to 0. From the line $y = 2$, let's use $(4, 2)$ as (x_1, y_1) and $(-2, 2)$ as (x_2, y_2).

$$m = \frac{y_2 - y_1}{x_2 - x_1} = \frac{2-2}{4-(-2)} = \frac{0}{6} = 0$$

SkillDrill 2.1-4

Directions: Based on the points in the figure below, find the equation of the line in Slope-Intercept Form (or $x = c$ form for vertical lines) that contains the two listed points, and find the coordinates of the x-intercept (if there is an x-intercept).

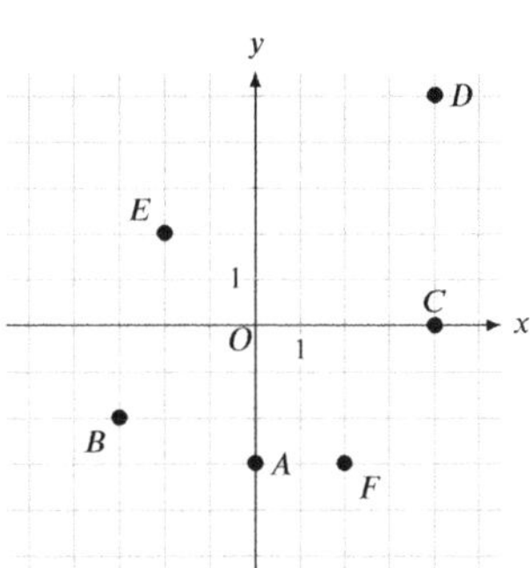

1. Points A and B

2. Points B and D

3. Points E and D

4. Points E and F

5. Points A and F

6. Points C and D

7. Points B and C

8. Points E and C

Section 2.1 Suggested Problems from Real Tests

View related real-test problems at 1600.io/p/smtex?topic=2.1

Section 2.1 Practice Problems

1 1600.io 2.1

In the xy-plane, what is the y-intercept of the line with the equation $y = 3x - 2$?

A) 3

B) $\frac{1}{3}$

C) $-\frac{1}{3}$

D) -2

2 1600.io 2.1

The line graphed in the xy-plane below models the total cost, in dollars, for a paddleboat rental, y, in a certain city park based on the number of hours the paddleboat is rented, x.

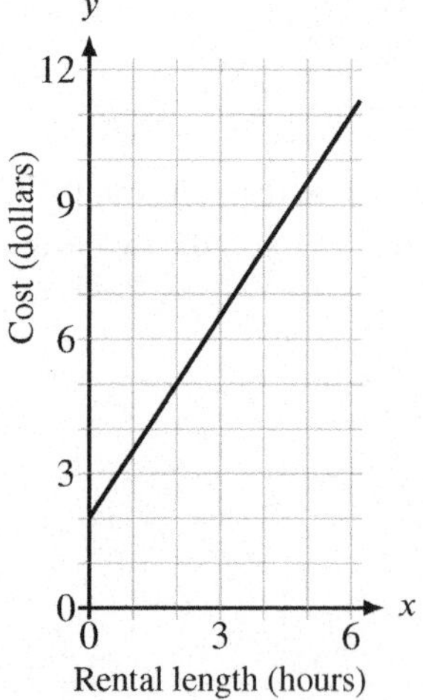

According to the graph, what is the cost for each additional hour, in dollars, of the rental?

A) \$0.50

B) \$1.00

C) \$1.50

D) \$2.00

3 2.1

Line t is shown in the xy-plane below.

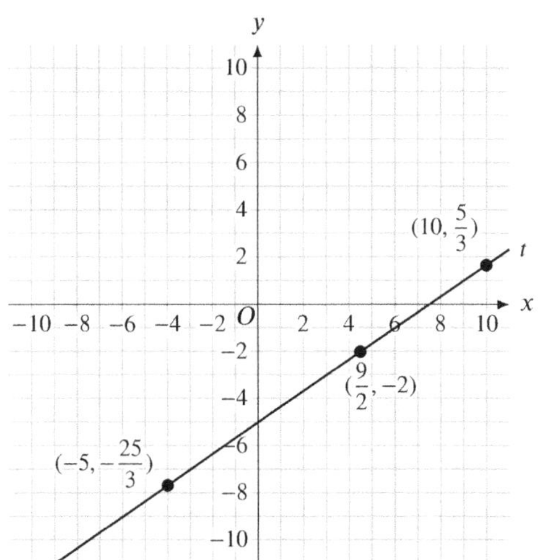

What is the slope of line t ?

4 2.1

The graph of $y = f(x)$ is a line in the xy-plane that passes through the point $(0, 7)$ and has a slope of 3. Which of the following equations could define the function f ?

A) $f(x) = -\frac{1}{7}x + 3$

B) $f(x) = -\frac{1}{3}x + 7$

C) $f(x) = 3x + 7$

D) $f(x) = 7x + 3$

2.2 Analyzing Graphs of Linear Equations

In a way, we have already walked through the process of making a graphical representation of a linear relationship, but we used real world examples like hills and ziplines, which both have natural slopes and automatically conjure up a mental image of a sloped line. However, we need to be able to identify the graphs of linear equations based on the equations themselves, without the aid of any real world context.

Luckily, the Slope-Intercept Form of lines provides us with enough useful information to identify the graph of a linear equation based on the slope and y-intercept, which are the two key visual features of line graphs.

Graphing Slope and *y*-intercept

When you have to identify the graph that corresponds to a linear equation, the key features to look out for are the slope and y-intercept.

Start by eliminating any choices that do not pass through the correct y-intercept value. Then check that the line slopes in the correct direction (positive or negative slope). Finally, if there are still multiple remaining choices, make sure that the slope is the correct value (i.e. if the slope is supposed to be -2, make sure that the graph goes down by 2 units for every 1 unit it goes to the right).

Example 2.2-1

2.2

Which of the following is the graph of the equation $y = -2x + 3$ in the xy-plane?

A)

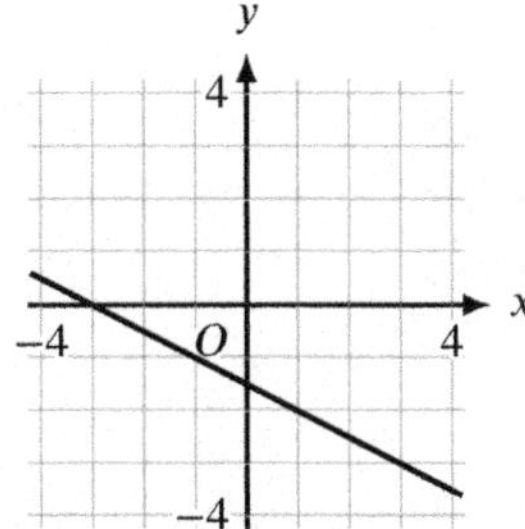

B)

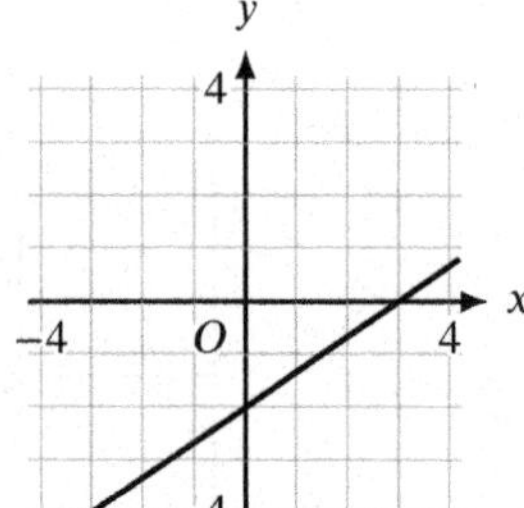

C)

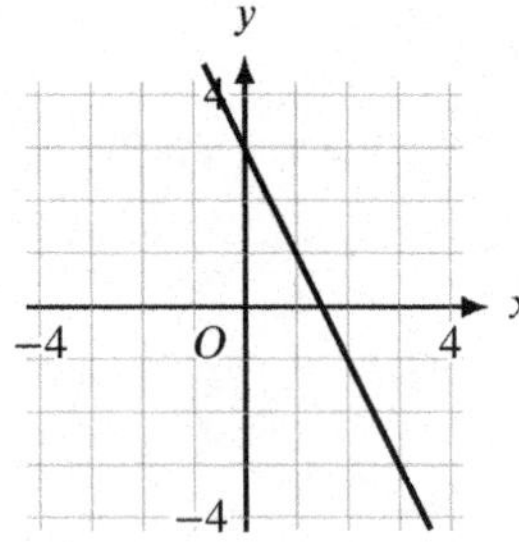

D)

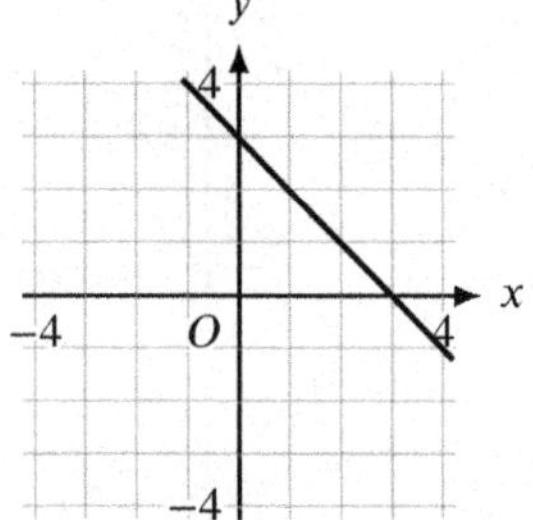

Solution

1. The y-intercept of the given equation is 3, so eliminate choices A and B, which do not pass through the y-axis at $y = 3$ (that is, at the point $(0, 3)$).

2. The slope of the line is negative (it's -2), but the remaining choices (C and D) have negative slopes, so we cannot eliminate either of them immediately. We need to choose the graph that has a slope of -2.
   Looking at the two remaining choices, we can start from the y-intercept and see how much the graphs go down and over to see which has a slope of -2. The correct answer will be the graph that goes down by 2 units for every 1 unit it goes over.

Choice C

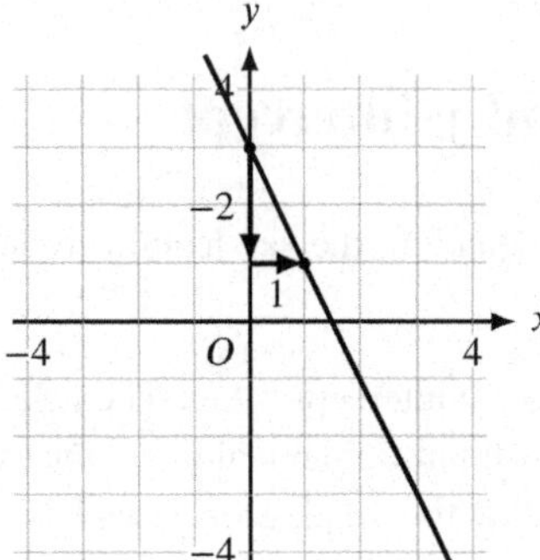

Choice D

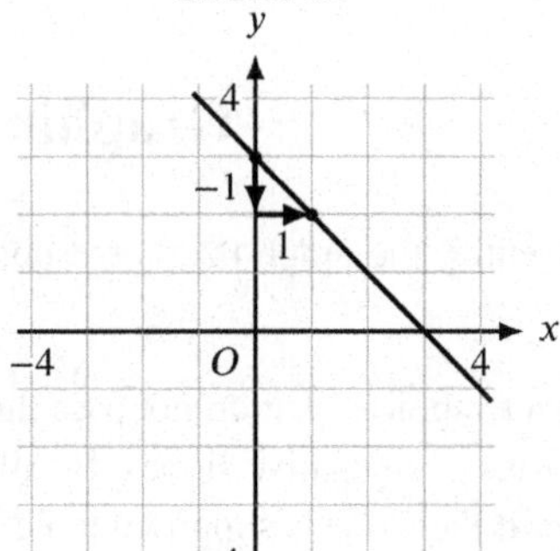

3. The graph of choice C is the one that has a slope of -2 because the graph goes down by 2 units for every 1 unit it goes over; the graph of choice D goes down by 1 unit for every 1 unit it goes over, so its slope is -1, and that does not match the slope we're looking for.

4. The answer is C.

View related real-test problems at 1600.io/p/smtex?topic=2.2

Section 2.2 Practice Problems

---

1 2.2

Which of the following is the graph of the equation $y = \frac{1}{2}x - 1$ in the xy-plane?

A)

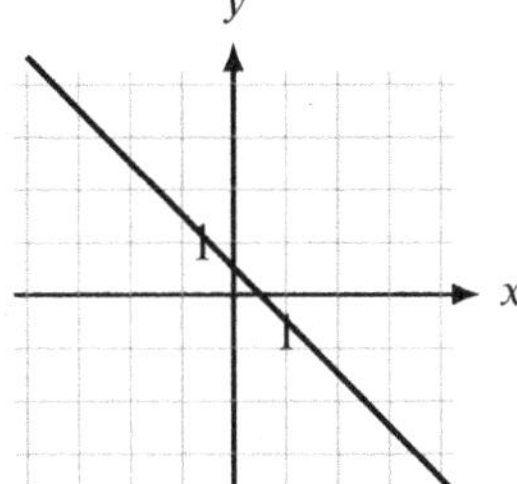

B)

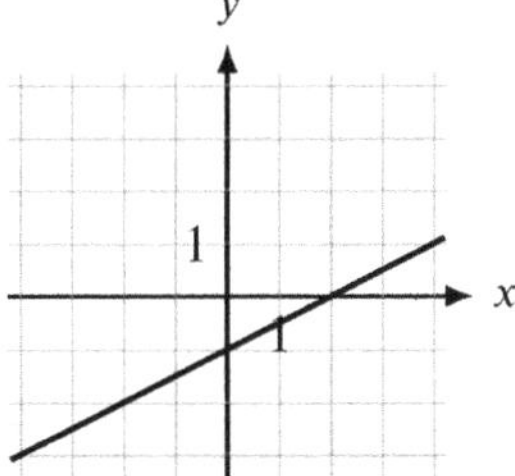

C)

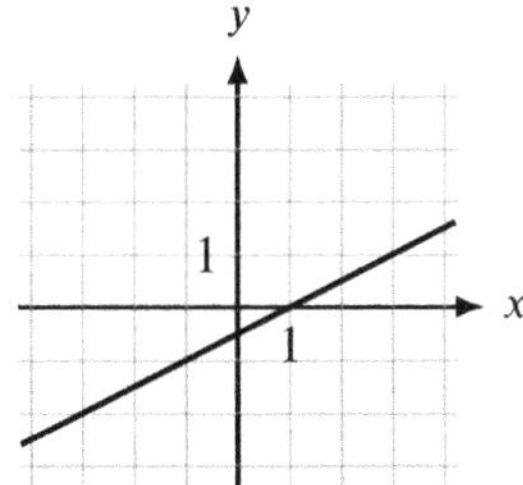

D)

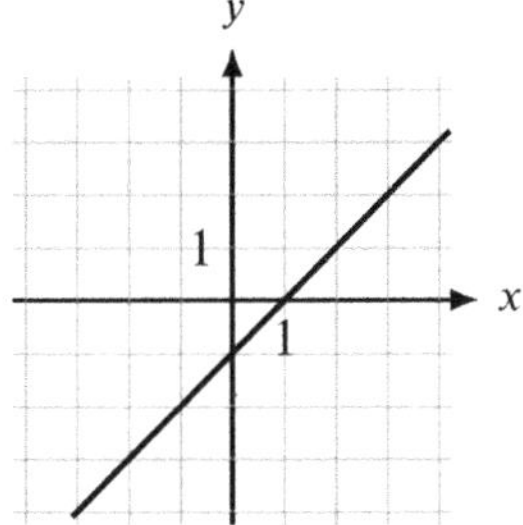

2 2.2

The function f is defined for all real numbers, and the graph of $y = f(x)$ in the xy-plane is a line with a positive slope. Which of the following must be true?

I. If $a < b$, then $f(a) > f(b)$

II. If $a < 0$, then $f(a) < 0$

III. If $a > 0$, then $f(a) > 0$

A) None

B) I only

C) II and III only

D) I, II, and III

2.3 Using Points and Tables

You don't need an actual graph to find the equation of a line. Sometimes you are just given two or more points and are told to find the equation of the line that goes through those points. **Any two points are sufficient to find the equation of a line.**

For example, let's find the slope of the line that goes through $(1, 3)$ and $(2, 5)$ using the Slope Formula by replacing y_2 with 5 and x_2 with 2 (from the point $(2, 5)$) and replacing y_1 with 3 and x_1 with 1 (from the point $(1, 3)$).

$$m = \frac{y_2 - y_1}{x_2 - x_1}$$

$$m = \frac{5 - 3}{2 - 1}$$

$$m = \frac{2}{1}$$

$$m = 2$$

Alternatively, we can draw a quick picture, plotting the points $(1, 3)$ and $(2, 5)$, and then using the over-and-up arrows to find the slope from Δy and Δx.

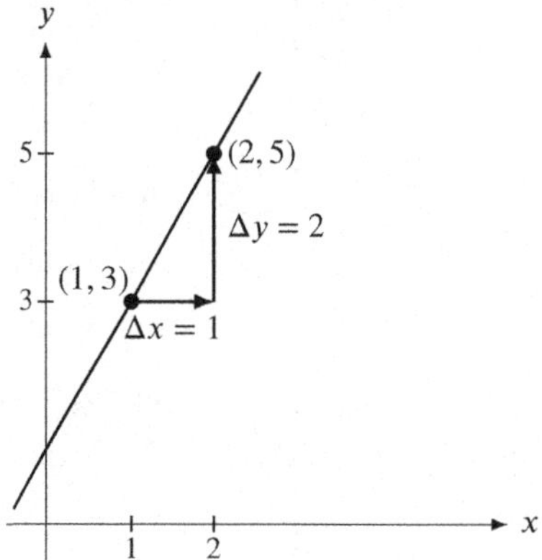

The x-values of the points increase by 1 (from 1 to 2) so $\Delta x = 1$. The y-values of the points increase by 2 (from 3 to 5) so $\Delta y = 2$. The slope of the line is $\frac{2}{1} = 2$. If we want to find the equation of this line in Slope-Intercept Form, we can replace m with 2 because the slope is 2.

$$y = mx + b$$

$$y = 2x + b$$

We can plug in the x and y-values of either given point, and once we have those three values (m, x, and y) substituted into the equation, we can solve for b, the y-intercept of the line. Let's use the point $(1, 3)$. **Note that any point on the line can be used**, but you can make smarter, easier choices if you choose points that have 0 or 1 as a value of the x- or y-coordinates because those values result in the simplest arithmetic.

$$y = 2x + b$$

$$3 = 2(1) + b$$

$$3 = 2 + b$$

$$1 = b$$

Since the slope is 2 and the y-intercept is 1, the equation of the line is $y = 2x + 1$.

Plugging In Points to Find Unknown Values

Once you have the slope (or y-intercept) of a line and you know a point on the line, the next logical step is to substitute the coordinates of the point into the Slope-Intercept Form. Replace the x variable with the x-value of the point you know, and replace the y variable with the y-value of the point you know.

You will have three of the four unknown values filled in and you can then solve for the remaining unknown value. In the previous example, we replaced m with the slope that we calculated, leaving us with the equation $y = 2x + b$.

Next comes the step where many students freeze up because they do not realize that they should substitute the coordinates of one of the points they know in order to figure out the y-intercept and complete the equation.

This tip does not just apply to lines but for all equations that will come up on the test: **if you are trying to fill in unknown values in an equation, you should substitute the coordinates of any points that are *given* to you by the text, graph, or table** (tables of points are discussed below).

SkillDrill 2.3-1

Directions: Based on the points given, find the equation of the line in Slope-Intercept Form.

1. $(-2, 3)$ and $(4, 1)$

2. $(0, -5)$ and $(2, 3)$

3. $(5, 14)$ and $(1, 11)$

4. $(-8, 0)$ and $(2, 0)$

5. $(-3, 4)$ and $(3, -4)$

6. $(5, -3)$ and $(3, 1)$

7. $(10, 2)$ and $(20, 3)$

8. $(8, 4)$ and $(-1, 5)$

Example 2.3-1

 2.3

The graph of a line in the xy-plane passes through the point $(5, 2)$ and crosses the x-axis at the point $(7, 0)$. The line crosses the y-axis at the point $(0, b)$. What is the value of b?

Solution 1

1. Recognize that this problem asks us to find the y-value of the point $(0, b)$, which is when the x-value is 0. **This is just another way of asking for the y-intercept of the line**. This means that the symbol b in the problem represents the y-value of the y-intercept, just as it does in the template $y = mx + b$ in the Slope-Intercept Form of a linear equation.

2. First we will find the slope of the line using the Slope Formula. The point (x_1, y_1) is $(5, 2)$, and the point (x_2, y_2) is $(7, 0)$.

$$m = \frac{0 - 2}{7 - 5}$$

$$m = \frac{-2}{2}$$

$$m = -1$$

3. Since we know the slope and a point on the line, we can substitute these values into the general Slope-Intercept Formula to find the y-intercept of the line. Replace m with -1, then, based on the point $(7,0)$, substitute 7 for x and 0 for y.

$$y = mx + b$$
$$y = (-1)x + b$$
$$y = -x + b$$
$$0 = -(7) + b$$
$$0 = -7 + b$$
$$7 = b$$

4. Since the slope is -1 and the y-intercept is 7, the equation of the line is $y = -x + 7$. Since the y-intercept is equal to 7, you can stop here and finalize 7 as your answer.

5. If you did not notice at the beginning of the problem that you were being asked for the y-intercept, which is the y-value of the point where the x-value is 0, you can find the y-value of the point $(0,b)$ by substituting 0 for x and b for y in the equation of this line (which is $y = -x + 7$).

$$y = -x + 7$$
$$(b) = -(0) + 7$$
$$b = 7$$

6. The answer is 7.

Solution 2

1. Recognize that this problem asks us to find the y-value of the point $(0,b)$, which is when the x-value is 0. This is just another way of asking for the y-intercept of the line.

2. First we will graph the points $(5,2)$ and $(7,0)$, and then use the picture to find the slope by drawing in the over-and-down arrows showing the change in y and the change in x.

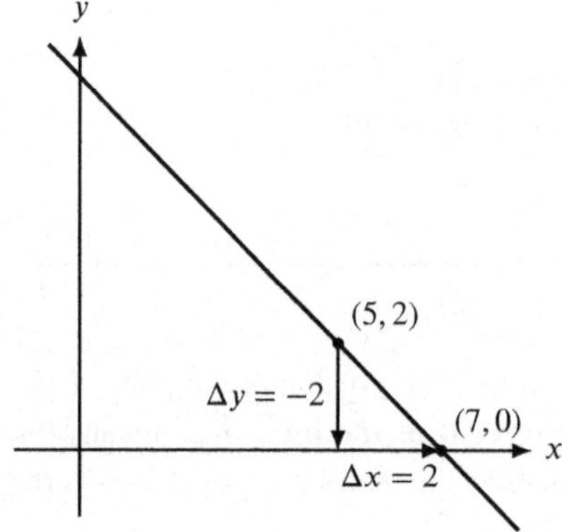

3. The y-value decreases by 2, so $\Delta y = -2$, and the x-value increases by 2, so $\Delta x = 2$. Therefore, the slope, which is Δy divided by Δx, is $\frac{-2}{2}$ or -1.

4. Since we know the slope and a point on the line, we can substitute these values into the general Slope-Intercept Formula to find the y-intercept of the line. Replace m with -1, then, based on the point $(7,0)$, substitute 0 for y and 7 for x.

$$y = mx + b$$
$$y = (-1)x + b$$
$$y = -x + b$$
$$0 = -(7) + b$$
$$0 = -7 + b$$
$$7 = b$$

5. Since the slope is -1 and the y-intercept is 7, the equation of the line is $y = -x + 7$. Since the y-intercept is equal to 7, you can stop here and finalize 7 as your answer.

6. If you did not notice at the beginning of the problem that you were being asked for the y-intercept, you can find the y-value of the point $(0, b)$ by substituting 0 for x and b for y in the equation of this line (which is $y = -x + 7$).

$$y = -x + 7$$
$$(b) = -(0) + 7$$
$$b = 7$$

7. The answer is 7.

Since we know how to find the equation of a line when we are given two points, we can also find the equation of a line when we are given a table of values that represent the x- and y- coordinates of a set of points on a line. The points will be represented as a column (or row) of x-values and a column (or row) of y-values that correspond to those x-values. Let's look at the following table of values.

x	y
-1	-2
0	2
1	6
2	10

Each row is a point, with the x-value in the left column and the y-value in the right column. For example, the first row shows us that $(-1, -2)$ is one point on the line. Similarly, the second row shows us that $(0, 2)$ is another point on the line. Also notice that $(0, 2)$ is the y-intercept of the line because the x-value of the point is 0. To find the equation of the line, we would start by using any two points (rows) from the table to find the slope of the line.

Remember that we found the slope from a graph by drawing a right triangle and finding Δy and Δx directly from the picture. We can similarly avoid formally plugging points into the Slope Formula on these problems. First, choose any two points from the table. By subtraction or counting, see how much the x- and y-values increase or decrease between those two points (finding the value of Δx and Δy, respectively). You can easily notate this by marking the change in x and y-values next to the table with brackets of some kind. Divide Δy by Δx to find the slope.

Let's use the first two points (rows). The y-value increases by 4 (from -2 to 2), so $\Delta y = 4$. The x-value increases by 1, so $\Delta x = 1$.

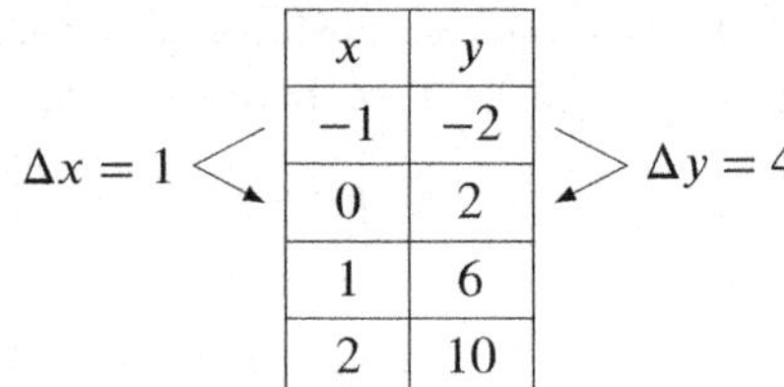

Since Δy is 4 and Δx is 1, the slope of this line is $\frac{4}{1}$ or 4. As it happens, we also know that the y-intercept is 2 because $(0, 2)$ is a point given to us in the table, so the equation of the line is $y = 4x + 2$.

Note that **you can always find the equation of a line when you are given any two points on the line (or the slope and any single point)**, so we could have used any two of the points in the table above to find the same equation of the line. If the y-intercept is not shown in the table, then you can substitute the slope (for m) and the x- and y coordinates of any point on the line (for x, and y, respectively) into the Slope-Intercept Form, $y = mx + b$, in order to solve for the y-intercept (b).

Using Tables of Points on Lines

Each row (or column) in a table is a point on a line. **Many tables show you the y-intercept of the line. Look out for the point where the x-value is 0.**

There is no need to use the Slope Formula when you are given a table of points on a line. **Subtract or count to see how much the x- and y-values increase or decrease between any two points to find Δx and Δy, repectively.**

Example 2.3-2

2 1600.io 2.3

Shipping Charges

Book Weight (pounds)	Shipping Charge ($)
2	2
4	3
8	5
16	9

The table above shows the shipping charges for an online retailer that sells books. There is a linear relationship between the shipping charge and the weight of the books. Which equation can be used to determine the total shipping charge y, in dollars, for an order with a book weight of x pounds?

A) $y = \frac{1}{2}x$

B) $y = \frac{1}{2}x + 1$

C) $y = x$

D) $y = x + 2$

Solution

1. The left column contains x-values and the right column contains y-values. Each row in the table is a point on the line. The first row tells us that $(2, 2)$ is a point, and the second row tells us that $(4, 3)$ is a point. We are told that the relationship between the cost and weight is linear, so we can use these points to find the slope of the line that describes the relationship.

2. Between the first and second row, the x-value increases by 2 (from 2 to 4), so $\Delta x = 2$, and the y-value increases by 1 (from 2 to 3), so $\Delta y = 1$.

$\Delta x = 2$ $\Delta y = 1$

Book Weight (pounds)	Shipping Charge ($)
2	2
4	3
8	5
16	9

Since $\Delta y = 1$ and $\Delta x = 2$, the slope, m, which is defined as $\frac{\Delta y}{\Delta x}$, is $\frac{1}{2}$.

Alternatively, substitute the coordinates of the two points into Slope Formula to find the slope of the line.

$$m = \frac{y_2 - y_1}{y_2 - y_1}$$

$$m = \frac{3 - 2}{4 - 2}$$

$$m = \frac{1}{2}$$

3. Since we know that the slope is $\frac{1}{2}$, we can replace m with $\frac{1}{2}$ in the general Slope-Intercept equation.

$$y = \frac{1}{2}x + b$$

4. Choose any point from the table to substitute into the equation so we can solve for b. Let's use $(2, 2)$. Replace the x-value with 2, and replace the y-value with 2.

$$y = \frac{1}{2}x + b$$

$$2 = \frac{1}{\cancel{2}}(\cancel{2}) + b$$

$$2 = 1 + b$$

5. Subtract 1 from both sides of the equation to solve for b, the y-intercept.

$$1 = b$$

6. Replace b with 1 in the general Slope-Intercept equation to find the equation of the line.

$$y = \frac{1}{2}x + 1$$

7. The answer is B.

Notes

If you are really comfortable working directly on the table, you can add an extra row to the table to work out what the y-value would be when the x-value is 0 in order to find the y-intercept more quickly.

	Book Weight (pounds)	Shipping Charge ($)	
	0	b	
$\Delta x = 2$	2	2	$\Delta y = 1$
$\Delta x = 2$	4	3	$\Delta y = 1$
$\Delta x = 4$	8	5	$\Delta y = 2$
$\Delta x = 8$	16	9	$\Delta y = 4$

The value of b has to be 1 because between the first row and the second row, the y-value has to increase by 1 because the x-value increases by 2 (the slope still has to be $\frac{1}{2}$).

Note also that the slope can be calculated using any two rows in the table. Even when Δx is different, the corresponding Δy will also change in such a way that the ratio of Δy to Δx (the slope) will always be constant because the slope of a line is the same everywhere by definition.

SkillDrill 2.3-2

Directions: Based on the points given in the tables below, find the equation of each line in Slope-Intercept Form and find the value of k either by counting the change in values between rows or by substituting into your equation the value of the known coordinate for the row (point) in which k appears.

1.

x	y
0	−5
1	−3
2	−1
3	k

2.

x	y
−2	10
−1	6
0	k
1	−2

3.

x	y
2	3
4	6
k	15
14	21

4.

x	y
−5	2
−1	1
3	0
k	−3

Section 2.3 Suggested Problems from Real Tests

View related real-test problems at 1600.io/p/smtex?topic=2.3

Section 2.3 Practice Problems

1 2.3

For a function f, $f(3) = 18$ and $f(5) = 26$. If the graph of $y = f(x)$ is a line in the xy-plane, what is the slope of the line?

2 2.3

x	$h(x)$
1	1
3	5
5	9
7	13

For the linear function h, the table above shows several values of x and their corresponding values of $h(x)$. Which of the following defines h?

A) $h(x) = 2x - 3$

B) $h(x) = 2x - 1$

C) $h(x) = 4x - 3$

D) $h(x) = 4x - 7$

3 2.3

In the xy-plane, line k intersects the y-axis at the point $(0, -4)$ and passes through the point $(3, 2)$. If the point $(15, w)$ lies on line k, what is the value of w?

4 2.3

x	$f(x)$
1	3
3	17
4	24

Some values of the linear function f are shown in the table above. Which of the following defines f?

A) $f(x) = x + 3$

B) $f(x) = 3x + 7$

C) $f(x) = 7x + 3$

D) $f(x) = 7x - 4$

2.4 Interpreting Linear Equations

Now that we know about slope and y-intercept and we can read and create graphs of linear equations, we can come back to real world problems to round out the topic of lines in Slope-Intercept Form. Some of the questions people struggle with the most are based on interpreting the *meaning* of the slope and y-intercept of linear equations that represent real world situations.

Remember the four parts of the equation that we talked about in the last chapter, and relate each part to a real world situation. The y-intercept (the value of b in the Slope-Intercept Form template) is the starting amount. The slope (m in the template) is the rate of change (how the y-value changes when the x-value changes) and is usually indicate by words like "each" or "per." Recall that slopes can be positive (to show an increase in a real world quantity) or negative (to show a decrease).

Example 2.4-1

1 1600.io 2.4

$$1500 - 32t = 220$$

In 1954, the population of a frog species was 1500. The population t years after 1954 was 220, and t satisfies the equation above. Which of the following is the best interpretation of the number 32 in this context?

A) The population t years after 1954

B) The value of t when the population was 220

C) The difference between the population in 1954 and the population t years after 1954

D) The average decrease in the population per year from 1954 to t years after 1954

Solution

1. The equation given to us is a linear equation. The terms are on the opposite side of the equals sign from what we are used to, but the pattern still fits: instead of being in the form $y = mx + b$, this line is in the form $b + mx = y$. The letter t is being used to represent the time, in years, instead of the generic x, in order to add meaning to the variable.
2. The coefficient of the x-, or in this case t-, variable is the slope, so, for this problem, we know that the slope is -32.
3. The slope is the change in y divided by the change in x. Since the y-value represents the population and the x-value (or t-value, in this case) is the number of years, **the slope of this line is the change in the population each year**. We choose to represent -32 as $\frac{-32}{1}$ in order to show the slope as a fraction that represents the change in y divided by the change in x.

$$\frac{\Delta y}{\Delta t} = \frac{\text{change in population}}{\text{change in years}} = \frac{-32}{1}$$

As you can see the population decreases by 32 every time the year increases by 1.

4. The answer is D.

Notes

For this example, let's identify each of the four parts of the equation and what those mean in the real world context.

The value 1500 is the y-intercept, or the starting population when the variable t is 0, which corresponds to the year 1954. The population in 1954 was 1500 and has been decreasing every year since then, until it finally reached a value of 220 after t years. The value 220 is like a particular y-value: it is the population that still exists after t years, so there exists a point $(t, 220)$, though note that we are never asked to find the value of t in this problem (spoiler alert: it's 40, which you should be able to figure out by solving the original equation for t). The variable t is acting as the x-variable: t represents the number of years since 1954, and there is a change in the population every year. If we want to know the remaining population after t years, we would have to subtract the population loss from the starting amount. The total loss would be found by multiplying the yearly decrease in population by the number of years since 1954. Since t is the number of years since 1954, then 32 must be the amount that the population decreases each year. Also recall that based on the general Slope-Intercept Form, the slope of the line is -32, which represents how much the population changes each year.

Example 2.4-2

2 2.4

Corinne is a computer technician. Each week, she receives a batch of computers that need repairs. The number of computers that she has left to fix at the end of each day can be estimated with the equation $C = 30 - 6d$, where C is the number of computers left and d is the number of days she has worked that week. What is the meaning of the value 30 in this equation?

A) Corinne will complete the repairs within 30 days.

B) Corinne starts each week with 30 computers to fix.

C) Corinne repairs computers at a rate of 30 per hour.

D) Corinne repairs computers at a rate of 30 per day.

Solution

1. We can see that this is a linear equation. We know that the y-variable is C, the number of computers left to fix after d days of work. We know that the x-variable is d, the number of days Corinne has worked.

2. The number of computers she has left to fix at the beginning of the week would be how many computers she has left to fix at the start of the week, or when $d = 0$. One way to contextualize the number 30 is to substitute 0 for d and see that when she has not worked any days yet, she still has 30 computers left to fix.

$$C = 30 - 6d$$
$$C = 30 - 6(0)$$
$$C = 30$$

3. Alternatively, you can just realize that the y-intercept (which is 30 based on the given linear equation) can be interpreted as the starting amount and immediately realize that she starts the week with 30 computers to fix.

4. The answer is B.

Some of the most difficult real-world linear equation interpretation questions involve complicated-looking fractional or decimal slopes. Remember that the slope is the change in y-values (Δy) divided by the change in x-values (Δx), so the change in y-values is measured in the same units as the y-value and the change in the x-values is measured in the same units as the x-value. Therefore, the slope will tell you how many units the y-value increases (or decreases) as the x-value increases by a certain number of units.

For example, if the weight, w, in pounds (or lbs), of a certain cactus that is currently in a pot of soil weighing 15 lbs increases by 13 lbs as the height, h, in inches, of the cactus increases by 2 in, then the linear equation representing the weight of the cactus and pot of soil (acting as the y-value) as a function of the height of the cactus (acting as the x-value) is $w = \frac{13}{2}h + 15$, where the slope is measured in units of lbs/in.

Because we know that the slope must be constant, we can use a simple proportion to see what change in the x-values (the change in height in this case) would produce a certain change in the y-values (the weight in this case). See the chapter on ratios and proportions if you're fuzzy on this type of setup.

$$\frac{\text{Change in Weight}}{\text{Change in Height}} = \frac{\Delta y}{\Delta x}$$

$$\frac{13}{2} = \frac{\Delta y}{\Delta x}$$

So, for example, if we wanted to know how much taller the cactus would have to grow in order to increase the weight by 1 lb, we would just substitute 1 for the change in weight (Δy), and solve for the corresponding change in height (Δx) by cross multiplying and then solving for Δx.

$$\frac{13}{2} = \frac{\Delta y}{\Delta x}$$

$$\frac{13}{2} = \frac{1}{\Delta x}$$

$$13(\Delta x) = 2(1)$$

$$13(\Delta x) = 2$$

$$\Delta x = \frac{2}{13}$$

In this example, if the height of the cactus increases by $\frac{2}{13}$ in, the weight of the cactus will increase by 1 lb.

We can verify this if we choose to input any two weights that are 1 lb different from each other into the equation $w = \frac{13}{2}h + 15$, and see that the heights corresponding to those weights are $\frac{2}{13}$ inches different from each other. Let's use the weights 15 lbs (the y-intercept, which makes our job easier because it corresponds to a cactus height of 0 in) and 16 lbs (which is 1 lb heavier than the other weight).

For the first plant and pot weighing 15 lbs, substitute 15 for w and solve for h (which will end up being 0).

$$w = \frac{13}{2}h + 15$$

$$15 = \frac{13}{2}h + 15$$

$$0 = \frac{13}{2}h$$

It should be obvious what h will be, but for completeness, let's multiply both sides of the equation by $\frac{2}{13}$ in order to solve for h.

$$\frac{2}{13}(0) = \frac{\cancel{2}}{\cancel{13}}\left(\frac{\cancel{13}}{\cancel{2}}h\right)$$
$$0 = h$$

The first plant and pot weighs 15 lbs when the height of the cactus is 0 in. For the second plant and pot, which weighs 16 lbs (1 lb more than the other plant and pot), substitute 16 for w and solve for h (which we predict should be $\frac{2}{13}$ in, which is $\frac{2}{13}$ in more than 0 in, the height of the other potted cactus).

$$w = \frac{13}{2}h + 15$$
$$16 = \frac{13}{2}h + 15$$
$$1 = \frac{13}{2}h$$

Multiply both sides of the equation by $\frac{2}{13}$ in order to solve for h.

$$\frac{2}{13}(1) = \frac{\cancel{2}}{\cancel{13}}\left(\frac{\cancel{13}}{\cancel{2}}h\right)$$
$$\frac{2}{13} = h$$

As we can see, in comparison to substituting x- and y-values into the linear equation, using the proportion based on the slope (which is constant for lines) was a much quicker and easier way to find corresponding changes in the x- and y-values. Problems that ask you to find how much one quantity changes in response to a specific change in the other are routine on the SAT, so it's important to become comfortable with using the proportion technique to rapidly solve such problems.

You don't always have to use the proportion in interpretation questions, but **you should be aware of the units of measurement for the x-and y-values so that you can easily interpret what the slope means in a real-world linear equation problem**. If we were just told that the relationship between the weight, w, of a potted cactus (measured in lbs) and the height, h, of the potted cactus (measured in in) is represented by the equation $w = \frac{13}{2}h + 15$, then we know that the meaning of the fraction $\frac{13}{2}$ is that the weight increases by 13 lbs for every 2 in increase in height.

Be aware that this slope could also be interpreted as a $\frac{13}{2}$-pound increase in weight for every 1-in increase in height, a 130-pound increase in weight for every 20-in increase in height, or even a 1-lb increase in weight for every $\frac{2}{13}$-in increase in height because all of the changes would still produce the same slope.

$$\text{Slope} = \frac{\Delta y}{\Delta x} = \frac{\text{Change in Weight}}{\text{Change in Height}} = \frac{13}{2} = \frac{\frac{13}{2}}{1} = \frac{130}{20} = \frac{1}{\frac{2}{13}}$$

Example 2.4-3

3 1600.io 2.4

$$d(t) = \frac{1}{248}t + 1{,}857$$

A geologist estimates that, as a result of erosion, the depth of the Grand Canyon has been increasing at a constant rate since it was first formed. The function above is used by the geologist to model the depth $d(t)$, in meters, of the canyon t years after the year 2000. According the the function, which of the following statements is true?

A) Every 248 years the depth of the canyon increases by 0.1 meters.

B) Every 2,480 years the depth of the canyon increases by 10 meters.

C) Every 100 years the depth of the canyon increases by 2.48 meters.

D) Every year the depth of the canyon increases by 248 meters.

Solution

1. In this equation, the d-value (acting as the y-value) is the depth of the canyon, measured in meters, and the t-value (acting as the x-value) is the number of years since the year 2000. Therefore, the slope, which is $\frac{\Delta d}{\Delta t}$, is measured in units of m/yr. As such, the fraction $\frac{1}{248}$ tells us that the depth of the canyon increases by 1 m every 248 yr.
2. Choice A is clearly wrong because we know that the depth increase by 1 full meter and not by 0.1 m every 248 yr. Eliminate choice A.
3. Choice D is frankly outlandish if you think about it, but more directly to the point, it inverts the units of the numerator and denominator of the slope, so eliminate choice D.
4. Choice C is not nearly as freakish as choice D; however, if we know that it takes 248 years for the depth to increase by 1 m, then the depth could not increase by more than 1 m in a smaller amount of time (only 100 years versus 248 years). Eliminate choice C.
5. The only remaining choice is B, which isn't immediately recognizable with our correct interpretation of the slope; however, if we set up the fraction representing the slope, $\frac{\Delta d}{\Delta t}$, we will see that a change in depth of 10 m (Δd) for a change in years of 2,480 yr still reduces to the correct slope.

$$\frac{\Delta d}{\Delta t} = \frac{10}{2{,}480}$$

$$\frac{\Delta d}{\Delta t} = \frac{1}{248}$$

6. The answer is B.

Notes

You could do this problem slowly by substituting values into the equation to check each answer choice. For example, to check choice A, you could input two values of t that are 248 years different from one another and see if the corresponding depths are 0.1 m different from one another (they will not be because this answer is not correct). To check choice B, you could input two values of t that are 2,480 yr different from one another and see if the corresponding depths are 10 m different from one another (they will be because this answer is correct). And so on...

View related real-test problems at 1600.io/p/smtex?topic=2.4

Section 2.4 Practice Problems

1 2.4

$$a = 20t + 130$$

Gregory made an initial deposit into his vacation fund jar. Each week thereafter he deposited a fixed amount to the jar. The equation above models the amount a, in dollars, that Gregory has deposited after t weekly deposits. According to the model, how many dollars was Gregory's initial deposit? (Disregard the $ sign when writing your answer.)

2 2.4

$$4{,}200 - 35k = 175$$

In 1806, the population of a fish species was 4,200. The population k years after 1806 was 175, and k satisfies the equation above. Which of the following is the best interpretation of the number 35 in this context?

A) The difference between the population in 1806 and the population k years after 1806

B) The average decrease in the population per year from 1806 to k years after 1806

C) The population k years after 1806

D) The value of k when the population was 175

CHAPTER 2 RECAP

- Slope-Intercept Form: $y = mx + b$
- Slope Formula: $m = \dfrac{y_2 - y_1}{x_2 - x_1} = \dfrac{\Delta y}{\Delta x}$
- A positive slope means that the y-value increases as x-value increases. Steeper lines have higher slopes because the y-value goes up more as the x-value increases. A line with a slope of 3 is steeper than a line with a slope of $\frac{1}{2}$.

  A negative slope means that the y-value decreases as the x-value increases. Steeper lines have lower (more negative) slopes because the y-value decreases more as the x-value increases. A line with a slope of -3 is steeper than a line with a slope of $-\frac{1}{2}$.

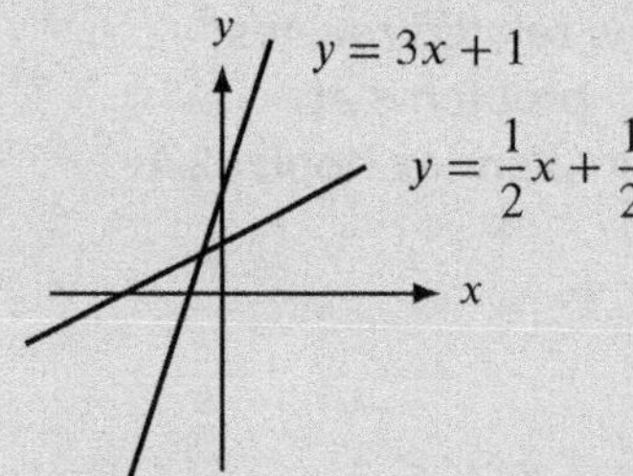

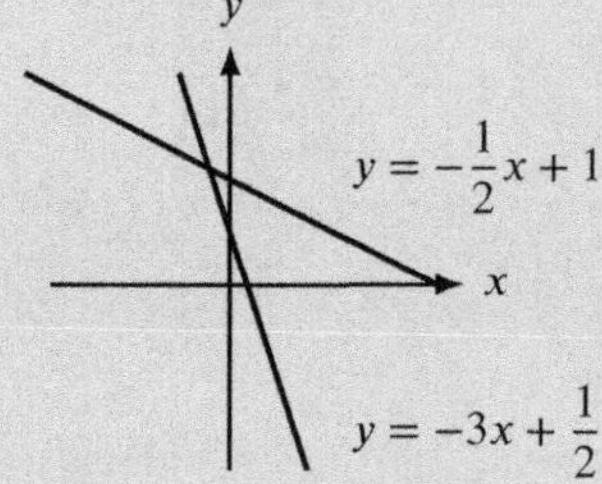

- Horizontal lines have a slope of zero and their equations are of the form $y = c$, where c is a constant (the y-value is the same for all points on the line).

  Vertical lines have an undefined slope and their equations are of the form $x = c$, where c is constant (the x-value is the same for all points on the line). Note that this is **not** a Slope-Intercept equation, because a vertical line cannot be represented in that form because the slope is undefined.

- The y-intercept is where a line crosses the y-axis. One useful way of thinking about this (especially for real world problems) is that the y-intercept is the starting amount or the value of y when the x-value is 0. To find the y-intercept when it is not clearly marked on a graph, substitute the slope and x- and y-coordinates of a point into the Slope-Intercept Form and solve for b.

  The x-intercept is where a line crosses the x-axis. Another useful way of thinking about this (especially for real world problems) is that this is the value of x when the y-value is equal to 0. Unlike the y-intercept, this value is not visible in any common representation of linear equations, but to find it when it is not clearly marked on a graph, substitute the slope and y-intercept into the Slope-Intercept Form, then set the y-value equal to 0 and solve for x.

- You can find the equation of any line as long as you know any two points on the line or know the slope and any one point. If you are given the slope and y-intercept, then you already have everything you need to make the equation.
- Using up-and-over arrows with graphical representations to find Δy and Δx, or counting differences between coordinate values between rows of tables, is often less error prone than substituting the coordinates of points into the long from of the Slope Formula. There is no mathematical difference between methods, but graphical methods are harder to mess up.
- When asked to interpret the meaning of a coefficient or constant in a Slope-Intercept Form linear equation, first determine which one of the four components of a linear equation it is (the y-value, the slope, the x-value, or the y-intercept).

  The y-intercept is the "starting amount" and is measured in the same units as the y-value.

  The slope is the rate of change of the y-value as the x-value changes and is measured in the units of the y-value divided by the units of the x-value (look for keywords like "per" which indicate division).

Additional Problems

1 2.1

A line in the xy-plane has a slope of 0. Which of the following could be the equation of the line?

A) $x = 0$

B) $y = x$

C) $y = 0$

D) $y = -x$

2 2.1

The line $y = kx + 5$, where k is a constant, is graphed in the xy-plane. If the line contains the point (c, d), where $c \neq 0$ and $d \neq 0$, what is the slope of the line in terms of c and d ?

A) $\frac{d-5}{c}$

B) $\frac{c-5}{d}$

C) $\frac{4-d}{c}$

D) $\frac{4-c}{d}$

3 2.1

Which of the following is an equation of the line in the xy-plane that has slope -5 and passes through the point $(0, 2)$?

A) $y = -5x - 2$

B) $y = -5x + 2$

C) $y = -5(x + 2)$

D) $y = -5(x - 3)$

4 2.3

$$C = 85h + 100$$

The equation above gives the amount C, in dollars, an HVAC technician charges for a job that takes h hours. Ms. Porter and Mr. Green each hired this technician. The technician worked 3 hours longer on Ms. Porter's job than on Mr. Green's job. How much more did the technician charge Ms. Porter than Mr. Green?

A) \$85

B) \$100

C) \$170

D) \$255

5 1600.io 2.3

The graph in the xy-plane of the linear function f contains the point $(1, 6)$. For every increase of 3 units in x, $f(x)$ increases by 4 units. Which of the following equations defines the function?

A) $f(x) = -\frac{4}{3}x + 10$

B) $f(x) = -\frac{3}{4}x + \frac{21}{4}$

C) $f(x) = \frac{3}{4}x + 2$

D) $f(x) = \frac{4}{3}x + \frac{14}{3}$

6 1600.io 2.4

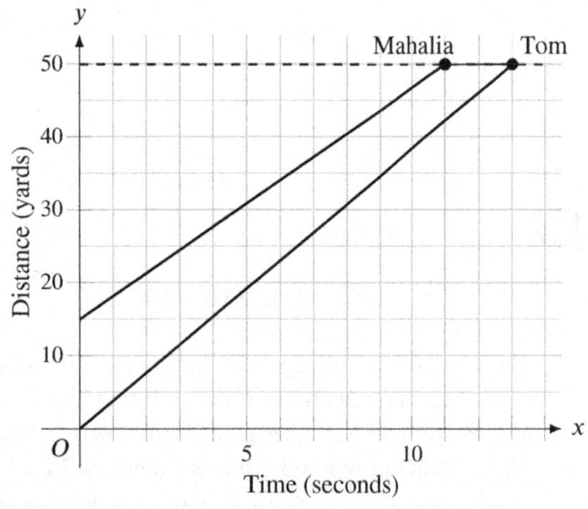

The graph above shows the positions of Tom and Mahalia during a race. Tom and Mahalia each rollerbladed at a constant rate, and Mahalia was given a head start to shorten the distance she needed to skate. Tom finished the race in 13 seconds, and Mahalia finished the race in 11 seconds. According to the graph, Mahalia was given a head start of how many yards?

A) 3

B) 10

C) 15

D) 20

7 1600.io 2.1

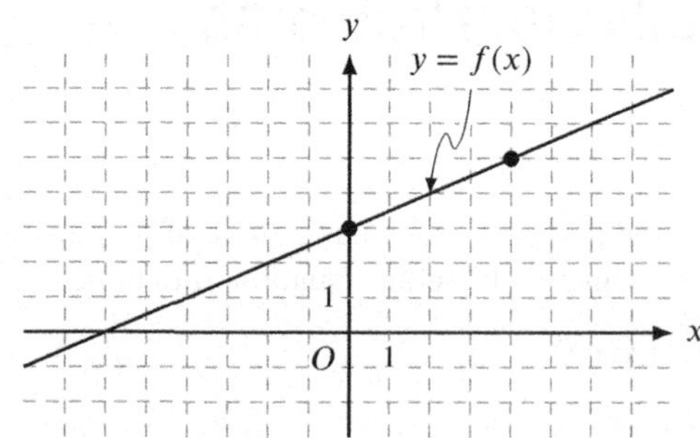

The graph of the function f is shown in the xy-plane above. The function f is defined by the equation $f(x) = \frac{a}{b}x + c$ for positive constants a, b, and c, where $\frac{a}{b}$ is a fraction in lowest terms. Which of the following orders a, b, and c from least to greatest?

A) $a < b < c$

B) $a < c < b$

C) $b < c < a$

D) $c < a < b$

8 1600.io 2.3

In the xy-plane, the points $(-1, 4)$ and $(2, -1)$ lie on the graph of which of the following linear functions?

A) $f(x) = -\frac{5}{3}x + \frac{7}{3}$

B) $f(x) = -\frac{3}{5}x + 1$

C) $f(x) = \frac{1}{2}x - 2$

D) $f(x) = 5x + 9$

9 2.4

The equation $p = 14.7 + 15.4d$ approximates the pressure p, in pounds per square inch, exerted on a peanut at a depth of d inches (in) below the surface of a chocolate syrup vat. What is the increase in depth that is necessary to increase the pressure by 1 pound per square inch?

A) $\frac{1}{14.7}$ in

B) $\frac{1}{15.4}$ in

C) 14.7 in

D) 15.4 in

10 2.3

x	$f(x)$
4	15
8	7

The table above shows two pairs of values for the linear function f. The function can be written in the form $f(x) = ax + b$, where a and b are constants. What is the value of $a + b$?

11 2.4

$$A = 205 + 24.14m$$

The equation above can be used to estimate the body surface area A, in square inches, of a child with mass m, in pounds mass, where $7 \leq m \leq 67$. Which of the following statements is consistent with the equation?

A) For each increase of 205 pounds in mass, A increases by approximately 1 square inch.

B) For each increase of 1 pound in mass, A increases by approximately 205 square inches.

C) For each increase of 1 pound in mass, A increases by approximately 24.14 square inches.

D) For each increase of 24.14 pounds in mass, A increases by approximately 1 square inch.

12 2.3

x	y
1	−2
k	10
5	n

The table above shows the coordinates of three points on a line in the xy-plane, where k and n are constants. If the slope of the line is 6, what is the value of $n - k$?

13 1600.io 2.3

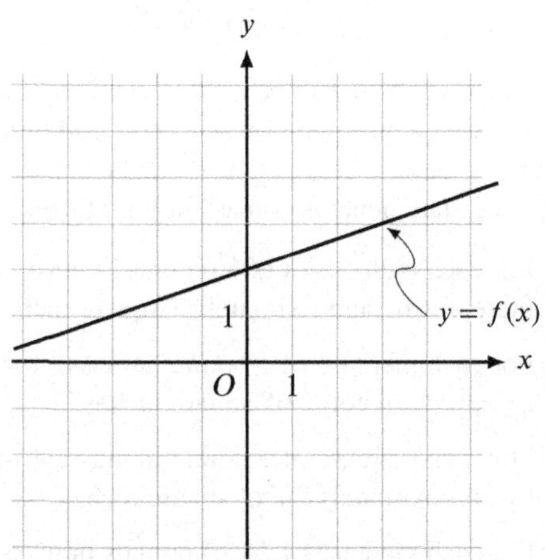

The graph of the linear function f is shown in the xy-plane above. The slope of the graph of the linear function g is 3 times the slope of the graph of f. If the graph of g passes through the point $(0, -8)$, what is the value of $g(6)$?

A) -8

B) -6

C) -2

D) 10

14 1600.io 2.1

A line in the xy-plane passes through the origin and has a slope $\frac{1}{10}$. Which of the following points lies on the line?

A) $(20, 2)$

B) $(10, 10)$

C) $(1, 10)$

D) $(0, 10)$

15 1600.io 2.3

The function f is linear, $f(1) = 20$, and $f(4) = 11$. If $f(x) = mx + b$, where m and b are constants, what is the value of b ?

A) $\frac{61}{3}$

B) 23

C) 17

D) $\frac{34}{3}$

16 1600.io 2.1

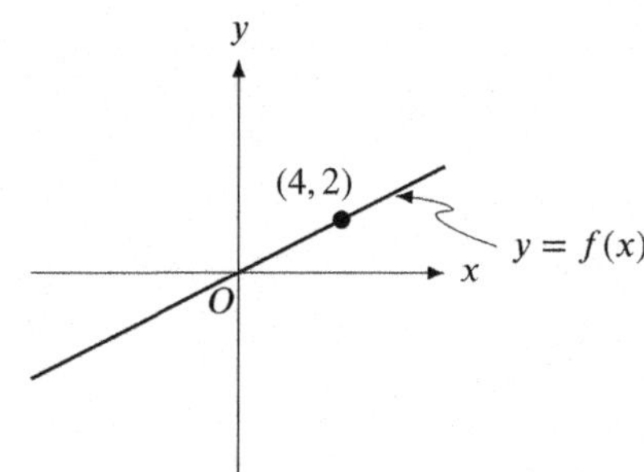

In the xy-plane above, a point (not shown) with coordinates (s, t) lies on the graph of the linear function f. If s and t are positive integers, what is the ratio of t to s ?

A) 1 to 2

B) 2 to 3

C) 2 to 1

D) 3 to 2

17 2.4

$$s = 32.2t$$

The equation above can be used to approximate the speed s, in feet per second (ft/s), of an object t seconds after being dropped into a free fall. Which of the following is the best interpretation of the number 32.2 in this context?

A) The speed, in ft/s, of the object when it hits the ground

B) The initial speed, in ft/s, of the object when it is dropped

C) The speed, in ft/s, of the object t seconds after it is dropped

D) The increase in speed, in ft/s, of the object for each second after it is dropped

18 2.3

x	$f(x)$
0	−2
3	7
7	19

Some values of the linear function f are shown in the table above. What is the value of $f(5)$?

A) 10

B) 13

C) 14

D) 15

Questions 19 and 20 refer to the following information.

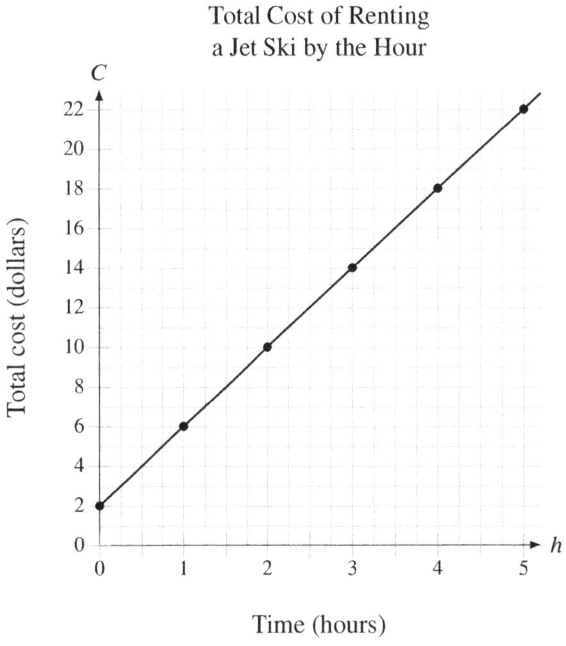

The graph above displays the total cost C, in dollars, of renting a jet ski for h hours.

19 2.4

What does the C-intercept represent in the graph?

A) The total number of jet skis rented

B) The total number of hours the jet ski is rented

C) The increase in cost to rent the jet ski for each additional hour

D) The initial cost of renting the jet ski

20 2.1

Which of the following represents the relationship between h and C ?

A) $h = 4C$

B) $C = h + 2$

C) $C = 2h$

D) $C = 4h + 2$

21 1600.io 2.3

A business owner purchased a vehicle valued at \$90,000. The values of the vehicle depreciates by the same amount each year so that after 5 years the value will be \$50,000. Which of the following equations gives the value, v, of the machine, in dollars, t years after it was purchased, for $0 \leq t \leq 5$?

A) $v = 50{,}000 - 8{,}000t$

B) $v = 90{,}000 - 50{,}000t$

C) $v = 90{,}000 - 8{,}000t$

D) $v = 90{,}000 + 8{,}000t$

22 1600.io 2.4

$$3n + 10 = 46$$

A snake had a length of 10 inches when it was hatched. The equation above can be used to find how many months n it took the snake to reach a length of 46 inches. Which of the following is the best interpretation of the number 3 in this context?

A) The number of months it took the snake to triple its length

B) The length, in inches, of the snake when the snake was 1 month old

C) The average number of months it takes similar snakes to grow 46 inches

D) The average number of inches that the snake grew per month

23 1600.io 2.3

x	$h(x)$
0	1
1	3
3	7

The table above shows selected values for the function h. In the xy-plane, the graph of $y = h(x)$ is a line. What is the value of $h(6)$?

A) 9

B) 11

C) 13

D) 14

24 1600.io 2.3

x	$f(x)$
0	c
1	$-2c$
2	$-5c$

For the linear function f, the table above gives some values of x and their corresponding values $f(x)$, where c is a constant. Which of the following equations defines f ?

A) $f(x) = -5cx - 5c$

B) $f(x) = -3cx + c$

C) $f(x) = -cx + c$

D) $f(x) = cx + c$

25 2.3

Which of the following is an equation of the line in the xy-plane that contains the points $(1, 4)$ and $(4, 16)$?

A) $y = 4x$

B) $y = x + 3$

C) $y = 3x + 4$

D) $y = \frac{1}{4}x$

26 2.3

Population of Hardlocke, Texas

Year	Population
1900	711
1910	687

The table above shows the population of Hardlocke, Texas, for the years 1900 and 1910. If the relationship between population and year is linear, which of the following functions P models the population of Hardlocke t years after 1900?

A) $P(t) = 711 - 2.4t$

B) $P(t) = 711 - 24t$

C) $P(t) = 711 - 2.4(t - 1900)$

D) $P(t) = 711 - 24(t - 1900)$

27 2.1

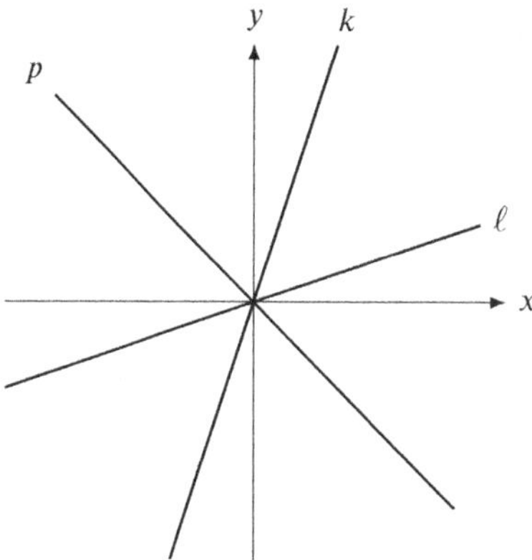

In the xy-plane, lines k, ℓ, and p are shown. Which of the following lists the slopes from least to greatest?

A) The slope of p, the slope of ℓ, the slope of k

B) The slope of ℓ, the slope of p, the slope of k

C) The slope of k, the slope of ℓ, the slope of p

D) The slope of p, the slope of k, the slope of ℓ

28 2.1

The graph of $y = mx + b$, where m and b are constants, is shown in the xy-plane.

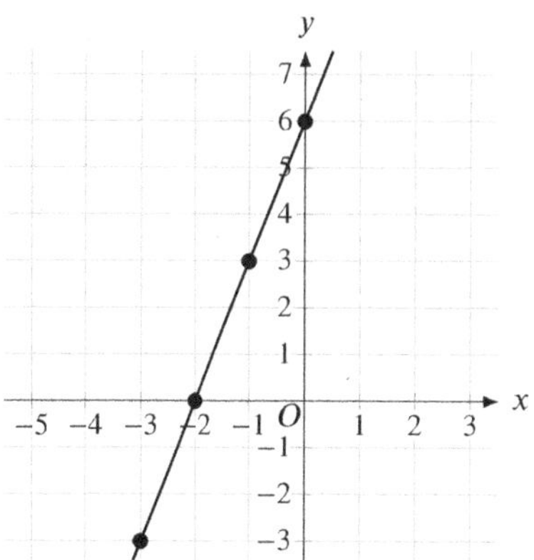

What is the value of m ?

29 1600.io 2.2

Which of the following is the graph of the equation $y = 3x + 1$ in the xy-plane?

A)

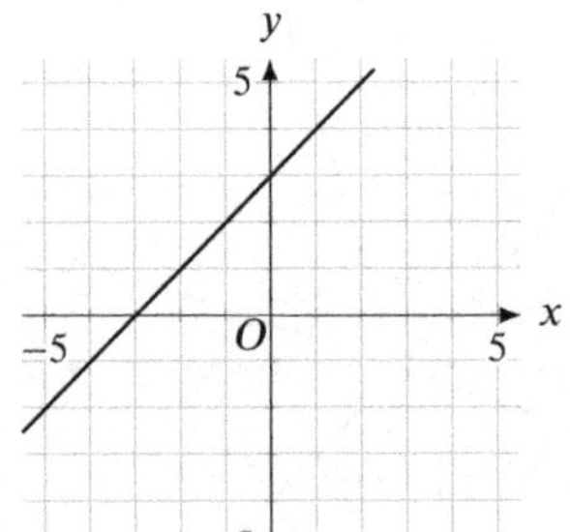

B)

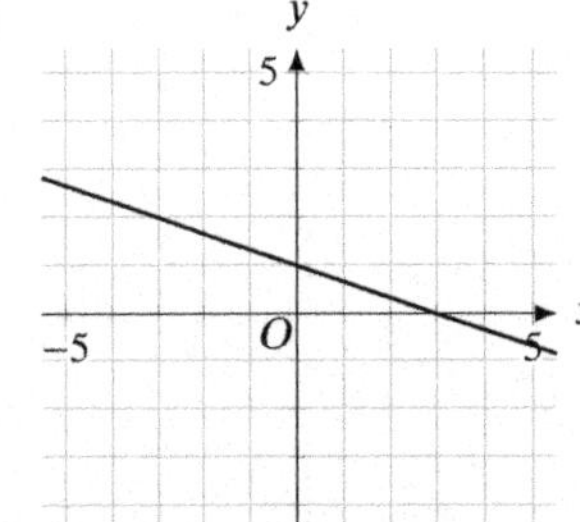

C)

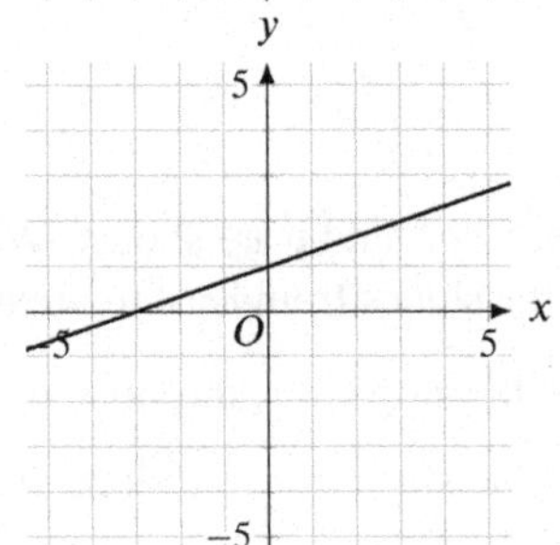

D)

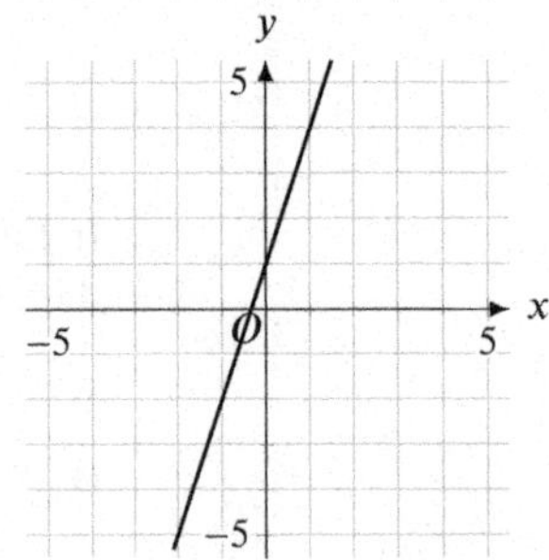

30 1600.io 2.3

Speed (mph)	Pulse (bpm)
4	65
8	77
12	89

The table lists selected values of Gina's rollerblading speed, in miles per hour (mph), and her corresponding pulse, in beats per minute (bpm). There is a linear relationship between Gina's speed, x, and her pulse, $f(x)$. Which of the following equations describes $f(x)$?

A) $f(x) = 12x + 65$

B) $f(x) = 12x + 53$

C) $f(x) = 3x + 65$

D) $f(x) = 3x + 53$

31 1600.io 2.4

Milk production in a certain area dropped from 10 million cartons in 2000 to 2.7 millions cartons in 2018. Assuming that the milk production decreased at a constant rate, which of the following linear functions f best models the production, in millions of cartons, t years after the year 2000?

A) $f(t) = \frac{73}{180}t + 10$

B) $f(t) = \frac{27}{180}t + 10$

C) $f(t) = -\frac{73}{180}t + 10$

D) $f(t) = -\frac{27}{180}t + 10$

Answer Key

SkillDrill 2.1-1

1. $(0, -3)$
2. $(-4, -2)$
3. $(3, 0)$
4. $(5, 3)$
5. $(0, 4)$
6. $(-3, 1)$
7. $(4, -4)$
8. $(-2, 0)$

SkillDrill 2.1-2

1. 1
2. 2
3. 5
4. 4
5. 3
6. 4
7. 1
8. 3

SkillDrill 2.1-3

1. $m = 2, b = 1$
2. $m = 3, b = 6$
3. $m = 1, b = -7$
4. $m = 5, b = 0$
5. $y = 5x - 4$
6. $y = 8x + 1$
7. $y = x$
8. $y = 2x - 2$

SkillDrill 2.1-4

1. $y = \frac{-1}{3}x - 3, x_{int} = (-9, 0)$
2. $y = x + 1, x_{int} = (-1, 0)$
3. $y = \frac{1}{2}x + 3, x_{int} = (-6, 0)$
4. $y = \frac{-5}{4}x - \frac{1}{2}, x_{int} = \left(\frac{-2}{5}, 0\right)$
5. $y = -3$, x_{int} does not exist
6. $x = 4, x_{int} = (4, 0)$
7. $y = \frac{2}{7}x - \frac{8}{7}, x_{int} = (4, 0)$
8. $y = \frac{-1}{3}x + \frac{4}{3}, x_{int} = (4, 0)$

Section 2.1 Practice Problems

1. D
2. C
3. $\frac{2}{3}$, .666, or .667
4. C

Section 2.2 Practice Problems

1. B
2. A

SkillDrill 2.3-1

1. $y = \frac{-1}{3}x + \frac{7}{3}$
2. $y = 4x - 5$
3. $y = \frac{3}{4}x + \frac{41}{4}$
4. $y = 0$
5. $y = \frac{-4}{3}x$
6. $y = -2x + 7$
7. $y = \frac{1}{10}x + 1$
8. $y = \frac{-1}{9}x + \frac{44}{9}$

SkillDrill 2.3-2

1. $y = 2x - 5, k = 1$
2. $y = -4x + 2, k = 2$
3. $y = \frac{3}{2}x, k = 10$
4. $y = \frac{-1}{4}x + \frac{3}{4}, k = 15$

Section 2.3 Practice Problems

1. 4
2. B
3. 26
4. D

Section 2.4 Practice Problems

1. 130
2. B

Additional Problems

1. C
2. A
3. B
4. D
5. D
6. C
7. A
8. A
9. B
10. 21
11. C
12. 19
13. C
14. A
15. B
16. A
17. D
18. B
19. D
20. D
21. C
22. D
23. C
24. B
25. A
26. A
27. A
28. 3
29. D
30. D
31. C

Standard Form/Parallel and Perpendicular Lines

3

3.1 Standard Form

Jimmy wants to buy notebooks that cost \$4 each. We've learned already how we could calculate the total amount that Jimmy would spend on notebooks by multiplying the cost of each notebook by the number of notebooks he buys. If Jimmy buys n notebooks, then he will spend $4n$ dollars.

Suppose he also needs to buy pens that cost \$2 each. The amount Jimmy would spend on p pens would be $2p$ dollars. Even though he is buying two different items, we can make one equation that represents the total amount he spends on both items by adding the total cost of the notebooks and pens together. If t is the total cost of the supplies, then the equation representing Jimmy's total cost is $2p + 4n = t$.

Let's say that Jimmy can only spend a total of \$40 on supplies. In the equation, the value of t would be 40:

$$2p + 4n = 40$$

Jimmy wants to use this equation to figure out how many pens and notebooks he can buy.

The first thing to note is that the more he buys of one thing, the fewer he could buy of the other. If he buys 0 notebooks, he can buy 20 pens because $2(\mathbf{20}) + 4(\mathbf{0}) = 40$. If he buys 1 notebook, he still has enough money for 18 pens ($2(\mathbf{18}) + 4(\mathbf{1}) = 40$), but if he buys 2 notebooks, he can only buy 16 pens ($2(\mathbf{16}) + 4(\mathbf{2}) = 40$).

As soon as we limit the total amount of money he is going to spend, the number of pens and notebooks has to strike a balance: the two values are related, much in the same way x and y-values are related to each other for the points on a line. That is because the equation we just wrote is a linear equation, but it's not in Slope-Intercept Form; it's in what we call **Standard Form**.

Standard Form Linear Equation

The following is the equation of a line in Standard Form, where A, B, and C are constants:

$$Ax + By = C$$

In a lot of word problems, it is easier to write the equation in Standard Form than in Slope-Intercept Form due to how the information is given to you. Once you have the equation, you can use it to solve for any values that are unknown.

SkillDrill 3.1-1

Directions: Write a Standard Form linear equation to represent the given situation. In order to make sure that you use variable letters that make sense (this is an important habit), we will provide them for you.

1. Bella gets paid \$2 for every backflip she does and \$3 for every front flip she does. In one day, she makes \$56 doing backflips and front flips. (Use b for the number of backflips and f for the number of front flips.)
2. In an eating contest, Ferdinand takes 1 minute to eat each hot dog and 3 minutes to eat each cake. It took Ferdinand 60 minutes to eat h hot dogs and c cakes.
3. It takes Paula 8 minutes to drink a small water bottle and 20 minutes to drink a big water bottle. In one week, it took her a total of 112 minutes to drink s small water bottles and b big water bottles.
4. A company loses \$100 for every inappropriate comment they make on social media and loses \$2.50 every time one of their employees exposes the hazardous working conditions in the company's overseas sweatshops. In one year, the company loses \$197.50 from c inappropriate comments and h reports of hazardous working conditions.
5. Jeremetrius gains 5 subscribers for every reaction video he posts and loses 10 subscribers for every prank video he posts. In one week, Jeremetrius loses a total of 42 subscribers. (Use r for the number of reaction videos and p for the number of prank videos.)

Example 3.1-1

1 1600.io 3.1

Nick spends \$57 per month on chips. A 10-bag pack of chips costs \$8.50, and a single bag of chips costs \$1.20. If p represents the number of 10-bag packs Nick buys in a month, and s represents the number of single bags Nick buys in a month, which of the following equations best represents the relationship between p and s?

A) $p + s = 8.50 + 1.20$

B) $p + s = 57$

C) $1.20p + 8.50s = 57$

D) $8.50p + 1.20s = 57$

Solution

1. We need to write an equation that represents the total amount of money Nick spends on chips in a month. To do this, we should start by finding the amount he spends on p 10-bag packs and s single bags of chips.
2. The cost of p 10-bag packs is equal to the cost per 10-bag pack (\$8.50) times the number of 10-bag packs (p), which is $8.50p$.
3. The cost of s single bags is equal to the cost per single bag (\$1.20) times the number of single bags (s), which is $1.20s$.
4. We know the total cost was \$57, so we can add the costs of buying p 10-bag packs ($8.50p$) and s single bags ($1.20s$) and set the sum equal to 57.

$$8.50p + 1.20s = 57$$

5. The answer is D.

For many word problems, it is easier to write linear equations in Standard Form; however, when lines are graphed, it is usually easier to write the equations first in Slope-Intercept Form and then convert the equations into Standard Form if necessary to match the format of the answer choices.

Converting from Slope-Intercept Form to Standard Form

We can convert from Slope-Intercept Form to Standard Form through simple algebraic steps by moving the x-variable to the same side of the equation as the y-variable.

We want to convert from a line in Slope-Intercept Form ($y = mx + b$) to a line in Standard Form ($Ax + By = C$), so we should subtract mx from both sides of the equation.

$$y = mx + b$$
$$-mx + y = b$$

The equation above is now in Standard Form ($Ax + By = C$) where $A = -m$, $B = 1$, and $C = b$.

For example, the line $y = -2x + 3$ is in Slope-Intercept Form, but by adding $2x$ to both sides of the equation (subtracting $-2x$ from both sides of the equation) we arrive at the same linear equation in Standard Form: $2x + y = 3$.

When the slope of a line in Slope-Intercept Form is a fraction, you may also wish to (or have to in order to match answer choices) **multiply both sides of the equation by the denominator of the x-coefficient to eliminate the fraction**.

For example, we can rewrite the linear equation $y = \frac{2}{3}x - 4$ in Standard Form in multiple equivalent ways. Start by subtracting $\frac{2}{3}x$ from both sides of the equation: $-\frac{2}{3}x + y = -4$. This is already in Standard Form, but it is not necessarily the stopping point (the answer choices for many questions asking you for the Standard Form equation of a line based on a graph will generally not have any fractional coefficients). We can multiply both sides of the equation by 3 (the denominator of the x-coefficient) in order to eliminate the fractional coefficient.

$$-\frac{2}{3}x + y = -4$$
$$3\left(-\frac{2}{3}x + y\right) = 3(-4)$$
$$\cancel{3}\left(-\frac{2}{\cancel{3}}x\right) + 3y = -12$$
$$-2x + 3y = -12$$

Similarly, we can (if necessary to match answer choices) multiply both sides of the equation by -1 in order to rewrite the equation into yet another equivalent representation.

$$-2x + 3y = -12$$
$$-1(-2x + 3y) = -1(-12)$$
$$-1(-2x) - 1(3y) = 12$$
$$2x - 3y = 12$$

This highlights the fact that while there is only **one** Slope-Intercept Form of a linear equation because one side of the equation must be just y, there are **infinite** equivalent Standard Form versions of the same equation because there are no constraints on the form or value of the variables' coefficients.

Example 3.1-2

2 1600.io 3.1

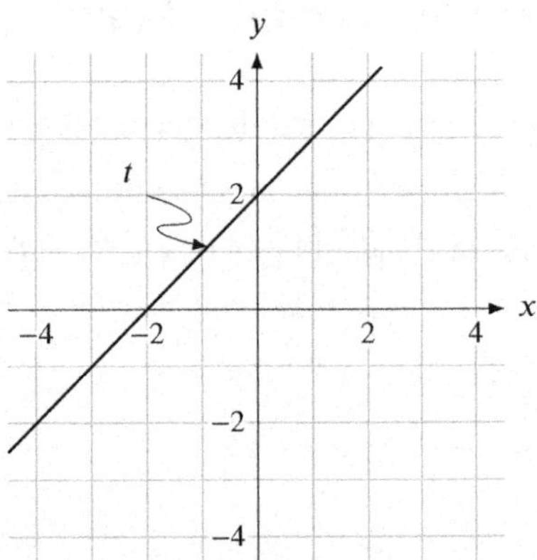

Which of the following is an equation of line t in the xy-plane above?

A) $x + y = 2$

B) $x + y = -2$

C) $x - y = 2$

D) $x - y = -2$

Solution 1

1. All of the answer choices are in Standard Form, $Ax + By = C$, where the value of A is 1 (because the coefficient of x is 1 in every choice). Therefore, we can simplify the equation of this line to $x + By = C$.

2. We can plug in points on the line to find the value of B and C. If we start with the point $(-2, 0)$, the y-term will drop out of the equation, helping us find the value of C easily.

$$x + By = C$$
$$-2 + B(0) = C$$
$$-2 = C$$

3. Since the value of C is -2, the equation of this line is $x + By = -2$ (limiting us to choices B and D), and we can solve for B by plugging in the point $(0, 2)$.

$$x + By = -2$$
$$0 + B(2) = -2$$
$$2B = -2$$
$$B = -1$$

4. Since the value of B is -1, the equation of this line is $x - y = -2$.

5. The answer is D.

Solution 2

1. Start by finding the equation of the line in Slope-Intercept Form, which can then be converted into Standard Form in order to match the answer choices.

2. Since the graph goes through the point $(0, 2)$, we know that the y-intercept of the line is 2.

3. We can draw in over-and-up arrows that show the changes in the y- and x-values so that we can find the slope of the line. Let's use the points $(0, 2)$ and $(-2, 0)$.

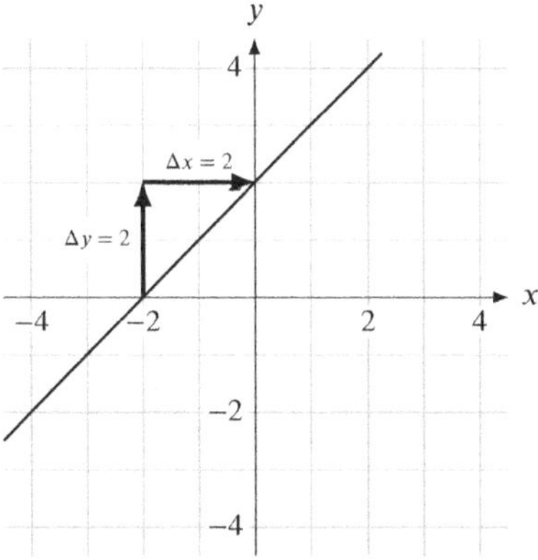

Since the slope is equal to $\frac{\Delta y}{\Delta x}$, the slope of this line is $\frac{2}{2}$ or 1.

4. We can write the equation of the line in Slope-Intercept Form ($y = mx + b$). We know that the slope is 1 and the y-intercept is 2, so we can plug in 1 for m (remember when the coefficient of a variable is 1, you do not have to write the coefficient) and 2 for b.

$$y = mx + b$$
$$y = (1)x + (2)$$
$$y = x + 2$$

5. In order to match the form of the answer choices, subtract x from both sides of the equation in order to rewrite the equation in Standard Form.

$$y = x + 2$$
$$-x + y = 2$$

6. None of the answer choices match this form. Since all of the answer choices start with a positive x instead of $-x$, multiply both sides of the equation by -1.

$$-x + y = 2$$
$$-1(-x + y) = -1(2)$$
$$-1(-x) - 1(y) = -2$$
$$x - y = -2$$

7. The answer is D.

Just as lines written in Slope-Intercept Form can be rewritten in Standard Form, lines written in Standard Form can be converted into Slope-Intercept Form.

Converting from Standard Form to Slope-Intercept Form

Sometimes we are given lines in Standard Form, but it is more useful for the problem to have them in Slope-Intercept Form. We can convert from Standard Form to Slope-Intercept Form through simple algebraic steps by isolating the y-variable.

We want to convert from a line in Standard Form ($Ax + By = C$) to a line in Slope-Intercept Form ($y = mx + b$), so we will complete the two following steps:

1. Subtract Ax from both sides of the equation: $By = -Ax + C$
2. Divide both sides of the equation by B: $y = \frac{-A}{B}x + \frac{C}{B}$

Remember, the slope of a line expressed in Slope-Intercept Form is the coefficient of x, so looking at the equation above, you can see that the **slope of a line in Standard Form is** $\frac{-A}{B}$.

Similarly, the y-intercept of a line expressed in Slope-Intercept Form is the constant term, so the ***y*-intercept of a line in Standard Form is** $\frac{C}{B}$.

You do not need to memorize this conversion formula; what's essential is that you understand the *procedure* involved, which is simply isolating the y term with no coefficient on one side of the equation. As long as you know that principle (and your algebra is solid), you can perform this conversion.

SkillDrill 3.1-2

Directions: Convert each linear equation from Standard Form to Slope-Intercept Form.

1. $4x - 2y = 8$ **2.** $9x - 3y = -21$ **3.** $-3x - 2y = 7$ **4.** $-5x - 6y = -18$

Directions: Convert each linear equation from Slope-Intercept Form to Standard Form, eliminating fractional coefficients if any. There are multiple correct answers; the answer key gives simple versions, with lowest non-fractional coefficients and non-negative x-coefficients.

5. $y = -5x - 10$ **6.** $y = 2x + 4$ **7.** $y = \frac{-1}{3}x - \frac{2}{3}$ **8.** $y = \frac{5}{2}x + 7$

Let's look back at the example of Jimmy buying pens and notebooks. We said if he buys p pens for $2 each and n notebooks for $4 each and spends a total of t dollars, then the equation that represents the relationship is $2p + 4n = t$. While this is a linear equation in Standard Form, it doesn't represent a specific line because t, the total amount that can be spent, is a variable, not a constant. As soon as we have a specific total amount that Jimmy can spend, the equation will represent a specific line that reflects the relationship.

For example, when we said that Jimmy has to spend exactly $40, we have the Standard Form linear equation $2p + 4n = 40$, and now we have a linear equation for a specific line (which can be graphed) for which the number of pens and notebooks must be in balance so that regardless of how many of each are bought, the total cost will come to $40.

It might be easier to visualize this if we write the equation in Slope-Intercept Form, which makes it easy to graph the line so we can select some points and plug them into the Standard Form equation; converting the equation to Slope-Intercept Form lets us find the value of p (which will be on the vertical axis) for any value of n (the horizontal axis), which lets us plot points and draw the line through them. Let's find the number of pens he buys as a function of the number of notebooks he buys by solving for p in terms of n, converting the equation into Slope-Intercept Form (where p is like the y-value and n is like the x-value). That is, we'd like an equation into which we can input the number of notebooks, and the equation will then produce the number of pens; to accomplish that, we will isolate the number of pens p on one side so when we evaluate the other side, we'll know the number of pens.

$$\begin{aligned} 2p + 4n &= 40 \\ 2p &= -4n + 40 \\ \frac{1}{\cancel{2}}(\cancel{2}p) &= \frac{1}{2}(-4n + 40) \\ p &= \frac{-4}{2}n + \frac{40}{2} \\ p &= -2n + 20 \end{aligned}$$

Now that the line is in Slope-Intercept Form, we can verify what we said before about how the number of pens is affected by the number of notebooks. The y-intercept is 20, because if Michael bought 0 notebooks, he could buy 20 pens (that is, n would equal zero, so the equation would be $p = 20$). The slope, given as the coefficient of the variable n, is -2, which means that the number of pens he can buy decreases by 2 every time he buys another notebook. This makes perfect sense, because a notebook costs \$2 and a pen costs \$1.

Let's now graph the line and pick a couple of points, so we can show how all of the points on the line also satisfy the Standard Form equation and provide ordered pairs of the number of pens and notebooks Jimmy can buy that will result in a total cost of \$40.

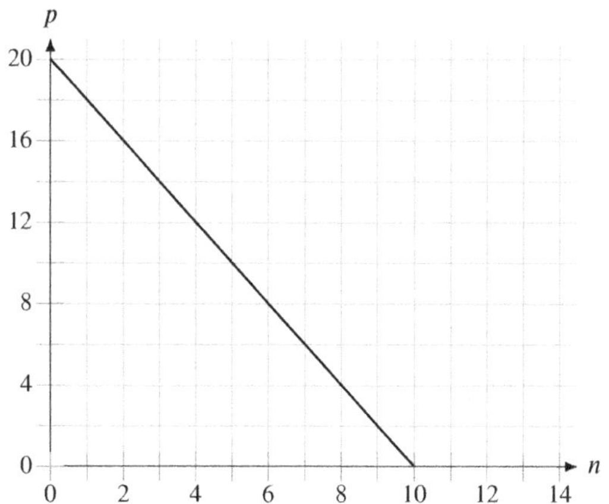

Remember that the cost of the supplies can be represented with the Standard Form equation $2p + 4n = t$. If we plug in any points from the graph into the Standard Form equation, we should see that the cost will add up to \$40. The two obvious points to look at are the p- and n-intercepts, $(0, 20)$ and $(10, 0)$, respectively. If we plug in the point $(0, 20)$, where $n = 0$ and $p = 20$, we will see that the cost of the supplies, t, is \$40.

$$\begin{aligned} 2p + 4n &= t \\ 2(20) + 4(0) &= t \\ 40 &= t \end{aligned}$$

If we plug in the point $(10,0)$, where $n = 10$ and $p = 0$, we will see agin that the cost of the supplies, t, is \$40.

$$\begin{aligned} 2p + 4n &= t \\ 2(0) + 4(10) &= t \\ 40 &= t \end{aligned}$$

Any point that we pick on the line will show that the total cost of supplies is \$40. Let's try $(5,10)$, where $n = 5$ and $p = 10$.

$$\begin{aligned} 2p + 4n &= t \\ 2(10) + 4(5) &= t \\ 20 + 20 &= t \\ 40 &= t \end{aligned}$$

Now let's check the point $(8,4)$, where $n = 8$ and $p = 4$.

$$\begin{aligned} 2p + 4n &= t \\ 2(4) + 4(8) &= t \\ 8 + 32 &= t \\ 40 &= t \end{aligned}$$

As soon as the total cost of the supplies was set at \$40, a single line was established, which could be graphed with the aid of a conversion to Slope-Intercept Form. Every point on the line could be plugged in to the Standard Form equation to show that any combination of notebooks and pens that appears as a point on the line would result in a total cost of \$40 (note that a point with a non-counting number coordinate value such as $(1.5,17)$ is on the line and satisfies the equation because $2(17) + 4(1.5) = 34 + 6 = 40$, but Jimmy probably can't buy one and half notebooks).

Example 3.1-3

3 3.1

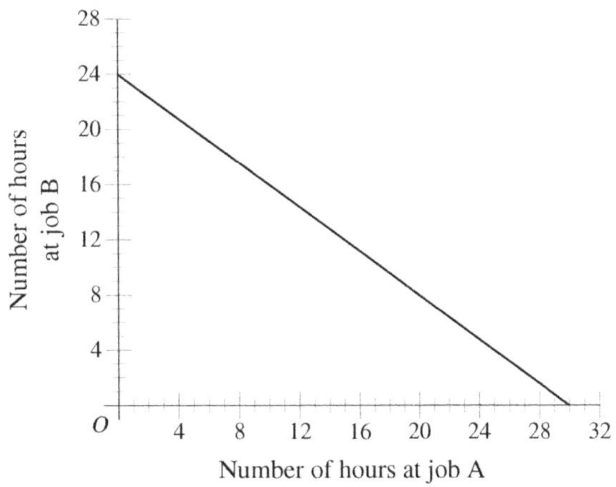

To earn money for piano lessons, Carlita works two part-time jobs: A and B. She earns \$8 an hour working at job A and \$10 an hour working at job B. In one week, Carlita earned a total of s dollars for working at the two part-time jobs. The graph above represents all possible combinations of numbers of hours Carlita could have worked at the two jobs to earn s dollars. What is the value of s ?

A) 192

B) 240

C) 300

D) 720

Solution

1. Normally, when there is a linear graph presented above a question, it is useful to find the equation of the line in Slope-Intercept Form. However, for this problem, that step would probably not be very useful to understanding the problem (it is not necessarily a waste of time or useless, and it should still generally be considered a good first step for many line problems).
   We can see that the horizontal axis (usually the x-axis) tells us the number of hours that Carlita worked at job A, which we will denote as a, and the vertical axis (usually the y-axis) tells us the number of hours that Carlita worked at job B, which we will denote as b. We are told that the line in the graph represents all possible combinations of hours that Carlita could have worked in order to earn a specific (but unknown) amount of money: s dollars.
   If we want to figure out the value of s, we need only pick any point (a, b) on this line and figure out how much money Carlita would make for working a hours at job A and b hours at job B (any and every point on the line tells us a combination of hours she could have worked to make s dollars). First, we need to write the Standard Form equation representing the line, which is easier to do based on the question's text than based on the Slope-Intercept Form of the line.

2. If Carlita works a hours at job A for \$8 an hour, then the total money she makes from job A is $8a$ dollars. If she works b hours at job B for \$10 an hour, then the total money she makes from job B is $10b$ dollars. In total, the amount of money she makes from working a hours at job A and b hours at job B, which is said to be s dollars, is equal to $8a + 10b$. Therefore, we can write the Standard Form linear equation $8a + 10b = s$ to represent the total amount of money she makes in a week.

3. Now that we have the Standard Form equation of the line (where s is still unknown), we can find the value of s by plugging in the a- and b-values of any point shown on the line. The easiest points to use would be either the a-intercept $(30, 0)$ (where the line hits the horizontal axis), or the b-intercept $(0, 24)$ (where the line hits the vertical axis). Note that any points on the line would work, but the lack of gridlines in the graph makes it harder to accurately choose any other points, and by choosing a point where one of the coordinate values is 0, we simplify the arithmetic we're about to perform. Let's check both intercepts just to verify that the total will be the same. First, let's use the point $(30, 0)$ by plugging in 30 for a and 0 for b.

$$\begin{aligned} 8a + 10b &= s \\ 8(30) + 10(0) &= s \\ 240 &= s \end{aligned}$$

We can comfortably choose choice B as the correct answer at this point, but for completeness, let's also check that the point $(0, 24)$ also produces the same value of s by plugging in 0 for a and 24 for b.

$$\begin{aligned} 8a + 10b &= s \\ 8(0) + 10(24) &= s \\ 240 &= s \end{aligned}$$

4. The answer is B.

Section 3.1 Suggested Problems from Real Tests

View related real-test problems at 1600.io/p/smtex?topic=3.1

Section 3.1 Practice Problems

1 3.1

Kenzie burns 3 calories per minute lifting weights and 15 calories per minute swimming. Which of the following equations represents the total number of calories, T, Kenzie has burned after lifting weights for 30 minutes and swimming for m minutes?

A) $T = 45m + 30$

B) $T = 15m + 90$

C) $T = 3m + 450$

D) $T = 18m + 30$

2 3.1

$$T = 4b + 10s$$

A manufacturer produces units of two different products. The equation above shows the total manufacturing cost T, in dollars, for manufacturing b units of the big product and manufacturing s units of the small product. If the total manufacturing cost was \$5,670 and 800 units of the big product were manufactured, how many units of the small product were manufactured?

3 3.1

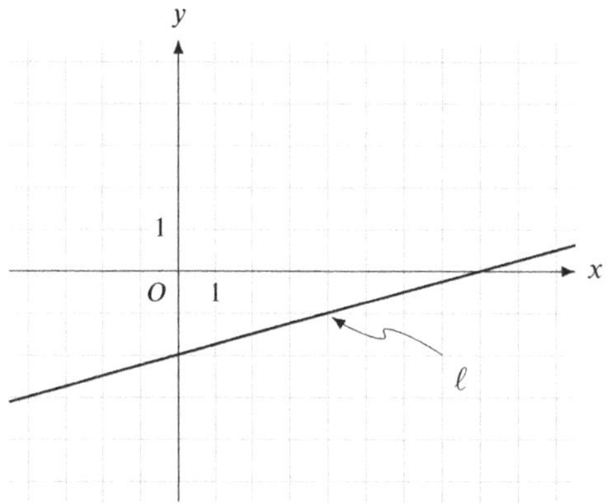

Line ℓ is shown in the xy-plane above. Which of the following is an equation of line ℓ?

A) $8x + 2y = 0$

B) $8x - 2y = 0$

C) $4x + y = 8$

D) $x - 4y = 8$

4 3.1

What are the slope and the y-intercept of the graph in the xy-plane of the equation $2x - 5y - 7 = 0$?

A) The slope is $-\frac{2}{5}$, and the y-intercept is $(0, -\frac{7}{5})$.

B) The slope is $-\frac{2}{5}$, and the y-intercept is $(0, \frac{7}{5})$.

C) The slope is $\frac{2}{5}$, and the y-intercept is $(0, -\frac{7}{5})$.

D) The slope is $\frac{2}{5}$, and the y-intercept is $(0, \frac{7}{5})$.

3.2 Parallel and Perpendicular Lines

One of the main reasons we may need to convert from Standard Form to Slope-Intercept Form is to solve problems that ask us about parallel or perpendicular lines. These problems usually need you to make use of the lines' slopes, which are most easily found when the lines are written in Slope-Intercept Form.

Parallel Lines

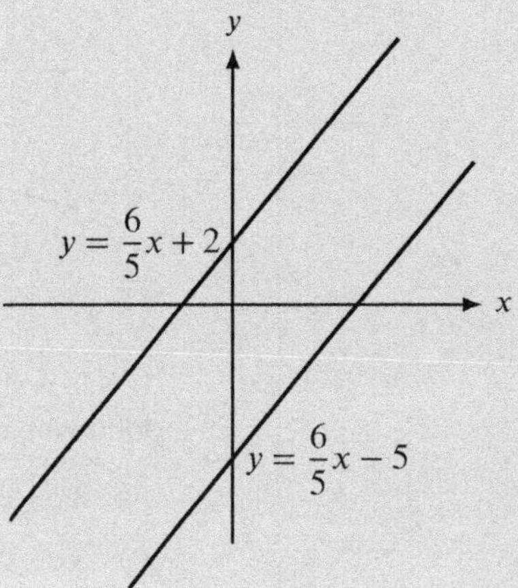

Parallel lines are the same distance apart everywhere, and thus they never intersect. Parallel Lines have the same slope. The line $y = \frac{6}{5}x + 2$ is parallel to the line $y = \frac{6}{5}x - 5$ because they have the same slope.

So we can see what parallel lines look like in Standard Form, convert both lines into Standard Form.

$$y = \frac{6}{5}x + 2 \qquad\qquad y = \frac{6}{5}x - 5$$

$$\frac{-6}{5}x + y = 2 \qquad\qquad \frac{-6}{5}x + y = -5$$

$$5\left(\frac{-6}{5}x + y\right) = 5(2) \qquad\qquad 5\left(\frac{-6}{5}x + y\right) = 5(-5)$$

$$\cancel{5}\left(\frac{-6}{\cancel{5}}x\right) + 5y = 10 \qquad\qquad \cancel{5}\left(\frac{-6}{\cancel{5}}x\right) + 5y = -25$$

$$-6x + 5y = 10 \qquad\qquad -6x + 5y = -25$$

We now have both equations in Standard Form, and we should notice that the x- and y-coefficients match in both equations.

$$\mathbf{-6}x + \mathbf{5}y = 10$$
$$\mathbf{-6}x + \mathbf{5}y = -25$$

If we were given these two lines in Standard Form, we would know that the lines are parallel because they x- and y-coefficients match. You can also verify this by remembering that the slope of a line in Standard Form, $Ax + By = C$, is equal to $\frac{-A}{B}$, so the slopes will match as long as the x- and y-coefficients are the same (or are in the same ratio to each other, which is covered more in the next chapter).

Perpendicular Lines

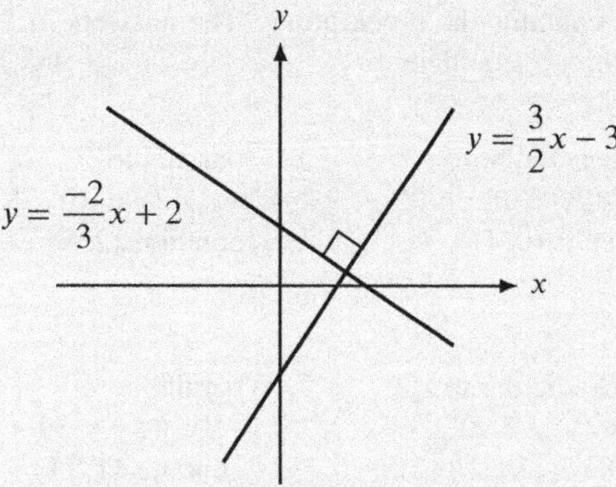

Perpendicular lines cross at a right angle. The slope of each line in a pair of perpendicular lines is the negative reciprocal of the slope of the other line. The **negative reciprocal** is found by swapping the values in the numerator and denominator of a slope and multiplying by -1. For example, a line with a slope of $\frac{-2}{3}$ is perpendicular to a line with a slope of $\frac{3}{2}$, which was found by flipping the fraction and multiplying by -1. Similarly, a line with a slope of 4 (or $\frac{4}{1}$) is perpendicular to a line with a slope of $\frac{-1}{4}$.

To consider what perpendicular lines look like when written in Standard Form, let's convert the perpendicular lines $y = 4x + 2$ and $y = \frac{-1}{4}x - 3$ into Standard Form.

$$y = 4x + 2$$
$$-4x + y = 2$$

$$y = \frac{-1}{4}x - 3$$
$$\frac{1}{4}x + y = -3$$
$$4\left(\frac{1}{4}x + y\right) = 4(-3)$$
$$\cancel{4}\left(\frac{1}{\cancel{4}}x\right) + 4y = -12$$
$$x + 4y = -12$$

These two lines in Standard Form are the following.

$$-4x + y = 2$$
$$x + 4y = -12$$

If we look at the two perpendicular lines in Standard Form, it looks like the x- and y-coefficients have swapped positions, and one of them has been multiplied by -1. In a way, you can think of this as a "horizontal negative reciprocal"—just as the negative reciprocal is found by swapping the numerator and denominator and multiplying by -1, the "horizontal negative reciprocal" here is found by swapping the x- and y-coefficients and multiplying one of them by -1. Remember again that the slope of a line in Standard Form, $Ax + By = C$, is equal to $\frac{-A}{B}$, so swapping the coefficients and multiplying one of them by -1 (to get the line $Bx - Ay = C$) effectively makes the slope equal to $\frac{B}{A}$, which is the negative reciprocal of $\frac{-A}{B}$.

SkillDrill 3.2-1

Directions: Given a linear equation in Standard Form, write the equation in both Standard Form and Slope-Intercept Form of the parallel or perpendicular line that contains the given point. The answers in Standard Form are written with lowest non-fractional coefficients and a non-negative x-coefficient.

1. parallel to
$3x - 2y = 7$
contains $(0, 4)$

2. perpendicular to
$3x - 2y = 7$
contains $(0, 4)$

3. parallel to
$4x + 2y = 10$
contains $(2, -6)$

4. perpendicular to
$4x + 2y = 10$
contains $(-1, 10)$

5. parallel to
$-5x - 4y = 90$
contains $(5, 4)$

6. perpendicular to
$-5x - 4y = 90$
contains $(10, 2)$

7. parallel to
$-8x + 5y = 35$
contains $(1, 1)$

8. perpendicular to
$-8x + 5y = 35$
contains $(-4, 0)$

Example 3.2-1

3.2

Lines t and w are parallel in the xy-plane. The equation of line t is $4x + 7y = 14$, and line w passes through $(7, 6)$. What is the value of the y-intercept of line w?

Solution 1

1. Remember that parallel lines in Slope-Intercept Form should have the same x- and y-coefficients (or be in the same ratio), so we know that for line w in Standard Form, $Ax + By = C$, the value of A should be 4 and the value of B should be 7 (we do not know C, but that is part of what is needed to solve the problem).

$$Ax + By = C$$
$$4x + 7y = C$$

2. In order to solve for C, we should plug in the only point on line w that we know (which we are given), $(7, 6)$. Plug in 7 for x, and plug in 6 for y.

$$4x + 7y = C$$
$$4(7) + 7(6) = C$$
$$28 + 42 = C$$
$$70 = C$$

3. Since $C = 70$, we can substitute 70 in for C to find the Standard Form equation of line w.

$$4x + 7y = C$$
$$4x + 7y = 70$$

4. The y-intercept is the y-value of the point on the line where $x = 0$, so plug in 0 for x in order to find the y-intercept of line w.

$$\begin{aligned} 4x + 7y &= 70 \\ 4(0) + 7y &= 70 \\ 7y &= 70 \\ y &= 10 \end{aligned}$$

5. The answer is 10.

Solution 2

1. First rewrite the equation of line t in Slope-Intercept Form, so we can find its slope (note that we don't actually need the entire equation including the constant that represents the y-intercept, because all we need to find is the slope, but we'll perform the conversion for completeness).

$$\begin{aligned} 4x + 7y &= 14 \\ 7y &= -4x + 14 \\ y &= \frac{-4}{7}x + 2 \end{aligned}$$

2. The slope of line t is $\frac{-4}{7}$, and since line w is parallel to line t, the slope of line w is also $\frac{-4}{7}$. Replace m with $\frac{-4}{7}$ in the general Slope-Intercept equation to begin writing the equation of line w.

$$y = \frac{-4}{7}x + b$$

3. Since we know that $(7, 6)$ is a point on line w, we can plug in 7 for x and 6 for y in order to solve for b, the y-intercept of line w.

$$\begin{aligned} y &= \frac{-4}{7}x + 2 \\ 6 &= \frac{-4}{7}(7) + b \\ 6 &= -4 + b \\ 10 &= b \end{aligned}$$

4. The answer is 10.

Notes

In Step 4 of Solution 1, instead of plugging in 0 for x to find the y-intercept, you could remember that the y-intercept of a line in Standard Form $Ax + By = C$ is equal to $\frac{C}{B}$ (but this doesn't save much time, is easy to screw up, and doesn't reinforce the fact the y-intercept of an equation is the y-value of the equation when the x-value is 0).

Example 3.2-2

2 1600.io 3.2

$$-4x + 3y = 8$$

In the xy-plane, the graph of which of the following equations is perpendicular to the graph of the equation above?

A) $3x + 4y = 8$

B) $3x - 4y = 8$

C) $4x + 3y = 8$

D) $4x - 3y = 8$

Solution 1

1. First we need to write the original equation in Slope-Intercept Form to find its slope.

$$-4x + 3y = 8$$
$$3y = 4x + 8$$
$$y = \frac{4}{3}x + \frac{8}{3}$$

2. The slope of the given line is $\frac{4}{3}$, so the slope of a perpendicular line is the negative reciprocal of $\frac{4}{3}$. Flip the fraction and multiply by -1 to determine that the slope of a perpendicular line is $\frac{-3}{4}$.

3. Start converting each answer choice from Standard Form to Slope-Intercept Form until you find one with a slope of $\frac{-3}{4}$. Let's begin with choice A: $3x + 4y = 8$.

$$4y = -3x + 8$$
$$y = \frac{-3}{4}x + 2$$

4. Luckily, the first choice was the correct choice, but if you want to double check, you could put all of the other lines in Slope-Intercept Form. None of the other lines will have a slope of $\frac{-3}{4}$.

5. The answer is A.

Solution 2

1. Instead of converting to Slope-Intercept Form, use the fact that the slope of a line in Standard Form, $Ax + By = C$, is equal to $\frac{-A}{B}$. In the given equation, $-4x + 3y = 8$, we know that $A = -4$ and $B = 3$, so the slope is equal to $\frac{-(-4)}{3}$ or $\frac{4}{3}$.
2. The slope of the given line is $\frac{4}{3}$, so the slope of a perpendicular line is the negative reciprocal of $\frac{4}{3}$. Flip the fraction and multiply by -1 to determine that the slope of a perpendicular line is $\frac{-3}{4}$.
3. Find the slope of the lines in the answer choices using the same method in order to see which choice has a slope of $\frac{-3}{4}$. Let's begin with choice A: $3x + 4y = 8$.
4. For this equation, $A = 3$ and $B = 4$, so the slope of the line is equal to $\frac{-3}{4}$, which is the slope of a line perpendicular to the line $-4x + 3y = 8$, which has a slope of $\frac{4}{3}$.
5. The answer is A.

Notes

Once you become familiar with finding the equation of a line perpendicular to a given line with both lines in Standard Form, you'll start to think about looking for (or creating) an equation where the coefficients of x and y are swapped and one of them is negated; inspect the coefficients in the given line equation and in answer choice A to see this relationship. This procedure streamlines the solving process, because you never actually need to determine the slopes explicitly.

View related real-test problems at 1600.io/p/smtex?topic=3.2

Section 3.2 Practice Problems

1 1600.io 3.1

Which of the following statements is true about the graph of the equation $3y + 5x = -12$ in the xy-plane?

A) It has a negative slope and a positive y-intercept.

B) It has a negative slope and a negative y-intercept.

C) It has a positive slope and a positive y-intercept.

D) It has a positive slope and a negative y-intercept.

2 1600.io 3.2

In the xy-plane, line ℓ has a slope of -3. If line k is perpedicular to line ℓ, which of the following could be an equation of line k ?

A) $-9x + 3y = 10$

B) $-2x + 6y = 12$

C) $-x - 3y = 4$

D) $12x + 4y = 7$

3 1600.io 3.2

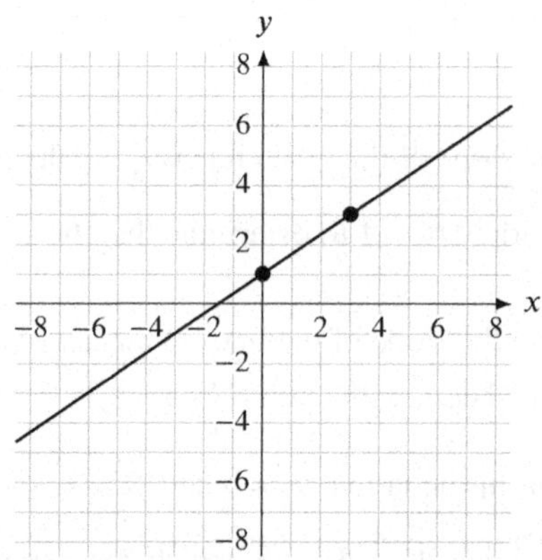

A line is shown in the xy-plane above. A second line (not shown) is parallel to the line shown and passes through the points $(0, 3)$ and $(4, c)$, where c is a constant. What is the value of c ?

CHAPTER 3 RECAP

- The Standard Form of Linear Equations is $Ax + By = C$.
- Standard Form can be converted into Slope-Intercept Form algebraically or by using the formula template $y = \frac{-A}{B}x + \frac{C}{B}$.
- The slope of a line in Standard Form is $\frac{-A}{B}$.
- The y-intercept of a line in Standard Form is $\frac{C}{B}$.
- Parallel lines are the same distance apart everywhere and thus they never intersect. Parallel Lines have the same slope.
- Perpendicular lines cross at a right angle. The slope of each line in a pair of perpendicular lines is the **negative reciprocal** of the slope of the other line. The negative reciprocal is found by swapping the values in the numerator and denominator of a slope and multiplying by -1.
- Parallel lines in Standard Form will have the same x- and y-coefficients (or the ratio of x- and y-coefficients will be the same).
- Perpendicular lines in Standard Form will have the x- and y-coefficients swapped, and one of the coefficients will be multiplied by -1 (or the ratio of the x- and y-coefficients will be flipped and multiplied by -1).

Additional Problems

1 1600.io 3.1

The line with the equation $\frac{3}{4}x + \frac{1}{5}y = 1$ is graphed in the xy-plane. What is the x-coordinate of the x-intercept of the line?

2 1600.io 3.1

$$x + y = 20$$

The equation above relates the number of minutes, x, Kevin spends showering each day and the number of minutes, y, he spends eating breakfast each day. In the equation, what does the number 20 represent?

A) The number of minutes spent showering each day

B) The number of minutes spent eating breakfast each day

C) The number of minutes spent eating breakfast for each minute spent showering

D) The total number of minutes spent showering and eating breakfast each day

3 1600.io 3.1

Gaston bought two types of candies: red candies that cost \$0.60 each and green candies that each cost z times as much as a red candy. If the cost of 3 red candies and 1 green candy was \$3, what is the value of z ?

4 1600.io 3.2

In the xy-plane, line k passes through the point $(5, 7)$ and is parallel to the line with the equation $y = \frac{7}{5}x - \frac{11}{5}$. What is the slope of line k ?

5 3.1

The headmaster of a wizarding school awarded a total of 1200 bonus points to the most upstanding students. The points were awarded in amounts of 50 points or 200 points. If at least one 50-point bonus and at least one 200-point bonus were awarded, what is one possible number of 50-point bonuses awarded?

6 3.2

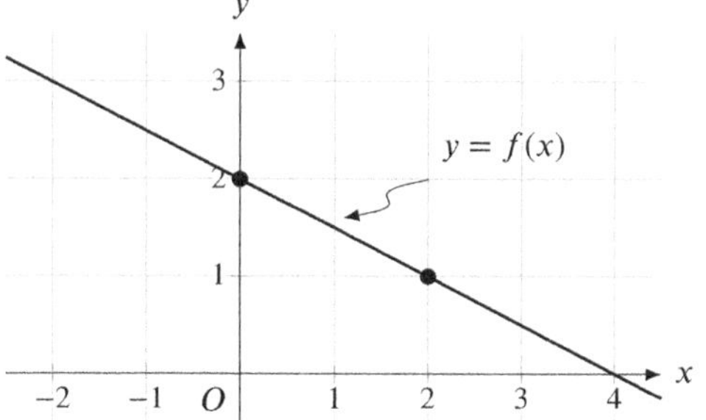

The graph of the linear function f is shown in the xy-plane above. The graph of the linear function g (not shown) is perpendicular to the graph of f and passes through the point $(2, 6)$. What is the value of $g(0)$?

7 3.1

The graph of the equation $ax + ky = -4$ is a line in the xy-plane, where a and k are constants. If the line contains the points $(2, 0)$ and $(0, -2)$, what is the value of k ?

A) -4

B) -2

C) 2

D) 4

8 3.2

Lines z and w are parallel in the xy-plane. The equation of line z is $2x + 5y = 10$, and line w passes through $(-4, 6)$. What is the value of the y-intercept of line w ?

9 1600.io 3.1

Which of the following is the graph of $y + 3x = 2$ in the xy-plane?

A)

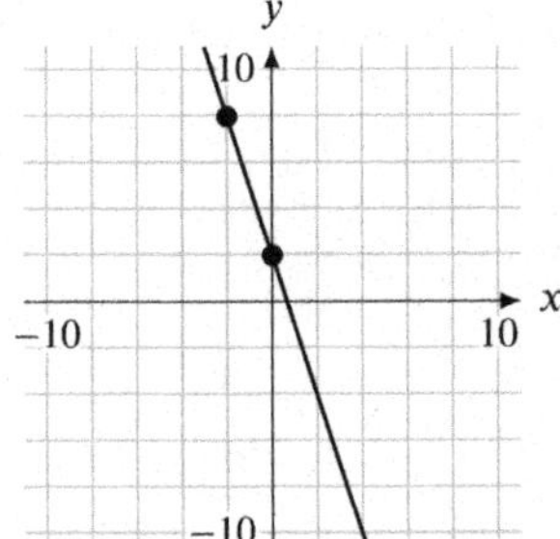

B)

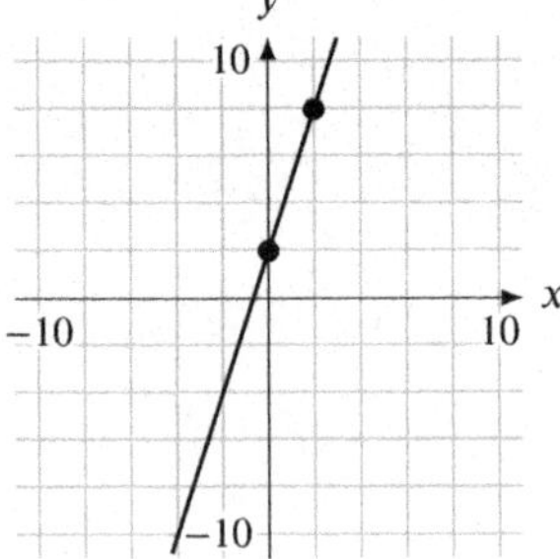

C)

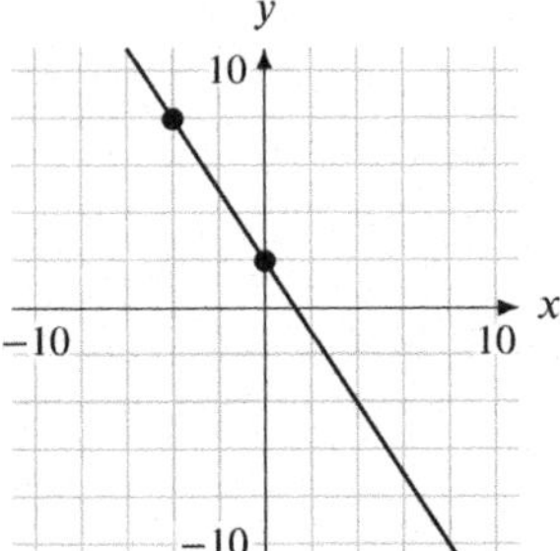

D)

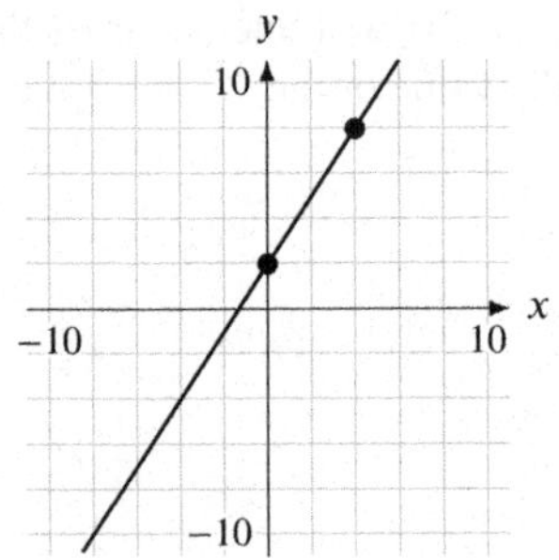

10 1600.io 3.1

$$-3x + 5y = -2$$

The graph of the equation above in the xy-plane is a line. What is the x-coordinate of the x-intercept of the line?

11 1600.io 3.2

In the xy-plane, line ℓ has a y-intercept of -2 and is perpendicular to the line with the equation $y = -\frac{3}{5}x$. If the point $(6, b)$ is on line ℓ, what is the value of b ?

12 3.2

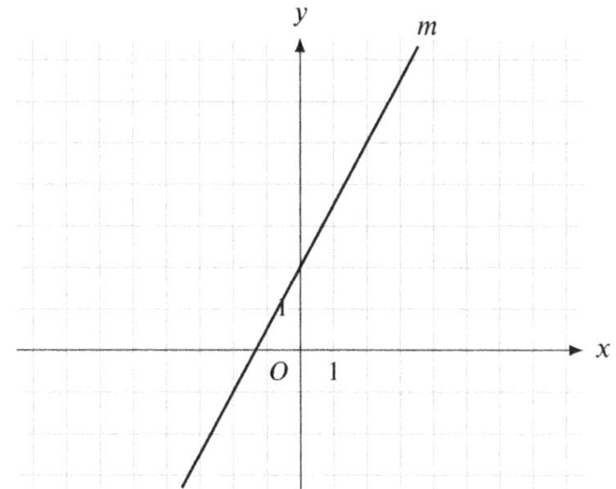

In the xy-plane above, line m is perpendicular to line ℓ (not shown). Which of the following could be an equation of line ℓ ?

A) $2x + 3y + 6 = 0$

B) $2x - 3y + 6 = 0$

C) $3x - 2y + 2 = 0$

D) $3x + 2y + 2 = 0$

13 3.1

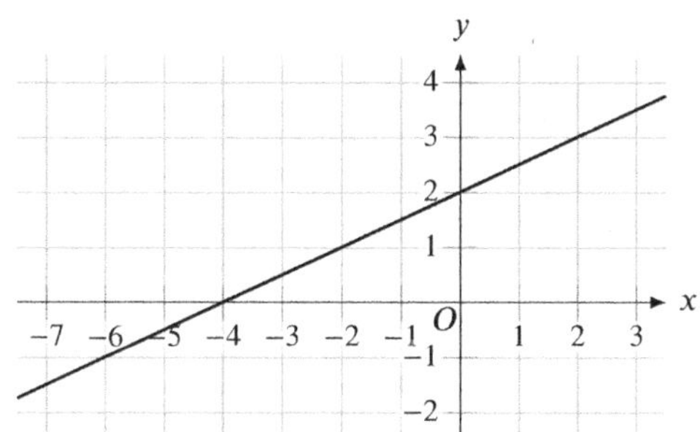

An equation of the graph shown is $ax + by = -8$, where a and b are constants. What is the value of b ?

A) −4

B) −2

C) 2

D) 4

14 3.1

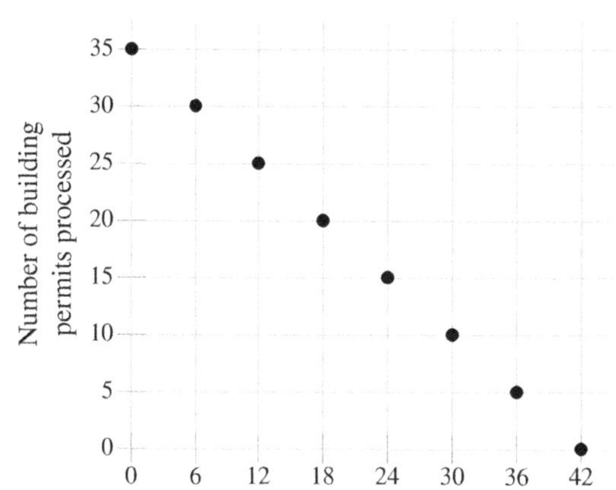

For his job, Kelvin spent a total of n minutes processing building permits and fishing permits. It takes Kelvin 30 minutes to process a building permit and 25 minutes to process a fishing permit. The graph above represents all possible combinations for the number of building permits and the number of fishing permits that Kelvin could have processed in the n minutes. What is the value of n ?

A) 1,470

B) 1,260

C) 1,050

D) 875

15 3.1

The graph of a line in the xy-plane has a negative slope and intersects the y-axis at a point that has a positive y-coordinate. Which of the following could be an equation of the line?

A) $-7x + 4y = -10$

B) $-7x + 4y = 10$

C) $7x + 4y = -10$

D) $7x + 4y = 10$

16 1600.io 3.1

x	y
$2b$	0
$4b$	$-b$
$6b$	$-2b$

Some values of x and their corresponding values of y are shown in the table above, where b is a constant and $b \neq 0$. If there is a linear relationship between x and y, which of the following equations represents the relationship?

A) $x + 2y = b$

B) $x + 2y = 2b$

C) $2x - y = -6b$

D) $2x - y = -b$

17 1600.io 3.2

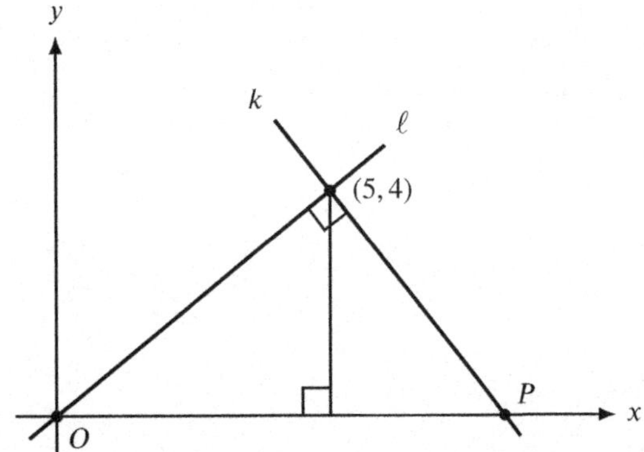

In the xy-plane above, lines k and ℓ are perpendicular. What is the x-coordinate of point P ?

A) 8.2

B) 8.25

C) 8.5

D) 8.8

Questions 18 and 19 refer to the following information.

Cost per Pound of Nuts

Nut	Dollars	Euros
Cashew	4.00	4.40
Brazil	3.00	3.30
Macadamia	4.00	4.40

The table above gives the typical costs per pound of nut, expressed in both dollars and euros, of the three nuts that a vendor sells.

18 1600.io 3.1

If x dollars is equivalent to k euros, of the following, which best represents the relationship between x and k ?

A) $k = 0.91x$

B) $xk = 1.1$

C) $k = 1.1x$

D) $x = 1.1k$

19 1600.io 3.1

If a client pays \$300 for a mixture of nuts consisting entirely of c pounds of cashews, b pounds of brazil nuts, and m pounds of macadamia nuts, which of the following expresses b in terms of c and m ?

A) $b = 100 - \frac{4}{3}(c + m)$

B) $b = 100 - \frac{4}{3}(c - m)$

C) $b = 100 + \frac{4}{3}(c + m)$

D) $b = 100 + \frac{3}{4}(c + m)$

Answer Key

SkillDrill 3.1-1

1. $2b + 3f = 56$
2. $h + 3c = 60$
3. $8s + 20b = 112$
4. $-100c - 2.50h = -197.50$
5. $5r - 10p = -42$

SkillDrill 3.1-2

1. $y = 2x - 4$
2. $y = 3x + 7$
3. $y = \frac{-3}{2}x - \frac{7}{2}$
4. $y = \frac{-5}{6}x + 3$
5. $5x + y = -10$
6. $2x - y = -4$
7. $x + 3y = -2$
8. $5x - 2y = -14$

Section 3.1 Practice Problems

1. B
2. 247
3. D
4. C

SkillDrill 3.2-1

1. $y = \frac{3}{2}x + 4$, $3x - 2y = -8$
2. $y = \frac{-2}{3}x + 4$, $2x + 3y = 12$
3. $y = -2x - 2$, $2x + y = -2$
4. $y = \frac{1}{2}x + \frac{21}{2}$, $x - 2y = -21$
5. $y = \frac{-5}{4}x + \frac{41}{4}$, $5x + 4y = 41$
6. $y = \frac{4}{5}x - 6$, $4x - 5y = 30$
7. $y = \frac{8}{5}x - \frac{3}{5}$, $8x - 5y = 3$
8. $y = \frac{-5}{8}x - \frac{5}{2}$, $5x + 8y = -20$

Section 3.2 Practice Problems

1. B
2. B
3. $\frac{17}{3}$, 5.66, or 5.67

Additional Problems

1. $\frac{4}{3}$ or 1.33
2. D
3. 2
4. $\frac{7}{5}$ or 1.4
5. 4, 8, 12, 16, or 20
6. 2
7. C
8. $\frac{22}{5}$ or 4.4
9. A
10. $\frac{2}{3}$, .666, or .667
11. 8
12. A
13. A
14. C
15. D
16. B
17. A
18. C
19. A

Systems of Linear Equations 4

4.1 Introduction to Systems of Linear Equations

A **system of linear equations** is a collection of two linear equations with the same set of variables. In previous chapters, we talked about the information that can be gleaned from a single linear equation and its graph, but what happens when we have two lines in the same system?

Let's look at a graph of two distinct lines: $y = 2x + 1$ and $y = -x + 4$.

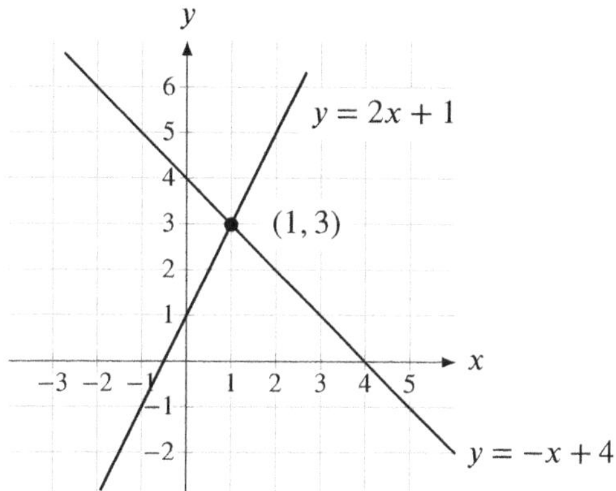

Notice that the two lines intersect at the point $(1, 3)$. This intersection point exists as a point on the graphs of both functions. Remember that the graph of a linear equation represents all of the points that are solutions to that linear equation. When two intersecting lines are graphed together to represent a system of linear equations, their intersection point gives one pair of x- and y-values that satisfies both equations. The intersection point is called a **solution to the system of equations** because it is a solution to both of the equations in the system.

Example 4.1-1

1 1600.io 4.1

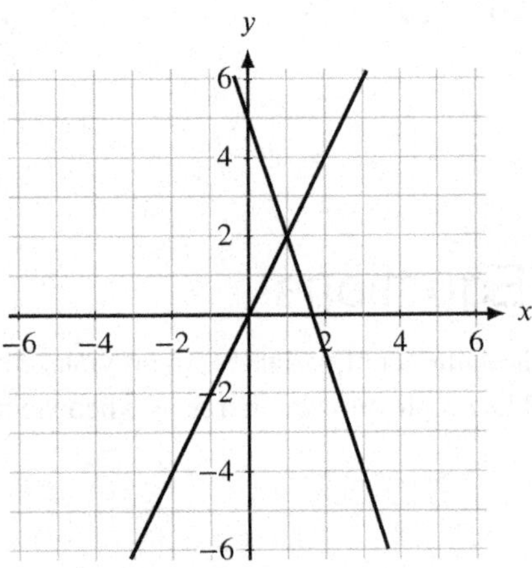

The lines in the xy-plane above are the graphs of two linear equations. What is the solution (x, y) to the system formed by the equations?

A) $(0, 5)$

B) $(0, 0)$

C) $(1, 2)$

D) $(2, 1)$

Solution

1. Since the solution point for a system of two linear equations is the point where the two lines intersect, we should check the gridlines to see if the intersection point is easily found.
2. Because the lines intersect at a meeting of gridlines, we can clearly see that the lines intersect at the point $(1, 2)$, so the x- and y-value pair that constitutes the solution to the system of linear equations is represented by the point $(1, 2)$.
3. The answer is C.

View related real-test problems at 1600.io/p/smtex?topic=4.1

Section 4.1 Practice Problems

1 4.1

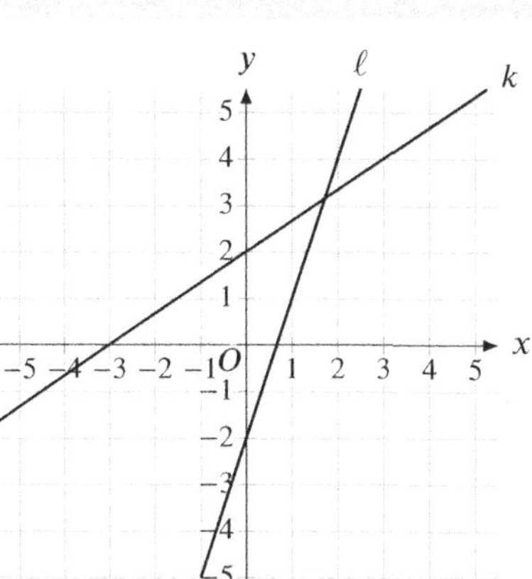

Lines ℓ and k in the xy-plane above are the graphs of the equations in a system. How many solutions does the system of equations have?

A) None

B) One

C) Two

D) More than two

2 4.1

$$-x + 2y = -2$$
$$3x - y = -2$$

Which of the following graphs in the xy-plane could be used to solve the system of equations above?

A)

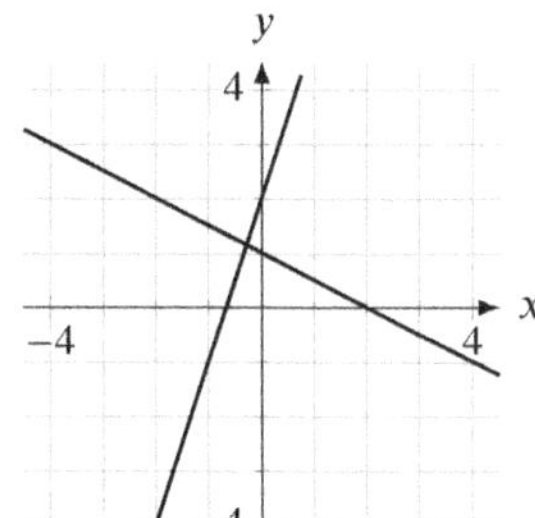

B)

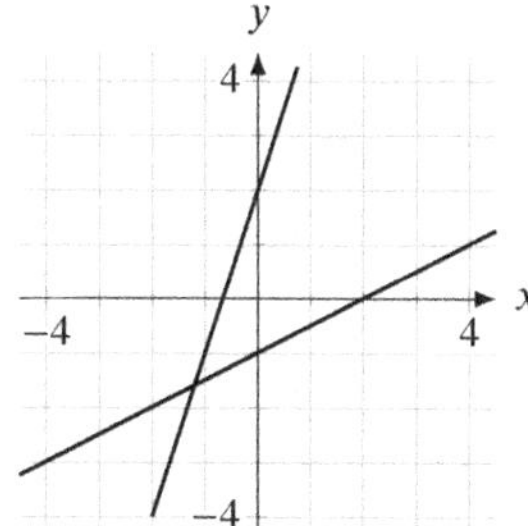

C)

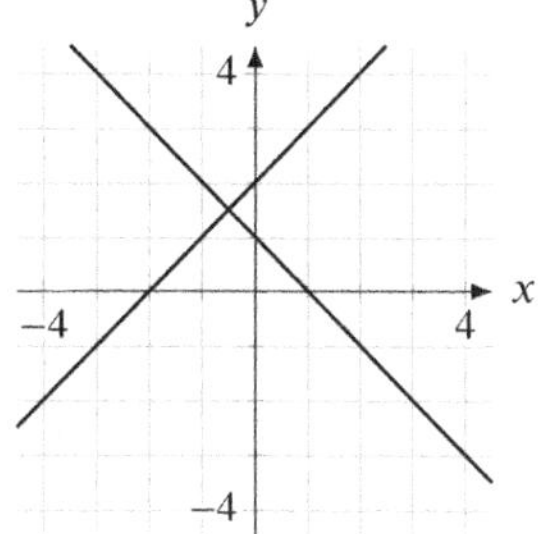

D)

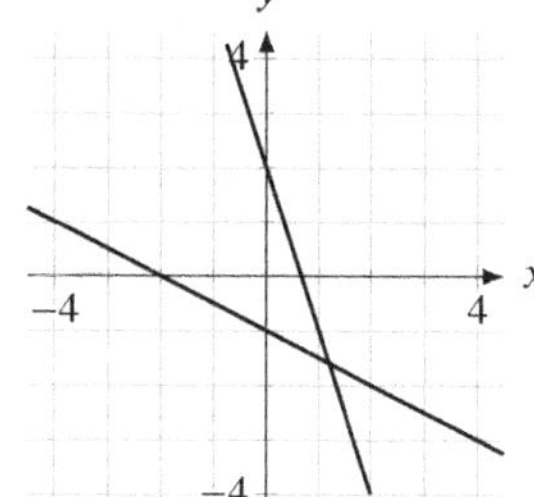

4.2 Using Substitution to Solve Systems of Linear Equations

Let's come back to our opening example with the lines $y = 2x + 1$ and $y = -x + 4$. We determined from the graph that the point $(1, 3)$ existed on both lines. But suppose the lines were not graphed on a carefully laid out grid, and we were asked to find the solution to the system if we only had the equations themselves. Perhaps there is a more mathematical approach to solving this system than sloppily drawing the lines ourselves and hoping we could draw a perfectly proportioned grid that would enable us to correctly identify the solution to the system (**NEVER** attempt to solve system of equations problem this way).

Instead of simply considering the solution to a system of linear equations as an intersection point on a graph, we can also consider that (as mentioned earlier) a solution to the system is also a pair of x- and y-values that satisfies both equations. Algebraically, we can solve the system using substitution. Since we are looking for an x- and y-coordinate pair that is a solution to both lines, the same x- and y-values that satisfy one of the equations also satisfy the other equation. When we are looking for this solution, we know that the y-value is the same in both equations (and so are the x-values), so we can plug one in for the other, which is very easy when both equations are written in Slope-Intercept Form.

When both lines are in Slope-Intercept Form, as in our current example, they are both solved for y in terms of x. For example, we know from one of our equations that y must be equal to $2x + 1$, and we know from the other equation that y must also be equal to $-x + 4$.

Here's what we're given:

$$y = 2x + 1$$
$$y = -x + 4$$

Let's just rewrite the first equation by switching the sides of the terms:

$$2x + 1 = y$$

Arranging our two equations:

$$\begin{aligned} 2x + 1 = y& \\ &y = -x + 4 \end{aligned}$$

Now, it should be apparent that

$$2x + 1 = -x + 4$$

because equality is transitive: generally, if we're given

$$y = u$$
$$y = v$$

we know that

$$u = v$$

Sometimes, this procedure is casually referred to as "setting the equations equal to each other," but that's not really right: we're not setting the two *equations* equal; we're setting the two *expressions* that are on the opposite side of the equals sign from y equal to each other, so be sure you understand that.

This procedure can equivalently be thought of as **substituting** an expression in terms of x for y in an equation, which has the effect of eliminating y from the equation, leaving x as the only variable. So, we have

$$y = 2x + 1$$

We also have

$$y = -x + 4$$

so we can substitute $-x + 4$ for y in the first equation:

$$\begin{aligned} y &= 2x + 1 \\ -x + 4 &= 2x + 1 \end{aligned}$$

Of course, we could do the same thing but switching the equations, so we could substitute $2x + 1$ for y in the second equation:

$$2x + 1 = -x + 4$$

The result is the same, except the sides of the expressions are swapped, which has no mathematical importance. Let's proceed with the solving using the first unified equation we made.

Now that the two expressions are set equal to each other, we can collect and combine all the x-terms on one side of the equation and all the constant terms on the other side of the equation in order to solve for x.

$$\begin{aligned} -x + 4 &= 2x + 1 \\ 4 &= 3x + 1 \\ 3 &= 3x \\ 1 &= x \end{aligned}$$

By setting the two expressions that represent y equal to each other or, equivalently, by substituting the expression that gives the value of y from one equation in for y in the other equation, we have determined the x-value of the solution point. Now that we know that $x = 1$ is *part* of the solution, we can **substitute this value for x in the equation for either line** (remember that the solution to the system is the coordinate pair that exists on **both** lines in the system) in order to find the y-value of the solution.

$$\begin{aligned} y &= 2x + 1 \\ y &= 2(1) + 1 \\ y &= 2 + 1 \\ y &= 3 \end{aligned}$$

By using substitution (instead of locating the intersection point on a graph), we have found the pair of x- and y-variables that form the solution to the system of equations.

SkillDrill 4.2-1

Directions: Use substitution to find the intersection point that is the solution to the system of linear equations.

1. $y = 8x + 2$
$y = -2x + 12$

2. $y = -3x$
$y = 2x + 25$

3. $y = x - 7$
$y = 3x - 14$

4. $y = 9x + 6$
$y = -3x + 5$

In the following example, we will solve for the solution to a system of linear equations by setting the expressions representing y equal to each other (we will have to write the second equation based on the question prompt before we can solve).

Example 4.2-1

 1600.io 4.2

$$y = x + 4$$

An equation of line ℓ in the xy-plane is shown above. Another line, k, has a slope equal to triple the slope of ℓ and a y-intercept equal to triple the y-intercept of ℓ. At which point (x, y) do lines ℓ and k intersect?

A) $(-4, 0)$

B) $\left(-\frac{1}{4}, 0\right)$

C) $\left(0, \frac{1}{4}\right)$

D) $(0, 4)$

Solution

1. Remember, the point of intersection of two lines represents the solution to the system the lines represent. Write the equation of the second line in the system based on the information given in the question. The slope of line k is triple (three times) the slope of line ℓ, and as the slope of line ℓ is 1, the slope of line k is 3. The y-intercept of line k is triple the y-intercept of line ℓ, and as the y-intercept of line ℓ is 4, the y-intercept of line k is 12. Since its slope is 3 and its y-intercept is 12, the equation of line k is $y = 3x + 12$.

2. Both equations are solved for y in terms of x. Since the y-values have to be equal at the intersection point, we can use substitution and set the right sides of both equations equal to each other.

$$x + 4 = 3x + 12$$

3. Combine the x-terms on one side of the equation and the constant terms on the other side of the equation, then solve for x.

$$\begin{aligned} x + 4 &= 3x + 12 \\ 4 &= 2x + 12 \\ -8 &= 2x \\ -4 &= x \end{aligned}$$

4. There is only one choice in which the x-value of the point is -4, so there is no need to solve for the y-value of the intersection point (by plugging the x-value into either of the original equations in the system), but you can if you like to play it safe.

$$\begin{aligned} y &= x + 4 \\ y &= -4 + 4 \\ y &= 0 \end{aligned}$$

5. The answer is A.

It is not necessary for both equations to be in Slope-Intercept Form (or, more generally, to be solved in terms of the same variable, whether it's x or y) in order to use substitution. **Whenever at least one of the equations in a system is solved for one variable in terms of another (one variable is isolated on one side of the equation), substitution will probably be the best method of solution** (we will discuss other cases later in the chapter). In the next example, neither linear equation is written in Slope-Intercept Form. DON'T PANIC; both of the equations are still linear, and we can still use substitution even when the linear equations are not written in either of the traditional forms of linear equations that we have discussed.

Example 4.2-2

2 4.2

$$\frac{1}{4}(x+3y) = \frac{9}{4}$$
$$x = 3y$$

The system of equations above has solution (x, y). What is the value of y?

Solution

1. Start by getting rid of the fractions in the first equation (a smart first step in most situations). Multiply both sides of the first equation by 4.

$$\not{4}\left(\frac{1}{\not{4}}\right)(x+3y) = \not{4}\left(\frac{9}{\not{4}}\right)$$
$$x + 3y = 9$$

2. Since the second equation tells us that x is equal to $3y$, substitute $3y$ in for x in the simplified version of the first equation ($x + 3y = 9$), then solve for y.

$$x + 3y = 9$$
$$(3y) + 3y = 9$$
$$6y = 9$$
$$y = \frac{9}{6}$$
$$y = \frac{3}{2}$$

3. The answer is $\frac{3}{2}$.

Notes

It was not essential that the fractions be eliminated as the first step; you could have started by substituting $3y$ for x in the first equation, which would result in $\frac{1}{4}(6y) = \frac{9}{4}$. At that point, you could multiply through by 4 to get $6y = 9$ and then proceed with solving for y from there.

View related real-test problems at 1600.io/p/smtex?topic=4.2

Section 4.2 Practice Problems

1 1600.io 4.2

$$7x + y = 53$$
$$x = 6$$

If (x, y) is the solution to the given system of equations, what is the value of y ?

2 1600.io 4.4

$$x - 4y = 16$$
$$4y = 12$$

If (x, y) is the solution to the system of equations above, what is the value of x ?

A) -4

B) 4

C) 28

D) 64

3 1600.io 4.2

$$x + 5y = 16$$
$$y = 3x$$

If the ordered pair (x, y) satisfies the system of equations above, what is the value of x ?

4 1600.io 4.2

In the xy-plane, the graph of $y = 3x - 2$ intersects the graph of $y = 2x + 4$ at the point (a, b). What is the value of a ?

A) -2

B) 2

C) 6

D) 16

5 1600.io 4.2

The graph of a line in the xy-plane has slope 4 and contains the point $(1, 10)$. The graph of a second line passes through the points $(1, 4)$ and $(2, 5)$. If the two lines intersect at the point (a, b), what is the value of $b - a$?

A) -3

B) -1

C) 2

D) 3

4.3 Number of Solutions to Systems of Linear Equations Part I

We know that a solution to a system of two linear equations is an x- and y-value pair that satisfies both linear equations, and the graphical representation of that solution is a point with that x- and y-value that lies on both lines. **When the lines intersect at a point, a single solution to the system exists.** But what happens if the lines in a system never intersect? There can be no solution to the system because there is no common point that exists on both lines.

The only way for two lines to never intersect (that is, for the system of equations to have no solution) is for them to be parallel: the two lines must have **the same slope and different y-intercepts**. For example, let's consider the lines $y = x + 1$ and $y = x + 3$.

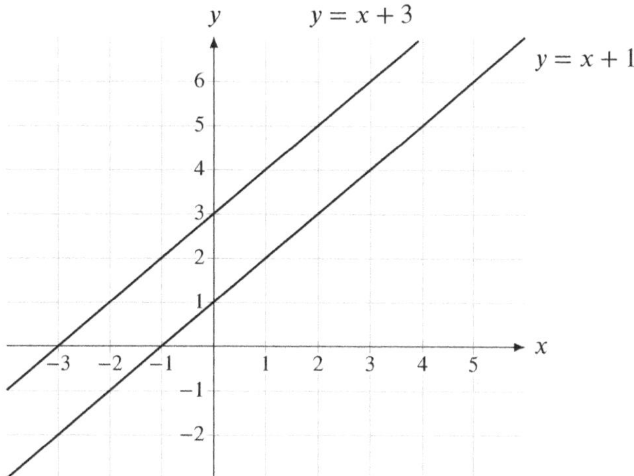

There are no x- and y-coordinate pairs that exist on both lines (there is no intersection point). Therefore, there is no solution to the system of equations.

If we tried to solve this system using substitution to create the equation $x + 1 = x + 3$, we would arrive at an impossible situation (which indicates that there is no solution) when we attempt to solve for x. When we subtract x from both sides of the equation (in an attempt to group the x-terms on one side of the equation), we end up with no x terms and have the irreconcilable, untrue equation $1 = 3$. Since 1 is obviously never equal to 3, there is no value of x for which $x + 1$ equals $x + 3$; there is no solution to the system of equations (no matter what value of x we plug into the equations).

Most of the time, problems about systems of linear equations with no solutions are disguised in the form of a single equation with only one variable. For example, if we are given the equation

$$ax + 5 = 2x + 3$$

and told that there are no solutions, and we are asked to find the value of a, then we need to understand that **this is actually a system of equations problem, but the first step of substitution is already done for us** (the expressions representing y for two separate linear equations have already been set equal to each other).

Essentially, it is as if we have been given a system of linear equations in which one equation is $y = ax + 5$ (based on the left side of the equation) and the other equation is $y = 2x + 3$ (based on the right side of the equation). If these two lines have no solution, then they must be parallel. **In order for the two lines to be parallel, their slopes must be the same, and their y-intercepts must be different.**

Since the slope of the first line is a, and the slope of the second line is 2, it must be true that $a = 2$ in order for the lines to have the same slope.

In essence, you do not have to actually split the equation into two separate equations; you simply need to **match the x-coefficients (the slopes) on both sides of the equation** (and verify that the constants, or y-intercepts, are not the same).

Indeed, if $a = 2$, we can see that plugging 2 in for a in the original single equation given to us, $ax + 5 = 2x + 3$, will once again produce an impossible situation.

$$ax + 5 = 2x + 3$$
$$(2)x + 5 = 2x + 3$$
$$5 = 3????$$

SkillDrill 4.3-1

Directions: All of the following equations have no solution. Find the value of a. Challenge questions are boxed.

1. $ax + 2 = 4x - 7$

2. $x + 2 = 2a(x - 7)$

3. $a(3x + 2) + 2x = 7x - 7$

4. $\boxed{ax + 2 = -7}$

Example 4.3-1

1 1600.io 4.3

$$a(-4x + 2) + 3x = 4x - 1$$

The equation above has no solutions, and a is a constant. What is the value of a ?

A) -1

B) $-\frac{1}{2}$

C) $-\frac{1}{4}$

D) 1

Solution

1. Our goal is to get both sides of the equation into the form $mx + b$ (as if the y-expressions for two lines have already been set equal to each other) so we can simply match the x-coefficients (and verify that the constants are not the same).
2. Distribute a on the left side of the equation.

$$a(-4x + 2) + 3x = 4x - 1$$
$$-4ax + 2a + 3x = 4x - 1$$

3. Subtract $3x$ from both sides of the equation to group the x-terms with numerical coefficients on the right side of the equation.

$$-4ax + 2a + 3x = 4x - 1$$
$$-4ax + 2a = x - 1$$

4. In order for there to be no solutions, the x-coefficients (which represent the slopes) must be the same (and the constants must not be equal). Set the x-coefficients ($-4a$ and 1) equal to each other to solve for a.

$$-4a = 1$$
$$a = -\frac{1}{4}$$

5. The answer is C.

Notes

You can double check the value of a by making sure that the constant terms (the y-intercepts) DO NOT match (if the slopes were the same and the y-intercepts were the same, the lines would be the same line instead of parallel lines). If $a = \frac{-1}{4}$, then the constant on the left side of the equation is $2\left(\frac{-1}{4}\right)$ or $\frac{-1}{2}$, which is not equal to the constant term on the other side of the equation (-1). The value we found for a passes this test, so we know that the two lines are parallel and are not the same line.

In Step 3, we subtracted $3x$ from both sides in order to avoid combining the x-coefficients ($-4a$ and 3) and factoring out x. This would not be wrong but is probably confusing for some students. In general, you want to try to keep unknown constants such as a, b, or c on one side of the equation (separate from numerical constants) when you have to match coefficients.

We've seen that a system of equations can have one solution where there's a single pair of values (x, y) that satisfies both equations, and we showed that the graphical representation of this is the point of intersection of the two lines that represent the equations. If the lines do not cross anywhere—they are parallel—there's no point that lies on both lines, and thus there is no solution.

There is only one other relationship between two linear equations: they're actually the same, and thus they produce the same line when graphed; such lines are called coincident lines. In that case, every solution to one of the equations is also a solution to the other equation; graphically, this is evident because the two lines are in fact the same, so every point lies on both, and is thus a solution to both. Because there are an infinite number of points on a line, this means that **there are infinitely many solutions to the system of equations in which the lines are exactly the same**. In the graph below, the line $y = -2x + 4$ is extra thick to show that the same line has been graphed twice (one on top of the other) and several of the infinite solution points are shown along the line.

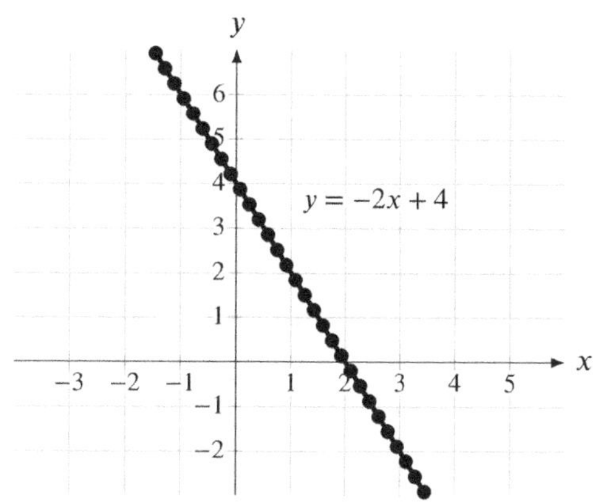

If we were given a system of linear equations in which both equations were the same, say $y = -2x + 4$ and $y = -2x + 4$ (it should be obvious the lines are the same if they are given in the same form, but let's continue anyway), we could try to solve the system with substitution.

$$-2x + 4 = -2x + 4$$

When we try to group the x-terms, they will once again cancel each other (as with a system of parallel lines), but this time we will be left with the undeniably true equation $4 = 4$. Since 4 is obviously always equal to 4 no matter what the value of x is, there are infinitely many solutions to the system of equations—no matter what value of x or y we plug into the equations, the two lines will always be equal because they are the same line.

Most of the time, problems about systems of linear equations with infinitely many solutions are disguised in the form of a single equation with only one variable. For example, if we are given the equation $ax + b = -3x + 5$ and told that there are infinitely many solutions, and we are asked to find the value of a, we need to understand that this is actually a systems of equations problem, but the first step of substitution is already done for us (the expressions that equal y for two separate linear equations have already been set equal to each other).

Essentially, it is as if we have been given a system of linear equations in which one equation is $y = ax + b$ (based on the left side of the equation) and the other equation is $y = -3x + 5$ (based on the right side of the equation). If these two lines have infinitely many solutions, then they must be exactly the same line. **In order for the two lines to be the same, their slopes *and* their y-intercepts must be the same.**

Since the slope of the first line is a, and the slope of the second line is -3, it must be true that $a = -3$ in order for the lines to have the same slope. Since the y-intercept of the first line is b, and the y-intercept of the second line is 5, it must be true that $b = 5$ for the lines to have the same y-intercept.

In essence, you do not have to actually split the equation into two separate equations; you simply need to **match the x-coefficients (the slopes) and the constant terms (the y-intercepts) on both sides of the equation when dealing with a system that has infinitely many solutions**.

Indeed, if $a = -3$ and $b = 5$, we can see that plugging -3 in for a and 5 in for b in the original single equation given to us, $ax + b = -3x + 5$, will once again produce a statement that is always true for any value of x.

$$ax + b = -3x + 5$$
$$-3x + 5 = -3x + 5$$
$$5 = 5$$

SkillDrill 4.3-2

Directions: Each of the following equations has infinite solutions. Find the values of a and b, reducing any fractions to lowest terms.

1. $ax - b = 4x - 7$ **2.** $a(x + 2) = 6x + b$ **3.** $ax + 2 = b(3x - 1)$ **4.** $abx + b = 3(5x + 3)$

Example 4.3-2

2 4.3

$$ax - 5(4 - 3x) = -20$$

In the equation above, a is a constant. For what value of a does the equation have infinitely many solutions?

A) -15

B) -3

C) 3

D) 5

Solution

1. Our goal is to get both sides of the equation into the form $mx + b$ (as if the expressions representing y for two lines have already been set equal to each other) so we can simply match the x-coefficients and constant terms on both sides of the equation (satisfying the conditions for infinitely many solutions).
2. Distribute -5 on the left side of the equation.

$$ax - 5(4 - 3x) = -20$$
$$ax - 20 + 15x = -20$$

3. Subtract $15x$ from both sides of the equation in order to have an x-term on both sides of the equation.

$$ax - 20 + 15x = -20$$
$$ax - 20 = -15x - 20$$

4. In order for there to be infinitely many solutions, the x-coefficients (a and -15), which represent the slopes, must be the same (so too must the constants, which, as expected, already match). Therefore $a = -15$.
5. The answer is A.

Notes

In Step 3, we subtracted $15x$ from both sides in order to avoid combining the x-coefficients (a and 15) and factoring out x. This would not be wrong but is probably confusing for some students. In general, you want to try to keep unknown constants such as a, b, or c on one side of the equation (separate from numerical constants) when you have to match coefficients.

Systems of Linear Equations with One Solution

In a system of equations with one solution, the lines intersect at one point, with the coordinates of the intersection point representing the x- and y-values of the solution. Remember, a solution represents a pair of x- and y-values that satisfies both equations, which, in graphical terms, means these values define a single point that lies on both lines; a point that's on both lines is a point of intersection.

***Any* two lines that have different slopes will intersect once.** Note that the lines do not have to be perpendicular.

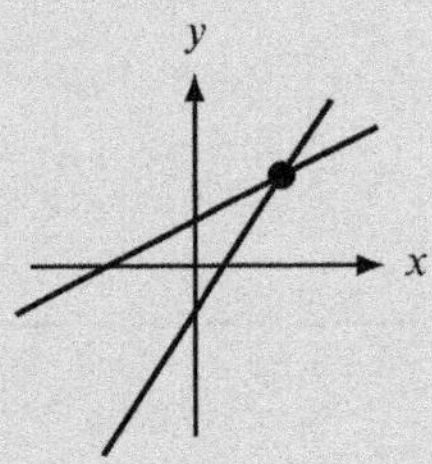

Systems of Linear Equations with No Solution

In a system of equations with no solutions, the lines are parallel, so they do not intersect. Because a solution is an x-value and a y-value that satisfies both linear equations, and the graphical representation of that solution is a point with that x- and y-value that lies on both lines, for a single solution to exist, the lines must intersect, with the point of intersection representing that solution. The only way two lines can never intersect is for the two lines to be parallel; **to be parallel, two lines must have the *same* slope and they must have *different* y-intercepts** (otherwise they'd be the same lines).

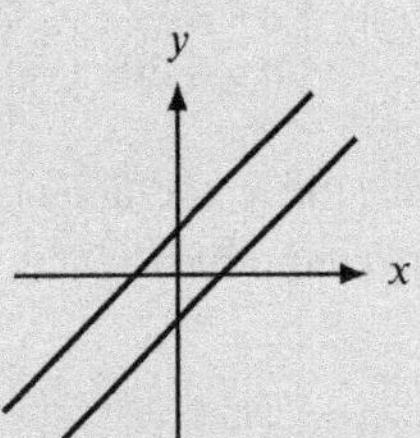

When the lines representing two linear equations are parallel, you will see when inspecting the equations in Slope-Intercept Form that the lines will have the same slope, but different y-intercepts. For example, the lines $y = x + 1$ and $y = x - 1$ are parallel and thus will never intersect because they have the same slope but different y-intercepts.

Systems of Linear Equations with Infinite Solutions

In a system of equations with infinitely many solutions, the lines must be exactly the same, and thus they produce the same line when graphed. Every solution to one of the equations is also a solution to the other equation; graphically, this is evident because the two lines are in fact the same (they're coincident), so every point on one line is common to the other line and is thus a solution to both. Because there are an infinite number of points on a line, this means that there are infinitely many solutions to the system of equations in this situation.

When two linear equations in Slope-Intercept Form are the same, you will see that **the lines will have the *same* slope and *same* y-intercept**. In the following picture, it may look like only one line is graphed, but in reality, the same line is graphed twice, and the two lines are actually drawn on top of each other.

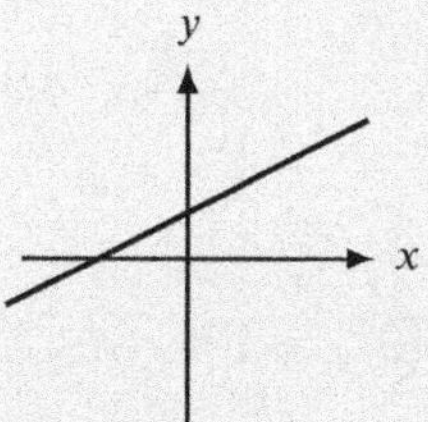

View related real-test problems at 1600.io/p/smtex?topic=4.3

Section 4.3 Practice Problems

1 1600.io 4.3

$$y = -\frac{1}{3}x + 1$$
$$y = ax - 4$$

In the system of equations above, a is a constant. If the system of equations has no solution, what is the value of a ?

A) -3

B) $-\frac{1}{3}$

C) 0

D) 3

2 1600.io 4.3

$$4k(x - 6) = x - 6$$

In the equation above, k is a constant. If the equation has infinitely many solutions, what is the value of k ?

3 1600.io 4.3

$$3ax - 12 = 2(x + 4) + 4(x - 3)$$

In the equation above, a is a constant. If no value of x satisfies the equation, what is the value of a ?

A) 0

B) 1

C) 2

D) 3

4 1600.io 4.3

$$5(x + b) = ax + 2c$$

In the equation above, a, b, and c are constants. If the equation has infinitely many solutions, which of the following must be equal to c ?

A) $5a$

B) $5b$

C) $\frac{5a}{2}$

D) $\frac{5b}{2}$

4.4 Solving Systems of Linear Equations by Elimination/Combination

The intersection of two graphs is one way to think about the solution to a system of linear equations. However, it is probably more useful to think about the solution to a system of equations as an ordered pair (x, y) of values that satisfies both equations because most systems of linear equations on the test are based on the Standard Form of lines and do not lend themselves to graphing and finding intersections (unlike lines in Slope-Intercept Form).

We will discuss the methods of solving systems of linear equations shortly, but for now let's briefly focus on writing our own system of linear equations in Standard Form (rather than in Slope-Intercept Form as in the previous example).

For many of the problems on the test, you need to write your own system of linear equations in Standard Form. Most of these are found in the form of word problems about how much money is made from selling a certain amount of two different items. The following example reflects something you are sure to see on every test. You will have to write one equation that represents the total number of items sold and one equation that represents the amount of money made from selling those things. It is easiest to write these equations in Standard Form based on how they are presented (not to mention that the answer choices will almost always be in Standard Form).

Example 4.4-1

1 4.4

A butcher sold 89 pounds of meat that consisted of b pounds of beef and p pounds of pork. The butcher sold the beef for \$2.39 per pound and the pork for \$1.39 per pound and collected a total of \$172.71. Which of the following systems of equations can be used to find the number of pounds of beef that were sold?

A) $b + p = 172.71$
$2.39b + 1.39p = 89$

B) $b + p = 89$
$2.39b + 1.39p = 172.71$

C) $b + p = 89$
$1.39b + 2.39p = 172.71$

D) $b + p = 172.71$
$1.39b + 2.39p = 89$

Solution

1. We need to write one equation that describes the total number of pounds of meat sold. We know that b is the number of pounds of beef, p is the number of pounds of pork, and 89 is the total number of pounds of meat sold. So one of the equations is the following:

$$b + p = 89$$

2. We also need to write an equation that describes the amount of money the butcher made. Since beef is sold for \$2.39 per pound and b pounds of beef are sold, the total amount of money made from beef is $2.39b$. Since pork is sold for \$1.39 per pound and p pounds of pork are sold, the total amount of money made from pork is $1.39p$. Add these two amounts and set them equal to 172.71, which is the total amount of money the butcher made from selling this meat.

$$2.39b + 1.39p = 172.71$$

3. The two equations that describe the number of pounds of meat sold and the amount of money made from selling the meat are the following:

$$b + p = 89$$
$$2.39b + 1.39p = 172.71$$

4. The answer is B.

In the previous example, we only had to write the system of linear equations, but notice that the question indicated that we were writing these equations in order to hypothetically solve for the number of pounds of beef that were sold.

How would we actually solve one of these systems of linear equations (find the values that satisfy both of the equations in the system)? In general, the process of solving systems of equations having two variables is performed by reducing the system of equations to a single equation with only one variable (and temporarily eliminating the other variable). Once we know the value of one of the variables, we can substitute the value back into either of the original equations (remember that the solution values will satisfy both of the original equations) and solve for the value of the remaining variable.

There are several ways to isolate the single variable and reduce the system to a single equation (namely, Elimination and Substitution), but the majority of the system of linear equations questions on the test (especially those in which the equations are written in Standard Form) can and should be solved using the **Elimination** method, which is based on the procedure of adding and subtracting entire linear equations; this technique can be leveraged to eliminate one of the variables. Before we outline the method, let's first understand why we can combine linear equations with addition or subtraction.

Combining Equations

Equations can be added together or subtracted from each other because both sides of an equation are equal. If we add the left sides of two equations and we add the right sides of two equations, the resulting equation will still be valid.

$$\begin{array}{rr} & a+b\ =4 \\ + & c+d\ =3 \\ \hline & (a+b)+(c+d)=7 \end{array}$$

Since $a+b$ is 4 and $c+d$ is 3, then we can substitute 4 for $a+b$ and 3 for $c+d$ and verify that the result is 7.

$$\begin{aligned} (a+b)+(c+d) &= 7 \\ 4 \quad + \quad 3 \quad &= 7 \\ 7 \quad &= 7 \end{aligned}$$

Note also that we can multiply both sides of any equation by a constant and the resulting equation is still the same equation as before, just with scaled coefficients and constant. Multiplying equations by constants is sometimes a necessary step in solving by elimination.

In order to solve linear equations by Elimination, we need to build off of the notion that we can combine linear equations by addition and subtraction. **Our goal is to add the equations in such a way that one of the variables will be eliminated**.

Solving Systems of Linear Equations by Elimination

Consider the following system of linear equations.

$$\begin{aligned} x+2y &= 5 \\ x-2y &= 3 \end{aligned}$$

Notice that the coefficients of y in the two equations are negatives of each other (the coefficient is 2 in the top equation and -2 in the bottom equation). If we add the two equations, then the y-terms will cancel each other out (their coefficients will sum to 0), eliminating the y-variables and leaving us with a single equation with only one variable remaining (the x-variable). We can use this new equation to solve for x.

$$\begin{array}{rr} & x+2y=5 \\ + & x-2y=3 \\ \hline & 2x+0y=8 \\ & \Downarrow \\ & 2x=8 \\ & x=4 \end{array}$$

Now that we have the value of x, we can plug it into either of the original two equations and solve for y. Let's use the first equation, $x + 2y = 5$.

$$\begin{aligned} x + 2y &= 5 \\ 4 + 2y &= 5 \\ 2y &= 1 \\ y &= \frac{1}{2} \end{aligned}$$

We sometimes need to multiply one or both equations in a system by a constant so that one of the variables will be canceled out when we add the the two equations to each other.

Consider the following system of linear equations.

$$\begin{aligned} 2x + 3y &= 6 \\ x - y &= 3 \end{aligned}$$

Let's solve for x by eliminating the y-variables. In order to eliminate the y-variable and solve for x, we need the y-coefficients to cancel each other. The easiest way to do that in this case is to multiply the bottom equation by 3 so that the top equation has the term $3y$ and the bottom equation has the term $-3y$. When we add the equations together, the y-terms will cancel.

$$\begin{aligned} 2x + 3y &= 6 \\ 3(x - y) &= 3(3) \end{aligned}$$

$$\Downarrow$$

$$\begin{aligned} 2x + 3y &= 6 \\ 3x - 3y &= 9 \end{aligned}$$

Now, we can add the two equations, and the y-variables will cancel, allowing us to solve for x.

$$\begin{array}{rr} & 2x + 3y = 6 \\ + & 3x - 3y = 9 \\ \hline & 5x + 0y = 15 \end{array}$$

$$\Downarrow$$

$$\begin{aligned} 5x &= 15 \\ x &= 3 \end{aligned}$$

We could have also eliminated the y terms by multiplying the top equation by $\frac{1}{3}$, but we chose the easier route of working with whole numbers instead of fractions. When it comes to systems of equations, working with whole-number coefficients is almost always the better option.

We could also have solved directly for y by multiplying both sides of the second equation by -2 in order for the x-coefficients to cancel when the equations are added, thus using the elimination strategy in order to solve for each variable separately instead of solving for one using elimination and then using substitution to find the other as above.

In the following example, we will find the solution of a system using Elimination, but we will have to multiply *both* of the equations by constants in order to eliminate a variable. As a generalized procedure that will allow you to eliminate a variable, multiply the first equation by the coefficient of that variable in the second equation, and multiply the second equation by the coefficient of that variable in the first equation; this will result in that variable having the same coefficient in both equations, allowing that variable to be eliminated (if one coefficient is a and the other is b, you'll end up with coefficients ab and ba, which have the same value because multiplication is commutative). If both of the coefficients have the same sign, multiply one of the equations by -1 as well before adding the two equations so the variable terms will cancel each other when summed.

Example 4.4-2

2 4.4

$$-5x + 2y = 10$$
$$4x + 5y = 25$$

If (x, y) is the solution to the system of equations above, what is the value of x?

Solution

1. Since we want to solve for x, we need to eliminate the y-terms. To do that while avoiding fractions as much as possible, we need to multiply both equations by constants that will cause the y-coefficients to be opposites that will cancel when we add the two equations. Multiply the **top** equation by 5 (which is the y-coefficient in the **bottom** equation) and multiply the **bottom** equation by 2 (which is the y-coefficient in the **top** equation) so that the y-coefficients will both be 10.

$$5(-5x + 2y) = 5(10)$$
$$2(4x + 5y) = 2(25)$$
$$\Downarrow$$
$$-25x + 10y = 50$$
$$8x + 10y = 50$$

2. We need to eliminate the y-variables, so multiply the top equation by -1 so the coefficients of the y-terms will cancel when they are added (we could have multiplied the bottom equation by -1, but we notice that if we use the top equation, the sign of the resulting x term will be positive, which is always preferred).

$$-1(-25x + 10y) = -1(50)$$
$$8x + 10y = 50$$
$$\Downarrow$$
$$25x - 10y = -50$$
$$8x + 10y = 50$$

3. Combine the equations and solve for x.

$$\begin{array}{r} 25x - 10y = -50 \\ +\quad 8x + 10y = 50 \\ \hline 33x + 0y = 0 \end{array}$$
$$\Downarrow$$
$$33x = 0$$
$$x = 0$$

4. The answer is 0.

Notes

Steps 1 and 2 could have been combined. If you notice that both of the coefficients of the variable you want to eliminate have the same sign (both positive or both negative), include a factor of -1 when multiplying one of the equations by the coefficient of the variable in the other equation. For example, in this problem, we could have multiplied the top equation by -5 instead of 5 if we kept in mind that we want the y-coefficients to be negatives of each other.

Alternatively, you could forego the multiplication by -1 and simply subtract the equations rather than adding them; just take care that you keep all the signs straight during the operation.

SkillDrill 4.4-1

Directions: Use elimination to find the intersection point that is the solution to the system of equations.

1. $2x + y = 6$
$x + y = 5$

2. $x - 3y = 4$
$x + 6y = 13$

3. $-2x - 3y = 13$
$4x + 9y = -35$

4. $4x + 5y = 2$
$2x - 3y = 1$

Example 4.4-3

3 1600.io 4.4

A group of 140 people are going to a wedding, where there are 30 tables. Some of the tables seat 4 people each, and the rest seat 6 people each. Assuming all the seats are filled and every person gets to sit in a seat, exactly how many of the tables were 4-person tables?

A) 10

B) 15

C) 20

D) 24

Solution

1. We need to write an equation that represents the total number of tables. Use the letter f to represent the number of 4-person tables and s to represent the number of 6-person tables. Since $f + s$ is the total number of tables, and there are 30 total tables, our first equation is $f + s = 30$.

2. We need to write an equation that represents the total number of seats. Since there are f tables that seat 4 people, the number of seats from those f tables is $4f$. Since there are s tables that seat 6 people, the number of seats from those s tables is $6s$. The total number of seats is $4f + 6s$, and there are 140 seats, so our second equation is $4f + 6s = 140$.

3. The system of equations is the following:

$$f + s = 30$$
$$4f + 6s = 140$$

4. Since we want to solve for f, we should multiply both sides of the top equation by -6 so the y-coefficients will cancel when we combine the equations.

$$-6(f+s) = -6(30)$$
$$4f + 6s = 140$$
$$\Downarrow$$
$$-6f - 6s = -180$$
$$4f + 6s = 140$$

5. Combine the equations and solve for f.

$$\begin{array}{rr} & -6f - 6s = -180 \\ + & 4f + 6s = 140 \\ \hline & -2f + 0s = -40 \end{array}$$
$$\Downarrow$$
$$-2f = -40$$
$$f = 20$$

6. The answer is C.

Notes

Take note of the fact that we did not have to find the value of s at any point in order to find the value of f. The true advantage of elimination over other methods of solving systems of equations is that there is no confusion about which variable you are actually solving for first. The answer is in the name "elimination": you eliminate the variable you don't want to solve for, leaving only the variable whose value you're seeking.

Occasionally, there is a test problem that asks you for the value of an expression rather than for the value of one variable. Most of the time, the expression has terms with both x- and y-variables. In almost all of these cases, it is much simpler to find the value of that expression directly rather than to first find the value of one variable, substitute, find the value of the other variable, then construct the desired expression and evaluate it. An example will illustrate this clearly. Usually, simply adding or subtracting the equations from each other will make the coefficients in the combined equation match up perfectly with the expression that you are asked to find.

For a deeper dive into the subject of problems for which there is a rapid, direct route to a solution that bypasses the more general approach, see the "Wormholes" chapter.

Example 4.4-4

4 4.4

$$2x + 3y = 100$$
$$4x + 3y = 360$$

In the system of equations above, what is the value of $6x + 6y$?

Solution 1

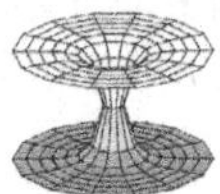

1. Notice that you are asked to solve for $6x + 6y$. You could solve this by finding the values of x and y independently and then plugging those values into the expression $6x + 6y$ and evaluating it, but notice that if we just combine the equations by adding them, the two x-terms will add up to $6x$, and the two y-terms will add up to $6y$.

$$\begin{array}{rr} & 2x + 3y = 100 \\ + & 4x + 3y = 360 \\ \hline & 6x + 6y = 460 \end{array}$$

2. The answer is 460.

Solution 2

1. We can choose to solve for either variable first if we decide to solve for them individually. Based on the starting conditions of the problem, it makes sense to eliminate y first because its coefficients already match. Multiply the top equation by -1, and then add the two equations in order to eliminate y and solve for x.

$$-1(2x + 3y) = -1(100)$$
$$4x + 3y = 360$$
$$\Downarrow$$
$$\begin{array}{rr} & -2x - 3y = -100 \\ + & 4x + 3y = 360 \\ \hline & 2x + 0y = 260 \end{array}$$
$$\Downarrow$$
$$2x = 260$$
$$x = 130$$

2. Now that we know the value of x, we can plug the value into either equation in order to solve for y. Let's use the top equation (because the coefficients are smaller).

$$2x + 3y = 100$$
$$2(130) + 3y = 100$$
$$260 + 3y = 100$$
$$3y = -160$$
$$y = \frac{-160}{3}$$

3. Now that we have the values of both x and y, we can substitute the values into the expression $6x+6y$ in order to find its value. Plug in 130 for x and $\frac{-160}{3}$ for y.

$$6x+6y = 6(130)+6\left(\frac{-160}{3}\right)$$
$$6x+6y = 780-320$$
$$6x+6y = 460$$

4. The answer is 460.

Notes

Solution 2 is not horribly long, but it involves messy fractions and large numbers that can be completely avoided if you know the test well and look for the shortcut provided by Solution 1.

Section 4.4 Suggested Problems from Real Tests

View related real-test problems at 1600.io/p/smtex?topic=4.4

Section 4.4 Practice Problems

1 1600.io 4.4

The Hartford ferry charges \$9 for an adult and \$1 for a child to ride one way. During a certain 8-hour shift, a ticket booth attendant collects \$1,051 from 155 passengers. Which of the following systems of equations could be used to determine the number of adult riders, A, and the number of child riders, C, during this 8-hour shift?

A) $9A + C = 8(1{,}051)$
$A + C = 8(155)$

B) $8(9A) + 8(C) = 1{,}051$
$8(A + C) = 155$

C) $9A + C = 155$
$A + C = 1{,}051$

D) $9A + C = 1{,}051$
$A + C = 155$

2 1600.io 4.4

$$5m + 3p = 24$$
$$m + p = 8$$

If (m_1, p_1) is the solution to the system of equations above, what is the value of p_1 ?

3 1600.io 4.4

The sum of two different numbers x and y is 80, and the difference when the smaller number is subtracted from the larger number is 40. What is the value of xy ?

A) 120

B) 320

C) 1,200

D) 3,200

4 1600.io 4.4

$$5x + 6y = 6$$
$$3x + 8y = 9$$

If (x, y) is the solution to the system of equations above, what is the value of $2x - 2y$?

A) -15

B) -3

C) 3

D) 15

5 1600.io 4.4

$$x + y = 13$$
$$x - 3y = -3$$

According to the system of equations above, what is the value of x ?

A) 2

B) 4

C) 9

D) 11

4.5 Number of Solutions to a System of Linear Equations Part II

We already know that the number of solutions to a system of linear equations can be thought of in terms of the slopes and y-intercepts of the lines in the system and the number of intersections of those lines: nonparallel lines will intersect once (one solution), parallel lines (lines with the same slope but different y-intercepts) will never intersect (0 solutions), and coincident lines (two equal lines with the same slope and y-intercept) share every point in common (infinitely many solutions). However, it is not so readily apparent (based on slope and y-intercept) how many solutions there will be to a system of linear equations in Standard Form because the slope and y-intercept do not exist as individual coefficients or constants in the equations.

Remember that lines in Standard Form can be easily rewritten in Slope-Intercept Form (though this is not a necessary step in the problems we are going to discuss), and that the slope and y-intercept are directly related to the constants and coefficients of the line in Standard Form.

For example, let's look at the symbolic Standard Form line $A_1x + B_1y = C_1$ and convert it into Slope-Intercept Form.

$$A_1x + B_1y = C_1$$

$$B_1y = -A_1x + C_1$$

$$y = \frac{-A_1}{B_1}x + \frac{C_1}{B_1}$$

The slope of a Standard Form line $A_1x + B_1y = C_1$ is equal to $\frac{-A_1}{B_1}$, and the y-intercept is equal to $\frac{C_1}{B_1}$.

Let's form a system of linear equations by also considering another line in Standard Form, $A_2x + B_2y = C_2$, whose slope is equal to $\frac{-A_2}{B_2}$ and whose y-intercept is equal to $\frac{C_2}{B_2}$ (based on the same conversion that was done for the line $A_1x + B_1y = C_1$).

We can use what we know about the number of solutions based on slope and y-intercept to draw some conclusions about how we can handle questions about the number of solutions to a system of linear equations in Standard Form.

We know that any two lines with **different slopes** (lines that are not parallel) will have **one solution**. In order for the system of equations consisting of the two lines mentioned above ($A_1x + B_1y = C_1$ and $A_2x + B_2y = C_2$) to have one solution, the ratios $\frac{-A_1}{B_1}$ and $\frac{-A_2}{B_2}$, which represent the slopes of their respective lines, must NOT be equal (we can actually omit the negative signs because they will cancel out anyway when the two ratios are set equal).

$$\frac{-A_1}{B_1} \neq \frac{-A_2}{B_2}$$

$$\frac{A_1}{B_1} \neq \frac{A_2}{B_2}$$

As long as the ratio of the x-coefficient to the y-coefficient is different for both equations, the system will have one solution (remember that if these ratios are not the same, it indicates that the slopes are not the same, despite the missing negative signs). For example, given the lines $4x + 2y = 5$ and $-3x + y = -5$, we can tell that the system will have one solution because the ratio of x- to y-coefficients is not the same for both equations: $\frac{4}{2} \neq \frac{-3}{1}$.

In order for the system to have **no solutions**, the lines would have to have the **same slope and different *y*-intercepts**, so we would know that **the ratio of *x*- to *y*-coefficients would have to be the same for both equations** (note again that the negative signs can be omitted): $\frac{A_1}{B_1} = \frac{A_2}{B_2}$ We also know that the *y*-intercepts of the lines must not be equal, and because the *y*-intercepts are equal to the ratio of the constant terms to the *y*-coefficients, these ratios must be different for both equations $\left(\frac{C_1}{B_1} \neq \frac{C_2}{B_2}\right)$.

For example, given the lines $4x + 2y = 5$ and $10x + 5y = 3$, we can tell that the system will have no solutions because not only is the ratio of the *x*- to *y*-coefficients the same for both equations $\left(\frac{4}{2} = \frac{10}{5} \text{ which reduces to } 2 = 2\right)$, which means that the slopes of these two line are the same, but the ratio of constant terms to *y*-coefficients is also not the same $\left(\frac{5}{2} \neq \frac{3}{5}\right)$, which means that the *y*-intercepts of these two lines are different. This means the lines are parallel and therefore have no intersection point, and thus there is no solution to the system.

Finally, in order for the system to have **infinitely many solutions**, the lines have to be **exactly the same, with the same slope and *y*-intercept**. Even if the coefficients in the equations are different, the coefficients and constant in one equation may have the same *ratio* among them as do the coefficients and constant in the other equation.

If the ratios of the *x*- and *y*-coefficients are equal $\left(\frac{A_1}{B_1} = \frac{A_2}{B_2}\right)$, which means that the slopes of these two lines are the same for both equations, and the ratios of the constant terms and *y*-coefficients are equal $\left(\frac{C_1}{B_1} = \frac{C_2}{B_2}\right)$, which means that the *y*-intercepts of these two lines are equal for both equations, then the lines are the same, and the system will have infinitely many solutions.

For example, given the lines $4x + 2y = 5$ and $10x + 5y = \frac{25}{2}$, we can see that the system will have infinitely many solutions because not only is the ratio of the *x*- to *y*-coefficients is the same for both equations $\left(\frac{4}{2} = \frac{10}{5}\right)$, but the ratio of the constant terms to the *y*-coefficients is also the same for both equations.

$$\frac{5}{2} = \frac{\frac{25}{2}}{5}$$

$$\frac{5}{2} = \frac{25}{10}$$

$$\frac{5}{2} = \frac{5}{2}$$

Systems of Linear Equations with One Solution

There will be **one solution** to a system of equations in Standard Form when the **ratio of *x*- to *y*-coefficients is different**.

For example, the lines $2x + 3y = 4$ and $-4x + 6y = 4$ will have one solution because the ratio of *x*- to *y*-coefficients for the first equation is $\frac{2}{3}$, but the ratio of *x*- to *y*-coefficients for the second equation is $\frac{-4}{6}$, which reduces to $\frac{-2}{3}$, which is not equal to $\frac{2}{3}$.

The *y*-intercept doesn't matter in this situation.

Systems of Linear Equations with No Solution

There will be **no solution** to a system of linear equations in Standard Form when the **ratio of x- to y-coefficients is the same for both equations, but the ratio of constant terms to y-coefficients is different for both equations**.

For example, the lines $2x + 3y = 4$ and $2x + 3y = 6$ will be parallel because the left sides of the equations are the same (so the ratio of the x- to y-coefficients is the same) but the right sides are different. If you want, you can convert the lines into Slope-Intercept Form to verify that they are parallel (they will have the same slope and different y-intercepts).

$$2x + 3y = 4 \quad \Rightarrow \quad y = \frac{-2}{3}x + \frac{4}{3}$$

$$2x + 3y = 6 \quad \Rightarrow \quad y = \frac{-2}{3}x + 2$$

Similarly, the lines $2x+3y = 4$ and $4x+6y = 10$ are also parallel lines (with the same slope), but how is this possible? Though the coefficients might be different in the two equations, the *ratio* of the coefficients is the same.

For the lines $2x + 3y = 4$ and $4x + 6y = 10$, the ratio of x-coefficient to y-coefficient for the first equation is 2 to 3 or $\frac{2}{3}$. The ratio of the x-coefficient to y-coefficient for the second equation is 4 to 6 or $\frac{4}{6}$, which reduces to $\frac{2}{3}$. Since these ratios match, these lines have the same slope.

Notice also that the ratio of constant to y-coefficient is 4 to 3 for the first equation but 10 to 6, which reduces to 5 to 3, for the second equation. These ratios aren't equal, so the y-intercepts are different.

Systems of Linear Equations with Infinite Solutions

There will be **infinite solutions** to a system of linear equations in Standard Form when **the ratio among the two variables' coefficients and the constant are the same in both equations**. In the simplest case, these values will simply be equal in both equations, but things will rarely be that simple, and you will usually have to test the ratios among the corresponding components of the equations to see if they are all identical.

For example, the lines $2x + 3y = 4$ and $2x + 3y = 4$ are very obviously the same line. However, the lines $2x + 3y = 4$ and $4x + 6y = 8$ are also the same line. In this example, it's easy to realize this; all the terms in the second equation are just double those in the first, so you can multiply both sides of the first equation by 2 to get the line $4x + 6y = 8$, which is exactly the same as the second equation.

In the general case, when you can't tell whether one equation is a scaled version of the other because the numbers are larger and/or are in non-integral ratios, you can scale one or both equations so as to match one of the terms, and then you can see if the other two terms also end up matching, which would indicate that the equations have the same solution set and thus that there are infinite solutions to the system.

You *could* choose any pair of corresponding coefficients, or the constants, and form a fraction that represents the scaling factor of one of the equations relative to the other, and then multiply the other two values by this scaling factor to see if the results match the corresponding elements in the other equation, which would indicate that the equations are the same. However, in some situations you will have to deal with fractions if you use this method, and fractions can make things messy. Alternatively, you can use one of the techniques used when performing elimination: you can pick any pair of corresponding coefficients, or the constants, and perform the complementary multiplication operations so the selected terms end up with exactly the same coefficients (be sure to preserve the signs of the coefficients when performing this procedure). Then, you can inspect the other terms to see if they, too, are now identical in both equations as a result of this equalizing procedure; if they are, the equations are the same and there are infinite solutions.

We need to determine if the ratio among these three components is the same in both equations; in the first equation in the example above, it's $2:3:4$, and in the second, it's $4:6:8$. Though the answer might be obvious here due to the simple numbers, let's work through it more rigorously to show the procedure so you're ready if you're faced with a less-pleasant situation.

Let's select the x-coefficients as our reference. We're going to perform what we call complementary intermultiplication, which is an appropriate term because we said so. We'll multiply the first equation by the x-coefficient of the second equation (which is 4), and we'll multiply the second equation by the x-coefficient of the first equation (which is 2). This will, of course, result in matching coefficients for the x terms in both equations (because $ab = ba$), but we need to determine if the *other* two terms end up matching as well.

$$4(2x + 3y = 4)$$
$$2(4x + 6y = 8)$$
$$\Downarrow$$
$$8x + 12y = 16$$
$$8x + 12y = 16$$

All the terms match, which means the equations represent the exact same relationship (the lines represented by the equations are coincident), and therefore there are infinite solutions to the system.

You can also realize that **the ratios of the x- to y-coefficients and the ratios of the constant terms to the y-coefficients is the same for the two equations**.

The ratio of the x- to y-coefficients for the first equation is $\frac{2}{3}$. The ratio of the x- to y-coefficients for the second equation is $\frac{4}{6}$, which reduces to $\frac{2}{3}$, so this ratio matches in the two equations, indicating that the slopes are the same. Similarly, the ratio of the constant terms to y-coefficient is $\frac{4}{2}$, which reduces to 2, and in the second equation, this ratio is equal to $\frac{8}{4}$, which also reduces to 2; this means the y-intercepts are the same as well. Since both of these ratios are the same for both equations, the lines are the same (they have the same slope and y-intercept) and will therefore have infinitely many solutions.

Finally, yet another option to check for infinitely many solutions is to convert both equations to Slope-Intercept Form and see if the slope and y-intercept are the same.

If you are told that a system has no solutions, but you need to determine the value of one of the coefficients, you can use the fact that the ratio of x- to y-coefficients must be equal to set up a simple proportion that will allow you to solve for the unknown quantity. For example, if you are given the following system with no solutions,

$$12x - 4y = 2$$
$$ax + 2y = 7$$

you can set up the following proportion which leverages the known ratio between the y-coefficients (we like to place the unknown in the numerator of the fraction on the left to facilitate solving):

$$\frac{a}{12} = \frac{2}{-4}$$

Solving for a,

$$a = 12\left(\frac{2}{-4}\right)$$
$$a = 2(-3)$$
$$a = -6$$

The use of a proportion keeps things organized, and more generally, writing down your work instead of relying on mental math is the better habit to maintain.

If you are told that a system has infinite solutions, not only will the x- and y-coefficients be in the same ratio, but the constants will be, too, so you can use the same procedure described above to determine the value of an unknown constant. If we have a system with infinite solutions such as this,

$$4x + 6y = 12$$
$$ax - 3y = b$$

you can set up a proportion to find either a or b by making use of the known ratio of the y-coefficients. We showed the procedure for finding a, the x-coefficient, above; here's what the proportion involving b would look like:

$$\frac{b}{12} = \frac{-3}{6}$$

Solving for b,

$$b = 12\left(\frac{-3}{6}\right)$$
$$b = -3(2)$$
$$b = -6$$

Generally, you will use a known ratio (whether of a pair of coefficients or of the constants) to set up a proportion to solve for an unknown value (coefficient or constant).

SkillDrill 4.5-1

Directions: All of the following systems of linear equations have no solution. Find the value of a.

1. $8x - 2y = 1$, $ax + y = 3$

2. $5x - 15y = 45$, $ax - 3y = 8$

3. $2x + 3y = 6$, $ax - y = 1$

4. $5x + 2y = 10$, $x + ay = 4$

Directions: All of the following systems of linear equations have infinite solutions. Find the values of a and b.

5. $3x - 9y = 12$, $ax + by = 4$

6. $2x + 3y = 6$, $ax - 3y = b$

7. $x + 5y = 8$, $ax - by = 1$

8. $-6x + 5y = 6$, $4ax + 2y = b$

Example 4.5-1

1 1600.io 4.5

$$-5x + y = 12$$
$$ax + 3y = 32$$

In the system of equations above, a is a constant. For which of the following values of a does the system have no solution?

A) −15

B) −10

C) −5

D) 0

Solution 1

1. In order for a system of linear equations to have no solution, the two lines must be parallel but have different y-intercepts. When the lines are in Standard Form, we can tell that they are parallel when the ratio of x- to y-coefficients is the same for both equations.

2. The ratio of x- to y-coefficients for the first equation is −5 to 1, or $\frac{-5}{1}$. The ratio of x- to y-coefficients for the second equation is a to 3, or $\frac{a}{3}$. Create a proportion by setting the two fractions equal to each other and solve for a. Remember to cross-multiply.

$$\frac{-5}{1} = \frac{a}{3}$$
$$-5(3) = a$$
$$-15 = a$$

3. The answer is A.

Solution 2

1. In order for a system of linear equations to have no solution, the two lines must be parallel but have different y-intercepts. When the lines are in Standard Form, we can take the approach of making x- and y-coefficients match in both equations. We just have to verify the constants on the right side of the equations are different from each other (technically, we know this will be true because the problem is set up so that there will be no solutions, and thus the constant terms will definitely not match).

2. We do not know how to make the x-coefficients match, since we do not know the value of a, but we can make the y-coefficients match by multiplying both sides of the first equation by 3. This is the first step in trying to get the left sides of the equations to look identical.

$$3(-5x + y) = 3(12)$$
$$ax + 3y = 32$$
$$\Downarrow$$
$$-15x + 3y = 36$$
$$ax + 3y = 32$$

3. The y-coefficients match, and the constants on the right side of the equation are different (again, this should be true given that the problem is set up to ensure there will be no solutions to the system of equations for a certain value of a), so there will be no solution when the x-coefficients are the same (making the lines parallel), which means that the value of a is -15.

4. The answer is A.

Solution 3

1. In order for a system of linear equations to have no solution, the two lines must be parallel but have different y-intercepts. We can convert both lines into Slope-Intercept Form and then check what value of of a would make the slopes equal.

2. Convert the first equation into Slope-Intercept Form.

$$-5x + y = 12$$
$$y = 5x + 12$$

3. Convert the second equation into Slope-Intercept Form.

$$ax + 3y = 32$$
$$3y = -ax + 32$$
$$y = \frac{-a}{3}x + \frac{32}{3}$$

4. The y-intercepts do not match, which is expected since the problem is about two lines that never intersect. In order for the lines to be parallel, the slopes must be the same. Set the two slopes equal to each other to find what value of a would make the slopes equal. The slope of the first line is 5. The slope of the second line is $\frac{-a}{3}$.

$$5 = \frac{-a}{3}$$
$$15 = -a$$
$$-15 = a$$

5. The answer is A.

Example 4.5-2

2 4.5

$$ax + by = 4$$
$$3x + 6y = 60$$

In the system of equations above, a and b are constants.

If the system has infinitely many solutions, what is the value of $\frac{a}{b}$?

Solution 1

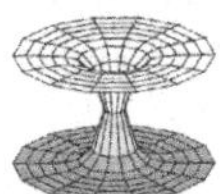

1. In order for a system of linear equations to have infinitely many solutions, the two lines must be exactly the same. The shortest way to handle this one is to remember that if the lines are in Standard Form, then the ratio of x and y-coefficients will be the same in both equations, so $\frac{a}{b} = \frac{3}{6}$, or (reducing the fraction) $\frac{a}{b} = \frac{1}{2}$.
2. The answer is $\frac{1}{2}$.

Solution 2

1. Since the problem states that there are infinitely many solutions, the two equations must be equal. If you are confused by the fact that the constants 4 and 60 don't match, then you can multiply both sides of the first equation by 15 (because $\frac{60}{4} = 15$) so that the 4 will match the 60 on the right side of the equation.

$$15(ax + by) = 15(4)$$
$$3x + 6y = 60$$
$$\Downarrow$$
$$15ax + 15by = 60$$
$$3x + 6y = 60$$

2. Now that the constants match, the next step is setting the ratios of x and y-coefficients for both equations equal to each other because the equations must be the same. Set $\frac{15a}{15b}$ equal to $\frac{3}{6}$, and reduce the fractions to solve for $\frac{a}{b}$.

$$\frac{\cancel{15}a}{\cancel{15}b} = \frac{3}{6}$$
$$\frac{a}{b} = \frac{1}{2}$$

3. The answer is $\frac{1}{2}$.

Notes

In Solution 1, we ignored the fact that the constant terms didn't match in the original forms of the equation. If the problem states that there are infinitely many solutions, you don't have to worry about making the constant terms match first before you start comparing the ratios of the coefficients.

The problem can also be done by converting both equations into Slope-Intercept Form and setting the two slopes equal to each other, then solving for $\frac{a}{b}$.

View related real-test problems at 1600.io/p/smtex?topic=4.5

Section 4.5 Practice Problems

1 4.5

In the system of equations below, a and c are constants.

$$\frac{1}{3}x + \frac{1}{5}y = \frac{1}{15}$$
$$ax + y = c$$

If the system of equations has an infinite number of solutions (x, y), what is the value of a ?

A) $-\frac{5}{3}$

B) $-\frac{1}{3}$

C) $\frac{1}{3}$

D) $\frac{5}{3}$

2 4.5

In the xy-plane, the equations $x + 5y = 8$ and $4x + 20y = c$ represent the same line for some constant c. What is the value of c ?

3 4.5

$$kx - 2y = 3$$
$$7x + 4y = 4$$

In the system of equations above, k is a constant and x and y are variables. For what value of k will the system of equations have no solution?

A) $-\frac{21}{4}$

B) $-\frac{7}{2}$

C) $\frac{7}{2}$

D) $\frac{21}{4}$

4 4.5

$$3x + 2y = 10$$
$$6x + cy = 21$$

In the system of equations above, c is a constant. For what value of c will there be no solution (x, y) to the system of equations?

A) 2

B) 3

C) 4

D) 6

CHAPTER 4 RECAP

- Solutions to systems of linear equations can be thought of as points where the graphs of the lines intersect. At these intersection points, both lines have the same x- and y- values.
- A system of linear equations has **one solution when the two lines are *not* parallel and cross at one point**.
- A system of linear equations has **no solutions when the lines are parallel**, because the lines do not intersect. If the equations of the lines are in Slope-Intercept Form, the equations of parallel lines will display the ***same* slope and *different* y-intercepts**.
- A system of linear equations has **infinite solutions when the two lines are exactly the same**. The **slopes and y-intercepts must be the same**.
- Set expressions for y equal to each other (substitution) to find the solution point when both equations are already in Slope-Intercept Form.
- Use substitution when the equations are in different forms, particularly when one variable is already solved for in terms of the other. Substitution is RARELY preferable to elimination for problems on the test.
- Use elimination to solve most systems of linear equations, particularly when both equations are in Standard Form. Multiply one or both equations by numbers that will cause the coefficients of the variable you want to eliminate to cancel out when the equations are combined through addition or subtraction.
- Use combination without eliminating either variable if possible when the problem asks for an expression involving terms with both variables.
- A system of linear equations in Standard Form has **one solution when the ratio of x- to y-coefficients is NOT the same for both equations** (this correlates to the fact that the slopes are not the same).
- A system of linear equations in Standard Form has **no solutions when the ratio of x- to y-coefficients is the same for both equations** (which correlates to the slopes being the same) **but the ratio of constant terms to y-coefficients is NOT the same for both equations** (which correlates to the y-intercepts being different).
- A system of linear equations in Standard Form has **infinitely many solutions when the ratio of x- to y-coefficients is the same for both equations** (which correlates to the slopes being the same) **and when the ratio of constant terms to y-coefficients is the same for both equations** (which correlates to the y-intercepts being the same).
- When asked to find unknown coefficient values in systems of linear equations in Standard Form that have no solutions or infinitely many solutions, use proportions of the ratios of the coefficients and constants to solve for unknown values.

  Alternatively, multiply one or both equations by scale factors so that any known coefficients or constants in the same position can be matched between the two equations.
- When you are asked about the number of solutions to a system of linear equations in Standard Form, you can always convert Standard Form linear equations into Slope-Intercept Form to make it easier to match the slope and y-intercept.

Additional Problems

 1 4.1

Which of the following is a graph of a system of equations with no solution?

A)

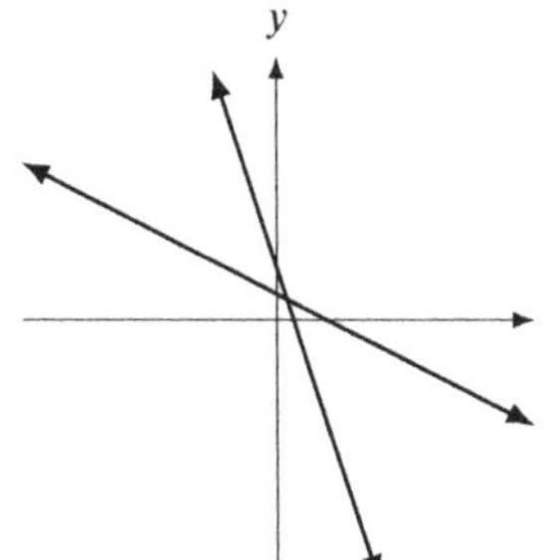

B)

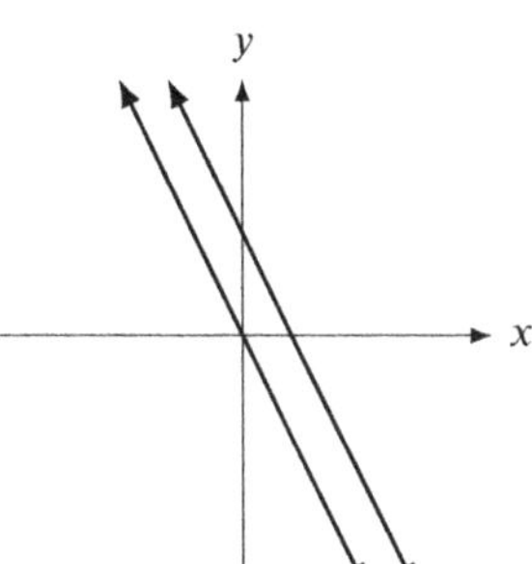

C)

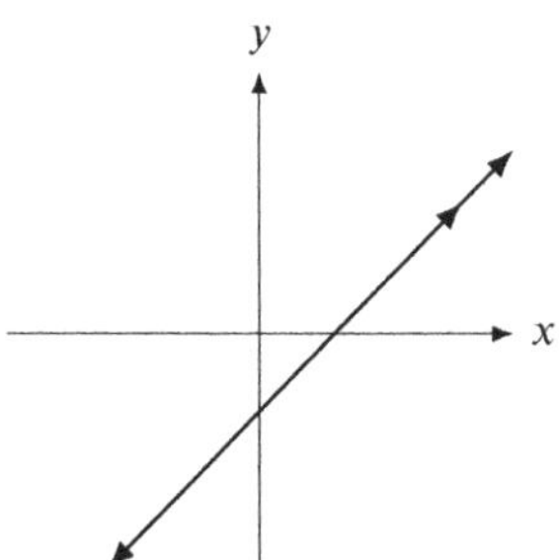

D)

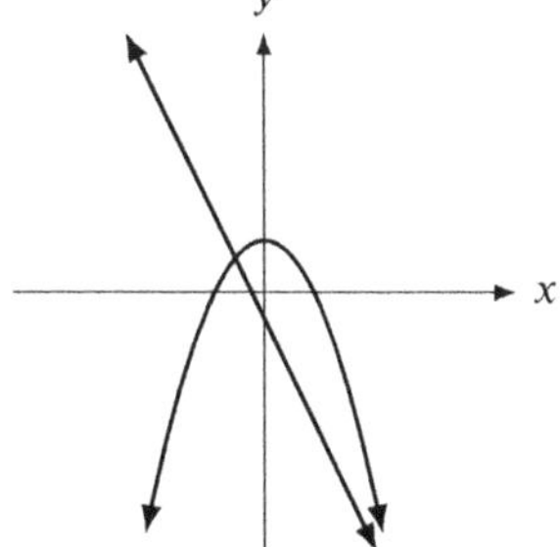

2 4.4

An aquarium sells two types of tickets. The standard ticket, for admission only, costs \$20. The premium ticket, which includes admission and a swim with angelfish, costs \$40. One Tuesday, the aquarium sold a total of 400 tickets and collected a total of \$9,000 from ticket sales. Which of the following systems of equations can be used to find the number of standard tickets, s, and premium tickets, p, sold on that Tuesday?

A) $s + p = 400$
$20s + 40p = 9{,}000$

B) $s + p = 400$
$40s + 20p = 9{,}000$

C) $20s + 40p = 400$
$s + p = 9{,}000$

D) $40s + 20p = 400$
$s + p = 9{,}000$

3 4.3

$$ax = 3$$

In the equation above, a is a constant. For which of the following values of a will the equation have no solution?

A) 0

B) 1

C) 3

D) 6

4 1600.io 4.4

$$\frac{1}{3}y = 6$$
$$x - \frac{1}{3}y = 2$$

The system of equations above has solution (x, y). What is the value of x ?

A) 4

B) $\frac{17}{3}$

C) 8

D) 20

5 1600.io 4.4

Marcus sells only hats and scarves on his website. Hats sell for \$15 each, and scarves sell for \$10 each. If Marcus sold 30 pieces of clothing and his sales totaled \$400, how many scarves did Marcus sell?

6 1600.io 4.3

$$12x - 4x(c - 2) = 3x$$

In the equation above, c is a constant. If the equation has infinitely many solutions, what is the value of c ?

A) $\frac{11}{4}$

B) $\frac{13}{4}$

C) $\frac{15}{4}$

D) $\frac{17}{4}$

7 1600.io 4.4

$$x = y - 5$$
$$\frac{x}{2} + 4y = 2$$

Which ordered pair (x, y) satisfies the system of equations shown above?

A) $(-5, 0)$

B) $(-4, 1)$

C) $(4, 0)$

D) $(5, 10)$

8 4.2

$$\frac{x}{y} = 4$$
$$3(y + 2) = x$$

If (x, y) is the solution of the system of equations above, what is the value of y?

A) 2

B) 6

C) 12

D) 24

9 4.4

$$2x + 5y = 800$$
$$5x + 2y = 1500$$

Based on the system of equations above, what is the value of $7x + 7y$?

10 4.2

$$4(x + y) = 56$$
$$\frac{x}{2} = 5$$

If (x, y) is a solution to the system of equations above, what is the value of y?

A) 16

B) 4

C) −4

D) −16

11 4.4

If $3w + 5t = 21$ and $5w - t = 7$, what is the value of $4w + 2t$?

A) 14

B) 18

C) 24

D) 28

12 1600.io 4.4

At a food truck, each empanada has 40 more calories than each taco. If 1 empanada and 8 tacos have a total of 1,570 calories, how many calories does an empanada have?

13 1600.io 4.4

$$x - 4y = 24$$
$$0.25x + y = 4$$

The solution to the system of equations above is (x, y). What is the value of x?

A) -4

B) 4

C) 20

D) 40

14 1600.io 4.4

$$-x + y = -4.75$$
$$x + 5y = 11.75$$

If (x, y) satisfies the system of equations above, what is the value of y?

15 1600.io 4.4

In the xy-plane, the point (p, r) lies on the line with equation $y = 2x + b$, where b is a constant. The point with coordinates $(4p, 3r)$ lies on the line with the equation $y = 3x + b$. If $p \neq 0$, what is the value of $\frac{r}{p}$?

A) 5

B) 2

C) $\frac{1}{2}$

D) $\frac{1}{5}$

16 4.3

The equation $7x - 4 = a(x - b)$, where a and b are constants, has no solutions. Which of the following must be true?

I. $a = 7$

II. $b = 4$

III. $b \neq \frac{4}{7}$

A) None

B) I only

C) I and II only

D) I and III only

17 4.2

In a wedding hall, during a reception, guests are seated at tables. If 6 guests are assigned to each table, 3 additional tables will be needed to seat all of the guests. If 12 guests are assigned to each table, 3 tables will not be used. How many guests will be attending the wedding reception?

18 4.5

$$\frac{2}{3}x - \frac{4}{5}y = 10$$
$$ax - by = 15$$

The system of equations above has no solutions. If a and b are constants, what is the value of $\frac{a}{b}$?

19 4.2

$$\frac{1}{4}y = \frac{21}{20} - \frac{1}{5}x$$
$$8y = 9x$$

In the xy-plane, the lines that correspond to the system of equations above intersect at the point (a, b). What is the value of $\frac{a}{b}$?

20 1600.io 4.4

The score on a history test is obtained by subtracting the number of incorrect answers from 4 times the number of correct answers. If a student answered all 25 questions and obtained a score of 65, how many questions did the student answer correctly?

21 1600.io 4.2

In one month, Dan and John spent a combined 500 hours writing a math book. If Dan spent 50 more hours writing the book than John did, how many hours did John spend writing the book?

22 1600.io 4.4

$$2x + y = a$$
$$-x + 2y = 4$$

In the system of equations above, a is a constant. What is the y-value of the solution to the system in terms of a?

A) $\frac{a+8}{5}$

B) $\frac{2a-4}{5}$

C) $\frac{4a+4}{5}$

D) $\frac{-3a-1}{5}$

23 1600.io 4.2

Ms. Morrissey has a bag containing n pieces of chocolate to distribute to the students in her second grade class. If she gives each student 2 pieces of chocolate, she will have 6 pieces of chocolate left over. In order to give each student 3 pieces of chocolate, she will need an additional 16 pieces of chocolate. How many students are in the class?

A) 10

B) 16

C) 19

D) 22

Answer Key

Section 4.1 Practice Problems

1. B
2. B

SkillDrill 4.2-1

1. $(1, 10)$
2. $(-5, 15)$
3. $\left(\frac{7}{2}, \frac{-7}{2}\right)$ or $(3.5, -3.5)$
4. $\left(\frac{-1}{12}, \frac{21}{4}\right)$ or $(-0.08\overline{33}, 5.25)$

Section 4.2 Practice Problems

1. 11
2. C
3. 1
4. C
5. D

SkillDrill 4.3-1

1. 4
2. $\frac{1}{2}$ or 0.5
3. $\frac{5}{3}$ or $1.\overline{66}$
4. 0

SkillDrill 4.3-2

1. $a = 4, b = 7$
2. $a = 6, b = 12$
3. $a = -6, b = -2$
4. $a = \frac{5}{3}, b = 9$

Section 4.3 Practice Problems

1. B
2. $\frac{1}{4}$ or .25
3. C
4. D

SkillDrill 4.4-1

1. $(1, 4)$
2. $(7, 1)$
3. $(-2, -3)$
4. $\left(\frac{1}{2}, 0\right)$ or $(0.5, 0)$

Section 4.4 Practice Problems

1. D
2. 8
3. C
4. B
5. C

SkillDrill 4.5-1

1. -4
2. 1
3. $\frac{-2}{3}$ or $-0.\overline{66}$
4. $\frac{2}{5}$ or 0.4
5. $a = 1, b = -3$
6. $a = -2, b = -6$
7. $a = \frac{1}{8}, b = \frac{-5}{8}$
   or
   $a = 0.125, b = -0.625$
8. $a = \frac{-3}{5}, b = \frac{12}{5}$
   or
   $a = -0.6, b = 2.4$

Section 4.5 Practice Problems

1. D
2. 32
3. B
4. C

Additional Problems

1. B
2. A
3. A
4. C
5. 10
6. D
7. B
8. B
9. 2300
10. B
11. A
12. 210
13. C
14. $\frac{7}{6}$, 1.16, or 1.17
15. A
16. D
17. 72
18. $\frac{5}{6}$ or .833
19. $\frac{8}{9}$, .888, or .889
20. 18
21. 225
22. A
23. D

Linear Inequalities and Absolute Value

5

5.1 Writing and Solving Linear Inequalities

Developing children are known to test their boundaries as a way of learning their limits. How many cookies can you sneak out of the kitchen before your stomach aches? How loud can you be before your dad loses his mind? Though the breaking point is important, the goal of this testing is to figure out what the safe zone is—as long as you eat fewer cookies than your limit, your mission can be considered a success.

When we work with linear expressions, sometimes we need to figure out boundaries, maximums, and minimums instead of just finding one particular value: we are interested in **inequalities** rather than equations. Writing and solving linear inequalities is extremely similar to writing and solving linear equations (in either Slope-Intercept Form or Standard Form). There are just a few key differences, the first being that we use inequality signs rather than equals signs.

Inequality Signs

Linear inequalities are written using one of four signs.

- **Less Than**
  The less-than sign is the following:

  $$<$$

  It signifies that the left side of the inequality is less than the right side. For example, $x < 8$ means that x is less than 8 (note that x cannot be equal to 8).

- **Less Than or Equal To**
  The less-than-or-equal-to sign is the following:

  $$\leq$$

  It signifies that the left side of the inequality is less than or equal to the right side. Another way the relationship might be phrased is that the value of the left side must be "at most" a certain number (or "no greater than" a certain number). The left side can match the right side, but cannot exceed its value. For example, $x \leq 8$ means that x is less than or equal to 8 (the maximum value of x is 8, but x can be any number that is no more than 8, including 8 itself).

- **Greater Than**
  The greater-than sign is the following:

  $$>$$

  It signifies that the left side of the inequality is greater than the right side. For example, $x > 8$ means that x is greater than 8 (note that x cannot be equal to 8).

- **Greater Than or Equal To**
  The greater-than-or-equal-to sign is the following:

  $$\geq$$

  It signifies that the left side of the inequality is greater than or equal to the right side. Another way the relationship might be phrased is that the value of the left side must be "at least" a certain number (or "no less than" a certain number). The left side can match the right side, but cannot be less than the right side. For example, $x \geq 8$ means that x is greater than or equal to 8 (the minimum value of x is 8, but x can be any number that is no less than 8, including 8 itself).

People often get confused which sign to use, but you only need to know two things. First, the small side of the inequality sign (the pointy end) is pointing to the smaller value side of the inequality, and the big side of the inequality (the open end) is on the same side as the greater value side of the inequality. Second, if the sign has a line underneath it, it means the two sides can also be equal.

SkillDrill 5.1-1

Directions: Write an inequality to represent the information given.

1. Bella gets paid \$2 for every backflip she does and \$3 for every front flip she does. In one day, she makes less than \$56 doing backflips and front flips. (Use b for the number of backflips and f for the number of front flips.)

2. In an eating contest, Ferdinand takes 1 minute to eat each hot dog and 3 minutes to eat each cake. It took Ferdinand at least 60 minutes to eat h hot dogs and c cakes.

3. A number x is at least three more than twice a number y.

4. Five less than three times a number n is no more than 35.

5. It takes Paula 8 minutes to drink a small water bottle and 20 minutes to drink a big water bottle. This week, she wants to spend fewer than 112 minutes drinking s small water bottles and b big water bottles.

Example 5.1-1

1 5.1

A cookware store is having a sale on knives and pans. During the sale, the cost of each knife is \$20, and the cost of each pan is \$30. Gordon can spend at most \$240 at the store. If Gordon buys k knives and p pans, which of the following must be true?

A) $20k + 30p \leq 240$

B) $20k + 30p \geq 240$

C) $30k + 20p \leq 240$

D) $30k + 20p \geq 240$

Solution

1. Start by writing an expression for the total cost of Gordon's items, but instead of writing an equation, we will form an inequality.
2. Since he is buying k knives for \$20 each, the total cost of k knives is $20k$. Since he is buying p pans for \$30 each, the cost of p pans is $30p$. Therefore, Gordon's total cost for knives and pans is $20k + 30p$.
3. The total amount he spends has an upper limit; he can spend at most \$240, so the total cost of buying k knives and p pans must be less than or equal to \$240. Set the expression $20k + 30p$ less than or equal to 240 in the inequality.

$$20k + 30p \leq 240$$

4. The answer is A.

Solving Linear Inequalities

When you have to solve inequalities, most operations can be applied just as you would apply them when solving equations, though there are a few notable exceptions.

Let's consider the true inequality $2 < 12$ and look at how performing operations on this inequality can result in other true inequalities. We will also graph the points 2 and 12 on a number line and verify that the inequality makes sense.

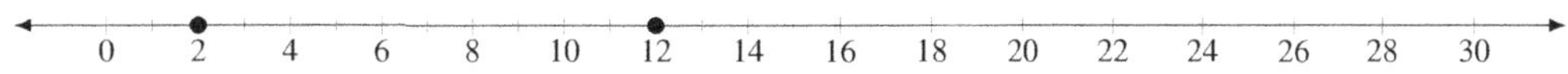

It is clear on the number line that 2 is further to the left than 12 (2 is less than 12). If we add 4 to both sides of the inequality, we have the inequality $6 < 16$, which is still true (the two original points are simply shifted, but maintain their positions relative to each other).

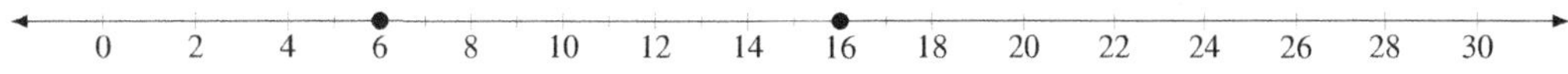

If we subtract 1 from both sides of this inequality, we have the inequality $5 < 15$, which is still true (again, the points have merely shifted).

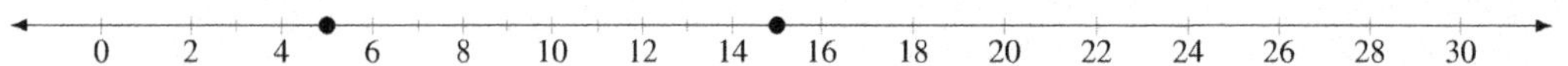

If we multiply both sides by 2, we have the inequality $10 < 30$, which is still true. Unlike when we added and subtracted, the points have not only shifted, but the distance between the points has grown due to the scale factor of 2 (they are now twice as far apart).

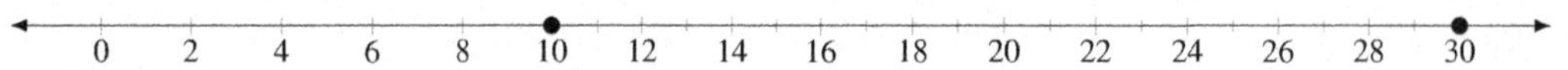

If we divide both sides of this inequality by 5, we have the inequality $2 < 6$, which is still true. Once again, the points have not only shifted, but the distance between them has shrunk (by a scale factor of 5).

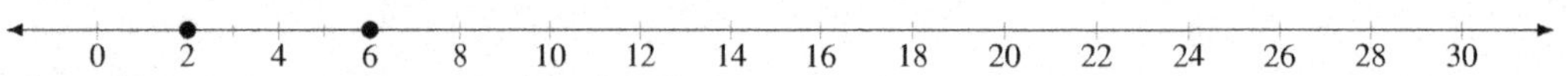

All of the operations we applied so far have produced valid inequalities. But what if we had multiplied both sides of the inequality by 0? The inequality breaks down because $0 \nless 0$ (0 is not less than 0).

Perhaps even more interesting is what happens when we multiply (or divide) an inequality by a negative number. Let's start back at the inequality $2 < 12$. If we multiply (or divide) both sides of the inequality by -1 (essentially mirroring both points, 2 and 12, about 0), we will see once again that the resulting inequality would not be true: $-2 \nless -12$ (notice that -2 is further to the right than -12).

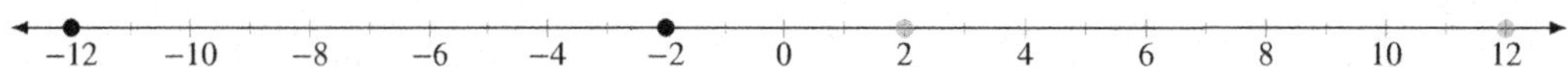

When multiplying (or dividing) an inequality by a negative number, you need to reverse the inequality sign in order to produce the correct inequality: $-2 > -12$. For a moment, let's consider what happens when we deal with some unknown constants, a and b, which for now, we will assume are both positive (though this is not important). If we know that $a < b$, then we can draw the following number line graph of the two values a and b.

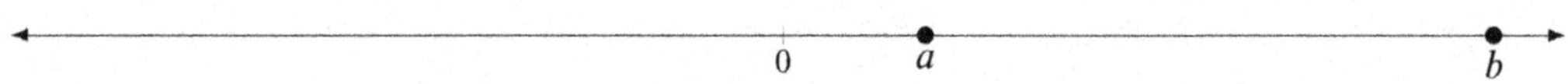

If we multiply both sides of the inequality by -1, we mirror both points, and we can see that $-a > -b$.

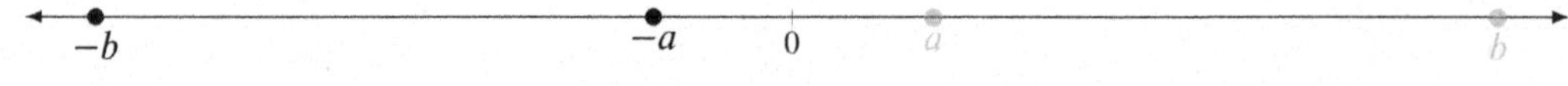

We can also prove this algebraically using subtraction instead of multiplication. Starting with the inequality $a < b$, let's subtract a from both sides.

$$a < b$$
$$0 < b - a$$

Now, subtract b from both sides of the inequality.

$$0 < b - a$$
$$-b < -a$$

Once again, we see that $-b$ is less than $-a$. Essentially, we have not "flipped the inequality sign," but reversed the sides of the terms by normal algebraic manipulation. Regardless, it is sufficient to say that **when we multiply (or divide) an inequality by a negative number, we need to reverse the inequality sign**.

Solving inequalities that contain variables is just like solving equations, but **if one of your algebraic steps involves multiplying or dividing both sides of the inequality by a negative number, you must remember to reverse the inequality sign**.

For example, if we are given the inequality $-8x + 3 \leq 59$ and are asked to solve for x, we can start by subtracting 3 from both sides of the equation.

$$-8x + 3 \leq 59$$
$$-8x \leq 56$$

Divide both sides of the inequality by -8. When we do that, we have to reverse the less-than-or-equal-to sign into a greater-than-or-equal-to sign to get the correct inequality: $x \geq -7$.

Any value of x that is greater than or equal to -7 is a solution to this inequality.

SkillDrill 5.1-2

Directions: Solve the given inequality for x (with x on the left side of the inequality) and find the maximum or minimum *integer* value of x that satisfies the inequality.

1. $3x + 2 \leq 8$

2. $5x - 3 \geq 4x + 5$

3. $10(x - 2) < 3x$

4. $3x - 5 < 4x - 7$

5. $3x + 2 \leq 8x$

6. $2x + 10 \geq 4x + 30$

7. $2x - 4 < 3x - 4$

8. $6x + 3 < 4x + 15$

Example 5.1-2

2 1600.io 5.1

Which of the following numbers is NOT a solution of the inequality $6x - 9 \leq 7x - 6$?

A) -1

B) -2

C) -3

D) -4

Solution

1. Group the x-terms on the right side of the inequality by subtracting $6x$ from both sides.

$$6x - 9 \leq 7x - 6$$
$$-9 \leq x - 6$$

2. Group the constant terms on the left side of the inequality by adding 6 to both sides in order to isolate and solve for x.

$$-9 \leq x - 6$$
$$-3 \leq x$$

3. Any value of x that *IS* greater than or equal to -3 is a solution of the inequality. Since the question asks us to pick the choice that is *NOT* a solution, we need to pick the only choice that is less than -3 (that is, not greater than or equal to -3), which is -4.

4. The answer is D.

Notes

You could do this problem by plugging in each choice and looking for the one that does not produce a valid inequality, but this method wastes time and is potentially confusing, especially since this inequality is very easy to solve.

Graphing Linear Inequalities

Let's extend the concept of inequalities into two dimensions (with two variables, x and y) by considering what it means to have a linear inequality, and what it means to be a solution to the linear inequality.

Let's consider the linear inequality (in Slope-Intercept Form) $y \leq 2x - 1$. We already know that if this were the linear equation $y = 2x - 1$, then the solution set could be represented with a line on the xy-plane that shows all possible pairs of x- and y-values that satisfy the equation.

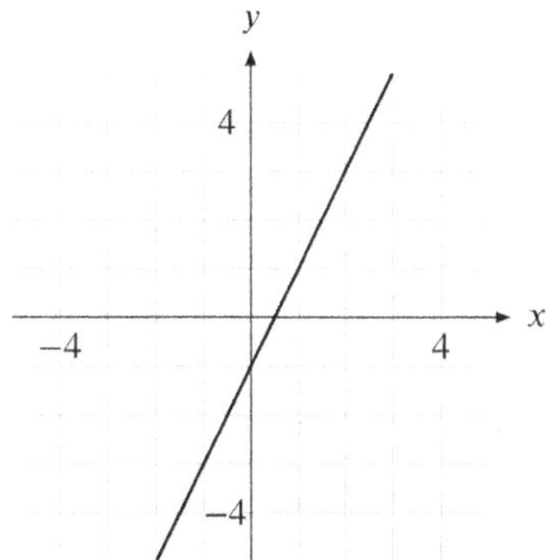

In the inequality, all of these points where the y-value is equal to $2x - 1$ are still solutions to the inequality because it includes the values of y that are **equal** to $2x - 1$, but they are not the only solutions to the inequality. Any point that is **below** a point on this line is also a solution to the system because the y-values at these points are **less than** the value of $2x - 1$ for any given x-value, so the solution region is represented by the entire shaded region under the line including the line itself.

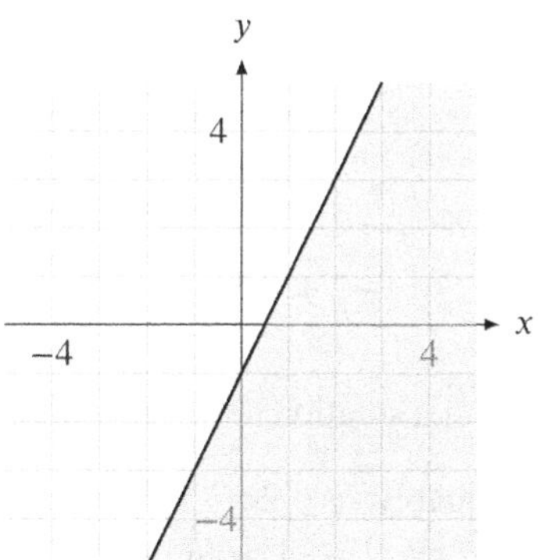

If we pick any point on the line or in the shaded region, we can plug the x- and y-values into the inequality to verify that it is still true. Let's use the point $(3, 2)$, which is located in the shaded region.

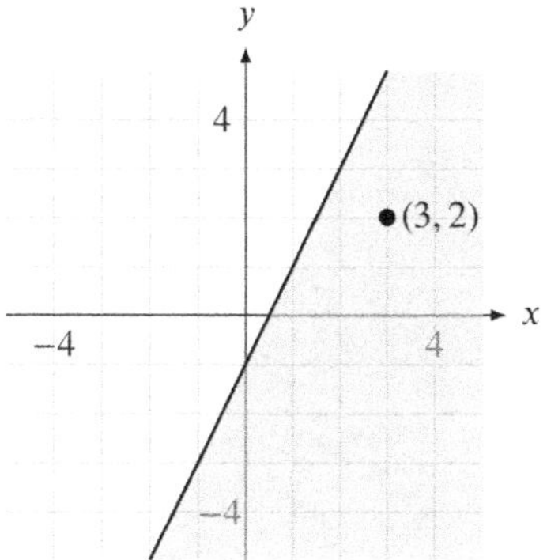

Let's plug in 3 for x and 2 for y in the linear inequality.

$$y \leq 2x - 1$$
$$(2) \leq 2(3) - 1$$
$$2 \leq 6 - 1$$
$$✓ \quad 2 \leq 5$$

It is true that $2 \leq 5$, so the point $(3, 2)$ is a solution to the inequality. But what if we choose a point outside of the shaded region (and not on the line)? Let's use the point $(-4, -2)$.

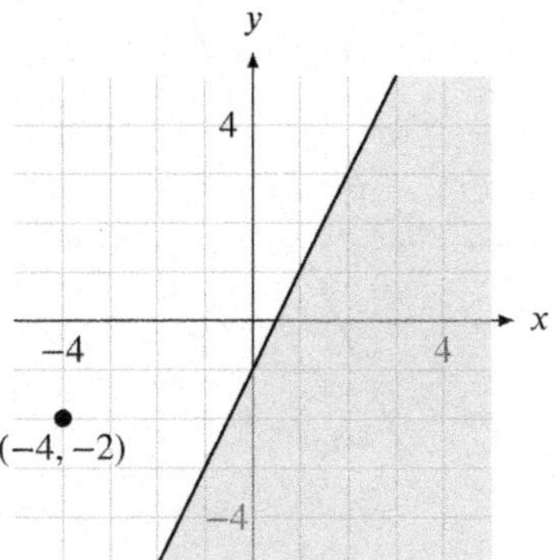

Let's plug in -4 for x and -2 for y in the linear inequality (note that we are simply plugging in negative values and not multiplying both sides by a negative, so we don't have to touch the inequality sign).

$$y \leq 2x - 1$$
$$(-2) \leq 2(-4) - 1$$
$$-2 \leq -8 - 1$$
$$✗ \quad -2 \leq -9$$
$$-2 \nleq -9$$

Since -2 is not less than or equal to -9, this point is not a solution to the system of inequalities.

If the inequality were not a "less than or equal to" inequality ($y \leq 2x - 1$), but instead were just a "less than" inequality ($y < 2x - 1$), the only difference would be that the line $y = 2x - 1$ would no longer be included in the solution set (because the y-values on the line are not strictly less than $2x - 1$ for any given value of x), so a dashed line instead of a solid line would be used to indicate the border of the region.

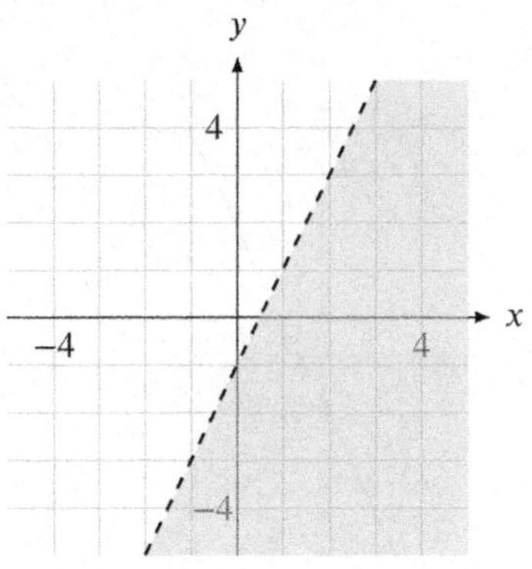

Graphing Linear Inequalities

When the sign in the inequality is $\leq$ or $\geq$, you will graph the line as a solid line because the points on the line are included in the solutions to the inequality, but if the symbol is $<$ or $>$, you will use a dashed line to graph the line because the points on the line will not satisfy the inequality and therefore are excluded from the solution set.

When we graph any linear inequality in Slope-Intercept Form with a greater-than or greater-than-or-equal-to sign, we shade above the line because any value of y that is above the y-values on the line is greater than the value of the y-coordinate of the point on the line below it, and thus will satisfy the inequality.

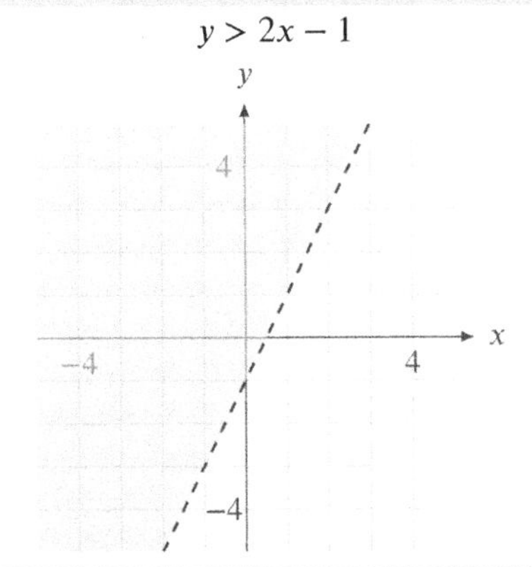

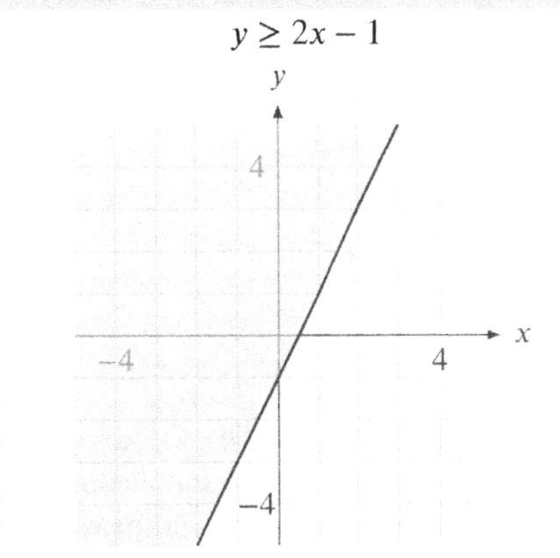

When we graph any linear inequality in Slope-Intercept Form with a less-than or less-than-or-equal-to sign, we shade below the line because any value of y that is below the y-values on the line will satisfy the inequality.

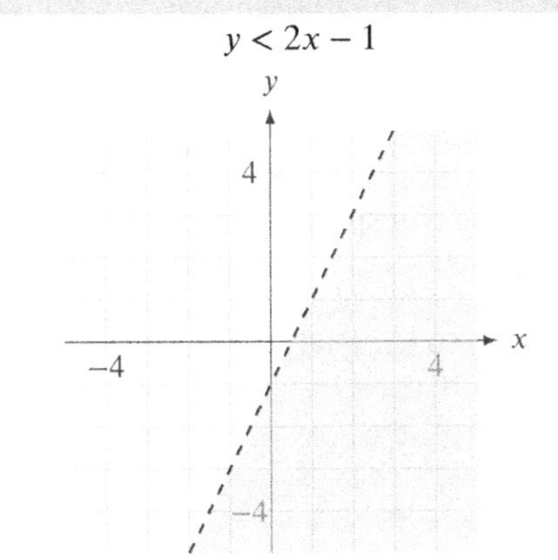

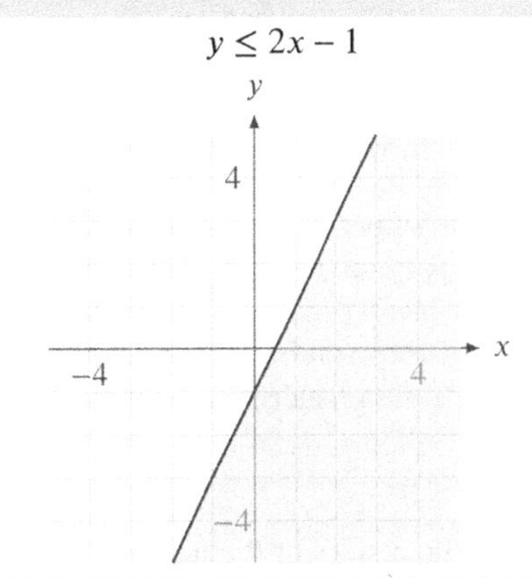

Most of the time, graphing is reserved for Systems of Linear Inequalities problems, which will be discussed later in the chapter. For now, it is sufficient that we know what it means for a point to be a solution to a linear inequality, and for many of the inequality problems, all we have to do is plug in values to check if the x- and y-values satisfy the inequality.

SkillDrill 5.1-3

Directions: For each inequality, see if each of the three following points is a solution to the inequality. List the Roman numerals of the points that are solutions to each inequality.

I. $(0, -5)$

II. $(1, 1)$

III. $(2, 4)$

1. $y < x$ **2.** $y \leq 2x$ **3.** $y < 2x - 5$ **4.** $y \geq 3x - 2$

Example 5.1-3

3 1600.io 5.1

Gretel rented an electric scooter. The scooter rental cost \$4 per hour, and she had to also pay for a helmet that costs \$8. Gretel spent more than \$42 for the rental and the helmet. If the scooter was available for only a whole number of hours, what was the minimum number of hours that Gretel could have rented the scooter?

Solution

1. Start by writing a linear expression for the total cost of Gretel's rental in Slope-Intercept Form, but instead of writing an equation, we will form an inequality.

2. There is a cost of \$4 per hour, so if she rents the scooter for h hours, she will spend $4h$ dollars plus the initial one-time fee of \$8 for the helmet. Therefore, the total cost of her rental was $4h + 8$.

3. The total amount she spends has a boundary; she spent more than \$42, so her total cost must be greater than \$42. Set the expression $4h + 8$ greater than 42 in the inequality.

$$4h + 8 > 42$$

4. Subtract 8 from both sides of the inequality.

$$4h > 34$$

5. Divide both sides of the inequality by 4 in order to solve for h.

$$4h > 34$$
$$h > \frac{34}{4}$$
$$h > \frac{17}{2}$$

6. Since $\frac{17}{2}$ is 8.5 and Gretel had to have rented the scooter for a whole number of hours, the least number of hours she could have rented the scooter that is still greater than 8.5 is 9.

7. The answer is 9.

Linear Inequalities can be written in Standard Form as well, and the math works the same (though graphing would require converting the inequality into Slope-Intercept Form, but graphing is rarely necessary). Simply plug in any given values and check if the points satisfy the inequality.

Example 5.1-4

4 5.1

Which of the following ordered pairs (x, y) satisfies the inequality $6x - 2y < 8$?

I. $(0, -4)$

II. $(1, 1)$

III. $(2, 2)$

A) I only

B) II only

C) I and II only

D) II and III only

Solution

1. Divide both sides of the inequality by 2 (because 2 is the greatest common factor of all of the coefficients) in order to simplify the inequality and make it easier to plug in points and evaluate the results (this step is not essential, but it simplifies the arithmetic to come, and why shouldn't you make life a little easier for yourself?).

$$6x - 2y < 8$$
$$\frac{1}{2}\left(6x - 2y\right) < \frac{1}{2}(8)$$
$$3x - y < 4$$

2. For each of the given points, plug in the x-coordinate for x and the y-coordinate for y in the simplified form of the inequality in order to check if the resulting inequality is true (which means the point is in the solution set).

3. Start with point I, $(0, -4)$: plug in 0 for x and -4 for y.

$$\begin{aligned} 3x - y &< 4 \\ 3(0) - (-4) &< 4 \\ 0 + 4 &< 4 \\ \text{✗} \quad 4 &< 4 \\ 4 &\not< 4 \end{aligned}$$

Since 4 is not less than 4, this point does not satisfy the inequality. Eliminate choices A and C, which include point I.

4. By process of elimination, point II, $(1, 1)$ will satisfy the inequality because it is included in both of the remaining answers, but if you want to be thorough, plug in 1 for x and 1 for y.

$$\begin{aligned} 3x - y &< 4 \\ 3(1) - (1) &< 4 \\ 3 - 1 &< 4 \\ \text{✓} \quad 2 &< 4 \end{aligned}$$

Point II satisfies the inequality because 2 is less than 4.

5. Check if point III, $(2, 2)$ satisfies the inequality by plugging in 2 for x and 2 for y.

$$\begin{aligned} 3x - y &< 4 \\ 3(2) - (2) &< 8 \\ 6 - 2 &< 4 \\ \text{✗} \quad 4 &< 4 \\ 4 &\not< 4 \end{aligned}$$

Since 4 is not less than 4, this point does not satisfy the inequality, so eliminate choice D, which includes point III.

6. The answer is B.

Notes

The points can simply be plugged into the inequality as provided (skipping Step 1), but here, as is sometimes the case with substitute-and-test problems, the inequality (or an equality, if that's what's being evaluated) can be simplified. While this adds a step up front (increasing the time needed and adding an opportunity for an error to be made), this investment is repaid with interest as it simplifies the substitution/evaluation procedure due to smaller (or no) coefficients and constants, making the method shown in the solution above more rapid and less error-prone.

When dealing with linear inequalities in Standard Form, sometimes you have to handle maximization or minimization problems. Remember a few chapters ago when we said that Standard Form linear equations can be though of as striking a balance between two variable quantities? The same holds true here: when two variable terms add up to a constant value, if one of those terms increases in value, the other term must decrease to compensate so the sum remains the same. In the following example, this means that in order to *maximize* one variable, we must *minimize* the other variable.

Example 5.1-5

5 5.1

$$C = 20x + 6y$$

The formula above gives the monthly cost C, in dollars, of operating a printer when the technician works a total of x hours and when y reams of paper are used. If, in a particular month, it cost no more than \$3,800 to operate the printer and at least 100 reams of paper were used, what is the maximum number of hours the technician could have worked?

A) 160

B) 300

C) 1,800

D) 3,200

Solution

1. Start by rewriting the given equation as an inequality. The total cost is no more than (less than or equal to) \$3,800, so set the expression $20x + 6y$ less than or equal to 3,800.

$$20x + 6y \leq 3{,}800$$

2. Since we want to maximize the number of hours the technician worked, we need to minimize the number of reams of paper used (so that the cost of paper will be as low as possible, meaning that the maximum portion of the budget will go towards the technician's pay, which indicates that the technician worked as many hours as possible). Since they used at least 100 reams, then 100 is the lowest possible number of reams of paper in order to maximize the number of hours. Substitute 100 for y.

$$20x + 6y \leq 3{,}800$$
$$20x + 6(100) \leq 3{,}800$$
$$20x + 600 \leq 3{,}800$$
$$20x \leq 3{,}200$$
$$x \leq 160$$

3. If $x \leq 160$, the maximum value x can have is 160, so the answer is A.

Be aware that in real world problems, the limit of an inequality is not necessarily the answer due to additional constraints, such as a requirement that the result must be a counting number (a non-negative integer). For example, if someone is buying b books that cost \$20 each, and they can spend at most \$75, then the inequality that represents the relationship is $20b \leq 75$. Solving for b, we see that $b \leq 3.75$, so as long as this person buys less than 3.75 books they will come in under budget. However, this person cannot buy three quarters of a book, so this person is limited to only buying 3 books. Be on the alert for problems that have an additional (sometimes implied but not directly stated) constraint that informs us that the answer must be an integer.

View related real-test problems at 1600.io/p/smtex?topic=5.1

Section 5.1 Practice Problems

1 1600.io 5.1

Fred harvests corn at a constant rate of 1.2 acres per day. He harvested 3 acres so far this month and plans to spend d days harvesting for the rest of the month. If Fred wants to harvest at least 10 acres of corn this month, which of the following inequalities best represents this situation?

A) $3d + 1.2 \geq 10$

B) $1.2d + 3 \geq 10$

C) $1.2d - 3 \geq 10$

D) $1.2d \geq 10$

2 1600.io 5.1

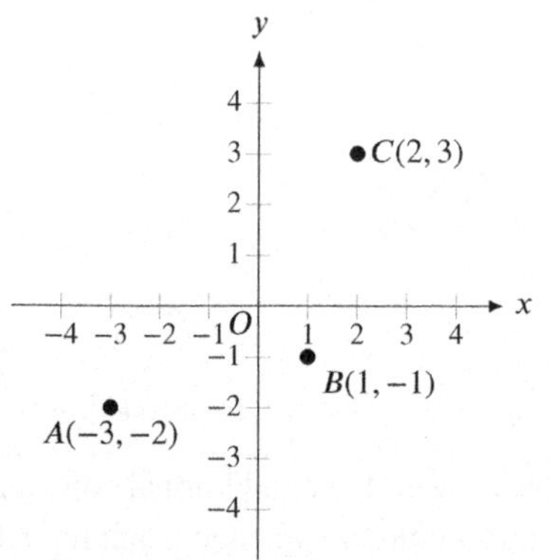

The coordinates of points A, B, and C are shown in the xy-plane above. For which of the following inequalities will each of the points A, B, and C be contained in the solution region?

A) $x > -3$

B) $y > x - 2$

C) $y < x + 2$

D) $y < x + 1$

3 1600.io 5.1

$$C = 5x + y$$

The formula above gives the weekly cost C, in dollars, of operating a lemon press when the lemonade maker works a total of x hours and when y lemons are used. If, in a particular week, it cost at least \$400 to operate the lemon press and no more than 100 lemons were used, what is the least number of hours the lemonade maker could have worked?

A) 40

B) 60

C) 100

D) 400

4 1600.io 5.1

If $5p - 7 \geq 4$, what is the least possible value of $5p + 1$?

A) $\frac{11}{5}$

B) 5

C) 11

D) 12

5.2 Compound Linear Inequalities

A **Compound Linear Inequality** is when a linear expression is bounded on both sides by both an upper and lower limit. The value of the expression must be between two values. For example, the compound inequality $3 \leq x < 7$ means that x is greater than or equal to 3, but x is also less than 7. By convention, the lower bound is written on the left, and the upper bound is written on the right, so only the less-than and less-than-or-equal-to signs are used.

When working with compound inequalities, it can be tempting to split the inequality up into two separate inequalities, but most of the time, it is easier to just work with what you are given. Doing algebraic work on compound inequalities is simple: just apply the same operations to all three parts of the inequality. Extending the principle that applies to simpler linear inequalities that we discussed earlier, if you multiply or divide by a negative number, you have to remember to flip **both** inequality signs; when you do this, re-write the inequality in the conventional orientation, with the lower bound on the left, thus using only less-than and less-than-or-equal-to signs.

For example, let's solve for x in the compound inequality $2 < -3x + 2 < 8$.

$$2 < -3x + 2 < 8$$

$$0 < -3x < 6$$ Subtract 2 from all three parts of the compound inequality.

$$\frac{0}{-3} > x > \frac{6}{-3}$$ Divide all three parts by -3 and flip the inequality signs.

$$0 > x > -2$$

$$-2 < x < 0$$ Rewrite the compound inequality in traditional orientation with only less-than signs.

SkillDrill 5.2-1

Directions: Solve each compound inequality for x.

1. $2 < 5x + 2 < 10$ **2.** $-6 < 4x - 3 < 9$ **3.** $0 < -7x - 1 < 6$ **4.** $-4 < 3 - 2x < 7$

Example 5.2-1

 5.2

Tickets for a school's winter concert cost \$2.50 for students and \$5 for adults. If Harold spends at least \$15 but no more than \$24 on x students tickets and 2 adult tickets, what is one possible value of x ?

Solution

1. Start by writing an expression to represent the total cost of tickets in Standard Form. Let's use s for the number of student tickets (even though they tell us to use x later), and let's use a for the number of adult tickets. If student tickets cost \$2.50 each, and Harold buys s student tickets, then the cost of those tickets is $2.5s$. Since adult tickets are \$5 each and Harold buys a of them, the price of those tickets is $5a$. Therefore, the total amount that Harold spends on tickets is $2.5s + 5a$.

2. The amount Harold spends must be between \$15 and \$24, inclusive, so we should set the expression $2.5s + 5a$ greater than or equal to 15, but also less than or equal to 24.

$$15 \le 2.5s + 5a \le 24$$

3. Since the problem tells us that Harold buys x student tickets, replace s with x. Since we know that Harold buys 2 adult tickets, replace a with 2.

$$\begin{aligned} 15 &\le 2.5s + 5a \le 24 \\ 15 &\le 2.5x + 5(2) \le 24 \\ 15 &\le 2.5x + 10 \le 24 \end{aligned}$$

4. Subtract 10 from all three parts of the inequality to isolate the x term.

$$\begin{aligned} 15 &\le 2.5x + 10 \le 24 \\ 5 &\le 2.5x \le 14 \end{aligned}$$

5. Divide all three parts of the inequality by 2.5 (if you like working without a calculator, you can convert 2.5 into the fraction $\frac{5}{2}$, then multiply all three parts by $\frac{2}{5}$ in order to isolate and solve for x).

$$\begin{aligned} 5 &\le 2.5x \le 14 \\ 2 &\le x \le 5.6 \end{aligned}$$

or

$$\begin{aligned} 5 &\le 2.5x \le 14 \\ 5 &\le \frac{5}{2}x \le 14 \\ \frac{2}{\cancel{5}}(\cancel{5}) &\le \frac{\cancel{2}}{\cancel{5}}\left(\frac{\cancel{5}}{\cancel{2}}x\right) \le \frac{2}{5}(14) \\ 2 &\le x \le \frac{28}{5} \end{aligned}$$

6. For your answer, you can fill in any whole number (integer) value between 2 and 5.6, inclusive (the valid answers must be whole numbers because x represents a number of tickets, and you can't buy part of a ticket). A number like 3 is a safe choice if you are unsure whether the boundaries should be included or not, though 2 is still a valid answer because the inequality indicates that x can be greater than *or equal to* 2.

View related real-test problems at 1600.io/p/smtex?topic=5.2

Section 5.2 Practice Problems

1 5.2

Jenny can shuck at least 20 dozen oysters per hour and at most 24 dozen oysters per hour. Based on this information, what is a possible amount of time, in hours, that it could take Jenny to shuck 120 dozen oysters?

2 5.2

A certain rhinoceros weighs 100 pounds at birth and gains more than 3 but less than 5 pounds per day during its first year. Which of the following inequalities represents all possible weights w, in pounds, for the rhinoceros 180 days after birth?

A) $640 < w < 1{,}000$

B) $540 < w < 900$

C) $300 < w < 500$

D) $280 < w < 900$

5.3 Systems of Linear Inequalities

We can write systems of linear inequalities just like we write systems of linear equations. The only difference is we also have to make sure that we use the correct inequality signs in all of the inequalities that we write.

Example 5.3-1

1 5.3

A maid service is buying window cleaner and floor polish from its supplier. The supplier will deliver no more than 450 pounds in a shipment. Each container of window cleaner weighs 5.65 pounds, and each container of floor polish weighs 8.4 pounds. The service wants to buy at least three times as many containers of floor polish as containers of window cleaner. Let w represent the number of containers of window cleaner, and let f represent the number of containers of floor polish, where w and f are non-negative integers. Which of the following systems of inequalities best represents this situation?

A) $8.4w + 5.65f \leq 450$
$f \geq 3w$

B) $8.4w + 5.65f \leq 450$
$3f \geq w$

C) $5.65w + 8.4f \leq 450$
$f \geq 3w$

D) $5.65w + 8.4f \leq 450$
$3f \geq w$

Solution

1. We need to write one inequality that describes the total number of pounds of product bought. We know that w is the number of containers of window cleaner, and each one weighs 5.65 pounds, so the total weight of window cleaner is $5.65w$. We know that f is the number of containers of floor polish, and each one weighs 8.4 pounds, so the total weight of floor polish is $8.4f$. Therefore, the total weight of the supplies is $5.65w + 8.4f$. The total weight must be no more than (less than or equal to) 450 pounds, so this expression should be set less than or equal to 450 to form the first linear inequality in the system.

   $$5.65w + 8.4f \leq 450$$

   Eliminate choices A and B, leaving only choices C and D.

2. This step is the crucial step in this problem, and it requires careful translation. We are told that the service wants to buy at least three times as many containers of floor polish as containers of window cleaner. The most common mistake made on questions like this is mistranslating this part into the wrong inequality. **Don't just try to write this relationship based on the order that the information appears in the sentence**. Because the number 3 is presented close to the words "floor polish," you might think that f should be multiplied by 3. However, this is incorrect.

   Visualize the situation before you write the inequality. For example, if you had one container of window cleaner, you would need at least 3 containers of floor polish. The number of floor polishes is larger, and it is three times the number of window cleaners, so therefore we would have to multiply the number of window cleaners by 3 in order to match the number of floor polishes. We have now rephrased the statement in a way that reflects its true meaning and helps us write the inequality: *the number of floor polish containers* ***is at least*** *(greater than or equal to) 3 times the number of window cleaner containers.*

   $$f \geq 3w$$

3. The set of inequalities that describe the given circumstances is the following:

   $$5.65w + 8.4f \leq 450$$
   $$f \geq 3w$$

4. The answer is C.

Notes

One straightforward way to approach the construction of inequalities (or equations) in scenarios like in Step 2 of the solution above is to start by setting up a proportion (they are covered in a later chapter); using proportions is really easy and you don't have to rely on intuition or plugging in actual values to figure out the solution. The given constraint that there must be at least three times as many containers of floor polish as containers of window cleaner simply means the ratio of the number of floor polish containers to the number of window cleaner containers must be at least 3 to 1. The phrase "at least" tells us to use a greater-than-or-equal-to sign.

$$\frac{\text{floor polish}}{\text{window cleaner}} \geq \frac{3}{1}$$

$$\frac{f}{w} \geq 3$$

Now, we just need to do some simple algebra to get the equation into the form of the answer choices. Multiply both sides of the equation by w.

$$f \geq 3w$$

Solving systems of linear inequalities can be confusing. Luckily, some problems gives you points as choices, and a lot of times, the easiest way to handle those problems is by plugging the answer choices into the two inequalities and seeing which points satisfy both inequalities. If a point only makes one of the inequalities true, then it is NOT a solution to the system.

Example 5.3-2

 5.3

$$y \geq -x + 3$$
$$y > 2x - 3$$

In the xy-plane, point A is contained in the graph of the solution set of the system of inequalities above. Which of the following could be the coordinates of point A ?

A) $(2, 1)$

B) $(3, 0)$

C) $(3, 3)$

D) $(3, 5)$

Solution

1. Try plugging the x-coordinate and y-coordinate of each answer choice into both inequalities to find the point that satisfies both inequalities.

2. Start with choice A, (2, 1); plug in 2 for x and 1 for y.

$$y \geq -x + 3$$
$$y > 2x - 3$$
$$\Downarrow$$
$$1 \geq -(2) + 3$$
$$1 > 2(2) - 3$$
$$\Downarrow$$
$$1 \geq -2 + 3$$
$$1 > 4 - 3$$
$$\Downarrow$$
$$1 \geq 1$$
$$1 > 1$$
$$\Downarrow$$
$$✓ \quad \mathbf{1 \geq 1}$$
$$✗ \quad \mathbf{1 \not> 1}$$

Even though the first inequality is true, the second inequality is not because 1 is not greater than 1. Eliminate choice A.

3. Try point B, $(3, 0)$; plug in 3 for x and 0 for y.

$$\begin{gathered} y \geq -x+3 \\ y > 2x-3 \\ \Downarrow \\ 0 \geq -(3)+3 \\ 0 > 2(3)-3 \\ \Downarrow \\ 0 \geq -3+3 \\ 0 > 6-3 \\ \Downarrow \\ 0 \geq 0 \\ 0 > 3 \\ \Downarrow \\ \checkmark \quad \mathbf{0 \geq 0} \\ \times \quad \mathbf{0 \not> 3} \end{gathered}$$

Even though the first inequality is true, the second inequality is not because 0 is not greater than 3. Eliminate choice B.

4. Try point C, $(3, 3)$; plug in 3 for x and 3 for y.

$$\begin{gathered} y \geq -x+3 \\ y > 2x-3 \\ \Downarrow \\ 3 \geq -(3)+3 \\ 3 > 2(3)-3 \\ \Downarrow \\ 3 \geq -3+3 \\ 3 > 6-3 \\ \Downarrow \\ 3 \geq 0 \\ 3 > 3 \\ \Downarrow \\ \checkmark \quad \mathbf{3 \geq 0} \\ \times \quad \mathbf{3 \not> 3} \end{gathered}$$

Even though the first inequality is true, the second inequality is not because 3 is not greater than 3. Eliminate choice C.

5. By process of elimination D is the answer, but you should check all the choices when you use plugging in as your solving method. Try point D, $(3, 5)$; plug in 3 for x and 5 for y.

$$\begin{gathered} y \geq -x+3 \\ y > 2x-3 \\ \Downarrow \\ 5 \geq -(3)+3 \\ 5 > 2(3)-3 \\ \Downarrow \\ 5 \geq -3+3 \\ 5 > 6-3 \\ \Downarrow \\ \checkmark \quad \mathbf{5 \geq 0} \\ \checkmark \quad \mathbf{5 > 3} \end{gathered}$$

Both inequalities are true, so point D satisfies the system of inequalities.

6. The answer is D.

Notes

Here, after we eliminated choice A, we could have observed that the x-value for all of the remaining three answer choices is 3, so we wouldn't need to recalculate the right side of the inequalities over and over—we could just do it once, so we'd be left with the following simplified inequalities:

$$y \geq -x + 3$$
$$y > 2x - 3$$
$$\Downarrow$$
$$y \geq -(3) + 3$$
$$y > 2(3) - 3$$
$$\Downarrow$$
$$y \geq -3 + 3$$
$$y > 6 - 3$$
$$\Downarrow$$
$$y \geq 0$$
$$y > 3$$

Now, we just need to substitute the y-values for each of the choices and determine if the inequalities are valid.

While systems of linear inequalities questions are rare, you do occasionally need to graph systems of linear inequalities and shade the region that contains the solution set. A good starting point is to write the inequalities in Slope-Intercept Form by isolating the y-variable. Once you have the inequalities in Slope-Intercept Form, you can begin graphing them.

When you graph a system of linear inequalities, you need to graph both linear inequalities. The region where the two shaded areas overlap is the solution set for the system of inequalities because it represents the set of all points that satisfy *both* inequalities in the system. When you need to pick a point that satisfies the system, you should limit your search to points that appear in this overlap region (or on any solid—not dashed—lines that bound the overlap region).

Graphing Systems of Linear Inequalities

For this demonstration of the graphical solution to a system of linear inequalities, let's look at the following system of linear inequalities and graph them (make sure the inequalities are written in Slope-Intercept Form if you have to graph them):

$$y \leq 2x - 1$$
$$y < -x + 2$$

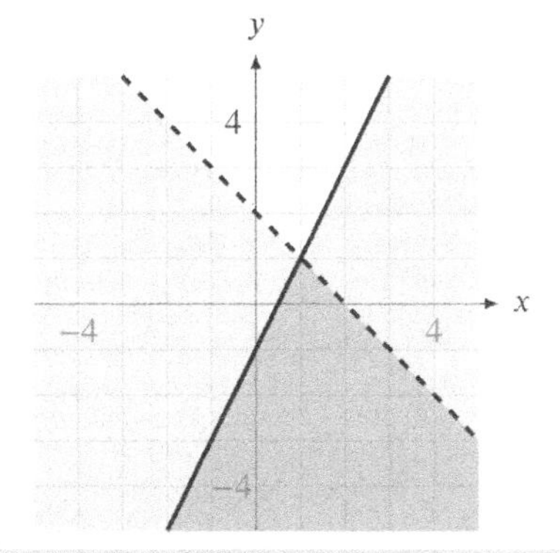

Notice the overlapping, darker region of shading. A point in this region will satisfy both inequalities, but points that are outside of the overlapping region will not. Look at the points $(0, -3)$, which is in the overlapping shaded region, and $(2, 0)$, which is in *a* shaded region, but on the dashed line and *not in the region of overlapping shading*.

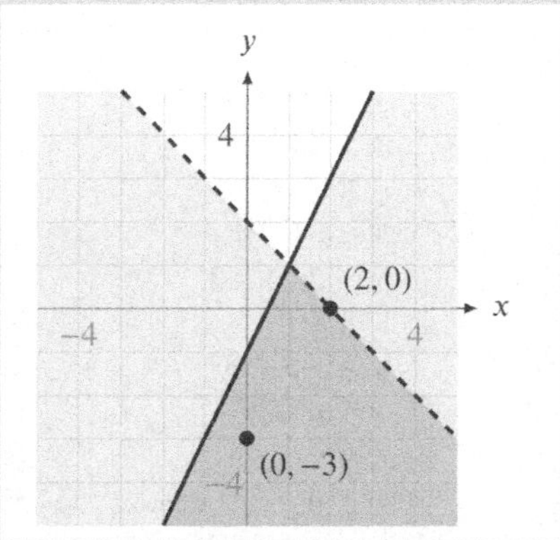

If we plug these points into both inequalities in the system, the point $(0, -3)$ will satisfy both inequalities, but the point $(2, 0)$ will only satisfy the first inequality.

$$\begin{array}{ll} y \leq 2x - 1 & y \leq 2x - 1 \\ y < -x + 2 & y < -x + 2 \\ \Downarrow & \Downarrow \\ -3 \leq 2(0) - 1 & 0 \leq 2(2) - 1 \\ -3 < -(0) + 2 & 0 < -(2) + 2 \\ \Downarrow & \Downarrow \\ \checkmark\ \mathbf{-3 \leq -1} & 0 \leq 4 - 1 \\ \checkmark\ \mathbf{-3 < 2} & 0 < -2 + 2 \\ & \Downarrow \\ & \checkmark\ \mathbf{0 \leq 3} \\ & \times\ \mathbf{0 \not< 0} \end{array}$$

Similar to systems of linear *equations*, the only time there will be no solutions to a system of linear *inequalities* is when the boundary lines are parallel (or the same line, with one or both not being solid), and no shaded regions or solid lines overlap each other at all.

SkillDrill 5.3-1

Directions: For each system of inequalities, check if each of the following points is a solution to the system (remember that a point must satisfy both inequalities in order to be a solution).

I. $(0, 6)$
II. $(1, 4)$
III. $(-2, -3)$

1. $2x + y \leq 6$, $x + y \geq 5$

2. $4x + 5y < 2$, $2x - 3y \geq 1$

3. $x + 6y > 10$, $2x + 3y < 2$

4. $7x - 2y \leq 4$, $y > -3$

Example 5.3-3

3 5.3

$$y \geq x + 1$$
$$x + 2y \leq 2$$

In which of the following does the shaded region represent the solution set in the xy-plane to the system of inequalities above?

A)

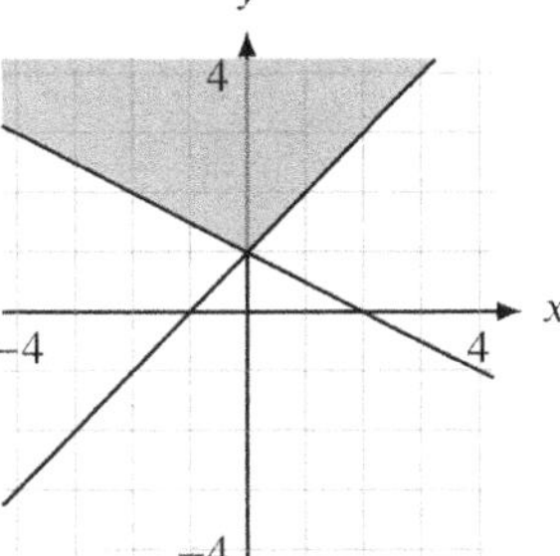

B)

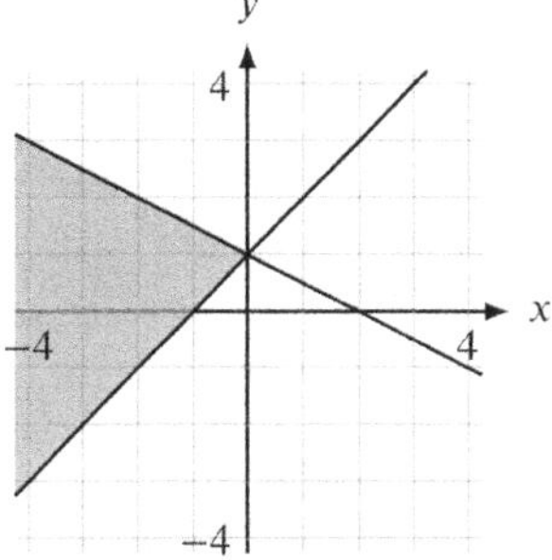

C)

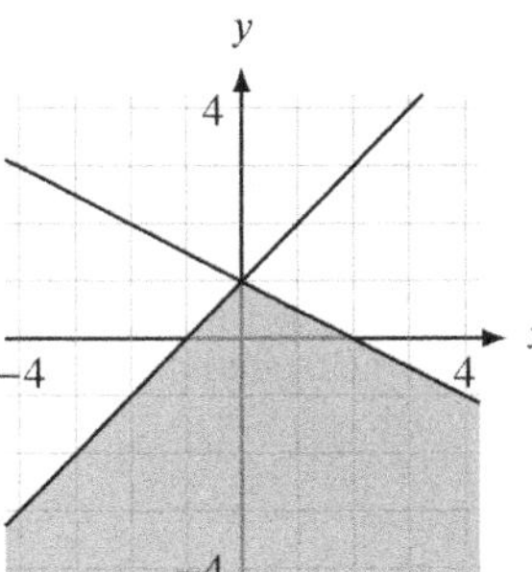

D)

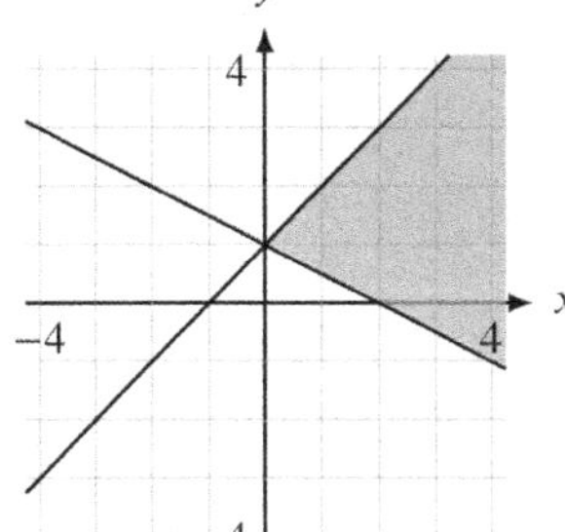

Solution 1

1. If you notice immediately that, in each of the answer choices, the same two lines are graphed, then you can cut out a lot of time on this problem. The first inequality is already given to us in Slope-Intercept Form, so we can identify the line $y = x + 1$ (the line going up from left to right), so we can narrow the possible choices to those that have shading above this line. That leaves choices A and B and eliminates choices C and D.

2. For the second inequality, the line is not in Slope-Intercept Form, but since we are not going to divide by a negative number, we know that the inequality will tell us that y is less than or equal to an expression, and therefore we will be shading below the second line (the line that goes down from left to right). Of the remaining choices, only choice B has shading below the second line, and we can eliminate choice A.

3. The answer is B.

Solution 2

1. The first inequality is already in Slope-Intercept Form. Write the second inequality, $x+2y \leq 2$, in Slope-Intercept Form.

$$x + 2y \leq 2$$
$$2y \leq -x + 2$$
$$y \leq \frac{-1}{2}x + 1$$

2. Graph the first inequality $y \geq x + 1$. Use a solid line to represent the line $y = x + 1$, then shade above the line.

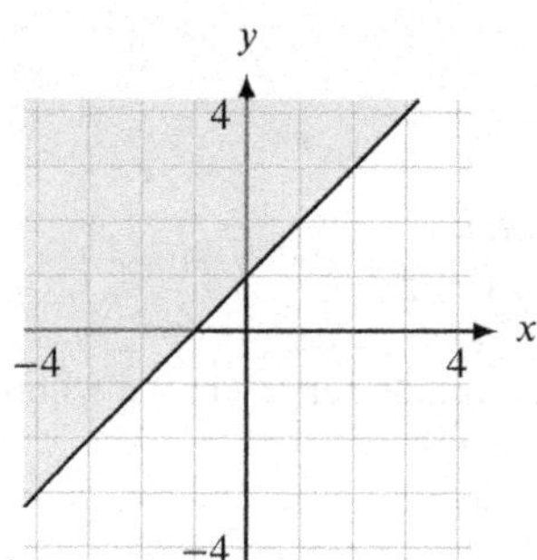

3. Add to the graph the second inequality, $y \leq \frac{-1}{2}x + 1$. Use a solid line to represent the line $y = \frac{-1}{2}x + 1$, then shade below the line.

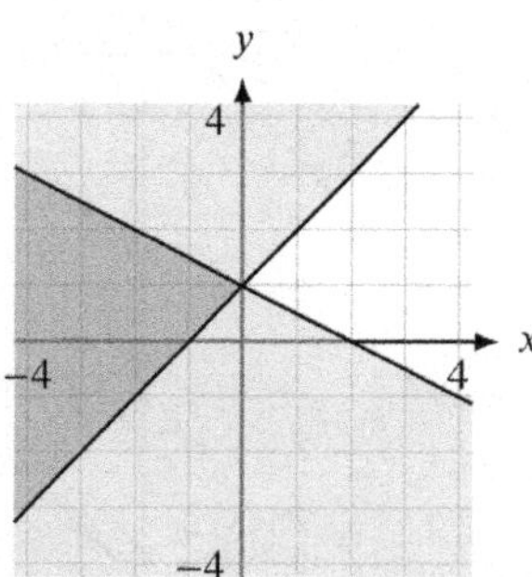

4. The darker shaded region (where the two shaded regions overlap) is the solution set of the system of inequalities.

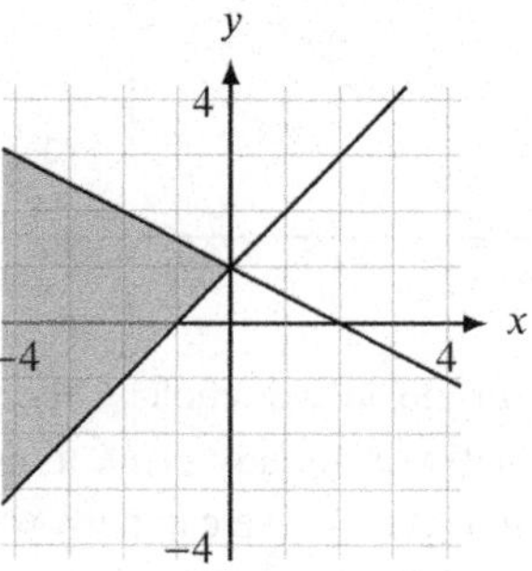

5. The answer is B.

Occasionally, the exact point where the two boundary lines intersect is actually the most important point to find when solving a system of linear inequalities problem, and to determine the coordinates of that point, you simply use the equations of those boundary lines (which are just the inequalities converted to equations) and then solve the resulting system of linear equations to find the intersection point. Specifically, if a question asks about the greatest (or least) possible value of x or y, then the intersection point of the boundary lines in the system of linear inequalities *must* be at an extreme point on the graph of the overlap region such that there is actually a maximum or minimum value of x or y, so you don't need to figure out whether that is the case or not. Therefore, **the intersection point of the boundary lines of the inequalities in a system will always represent the maximum or minimum coordinate value you are asked to find**; you will never be asked to determine whether or not such a finite extreme value exists, so you can always assume that it does and just convert the system to one of equations and solve it. Problems of this type rarely appear on the test, but there have been a few sightings of them over the years, so we will cover the needed concepts here.

If we graph the system of linear inequalities below, we will see that the overlap region has a maximum y-value (there is, however, no maximum or minimum x-value).

$$y \leq 2x + 1$$
$$y \leq -x + 5$$

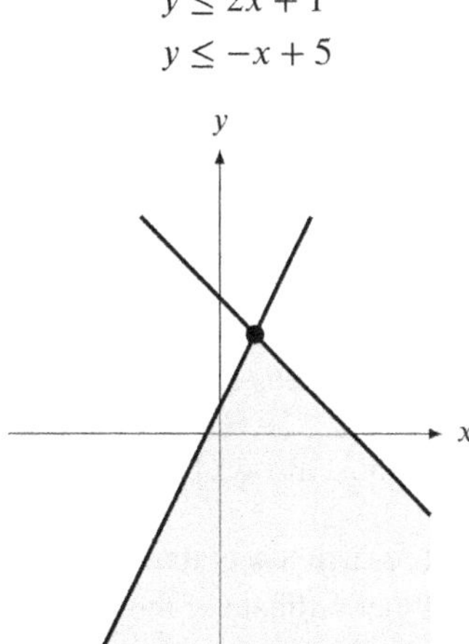

If we look at the bounded region, we can see that the point where the two lines meet has the greatest y-value of any point in the bounded region (which includes both of the graphed lines) because all of the other points in the shaded region lie below the intersection point.

If we treat the system of linear inequalities as a system of linear equations which represent the boundary lines, we can find the intersection point with substitution (setting $2x + 1$ equal to $-x + 5$) in order to find the x-value of the intersection point and then we can plug that x-value back into either boundary line equation to find the maximum value of y (alternatively, we could use elimination to solve directly for the y-value of the intersection point).

$$2x + 1 = -x + 5$$
$$3x + 1 = 5$$
$$3x = 4$$
$$x = \frac{4}{3}$$

$$\Rightarrow \text{Substitute } \frac{4}{3} \text{ for } x \Rightarrow$$

$$y = 2x + 1$$
$$y = 2\left(\frac{4}{3}\right) + 1$$
$$y = \frac{8}{3} + \frac{3}{3}$$
$$y = \frac{11}{3}$$

The intersection point of the two boundary lines is $\left(\frac{4}{3}, \frac{11}{3}\right)$, and every y-value in the bounded region must be less than or equal to $\frac{11}{3}$.

Of course, the x-value can also have a maximum or minimum in a system of inequalities (without the y-value having a maximum or minimum). If we graph the system of inequalities below (which has the same two boundary lines as in the previous example, but the second inequality has a different sign), we will see that the bounded region has a minimum x-value (while the y-value has no maximum or minimum).

$$y \leq 2x + 1$$
$$y \geq -x + 5$$

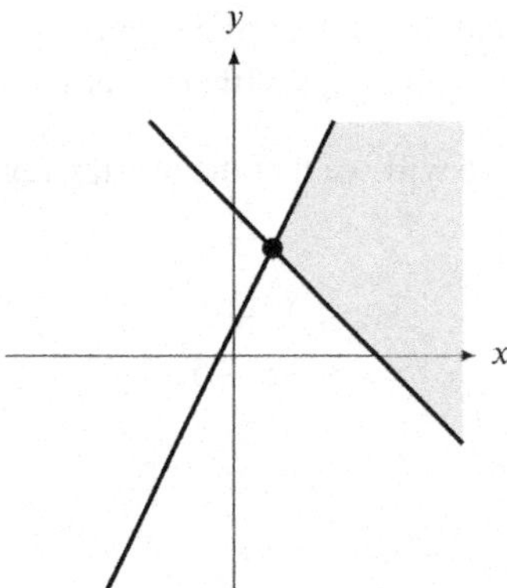

Since the two boundary lines are the same as those in the previous example, we know that the intersection point is $\left(\frac{4}{3}, \frac{11}{3}\right)$, and, in this case, the x-value of all points in the solution area must always be greater than or equal to $\frac{4}{3}$.

Finally, it is possible for two linear inequalities to meet in such a way that the intersection point's x-coordinate and y-coordinate *both* represent extreme values—that is, both the x- and y-coordinate of the intersection point are a maximum or minimum.

Let's graph the system of linear inequalities below.

$$y \leq x + 4$$
$$y \geq 3x - 2$$

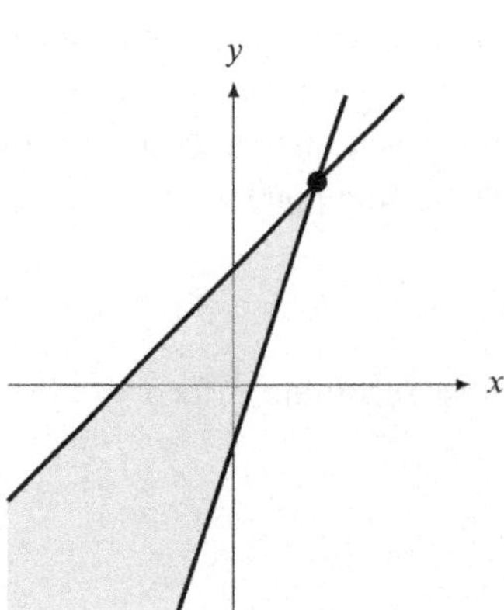

Notice that the intersection point is both the highest up (greatest y-value) and furthest right (greatest x-value) of any of the points in the shaded region. Let's use the equations of the boundary lines, $y = x + 4$ and $y = 3x - 2$, set the expressions $x + 4$ and $3x - 2$ equal to each other to solve for the x-value of the intersection point, and then substitute the x-value into either equation to find the y-value of the intersection point.

$$x + 4 = 3x - 2 \qquad\qquad y = x + 4$$
$$4 = 2x - 2 \quad \Rightarrow \text{Substitute 3 for } x \Rightarrow \quad y = (3) + 4$$
$$6 = 2x \qquad\qquad y = 7$$
$$3 = x$$

The intersection point is (3, 7), and for every point in the solution region, the x-coordinate must be less than or equal to 3, and the y-coordinate must be less than or equal to 7.

One more note: because, in this last case, there is a maximum x-value and a maximum y-value, you could be asked for the maximum value of $x + y$; you couldn't answer such a question if either value did not have a maximum in the system of inequalities.

To reiterate the central principle here: **if you're asked for a maximum or minimum coordinate value in a system of linear inequalities, that coordinate *must* be at the intersection point of the boundary lines, and that's found by converting the system to one of equations and solving that.**

Example 5.3-4

5.3

$$y \leq -15x + 2000$$
$$y \leq 5x$$

In the xy-plane, if a point with coordinates (a, b) lies in the solution set of the system of inequalities above, what is the maximum possible value of b?

Solution

1. We need to find the point in the solution set that has the greatest y-value because b is the y-value of a point in the solution set. This maximum value of y *must* be the y-coordinate of the point of intersection of the boundary lines of the system, so we could forge ahead with converting the system to one of equations and solving. However, both of the linear inequalities in the system are in Slope-Intercept Form, so visualizing the graph of the systems is a good and simple start, even if it doesn't directly provide the answer to the question.

   Start by roughly drawing the line $y = -15x + 2000$, which has a steep negative slope of -15 and goes through the point $(0, 2000)$ (because the y-intercept is 2,000). Shade below this line.

   Next, roughly draw the line $y = 5x$, which has a much less steep positive slope of 5 (the axes do not have to be on the same scale as each other, as this is just a rough sketch to get an idea of what the graph looks like) and goes through the origin (because the y-intercept is 0). Shade below this line as well, then look at the area of overlapping shading.

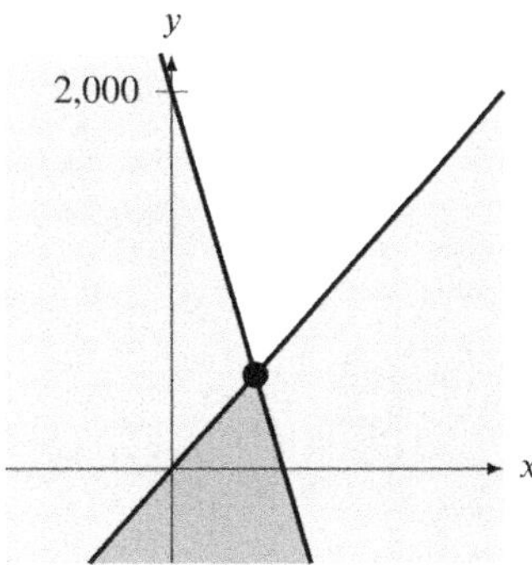

2. We can see that the maximum y-value for any points in the solution area exists at the point where the two boundary lines intersect. Therefore, we can find this value by treating the two inequalities like equations and using elimination to solve for y.

$$\begin{aligned} y &= -15x + 2000 \\ y &= 5x \\ &\Downarrow \\ y &= -15x + 2000 \\ 3(y) &= 3(5x) \\ &\Downarrow \\ y &= -15x + 2000 \\ + \quad 3y &= 15x \\ \hline 4y &= 2000 \\ &\Downarrow \\ y &= 500 \end{aligned}$$

3. The answer is 500.

Notes

Of course, you can use substitution to solve for the x-value of the intersection point, but you have to remember to plug the value back into either equation in order to find the y-value that is the correct answer to the question.

Section 5.3 Suggested Problems from Real Tests

View related real-test problems at 1600.io/p/smtex?topic=5.3

Section 5.3 Practice Problems

1 5.3

Hurston has 500 beads. He wants to make at least 4 bracelets and at least 5 necklaces. Each bracelet requires 20 beads, and each necklace requires 40 beads. If b represents the number of bracelets and n represents the number of necklaces, which of the following systems of inequalities represents this situation?

A) $b + n \leq 500$
$b \geq 4$
$n \geq 5$

B) $2b + 4n \leq 500$
$b \geq 4$
$n \geq 5$

C) $2b + 4n \leq 500$
$b \geq 20$
$n \geq 40$

D) $20b + 40n \leq 500$
$b \geq 4$
$n \geq 5$

2 5.3

Gina is a car dealer who sells two types of cars: a \$35,000 car and a \$65,000 car. Last month, her goal was to sell at least 40 cars. While she did not meet her goal, the total value of the cars she sold was over \$1,800,000. Which of the following systems of inequalities describes x, the possible number of \$35,000 cars, and y, the possible number of \$65,000 cars, that Gina sold last month?

A) $x + y \geq 40$
$35{,}000x + 65{,}000y > 1{,}800{,}000$

B) $x + y < 40$
$35{,}000x + 65{,}000y < 1{,}800{,}000$

C) $x + y \geq 40$
$35{,}000x + 65{,}000y < 1{,}800{,}000$

D) $x + y < 40$
$35{,}000x + 65{,}000y > 1{,}800{,}000$

3 5.3

$$y \leq -x + a$$
$$y \leq x + b$$

In the xy-plane, if $(0, 0)$ is a solution to the system of inequalities above, which of the following relationships between a and b must be true?

A) $a - b = 0$

B) $a \leq b$

C) $a \geq b$

D) $a + b \geq 0$

5.4 Absolute Value

Absolute value refers to the *distance from zero* of a value. As such, it is **always a positive value or zero**. The absolute value of 7 is 7 because its distance from zero is 7; the absolute value of −9 is 9 because its distance from zero is 9.

The absolute value of an expression is indicated by enclosing the expression in a pair of vertical bars. So, $|5|$ indicates the absolute value of 5, which is 5; $|-5|$ indicates the absolute value of −5, which is also 5.

This last example demonstrates a very important characteristic of the absolute value operation: because absolute value represents distance from zero, **there are always *two* values that have the same absolute value**: a positive number and the negative of that number (which happens to be called the additive inverse). The only exception to this is that zero itself is neither negative nor positive, so only the absolute value of zero yields zero.

The fact that there can be two values of an expression that yield the same absolute value means that **when solving an equation for a variable, you need to take into account both of these values**. Using the previous example, if we're told that $|x| = 5$, we must realize that this means that x could be 5 or −5:

$$|x| = 5$$
$$\Downarrow$$
$$x = 5$$
$$x = -5$$

This splitting of the given equation into two equations is the primary mechanism for solving problems that involve an absolute value. To illustrate this, let's look at a more realistic example of a test problem.

Example 5.4-1

 5.4

$$|3x - 2| = 7$$

If a and b are the solutions to the equation above, what is the value of $|a - b|$?

Solution 1

This solution makes clever use of equation combination to solve for the expression $a - b$ directly rather than solving for a and b individually first.

1. Make two equations from the original, one where the expression $3x - 2$ is set equal to 7, and one where it is set equal to −7.

$$3x - 2 = 7$$
$$3x - 2 = -7$$

2. Since one solution value of x is a and the other solution value of x is b, plug a in for x in the first equation and plug b in for x in the second equation. Note that it does not matter which value goes into which equation (it doesn't matter if a or b is the greater value), because when we take the absolute value of the difference between them, the result would be the same regardless.

$$3a - 2 = 7$$
$$3b - 2 = -7$$

3. Subtract the second equation from the first in order to arrive at an equation containing the expression $3a-3b$, from which we can factor out a 3 and arrive at the desired expression $a - b$.

$$\begin{array}{r} 3a - 2 = 7 \\ -\quad (3b - 2 = -7) \\ \hline 3a - 3b = 14 \end{array}$$

4. Factor a 3 out of both terms on the left side of the equation in order to isolate the expression $a - b$.

$$3a - 3b = 14$$
$$3(a - b) = 14$$

5. Divide both sides of the equation by 3 in order to find the value of $a - b$.

$$3(a - b) = 14$$
$$a - b = \frac{14}{3}$$

6. The value of $a - b$ is $\frac{14}{3}$, so $|a - b| = \frac{14}{3}$.

7. The answer is $\frac{14}{3}$.

Solution 2

1. Make two equations from the original, one where the expression $3x - 2$ is set equal to 7, and one where it is set equal to -7.

$$3x - 2 = 7$$
$$3x - 2 = -7$$

2. Solve each equation to find the two solutions. Start with the first equation, $3x - 2 = 7$.

$$3x - 2 = 7$$
$$3x = 9$$
$$x = 3$$

One of the solutions is 3.

3. Now solve the second equation, $3x - 2 = -7$ to find the second solution.

$$3x - 2 = -7$$
$$3x = -5$$
$$x = \frac{-5}{3}$$

The second solution is $\frac{-5}{3}$.

4. We are asked for the value of $|a - b|$. We know that a and b are the solutions of the equation, but which solution is a and which one is b? The good news is that it doesn't matter which solution you choose for a because taking the absolute value of the expression $a - b$ will ensure that we get the same value either way. Let's substitute 3 for a and $\frac{-5}{3}$ for b.

$$|a - b|$$

$$\left|3 - \left(\frac{-5}{3}\right)\right|$$

$$\left|\frac{9}{3} + \frac{5}{3}\right|$$

$$\left|\frac{14}{3}\right|$$

$$\frac{14}{3}$$

5. The answer is $\frac{14}{3}$.

Notes

If you are skeptical about the respective values of a and b not being important to this problem, then you can try swapping them by plugging in $\frac{-5}{3}$ for a and 3 for b, and you will see (if you do it correctly) that in the end we will have $\left|\frac{-14}{3}\right|$, which also evaluates to $\frac{14}{3}$.

Be aware, however, that some problems may have added conditions such as $a > b$. In these cases, you do have to assign values to the variables that agree with any conditions like $a > b$ that are given to you in the problem statement.

SkillDrill 5.4-1

Directions: Find the solution(s) to each absolute value equation.

1. $|x + 2| = 5$ **2.** $|-4x + 1| = 7$ **3.** $|2x - 5| = 17$ **4.** $|3x - 3| = 0$

Absolute value inequalities again work in a similar way to absolute value equations, except that when we produce the second resulting inequality, we have to remember to flip the inequality sign (as if we multiplied by -1). If you think about the meaning of absolute value, which is that it represents distance from zero, this makes perfect sense: a negative number's absolute value increases when the number becomes more negative, smaller, or farther from zero on the left side of the number line, while a positive number's absolute value increases when the number becomes more positive, larger, or farther from zero on the right side of the number line.

For example, the inequality $|x-4|>2$ tells us that $x-4$ is either greater than 2 or less than -2, because any values greater than 2 or less than -2 have an absolute value that is greater than 2.

$$|x-4|>2 \quad \Rightarrow \quad \begin{cases} x-4 & >2 \\ x-4 & <-2 \end{cases}$$

Absolute value inequalities that contain the greater-than sign result in two discontiguous simple inequalities; that is, there will be one inequality that's unbounded on the lower end and bounded by a negative value on the upper end, and there will be a second inequality that has a positive lower bound, and it will be unbounded on the upper end. In-between the two ranges will be the values that are excluded. For example, $|x-4|>2$ is equivalent to the two inequalities shown just above, and together they cover the range $-\infty$ to -2 (exclusive) and 2 (exclusive) to ∞, thereby excluding the range -2 to 2.

By contrast, absolute value inequalities with less-than signs also produce two inequalities, but they end up collapsing into a compound inequality because they define one contiguous range of values. For example, the inequality $|x-4|<2$ tells us that $x-4$ must be less than 2 and also greater than -2.

$$|x-4|<2 \quad \Rightarrow \quad \begin{cases} x-4 & <2 \\ x-4 & >-2 \end{cases}$$

These two inequalities will collapse into one compound inequality because the value of x has a lower bound at -2 and an upper bound at 2, which produces the compound inequality $-2<x-4<2$.

SkillDrill 5.4-2

Directions: Find all values of x that are solutions to each absolute value inequality.
Challenge problems are boxed.

1. $|x+2|<5$

2. $|-4x+1|\geq 7$

3. $|2x-5|\leq 17$

4. $\boxed{|3x-3|>0}$

Section 5.4 Suggested Problems from Real Tests

View related real-test problems at 1600.io/p/smtex?topic=5.4

Section 5.4 Practice Problems

1 1600.io 5.4

For what value of n is $|n-4|+2$ equal to 0 ?

A) 2

B) 3

C) 4

D) There is no such value of n

2 1600.io 5.4

$$|8-x|=3$$

The value of one solution to the equation above is 5. What is the value of the other solution?

3 1600.io 5.4

Two different points on a number line are both 2 units from the point with coordinate −5. The solution to which of the following equations gives the coordinates of both points?

A) $|x+5|=2$

B) $|x-5|=2$

C) $|x+2|=5$

D) $|x-2|=5$

CHAPTER 5 RECAP

- Solve inequalities like you solve equations, but remember to flip the sign if you multiply or divide by a negative number.
- The pointy or small end of the inequality sign is the lesser side of the inequality; the open or big end of the inequality sign is the greater side of the inequality.
- Plugging in values is an easy way to check answers for inequality problems.
- In real world problems, correct answers often have to be integers, particularly if the problem involves items that cannot be divided into fractional amounts (books, shirts, etc.).
- Compound inequalities can be solved in one step as long as you are careful about flipping both inequality signs if you multiply or divide by negative numbers. Just make sure to apply the same operation to all three parts of the compound inequality.
- A point is in the solution set of a system of inequalities only if it satisfies both inequalities.
- When graphing linear inequalities in the xy-plane, use a solid line if there is a $\leq$ or $\geq$ sign in the inequality (because points on the line **are** solutions to the inequality), and use a dashed line if there is a $<$ or $>$ sign in the inequality (because points on the line **are NOT** solutions to the inequality). Shade **above** the line to show the solution region when the y-variable is **greater than** the linear expression. Shade **below** the line to show the solution region when the y-variable is **less than** the linear expression.
- Solutions to a system of linear inequalities must satisfy all the inequalities in the system. If the inequalities are graphed on the same xy-plane, the solutions are located within the overlapping shaded regions and on any solid lines bounding those regions.
- You can solve absolute value equations by making two equations: one where the expression in the absolute value bars is set equal to the original value on the other side of the equation, and one where the expression is set equal to the negative of that value. For example, $|x| = 5$ yields both $x = 5$ and $x = -5$.

  Note that while the expression *within* the absolute value bars can have any value, positive or negative, **the absolute value of the expression can never be negative, by definition**. For example, while $|x| = 5$ yields two possible solutions ($x = 5$ and $x = -5$), the equation $|x| = -5$ yields **zero solutions** because the absolute value of an expression can never be negative.
- $|x+a| > b \quad \Rightarrow \quad \begin{cases} x+a > b \\ x+a < -b \end{cases}$
- $|x+a| < b \quad \Rightarrow \quad \begin{cases} x+a < b \\ x+a > -b \end{cases} \quad \Rightarrow \quad -b < x+a < b$

Additional Problems

1 1600.io 5.1

The average annual cable television cost for a certain home is $1,347. The homeowner plans to spend $2,400 to install satellite television. The homeowner estimates that the average annual satellite television cost will then be $1,031. Which of the following inequalities can be solved to find t, the number of years after installation at which the total amount of television cost savings will exceed the installation cost?

A) $2{,}400 < 1{,}347 - 1{,}031t$

B) $2{,}400 > (1{,}347 - 1{,}031)t$

C) $2{,}400 < (1{,}347 - 1{,}031)t$

D) $2{,}400 > \frac{1{,}347}{1{,}031}t$

2 1600.io 5.1

Carol has $12.00 to spend on peaches and plums. Peaches cost $0.80 each, and plums cost $0.45 each. If there is no tax on this purchase and she buys 12 peaches, what is the maximum number of whole plums she can buy?

3 1600.io 5.1

At the beginning of a recipe, Leslie had 8 cups of wine in a measuring cup. The first step of the recipe consisted of Leslie pouring x cups of the wine into a saucepan and y cups of the wine into a different saucepan. There remained at least 2 cups of wine in the measuring cup after the first step. Which of the following inequalities can be used to correctly represent this situation?

A) $2 - x - y \geq 4$

B) $2 - x + y \geq 4$

C) $8 - x - y \geq 2$

D) $8 - x + y \geq 2$

4 1600.io 5.3

$$y \geq 2x - 2$$
$$x - y < 2$$

Which of the following ordered pairs (x, y) satisfies the system of inequalities above?

A) $(0, -2)$

B) $(-1, -3)$

C) $(1, 2)$

D) $(3, 3)$

5 5.1

When 45 is decreased by $4x$, the result is greater than 25. What is the greatest possible integer value for x ?

6 5.3

$$y \leq -24x + 4500$$
$$y \leq 6x$$

In the xy-plane, if a point with coordinates (a, b) lies in the solution set of the system of inequalities above, what is the maximum possible value of b ?

7 5.4

Which of the following expressions is equal to 0 for some value of x ?

A) $|x - 10| + 2$

B) $|x + 7| - 2$

C) $|x - 2| + 1$

D) $|x - 4| + 0.5$

8 5.1

A delivery van carries only 50-pound packages and 80-pound packages. For each delivery trip, the van must carry at least 20 packages, and the total weight of the packages can be at most 1,400 pounds. What is the maximum number of 80-pound packages that the van can carry per trip?

A) 13

B) 14

C) 17

D) 18

9 5.3

$$y < -x + 2$$
$$2x > -7$$

Which of the following consists of the y-coordinates of all the points that satisfy the system of inequalities above?

A) $y < \frac{11}{2}$

B) $y < \frac{9}{2}$

C) $y < \frac{7}{2}$

D) $y > \frac{-7}{2}$

10 1600.io 5.1

$$4x - 12y < 36$$

Which of the following inequalities is equivalent to the inequality above?

A) $x - y < 9$

B) $3x - y < 3$

C) $3y - x < 9$

D) $x - 3y < 9$

11 1600.io 5.3

Students in a baking class are working in groups to make both a small cake and a large cake. A large cake requires 6 eggs and 2 cups of milk, and a small cake requires 4 eggs and 1 cup of milk. There are 66 eggs and 17 cups of milk available, and each group must have enough eggs and cups of milk to bake one large and one small cake. What is the maximum number of groups that could participate in this baking class?

12 1600.io 5.3

Charlotte needs to buy at least 12 new pieces of furniture for her office. The furniture will be made up of chairs, which cost \$64 each, and tables, which cost \$210 each. Her budget for the furniture is no more than \$2,200. She must buy at least 6 chairs and at least 3 tables. Which of the following systems of inequalities represents the conditions described if x is the number of chairs and y is the number of tables?

A) $64x + 210y \geq 2{,}200$
$x + y \leq 12$
$x \geq 6$
$y \geq 3$

B) $64x + 210y \leq 2{,}200$
$x + y \leq 12$
$x \leq 6$
$y \leq 3$

C) $64x + 210y \geq 2{,}200$
$x + y \geq 12$
$x \leq 6$
$y \leq 3$

D) $64x + 210y \leq 2{,}200$
$x + y \geq 12$
$x \geq 6$
$y \geq 3$

13 1600.io 5.1

Polly can spend up to a total of \$25 on beans and tortillas for a burrito dinner. Beans cost \$0.89 per can, and tortillas cost \$3.59 per pack. Which of the following inequalities represents this situation, where b is the number of cans of beans Polly can buy and t is the number of packs of tortillas Polly can buy? (Assume there is no sales tax.)

A) $0.89b + 3.59t \leq 25$

B) $0.89b - 3.59t \leq 25$

C) $0.89t + 3.59b \geq 25$

D) $0.89t - 3.59b \geq 25$

14 5.4

A hole digger estimates that a hole will take x minutes to dig, where $x > 240$. The goal is for the estimate to be within 20 minutes of the time it will actually take to dig the hole. If the digger meets the goal and it takes y minutes to dig the hole, which of the following inequalities represents the relationship between the estimated time and the actual completion time?

A) $y \leq x - 20$

B) $y \geq x + 20$

C) $x - y \leq 20$

D) $-20 \leq y - x \leq 20$

15 5.1

$$T = \frac{S}{B}$$

The formula above is Julian's law for download speed with time T, in seconds, download size S, in megabits, and bandwidth B, in megabits per second (Mbps). A music pirate has a bandwidth of 40 Mbps, and his download size will be generated by n two-megabit songs that produce a total download size of $2n$ megabits. If the download must take no longer than 0.67 seconds, what is the greatest number, n, of two-megabit songs that can be downloaded?

16 5.1

Olivier currently has 100 followers on a social media app. His goal is to have at least 2,200 followers. If he wants to meet this goal in 30 weeks, what is the minimum number of followers per week, on average, he should gain?

A) 69

B) 70

C) 71

D) 73

17 5.1

$$\frac{a+b}{a} = c$$

In the equation above, if a is positive and b is negative, which of the following must be true?

A) $c < 0$

B) $c < 1$

C) $c = 1$

D) $c > 1$

18 1600.io 5.1

Every Sunday, Susie makes seashell sculptures to sell at the flea market. Each sculpture costs her \$0.50 to make, and she sells the sculptures for \$6.50 each. She also pays a vendor's fee of \$80 every Sunday to set up her booth. What is the least number of seashell sculptures Susie needs to sell every Sunday to cover the cost of the vendor's fee?

A) 14

B) 13

C) 12

D) 11

19 1600.io 5.2

A brewer is gathering the ingredients to make 17 batches of ale and 1 batch of stout. The stout will require one-third pound of hops. The brewer needs a total of more than 5 but less than 6 pounds of hops. What is one possible value for the fraction of one pound of hops required for each batch of ale?

20 1600.io 5.1

The posted weight limit for a ladder in a warehouse is 300 pounds. A worker will climb the ladder while carrying x identical boxes each weighing 4 pounds. If the weight of the worker is 215 pounds, what is the maximum possible value for x that will keep the combined weight of the worker and boxes below the ladder's posted weight limit?

21 1600.io 5.4

If $|3x - 2| = 7$ and $|y + 4| = 1$, what is one possible value of $|xy|$?

Questions 22 and 23 refer to the following information.

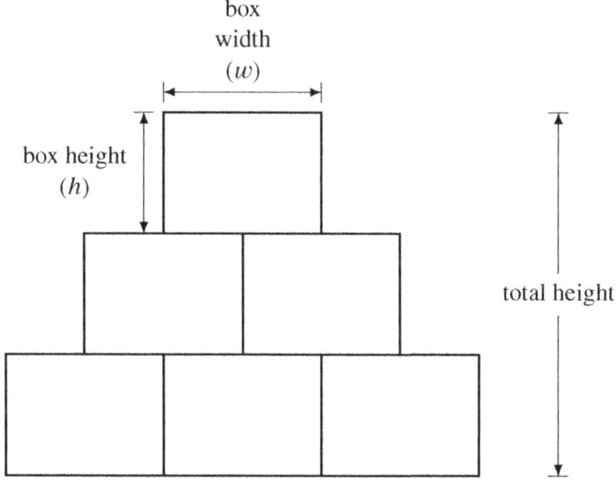

Note: Figure not drawn to scale.

In a box-stacking competition, legal box pyramids must conform to the box pyramid formula $3h + w = 35$, where h is the height of each box, in inches, and w is the width of each box, in inches. The dimensions of every box in the pyramid are the same.

The height of each level in the pyramid is equal to the height of the boxes in the pyramid. For example, there are 3 levels in the figure above, each with a height of h. The total height of the box pyramid is the sum of each level's height as shown in the figure.

22 5.2

Some competitions require that the width of the boxes used to stack must be no more than 14 inches, and the height of the boxes used to stack must be no more than 10 inches. According to the box pyramid formula, which of the following inequalities represents the set of all possible values for the box height that meets this requirement?

A) $h \leq 10$

B) $0 \leq h \leq 10$

C) $7 \leq h \leq 10$

D) $10 \leq h \leq 21$

23 5.2

A box pyramid stacker wants to use the box pyramid formula to design a pyramid with a total height of 11 feet, a box height between 8 and 9 inches, and an even number of levels. With the stacker's constraints, which of the following must be the box width, in inches, of the boxes in the pyramid?

A) 8.25

B) 8.6

C) 10.25

D) 16

24 5.1

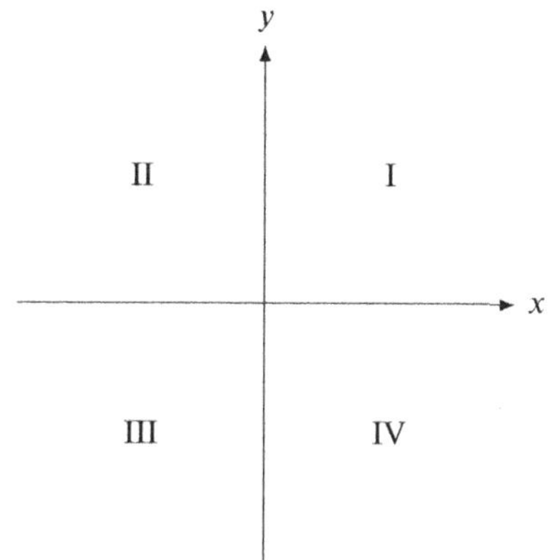

If the system of inequalities $y \leq -3x + 1$ and $y < \frac{1}{4}x + 2$ is graphed in the xy-plane above, which quadrant contains no solutions to the system?

A) Quadrant I

B) Quadrant II

C) Quadrant IV

D) There are solutions in all four quadrants.

Answer Key

SkillDrill 5.1-1

1. $2b + 3f < 56$
2. $h + 3c \geq 60$
3. $x \geq 2y + 3$
4. $3n - 5 \leq 35$
5. $8s + 20b < 112$

SkillDrill 5.1-2

1. $x \leq 2$, $x_{max} = 2$
2. $x \geq 8$, $x_{min} = 8$
3. $x < \frac{20}{7}$, $x_{max} = 2$
4. $x > 2$, $x_{min} = 3$
5. $x \geq \frac{2}{5}$, $x_{min} = 1$
6. $x \leq -10$, $x_{max} = -10$
7. $x > 0$, $x_{min} = 1$
8. $x < 6$, $x_{max} = 5$

SkillDrill 5.1-3

1. Point I only
2. Points I, II, and III
3. None
4. Points II and III

Section 5.1 Practice Problems

1. B
2. C
3. B
4. D

SkillDrill 5.2-1

1. $0 < x < \frac{8}{5}$
2. $\frac{-3}{4} < x < 3$
3. $-1 < x < \frac{-1}{7}$
4. $-2 < x < \frac{7}{2}$

Section 5.2 Practice Problems

1. $5 \leq h \leq 6$
2. A

SkillDrill 5.3-1

1. Points I and II
2. Point III only
3. None
4. Points I and II

Section 5.3 Practice Problems

1. D
2. D
3. D

SkillDrill 5.4-1

1. $x = -7$, $x = 3$
2. $x = \frac{-3}{2}$, $x = 2$
3. $x = -6$, $x = 11$
4. $x = 1$

SkillDrill 5.4-2

1. $-7 < x < 3$
2. $x \leq \frac{-3}{2}$ or $x \geq 2$
3. $-6 \leq x \leq 11$
4. $x < 1$ or $x > 1$ which means $x \neq 1$

Section 5.4 Practice Problems

1. D
2. 11
3. A

Additional Problems

1. C
2. 5
3. C
4. C
5. 4
6. 900
7. B
8. A
9. A
10. D
11. 5
12. D
13. A
14. D
15. 13
16. B
17. B
18. A
19. $\frac{14}{51} < a < \frac{1}{3}$ or $.275 \leq a \leq .333$
20. 21
21. 5, $\frac{25}{3}$, 8.33, 9, or 15
22. C
23. C
24. D

Exponents and Radicals/Roots 6

6.1 What are Exponents?

Up until this point, we have dealt exclusively with linear equations, but in order to round out the skills needed to master this test, we need to go beyond just x and y, and learn how to solve equations that have x^n terms, where n is any real number acting as the power of x.

For those who are unaware, that little n above the x in the expression x^n is the **exponent** and x is the **base**. The value of such a term is a **power** of the base, and the expression x^n is read as "the n-th power of x" or "x to the n-th power" and refers to the product of multiplying the base, x, n times. The bases and exponents can be any number (including fractions, zero, and negative numbers, which we will talk more about later).

For example, the expression 3^4 is read as "the fourth power of three" or "three to the fourth power" (often shortened to "three to the fourth") and is equal to $3 \times 3 \times 3 \times 3$ (the product of multiplying the base, 3, four times) or 81, and the expression 2^5 is read as "the fifth power of two" or "two to the fifth power" ("two to the fifth") and is equal to $2 \times 2 \times 2 \times 2 \times 2$ (the product of multiplying the base, 2, five times) or 32.

If the base is raised to the second power, such as in the expression x^2, we will usually read the expression as "x squared" instead of "x to the second power" because the area of a square with side length x would be equal to x^2. Similarly, if the base is raised to the third power, such as in the expression x^3, we will usually read the expression as "x cubed" instead of "x to the third power" because the volume of a cube with side length x is equal to x^3.

Exponents

Exponential terms, or powers, are of the form a^b, where a is the base number and b is the exponent. The value of a^b is found by multiplying the base (a) by itself b times.

For example, 2^4 is equal to $2 \times 2 \times 2 \times 2$ or 16.

Take note that **any base (including a base of 0) raised to the zeroth power is equal to 1**, and **any base raised to the first power is equal to itself**.

2^0	$= 1$	3^0	$= 1$	40^0	$= 1$
2^1	$= 2$	3^1	$= 3$	40^1	$= 40$
$2^2 = 2 \times 2$	$= 4$	$3^2 = 3 \times 3$	$= 9$	$40^2 = 40 \times 40$	$= 1600$
$2^3 = 2 \times 2 \times 2 = 8$		$3^3 = 3 \times 3 \times 3 = 27$		$40^3 = 40 \times 40 \times 40 = 64{,}000$	

The base **1 raised to any power is always equal to 1**.

The base **0 raised to any *positive* power is always equal to 0**. Remember that we already established that any base (including 0) raised to the zeroth power is 1 ($0^0 = 1$). Negative powers of 0, which are discussed later in the chapter, result in undefined values.

Positive numbers raised to any power are always positive.

Negative numbers raised to even powers are positive because all negative factors will be be present in pairs (the product of two negative factors is positive). For example, $(-3)^2 = -3 \times -3 = 9$. When you are using your calculator, make sure to put the negative base in parentheses just in case; entering -3^2 may get a result of -9, which is different from entering $(-3)^2$, which will yield 9.

Negative numbers raised to odd powers are negative because there will always be one unpaired negative factor. For example, $(-3)^3 = -3 \times -3 \times -3 = -27$.

For any values of x (where x is not equal to 0, 1, or -1), we know that **if $x^a = x^b$, then $a = b$**, because x raised to one power cannot be equal to x raised to a different power.

Of course, we can add terms like 2^3 and 2^2, where the base is a number, by evaluating the two exponential terms and then summing the two numbers.

$$2^3 + 2^2$$
$$8 + 4$$
$$12$$

Note that **if the base is an unknown value such as x, we CANNOT simply combine terms with different exponents**. For example, $x^3 + x^2$ can be rewritten in various ways, but we cannot collapse these two into one term with x raised to a power, even though the base is the same in both terms.

However, **if the bases and exponents are the same, the terms can be grouped with addition**. Just as $2x + 3x = 5x$, and $2xy + 3xy = 5xy$, so too does $2x^2 + 3x^2 = 5x^2$.

SkillDrill 6.1-1

Directions: Evaluate the given exponential expression as a quantity with no exponent (an exponent of 1). For example, rewrite 2^2 as 4.

1. 3^3 **2.** 4^2 **3.** 10^0 **4.** $(-3)^4$

5. 0^{20} **6.** 1^{100} **7.** $(-5)^3$ **8.** 17^1

9. $2^2 + 2^3$ **10.** $3^3 - 4^2$ **11.** $0^0 + 0^1$ **12.** $1^3(2^5)$

Directions: Rewrite the expressions in the form a^b if possible and evaluate any numerical values. For example, rewrite $x \cdot x$ as x^2 and rewrite $2 \cdot 2 \cdot 2 \cdot x \cdot x$ as $8x^2$.

If there is more than one base involved in a multiplication, rewrite the expressions in the form $a^b \cdot c^d \cdot \ldots \cdot y^z$. For example, rewrite $x \cdot x \cdot y \cdot y$ as x^2y^2.

Combine added terms if possible. For example, you should go no further if you arrive at an expression like $x^2 + x^3$ or $x^2 + y^2$; however, you should combine terms like $2^4 + 5^2$ as 41 or $x^2 + x^2$ as $2x^2$.

13. $x \cdot x$

14. $4 \cdot 4 \cdot y \cdot y$

15. $x + x$

16. $x \cdot x \cdot x \cdot y$

17. $(a \cdot a) + (a \cdot a) + (a \cdot a)$

18. $(b \cdot b) - (b \cdot b \cdot b)$

19. $x \cdot y + y \cdot x$

20. $x \cdot x \cdot y + x \cdot y \cdot y$

21. $a \cdot a \cdot b \cdot b \cdot c \cdot c$

22. $2 \cdot x \cdot y \cdot 2 \cdot x$

23. $d \cdot x + d \cdot d \cdot d$

24. $5 \cdot x \cdot x - 3 \cdot x \cdot x$

6.2 Exponent Rules

Rule 1: To Multiply Terms with the Same Base, Add Their Exponents

When two terms with the same base are multiplied by each other, their exponents will be added together. You probably already use this rule without realizing it when you multiply terms that have an implied exponent of 1; it will not come as any surprise that $x \cdot x = x^2$, but you might not have realized that this could be written as $x^1 \cdot x^1 = x^{1+1} = x^2$. The rule is being used right there, hiding in plain sight.

Let's look at an example where the exponents are something other than 1:

$$2^3 \cdot 2^2 = 2^{3+2} = 2^5$$

To demonstrate why this is true, let's expand out both of the terms and recombine them.

$$2^3 \times 2^2$$
$$(2 \times 2 \times 2) \times (2 \times 2)$$
$$2 \times 2 \times 2 \times 2 \times 2$$
$$2^5$$

Add Exponents When Multiplying Terms with the Same Base

When two exponential terms with the same base, a, are multiplied by each other, the exponents are added to each other.

$$a^b \cdot a^c = a^{b+c}$$

For example, $3^4 \cdot 3^5 = 3^{4+5} = 3^9$. Similarly, $x^5 \cdot x^2 = x^{5+2} = x^7$.

In order for the exponents to be added, the bases MUST be the same.

As has been previously shown, $x^1 = x$. If we have an expression that requires the multiplication of terms with the same base, and one or more of those terms has a variable without an explicitly indicated exponent, it can be considered to be raised to the first power and written as such to facilitate the adding of the exponents (you probably won't do this if you are comfortable working with exponents, but we'll do it for demonstration purposes).

For example, to evaluate the expression $6x(2x^3)$, we can rewrite $6x$ as $6x^1$ in order to make it clear what the exponents will be when multiplying the two x terms. The coefficients 6 and 2 will be multiplied by each other normally, and we will use the exponent addition rule to find the product of the x terms.

$$6x(2x^3)$$
$$6x^1(2x^3)$$
$$6(2)(x^1 \cdot x^3)$$
$$12(x^{1+3})$$
$$12x^4$$

SkillDrill 6.2-1

Directions: Rewrite the expressions in the form a^b if possible and evaluate any numerical values. For example, rewrite $x^2 \cdot x^3$ as x^5 and rewrite $2^2 \cdot 2^3 \cdot x^2 \cdot x^3$ as $32x^5$.

If there is more than one base involved in a multiplication, rewrite the expression in the form $a^b \cdot c^d \cdot \ldots \cdot y^z$. For example, rewrite $x^2 \cdot x \cdot y^4 \cdot y^6$ as x^3y^{10}.

Combine added terms if possible. For example, you should go no further if you arrive at an expression like $x^2 + x^3$ or $x^2 + y^2$; however, you should combine terms like $2^4 + 5^2$ as 41 or $x^2 + x^2$ as $2x^2$.

Challenge problems are boxed.

1. $x^2 \cdot x^2$

2. $4^2 \cdot 4 \cdot y^3 \cdot y^4$

3. $x \cdot x^4 + x^2 \cdot x^3$

4. $x^2 \cdot x^5 \cdot x^7 \cdot y^5$

5. $(a^2 \cdot a^4) \cdot (a^4 \cdot a)$

6. $(b \cdot b^3) - (b^2 \cdot b \cdot b^2)$

7. $(x^2 \cdot y^5) \cdot (x^3 \cdot y^2)$

8. $2^0 \cdot 2^0$

9. $\boxed{x^3 \cdot x^5 \cdot y + x \cdot y \cdot y^4}$

10. $\boxed{2^3 \cdot a^3 \cdot a^3 \cdot 2^2 \cdot b^2 \cdot b^4 \cdot 2 \cdot c \cdot c}$

11. $\boxed{3 \cdot d^4 \cdot d^3 \cdot x \cdot x^2 + 3^2 \cdot d^2 \cdot d^5 \cdot x^2 \cdot x}$

12. $\boxed{5 \cdot x^3 \cdot x^6 - 5 \cdot x^8 \cdot x}$

Example 6.2-1

6.2

Which of the following is equivalent to $3x\left(x^2+4x\right)$?

A) $15x^2$

B) $7x^3+x^2$

C) $3x^3+4x$

D) $3x^3+12x^2$

Solution

1. Distribute $3x$ to both terms in the parentheses.

$$3x\left(x^2+4x\right)$$
$$3x\left(x^2\right)+3x(4x)$$

2. The $3x$ terms are really 3 times x^1 (the 3 is not part of the base), and by the same token, the $4x$ term can be considered to be 4 times x^1. The constants can just be multiplied by each other, but we need to make use of the exponent addition rule to combine and simplify the exponential terms.

$$3x\left(x^2\right)+3x(4x)$$
$$3x^1\left(x^2\right)+3x^1\left(4x^1\right)$$
$$3\left(x^1\cdot x^2\right)+3(4)\left(x^1\cdot x^1\right)$$
$$3x^{1+2}+12x^{1+1}$$
$$3x^3+12x^2$$

3. The answer is D.

Rule 2: To Raise an Exponential Term to Another Power, Multiply the Exponents

When an exponential term is raised to another power, the exponents are multiplied. For example, $\left(2^3\right)^2=2^{3(2)}=2^6$.

This can be demonstrated as follows:

$$\left(2^3\right)^2$$
$$(2\times2\times2)\times(2\times2\times2)$$
$$2\times2\times2\times2\times2\times2$$
$$2^6$$

If there are multiple terms to which the exponentiation applies, and the terms are all subject only to multiplication or division, every such term's exponent gets multiplied by the exponent of the whole expression; that is, the exponent is distributed through the exponents of the multiplied terms.

For example,

$$(xy)^2 = x^2y^2$$

This can be demonstrated as follows:

$$(xy)^2$$
$$(xy) \cdot (xy)$$
$$x \cdot y \cdot x \cdot y$$
$$x \cdot x \cdot y \cdot y$$
$$x^2y^2$$

As another example, if we have $\left(x^2y^4\right)^3$, we can distribute the multiplication by the whole expression's exponent of 3 to the exponent of each of the terms in the base expression because they are multiplied by each other.

$$(x^2y^4)^3$$
$$(x^2)^3(y^4)^3$$
$$x^{2(3)}y^{4(3)}$$
$$x^6y^{12}$$

On the other hand, if the expression has addition or subtraction, you CANNOT distribute the multiplication of the exponent.

For example, if we have $(x + y)^2$, we can't distribute the multiplication of the whole expression's exponent of 2 to get $x^2 + y^2$ because the terms inside the original expression are added to each other (we'll see how to evaluate $(x + y)^2$ correctly in the next chapter).

This idea is more easily demonstrated using numerical constants instead of variables. For example, we can show that $(2 + 5)^2 \neq 2^2 + 5^2$.

Add the two terms in the parentheses to see that $(2 + 5)^2$ must be equal to $(7)^2$, which is 49. However, $2^2 + 5^2 = 4 + 25$, which is 29, so the two expressions are not equal to each other.

Multiply Exponents When Raising an Exponential Term to a Power

When an exponential term a^b is raised to another power c, the exponents are multiplied.

$$\left(a^b\right)^c = a^{bc}$$

One interesting consequence of this fact is that $\left(a^b\right)^c = \left(a^c\right)^b$, because multiplication is commutative. Note that this holds true all the time when the base, a is non-negative, but may have weird consequences when $a < 0$. Most likely, you will not have to deal with any of those consequences on the test, and the rule should be good enough as presented above.

If there are multiple terms to which the exponentiation applies, and the terms are all subject only to multiplication or division, every such term's exponent gets multiplied by the exponent of the whole expression:

$$(ab)^c = a^cb^c$$

$$\left(\frac{a}{b}\right)^c = \frac{a^c}{b^c}$$

SkillDrill 6.2-2

Directions: Rewrite the expressions in the form a^b if possible and evaluate any numerical values. For example, rewrite $\left(x^2\right)^4$ as x^8 and rewrite $\left(2^2 \cdot x^3\right)^3$ as $64x^9$.

If there is more than one base involved in a multiplication, rewrite the expression in the form $a^b \cdot c^d \cdot \ldots \cdot y^z$. For example, rewrite $\left(x^2 \cdot y^4\right)^6$ as $x^{12}y^{24}$.

Combine added terms if possible, but do not expand or factor. For example, you should go no further if you arrive at an expression like $\left(x^2 + x^3\right)^2$ or $\left(x^2 + y^2\right)^3$; however, you should combine terms like $\left(2^4 + 3^2\right)^2$ as 625 or $\left(x^2 + x^2\right)^4$ as $16x^8$.

Challenge problems are boxed.

1. $\left(x^3\right)^2$ **2.** $\left(2^2 \cdot 2\right)^2$ **3.** $\left(a^2 \cdot a^4\right)^3$ **4.** $(x^2 \cdot y^5)^7$

5. $\left(2b \cdot b^3\right)^4 - (b \cdot b)^8$ **6.** $\boxed{\left(x^3 \cdot y^5\right)^2 + (x \cdot y \cdot y)^5}$ **7.** $\boxed{\left(x \cdot x^4 + x^2 \cdot x^3\right)^3}$ **8.** $\boxed{\left((x^2)^4 + (y^5)^2\right)^2}$

Example 6.2-2

2 6.2

If $\left(x^{16}\right)^a = \left(x^4\right)^4$, and $x > 1$, what is the value of a?

A) 0

B) $\frac{1}{2}$

C) 1

D) 2

Solution

1. Distribute the exponents on each side of the equation.

$$x^{16a} = x^{16}$$

2. The two exponents must be equal since x raised to one power cannot be equal to x raised to a different power (the exceptions of x being equal to -1, 0, or 1 are taken out of play due to the restriction that $x > 1$). Therefore, $16a = 16$, and dividing both sides of this equation by 16 tells us that $a = 1$.

3. The answer is C.

Rule 3: Fractional Exponents Can Be Written as Roots and Vice Versa

When a base is raised to an exponent that is a fraction, the expression can be written as a radical (or root) expression (which is denoted by the symbol $\sqrt{\ }$) and vice versa.

The square root is probably the most familiar radical. Taking the square root of a number is the same as raising the number to the $\frac{1}{2}$ power:

$$a^{\frac{1}{2}} = \sqrt{a}$$

Taking a square root is the opposite of squaring a number. For example, $\sqrt{4} = 2$ because $2^2 = 4$; notice that when squaring, the exponent is 2, and when taking a square root, the exponent is the reciprocal of 2, or $\frac{1}{2}$. While it is technically true that $(-2)^2 = 4$ as well, by convention, **any even roots of numbers are always positive only** (we will discuss this in more depth in a later chapter).

Note that this rule about even roots being positive by convention applies regardless of how the root is written; just as $\sqrt{4}$ evaluates to 2 only (not also to -2), $4^{\frac{1}{2}}$ also evaluates to 2 only, because it means exactly the same thing. This can produce puzzling outcomes; for example, if we apply the exponentiation of a term with exponents rule to simplify $\left(x^2\right)^{\frac{1}{2}}$, we would conclude that $\left(x^2\right)^{\frac{1}{2}} = x^{\frac{2}{2}} = x^1 = x$, and this seems to make sense (squaring and square-rooting appear to be reverse operations of each other), but this is not necessarily true, because the squaring operation x^2 produces the same result regardless of whether x is positive or negative. When we then apply the square root operation (raising x^2 to the $\frac{1}{2}$ power), and we end up with only the positive root by convention, that wouldn't match the original value of x if x were a negative number. For example, while $\left(2^2\right)^{\frac{1}{2}} = 2$, interestingly enough, $\left((-2)^2\right)^{\frac{1}{2}}$ also evaluates to 2, and, of course, $-2 \neq 2$. This information will not change how any problems are solved on the test, but you might spot an unexpected absolute value operation in an answer choice (which deals with this behavior for you), so students do not need to be concerned with navigating such cases. Nevertheless, it is an interesting phenomenon to be aware of.

Let's return to our discussion of roots/radicals and fractional exponents. Just as the square (second) root can be written in two ways, the cubed root of a is written as $\sqrt[3]{a}$ (notice the small 3 above the hook which differentiates it from the square root), and is the same as raising a to the $\frac{1}{3}$ power:

$$a^{\frac{1}{3}} = \sqrt[3]{a}$$

Taking a cubed root of a number is the opposite of cubing a number. For example $\sqrt[3]{8} = 2$ because $2^3 = 8$, and $\sqrt[3]{-8} = -2$ because $(-2)^3 = -8$. Again, these complementary operations are reflected in the exponents being the reciprocals of each other: cubing a number means the exponent will be 3, and taking the cube root means the exponent will be $\frac{1}{3}$.

In general, it is true that $x^{\frac{1}{c}} = \sqrt[c]{x}$.

But what happens when the numerator of the fraction is not 1? For example, the expression $a^{\frac{4}{3}}$ could be written as either $\left(a^4\right)^{\frac{1}{3}}$ or as $\left(a^{\frac{1}{3}}\right)^4$ (an infinite number of less useful representations exist also) because in both these cases the exponents would multiply to $\frac{4}{3}$. Therefore, the expression $a^{\frac{4}{3}}$ can be rewritten as either $\sqrt[3]{a^4}$ or $\left(\sqrt[3]{a}\right)^4$. Note once again that there are exceptions to this rule when $a < 0$, but the rule will hold as long as the base, a, is non-negative (you should not have to deal with any other cases, or at least not often).

Fractional Exponents & Roots/Radicals

When a positive base a is raised to an exponent that is a fraction $\frac{b}{c}$, the expression can be written as a radical (or root) expression (which is denoted by the symbol $\sqrt{\ }$) and vice versa.

$$a^{\frac{b}{c}} = \sqrt[c]{a^b} = \left(\sqrt[c]{a}\right)^b$$

In order to apply the rules for multiplying and exponentiating terms with exponents, we first have to have terms with exponents! Therefore, if you have any terms that are written in radical format, convert them to exponent form so those rules can be applied. Remember, when a radical is converted to exponent form, you'll get a fractional exponent. **Always rewrite radical expressions as fractional exponents before attempting to apply exponent rules and simplify expressions.**

For example, the expression $x\sqrt{x}$ can be simplified to just x raised to a power if we start by rewriting $\sqrt{x}$ as $x^{\frac{1}{2}}$ and we then apply the rule for adding exponents when two terms with the same base are multiplied.

$$x\sqrt{x}$$
$$x^1 \cdot x^{\frac{1}{2}}$$
$$x^{1+\frac{1}{2}}$$
$$x^{\frac{2}{2}+\frac{1}{2}}$$
$$x^{\frac{3}{2}}$$

Working in the reverse direction, if the exponent is an improper fraction (a fraction that has a larger numerator than denominator), the exponent can be split into a whole number part and the remaining proper fraction, which allows the term to be re-written as the product (multiplication) of the base with an integer exponent and a radical.

For example, if we have $x^{\frac{8}{3}}$, we can rewrite the improper fraction exponent of $\frac{8}{3}$ as the sum of a whole number and a proper fraction, $\frac{6}{3} + \frac{2}{3}$ or $2 + \frac{2}{3}$, giving us $x^{\left(2+\frac{2}{3}\right)}$. Recall that when multiplying terms with exponents, we add the exponents, and the reverse is true, too: we can convert a base with an addition expression in the exponent into a multiplication. Therefore, we can rewrite this expression as $x^2 \cdot x^{\frac{2}{3}}$. We can then convert the second term into a radical, giving us $x^2\sqrt[3]{x^2}$.

SkillDrill 6.2-3

Directions: Rewrite the radical expressions in the form a^b, where b is a fraction, if possible, and evaluate any numerical values. For example, rewrite $\sqrt[3]{x^2}$ as $x^{\frac{2}{3}}$.

Challenge problems are boxed.

1. $\sqrt{a}$ **2.** $\sqrt[3]{a^2}$ **3.** $\sqrt[3]{8h^3}$ **4.** $\sqrt[9]{x^3}$

5. $\sqrt{16x^4}$ **6.** $\sqrt[4]{a^3}$ **7.** $\boxed{\sqrt[4]{16x^3}}$ **8.** $\sqrt[5]{x^2y^{10}}$

Directions: Rewrite the following improper fractions as an integer plus a proper fraction in lowest terms. For example, rewrite $\frac{14}{4}$ as $3 + \frac{1}{2}$.

9. $\frac{4}{3}$

10. $\frac{7}{5}$

11. $\frac{5}{2}$

12. $\frac{13}{10}$

13. $\frac{9}{6}$

14. $\frac{11}{5}$

15. $\frac{10}{4}$

16. $\frac{23}{5}$

Just as exponents are applied across multiplied terms—for example, $(xy)^n = x^n y^n$—so too are radicals (which are just an alternative representation of exponents). For example, the expression $\sqrt{4x}$ can be split into $\sqrt{4}\sqrt{x}$ and then rewritten as $2\sqrt{x}$.

Sometimes, you'll encounter a base in a square root and the base won't be a perfect square (that is, the square root of the base isn't an integer), so you can't just evaluate the term and get a nice round number. In order to match the formats of given answer choices, you may need to split the number into factors (looking for perfect square factors like 4, 9, 25, etc.) which will allow you to rewrite the expression to make it more useful.

For example, 24 is not a perfect square (there is no integer which, when squared, equals 24), so we can't evaluate $\sqrt{24}$ and end up with a nice integer result. However, there might be a factor of 24 that *is* a perfect square, and we could therefore pull that factor out of the radical by taking its convenient, integer square root in order to make the expression more useful. Indeed, by examining the factors of 24 (which are 2, 3, 4, 6, 8, and 12), we notice that 4 *is* a perfect square (4 is equal to 2^2). If we factor 24 into 4(6), we can exfiltrate (as they say in the CIA) the 4 from within the radical.

The square root is distributed to both factors; remember that radicals and exponents are just two different ways of writing the same thing so the same rules apply regardless of which notation is used. Therefore, the radical can distribute to both the 4 and the 6 because they are multiplied by each other.

$$\sqrt{24} = \sqrt{4(6)} = \sqrt{4}\sqrt{6} = 2\sqrt{6}$$

Note that this is exactly equivalent to distributing a fractional exponent; it's just another way of writing the terms.

$$[4(6)]^{\frac{1}{2}} = 4^{\frac{1}{2}}6^{\frac{1}{2}} = 2 \cdot 6^{\frac{1}{2}}$$

This is true for other roots as well, not just for square roots. For example, if we have $\sqrt[3]{16}$, we can't evaluate it, because 16 isn't a perfect cube (there's no integer which, when cubed, equals 16). However, there might be a factor of 16 that *is* a perfect cube, and we could therefore pull that factor out of the radical in order to make the expression more useful. Indeed, by examining the factors of 16 (which are 2, 4, and 8), we notice that 8 *is* a perfect cube (it's 2 cubed), so if we factor 16 into 8(2), we can exfiltrate 8 from within the radical

$$\sqrt[3]{16} = \sqrt[3]{8(2)} = \sqrt[3]{8}\sqrt[3]{2} = 2\sqrt[3]{2}$$

Again, because radicals and exponents are just two ways of writing the exact same thing, the above is completely equivalent to the following:

$$16^{\frac{1}{3}} = [8(2)]^{\frac{1}{3}} = 8^{\frac{1}{3}} \cdot 2^{\frac{1}{3}} = 2 \cdot 2^{\frac{1}{3}}$$

Be aware that **it does you no good to rewrite the base as an expression involving addition or subtraction**, because the radical—which, you'll recall, is just another way to write an exponent—**CANNOT** be distributed to added terms. For example, $\sqrt{10}$ should NOT be rewritten as $\sqrt{4+6}$ because the radical cannot be distributed to added terms; that is, $\sqrt{4+6} \neq \sqrt{4} + \sqrt{6}$.

Splitting Radical Expressions

Radicals are another way to represent fractional exponents, so radicals can be distributed across terms that are multiplied.

When taking a square root of a number that is not a perfect square, look for any factors of the number that are perfect squares and rewrite the number as the perfect square factor times another number so that the square root can be distributed to both factors. For example, $\sqrt{18} = \sqrt{9(2)} = \sqrt{9}\sqrt{2} = 3\sqrt{2}$

When taking a cube root of a number that is not a perfect cube, look for any factors of the number that are perfect cubes and rewrite the number as the perfect cube factor times another number so that the cube root can be distributed to both factors. For example, $\sqrt[3]{54} = \sqrt[3]{27(2)} = \sqrt[3]{27}\sqrt[3]{2} = 3\sqrt[3]{2}$

SkillDrill 6.2-4

Directions: Factor the following integers into a perfect square and another number. For example, rewrite 27 as $9 \cdot 3$, where 9 is the perfect square and 3 is the other number.

Some items have multiple answers; see if you can find them all.

1. 24 **2.** 12 **3.** 45 **4.** 50

5. 32 **6.** 98 **7.** 72 **8.** 48

Directions: Factor the following integers into a perfect cube and another number. For example, rewrite 24 as $8 \cdot 3$, where 8 is the perfect cube and 3 is the other number. (The most likely perfect cubes that you will encounter are $8 = 2^3$ and $27 = 3^3$, but possibly $64 = 4^3$ and $125 = 5^3$).

9. 32 **10.** 80 **11.** 54 **12.** 250

Directions: Simplify the square root expression by splitting the radical into the square root of a perfect square times the square root of another number. For example, rewrite $\sqrt{27}$ as $\sqrt{9}\sqrt{3}$, where 9 is the perfect square and 3 is the other number, and then simplify to $3\sqrt{3}$ as your answer. If the other number can also be split and simplified, then continue the process until the number in the radical sign has no more perfect square factors.

13. $\sqrt{24}$ **14.** $\sqrt{12}$ **15.** $\sqrt{45}$ **16.** $\sqrt{50}$

17. $\sqrt{32}$ **18.** $\sqrt{98}$ **19.** $\sqrt{72}$ **20.** $\sqrt{48}$

Directions: Rewrite the exponential expressions in the form $a^b\sqrt[c]{a^d}$, where b, c, and d are whole numbers, and evaluate any numerical values. If the numerator of a fractional exponent is larger than its denominator (an "improper" fraction), break the fraction into a whole number and a proper fraction in lowest terms, then split off and convert the proper fraction portion of the exponent into a radical expression. For example, rewrite $\left(x^5\right)^{\frac{1}{2}}$ as $x^2\sqrt{x}$

$$\left(x^5\right)^{\frac{1}{2}} \Rightarrow x^{\frac{5}{2}} \Rightarrow x^{2+\frac{1}{2}} \Rightarrow x^2\left(x^{\frac{1}{2}}\right) \Rightarrow x^2\sqrt{x}$$

and rewrite $\left(32x^4\right)^{\frac{1}{3}}$ as $2x\sqrt[3]{4x}$.

$$\left(32x^4\right)^{\frac{1}{3}} \Rightarrow 32^{\frac{1}{3}}x^{\frac{4}{3}} \Rightarrow [8(4)]^{\frac{1}{3}}x^{1+\frac{1}{3}} \Rightarrow 8^{\frac{1}{3}}4^{\frac{1}{3}}x\left(x^{\frac{1}{3}}\right) \Rightarrow 2x\sqrt[3]{4x}$$

21. $x^{\frac{1}{2}}$

22. $y^{\frac{2}{3}}$

23. $a^{\frac{3}{2}}$

24. $b^{\frac{11}{3}}$

25. $x^{\frac{4}{3}}$

26. $a^{\frac{7}{2}}$

27. $\left(27x^5\right)^{\frac{1}{2}}$

28. $\left(16b^8\right)^{\frac{1}{3}}$

Example 6.2-3

3 1600.io 6.2

$$\sqrt{16x^4}$$

If $x > 0$, which of the following is equivalent to the given expression?

A) $4x$

B) $4x^2$

C) $16x$

D) $16x^2$

Solution

1. The first step when we see a term composed of both constants and variables in a radical (or, equivalently, such a term being exponentiated) is usually to separate the constant part and the variable part so that we can attempt to evaluate or simplify each of those parts individually. When we do this, we take advantage of the principle that when terms are multiplied and then raised to a power, the result is equivalent to first raising each term to that power, and then multiplying those results (this is because exponentiation is a form of multiplication, and multiplications can be done in any order because multiplication is commutative, but you knew that). Here, we'll split the constant, 16, and the variable, x^4, into separate radicals that are then multiplied. Conveniently, 16 is a perfect square, so once $\sqrt{16}$ is split off, we can evaluate it and replace it with 4.

   Split the radical expression into two parts, one with the constant, 16, in a radical sign, and one with x^4 in a second radical sign. Evaluate the radical containing the constant (the square root of 16 is 4).

$$\sqrt{16x^4}$$

$$\sqrt{16}\sqrt{x^4}$$

$$4\sqrt{x^4}$$

2. Rewrite the radical expression as an exponential expression with a fractional exponent. Remember, the square root is just the second root, so taking a square root of an expression is the same as raising the expression to the $\frac{1}{2}$ power.

$$4\sqrt{x^4}$$

$$4\left(x^4\right)^{\frac{1}{2}}$$

$$4x^{4\left(\frac{1}{2}\right)}$$

$$4x^{\frac{4}{2}}$$

$$4x^2$$

3. The answer is B.

Notes

Sometimes, you can simplify the radical with the variable without having to convert it to an exponential term, as when it's simple and obvious. For example, we wouldn't normally rewrite $\sqrt{x^2}$ as $\left(x^2\right)^{\frac{1}{2}}$, because we can recognize that the square root of x^2 is equal to x (or $|x|$ if the test makers don't include the caveat that $x > 0$); similarly, though it's not quite as obvious, you might recognize that here, $\sqrt{x^4}$ is equal to x^2, but it's still important to be adept at using the more generalized procedure shown above.

Rule 4: To Divide Terms with the Same Base, Subtract the Denominator's Exponent From the Numerator's

When a term is divided by another term with the same base, subtract the exponent of the term in the denominator from the exponent of the term in the numerator.

For example, $\frac{3^4}{3^3} = 3^{4-3} = 3^1 = 3$, which can be demonstrated by expanding the numerator and denominator.

$$\frac{3^4}{3^3} = \frac{3 \times 3 \times 3 \times 3}{3 \times 3 \times 3} = \frac{3 \times \cancel{3} \times \cancel{3} \times \cancel{3}}{\cancel{3} \times \cancel{3} \times \cancel{3}} = 3$$

Similarly, $\frac{x^5}{x^2} = x^{5-2} = x^3$.

In order for the exponents to be subtracted, the bases MUST be the same, just as when multiplying numbers with exponents by adding their exponents.

Subtract Exponents When Dividing Terms with the Same Base

When two exponential terms with the same base, a, are divided by each other, the exponent of the term in the denominator is subtracted from the exponent of the term in the numerator.

$$\frac{a^b}{a^c} = a^{b-c}$$

SkillDrill 6.2-5

Directions: Rewrite the expressions in the form a^b, where b can be any fraction or whole number, and evaluate any numerical values. For example, rewrite $\frac{x^3}{x^2}$ as x and rewrite $\frac{32x^6}{4\sqrt{x}}$ as $8x^{\frac{11}{2}}$. Do not convert fractional exponents back into radical expressions.

Challenge problems are boxed.

1. $\frac{x^5}{x^3}$

2. $\frac{y^7}{y^2}$

3. $\frac{32a^3b^4}{8ab}$

4. $\frac{a^3a^7}{a^2}$

5. $\frac{3x^2}{\sqrt{3x}}$

6. $\frac{\sqrt{y}}{\sqrt[4]{y}}$

7. $\boxed{\frac{\sqrt[3]{a^2b^3}}{\sqrt{ab}}}$

8. $\boxed{\frac{x^4\sqrt{y}}{x\sqrt[5]{y^2}}}$

Example 6.2-4

4 6.2

If $\dfrac{\sqrt[3]{x^2}}{\sqrt[8]{x^5}} = x^{\frac{a}{b}}$ for all positive values of x, what is the value of $\dfrac{a}{b}$?

Solution

1. Rewrite both radical terms as exponential terms on the left side of the equation.

$$\frac{\sqrt[3]{x^2}}{\sqrt[8]{x^5}} = x^{\frac{a}{b}}$$

$$\frac{x^{\frac{2}{3}}}{x^{\frac{5}{8}}} = x^{\frac{a}{b}}$$

2. Since two terms with the same base are being divided, the terms can be combined by subtracting the exponents. Rewrite the fractions in terms of a common denominator in order to carry out the subtraction.

$$\frac{x^{\frac{2}{3}}}{x^{\frac{5}{8}}} = x^{\frac{a}{b}}$$

$$x^{\frac{2}{3}-\frac{5}{8}} = x^{\frac{a}{b}}$$

$$x^{\frac{16}{24}-\frac{15}{24}} = x^{\frac{a}{b}}$$

$$x^{\frac{1}{24}} = x^{\frac{a}{b}}$$

3. Excepting the bases -1, 0, and 1, a base raised to one power cannot be equal to the same base raised to a different power, and here, the base, x, can be any positive number, so therefore the exponents must be equal.

$$\frac{1}{24} = \frac{a}{b}$$

4. The answer is $\frac{1}{24}$.

The subtraction of the exponents leads us to the idea of negative exponents and what it means for a number to be raised to a negative power.

You might wonder what a negative exponent even means; 3^2 makes sense, because it's just $3 \cdot 3$; similarly, 3^3 is $3 \cdot 3 \cdot 3$; and so on. We just multiply base by itself the number of times indicated by the exponent. What, then, does 3^{-2} mean? How do we multiply something a negative number of times?

Let's look at what's happening when we start with an exponent of 0 and then incrementally increase that exponent:

$$3^0 = 1$$

To increase the exponent by 1 on the left side of the equation, we multiply both sides by 3:

$$3^1 = 1 \cdot 3$$

To increase it again, we again multiply by 3:

$$3^2 = 3 \cdot 3$$

So far, so good. Now, let's reverse course and decrease the exponent by one. To do that, we need to undo the previous operation, so we must perform the reverse operation of multiplication, which, of course, is division:

$$3^1 = \frac{3 \cdot 3}{3} = \frac{3}{1} = 3$$

Let's decrease the exponent again, which means dividing by 3 again:

$$3^0 = \frac{3}{3} = 1$$

Things are about to get interesting, because our exponent is going to become negative. Let's repeat the same division operation as we once again decrement the exponent:

$$3^{-1} = \frac{1}{3}$$

Let's do it one more time just for clarity:

$$3^{-2} = \frac{\frac{1}{3}}{3} = \frac{1}{3 \cdot 3} = \frac{1}{3^2}$$

Negative Exponents

When a base a is raised to a negative exponent $-b$, the expression is equal to its reciprocal with a positive exponent.

$$a^{-b} = \frac{1}{a^b}$$

For example, if $a = 3$ and $b = 2$, then $a^{-b} = 3^{-2} = \frac{1}{3^2} = \frac{1}{9}$.

By the same token, we can observe that the same principle applies when the term with the negative exponent is in the denominator (this is just another arrangement of the equation above):

$$\frac{1}{a^{-b}} = a^b$$

As you can see, the general principle is very simple—we can create an equivalent term by taking the reciprocal and negating the sign of the exponent.

Importantly, when performing these transformations, you only take the reciprocal of the exponentiated variable or constant, but not of any coefficient. So, this is correct:

$$3x^{-4} = \frac{3}{x^4}$$

but this is not:

$$3x^{-4} \neq \frac{1}{3x^4}$$

This applies regardless of whether the exponentiated term starts out in the numerator or the denominator, so this is correct:

$$\frac{1}{7r^{-3}} = \frac{r^3}{7}$$

but not this:

$$\frac{1}{7r^{-3}} \neq \frac{7r^3}{1}$$

Generally speaking, this principle that converts a negative exponent into a positive one is useful anytime you have a term with a negative exponent, because converting that term into one with a positive exponent facilitates evaluating it. Here are a few examples:

$$5^{-2} = \frac{1}{5^2} = \frac{1}{25} \qquad 16 \cdot 2^{-3} = \frac{16}{2^3} = \frac{16}{8} = 2 \qquad \frac{1}{4^{-3}} = 4^3 = 64 \qquad \frac{1}{9 \cdot 3^{-4}} = \frac{3^4}{9} = \frac{81}{9} = 9$$

SkillDrill 6.2-6

Directions: Rewrite any terms with negative exponents as terms with positive exponents. Continue on from there to rewrite the expressions in the form $\frac{a^b}{c^d}$, where b and d can be any fractions or whole numbers, based on any of the established exponent rules. Do not convert fractional exponents back into radical expressions, and express any fractions in lowest terms.

Challenge problems are boxed.

1. x^{-2}

2. $\frac{1}{y^{-3}}$

3. $\frac{4x^{-2}}{12y^{-3}}$

4. $\frac{r^{-3}}{r^4}$

5. $\frac{x^2}{x^{\frac{-1}{2}}}$

6. $\boxed{\frac{x^{-7}y^{\frac{-2}{5}}}{x^3y^{\frac{-1}{5}}}}$

7. $\boxed{\frac{a^{-4}b^{\frac{3}{4}}}{a^{-1}b^{\frac{-1}{4}}}}$

8. $\boxed{3x^{-6}\sqrt[3]{27y^{-4}}}$

"Equivalent to" problems are challenging, because there are many possible equivalent expressions, but only one is present in the answer choices. So, one should examine the answer choices to ascertain what commonality they have in order to know in which direction to set out. Start by reviewing the answer choices to determine what attributes they share, so you'll know at least what *not* to have in any answer candidate. In the following example, we see that there are no negative exponents in the answer choices, so we should set out to eliminate those. Then, note that radical notation is used for fractional exponents, so be sure to match that as well.

Example 6.2-5

5 1600.io 6.2

The expression $\dfrac{x^{-1}y^{\frac{1}{3}}}{x^{\frac{1}{3}}y^{-1}}$, where $x > 1$ and $y > 1$, is equivalent to which of the following?

A) $\dfrac{\sqrt[3]{y}}{\sqrt[3]{x}}$

B) $\dfrac{y\sqrt[3]{y}}{\sqrt[3]{x^2}}$

C) $\dfrac{y\sqrt[3]{y}}{x\sqrt[3]{x}}$

D) $\dfrac{\sqrt[4]{y^3}}{x^3}$

Solution

1. Since none of the answer choices contain negative exponents and they all make use of radical notation for fractional exponents, we should look to eliminate negative and fractional exponents by rewriting them.
2. Begin by using the negative exponent rule to move x^{-1} to the denominator as x^1 and y^{-1} to the numerator as y^1.

$$\frac{x^{-1}y^{\frac{1}{3}}}{x^{\frac{1}{3}}y^{-1}} = \frac{y^1y^{\frac{1}{3}}}{x^1x^{\frac{1}{3}}}$$

3. Rewrite the terms wth fractional exponents as radical expressions.

$$\frac{y^1y^{\frac{1}{3}}}{x^1x^{\frac{1}{3}}} = \frac{y\sqrt[3]{y}}{x\sqrt[3]{x}}$$

4. The answer is C.

Section 6.2 Suggested Problems from Real Tests

- Test 3 NC-5
- Test 7 NC-11
- Test 10 NC-5
- Test 10 C-6
- Apr 2017 NC-12
- May 2017 NC-14
- May 2019 (US) C-8
- May 2019 (Int) NC-20

View related real-test problems at 1600.io/p/smtex?topic=6.2

6.3 Methods of Solving Exponent Equations

Throughout the chapter we have seen exponent equations where both sides boiled down to the same base being raised to a power, so we knew that the two exponents must be equal. However, there are sometimes equations which do not fit that pattern: the bases of the exponential terms may not always be the same,

Raising Both Sides to a Power

When solving equations with exponential terms, we can apply exponent rules in order to isolate a variable term that has the correct exponent, usually done by raising both sides of the equation to a power that will transform (through multiplication) the exponent on the variable so that it matches the exponent we want.

Let's take a look at a simple example. If we know that $x = 4$, then we can find the value of x^2 by squaring both sides of the equation.

$$x = 4$$
$$x^2 = 4^2$$
$$x^2 = 16$$

By the same principle, if we are told $x^3 = 27$, then we can find the value of x (which can also be represented as x^1) by raising both sides of the equation to the one-third power, which would cause the exponents on the left side of the equation to multiply to 1.

$$x^3 = 27$$
$$\left(x^3\right)^{\frac{1}{3}} = 27^{\frac{1}{3}}$$
$$x^{3\left(\frac{1}{3}\right)} = 27^{\frac{1}{3}}$$
$$x^1 = 3$$
$$x = 3$$

In the following example, we will work through the problem in two ways, one more direct than the other.

Example 6.3-1

1 6.3

For a positive real number x, where $x^5 = 2$, what is the value of x^{25} ?

A) $\sqrt[5]{25}$

B) 5

C) 16

D) 32

Solution 1

1. We need to find a way to transform x^5 into x^{25} by applying some exponent rule to both sides of the given equation. We should raise both sides of the equation to the fifth power because, based on exponent rules, raising x^5 to the fifth power will cause the exponents to multiply on the left side of the equation, producing the desired term x^{25} on the left side of the equation.

$$x^5 = 2$$
$$\left(x^5\right)^5 = 2^5$$
$$x^{5(5)} = 32$$
$$x^{25} = 32$$

2. The answer is D.

Solution 2

1. In this approach, we'll first solve for x, and then we'll raise both sides of the equation to the 25th power. This is a longer procedure than the one shown above, but some students might be more comfortable with this method.

   We can isolate the term x or x^1 on the left side of the equation if we raise both sides of the equation to the one-fifth power.

$$x^5 = 2$$
$$\left(x^5\right)^{\frac{1}{5}} = 2^{\frac{1}{5}}$$
$$x^{5\left(\frac{1}{5}\right)} = 2^{\frac{1}{5}}$$
$$x = 2^{\frac{1}{5}}$$

2. Now that we know the value of x, we can raise it to the twenty-fifth power to find the value of x^{25}.

$$x = 2^{\frac{1}{5}}$$
$$x^{25} = \left(2^{\frac{1}{5}}\right)^{25}$$
$$x^{25} = 2^{\frac{1}{5}(25)}$$
$$x^{25} = 2^5$$
$$x^{25} = 32$$

3. The answer is D.

Notes

You might have wondered if we could have multiplied both sides of the equation by x^{20} to apply the exponent addition rule, but though this would be a mathematically valid operation, it would not be helpful to do so because even if we were to transform the exponent on one side of the equation, we would fail to isolate the term we are looking for because we would also produce an x^{20} term on the other side of the equation.

$$x^5 = 2$$
$$x^5 \cdot x^{20} = 2x^{20}$$
$$x^{5+20} = 2x^{20}$$
$$x^{25} = 2x^{20}$$

This is mathematically valid, but it does not get us any closer to solving the problem.

Rewriting Exponential Terms In Terms of Another Base

In order to apply exponent rules to combine terms, the terms must all have the same base, so sometimes it is useful to rewrite numbers in terms of their factors, specifically those which may be roots of the number. For example, the number 16 has the factors 2, 4, and 8, and both 2 and 4 are roots of 16 because $2^4 = 16$ and $4^2 = 16$.

We can take advantage of the fact that $\left(a^b\right)^c = a^{bc}$ (and remember that the rules can be applied in both directions in order to write exponential terms in the way that is most useful for the situation at hand) in order to rewrite an exponential term with a different base that allows us to either match answer choices or make equations easier to solve.

It could be advantageous to write relatively large bases in terms of smaller bases in order to rewrite exponential terms with fractional exponents (without using a calculator) in order to match answer choices. For example, if we wanted to simplify the term $9^{\frac{3}{4}}$, we could rewrite the 9 as 3^2, allowing us to break the exponent up and rewrite $9^{\frac{3}{4}}$ as a radical expression with a base of 3.

	$9^{\frac{3}{4}}$
Replace 9 with 3^2:	$\left(3^2\right)^{\frac{3}{4}}$
Apply exponentiation of exponent rule by multiplying exponents:	$3^{2\left(\frac{3}{4}\right)}$
	$3^{\frac{6}{4}}$
Reduce fraction in exponent:	$3^{\frac{3}{2}}$
Split improper fraction into integer and proper fraction:	$3^{\left(\frac{2}{2}+\frac{1}{2}\right)}$
	$3^{\left(1+\frac{1}{2}\right)}$
Apply (in reverse) multiplication of terms with exponents rule:	$3 \cdot 3^{\frac{1}{2}}$
Convert fractional exponent part to radical notation:	$3\sqrt{3}$

It is also advantageous to write terms in the another base whenever you have two different base numbers that share a common factor. For example, we can combine the terms in the expression below if we rewrite 27 as a base of 3 raised to the third power, allowing us to apply exponent rules to combine the terms (particularly if the problem asks us to find the value of $3x + 4y$, which will be the exponent when the terms are combined).

$$27^x \cdot 3^{4y} = 3^5$$
$$\left(3^3\right)^x \cdot 3^{4y} = 3^5$$
$$3^{3x} \cdot 3^{4y} = 3^5$$
$$3^{3x+4y} = 3^5$$

Changing the base was useful in this example because it allowed us to write both sides of the equation as 3 raised to a power, which allows us to very easily see that $3x + 4y$ must be equal to 5 (since 3 to one power can't be equal to 3 to a different power).

Example 6.3-2

2 1600.io 6.3

If $4x - y = 8$, what is the value of $\frac{16^x}{2^y}$?

A) 2^8

B) 8^2

C) 4^2

D) The value cannot be determined from the information given.

Solution

1. The first equation might not seem useful at first, but when you are given information like this at the beginning of the problem, it will be useful later. The expression $4x - y$ should appear at some point in the course of solving the problem, so keep an eye out for it.

2. The expression $\frac{16^x}{2^y}$ has to be rewritten to be useful: the two bases are not equal, so we cannot simplify unless we have the numerator and denominator both in the same base.

3. Since $16 = 2^4$, we can replace the 16 with 2^4. This way, the bases of the numerator and denominator will both be 2.
$$\frac{16^x}{2^y} = \frac{\left(2^4\right)^x}{2^y} = \frac{2^{4x}}{2^y}$$

4. Now that the numerator and denominator are written in terms of the same base, we can subtract the exponents in order to simplify.
$$\frac{2^{4x}}{2^y} = 2^{4x-y}$$

5. The first given equation tells us that $4x - y = 8$, so substitute 8 in for $4x - y$ to find the value of the expression.
$$2^{4x-y} = 2^8$$

6. The answer is A.

View related real-test problems at 1600.io/p/smtex?topic=6.3

6.4 Table of Exponent Rules

<table>
<tr><th>Rule</th><th>Example</th><th>Demonstration</th></tr>
<tr><td>$a^b \cdot a^c = a^{b+c}$</td><td>$3^2 \cdot 3^4 = 3^6$</td><td>$3^2 \cdot 3^4$
$(3 \times 3) \times (3 \times 3 \times 3 \times 3)$
$3 \times 3 \times 3 \times 3 \times 3 \times 3 = 3^6$</td></tr>
<tr><td>$\left(a^b\right)^c = a^{bc}$</td><td>$\left(4^2\right)^3 = 4^6$</td><td>$\left(4^2\right)^3$
$(4 \times 4)^3$
$(4 \times 4) \times (4 \times 4) \times (4 \times 4)$
$4 \times 4 \times 4 \times 4 \times 4 \times 4 = 4^6$</td></tr>
<tr><td colspan="3">Powers ARE distributed across multiplied or divided factors. ✓ $(ab)^c = a^c b^c$ ✓ $\left(\frac{a}{b}\right)^c = \frac{a^c}{b^c}$</td></tr>
<tr><td>$(ab)^c = a^c b^c$</td><td>$(2 \cdot 3)^3 = 2^3 \cdot 3^3$</td><td>$(2 \cdot 3)^3$
$(2 \cdot 3) \times (2 \cdot 3) \times (2 \cdot 3)$
$2 \times 3 \times 2 \times 3 \times 2 \times 3$
$2 \times 2 \times 2 \times 3 \times 3 \times 3 = 2^3 \cdot 3^3$</td></tr>
<tr><td colspan="3">Powers are NOT distributed to added or subtracted terms: ✗ $(a+b)^2 \neq a^2 + b^2$ ✓ $(a+b)^2 = (a+b)(a+b)$

Carrying out the multiplication of expressions like this is discussed in the next chapter.</td></tr>
<tr><td>$(a+b)^c \neq a^c + b^c$</td><td>$(2+3)^3 \neq 2^3 + 3^3$</td><td>$(2+3)^3 \neq 2^3 + 3^3$
$(5)^3 \neq 8 + 27$
$125 \neq 35$</td></tr>
<tr><td>$\sqrt[c]{a^b} = a^{\frac{b}{c}}$</td><td>$\sqrt[3]{8^4} = 8^{\frac{4}{3}}$</td><td></td></tr>
<tr><td>$\frac{a^b}{a^c} = a^{b-c}$</td><td>$\frac{4^5}{4^3} = 4^2$</td><td>$\frac{4^5}{4^3} = \frac{4 \times 4 \times \cancel{4} \times \cancel{4} \times \cancel{4}}{\cancel{4} \times \cancel{4} \times \cancel{4}} = \frac{4 \times 4}{1} = 4^2$</td></tr>
<tr><td>$a^{-b} = \frac{1}{a^b}$</td><td>$2^{-2} = \frac{1}{2^2}$</td><td></td></tr>
<tr><td>$\frac{1}{a^{-b}} = a^b$</td><td>$\frac{1}{2^{-2}} = 2^2$</td><td></td></tr>
</table>

CHAPTER 6 RECAP

- Exponential terms consist of a base a and exponent b and are in the form a^b.
- Exponents tell you how many factors of the base should be multiplied by each other. For example, $2^5 = 2\times2\times2\times2\times2$ (there are 5 factors of 2 multiplied by each other).
- $a^b a^c = a^{b+c}$
- $\left(a^b\right)^c = a^{bc}$
- $(ab)^c = a^c b^c$ BUT WATCH OUT FOR THIS MISTAKE: $(a+b)^c \neq a^c + b^c$
- $a^{\frac{b}{c}} = \sqrt[c]{a^b} = \left(\sqrt[c]{a}\right)^b$ Note that the rule will hold as long as the base, a, is non-negative.
- Rewrite radical expressions as terms with fractional exponents.
- Look for perfect square or perfect cube factors when taking square roots or cube roots of numbers, respectively.
- You can solve exponential equations by raising both sides to a power such that the exponents of the variable term will multiply to the correct power (the power you are looking for) on one side of the equation.
- $\dfrac{a^b}{a^c} = a^{b-c}$
- $a^{-b} = \dfrac{1}{a^b}$ and $\dfrac{1}{a^{-b}} = a^b$
- Rewrite expressions in terms of the same base if possible so that you can use the preceding rules to simplify. For example, if you are asked for the value of $\dfrac{25^3}{5^2}$, the simplest way to evaluate the expression (without a calculator) would be to rewrite 25 as 5^2 and progress from there, applying exponent rules to arrive at an easily calculable value.

$$\frac{25^3}{5^2} \Rightarrow \frac{\left(5^2\right)^3}{5^2} \Rightarrow \frac{5^6}{5^2} \Rightarrow 5^{6-2} \Rightarrow 5^4 \Rightarrow 625$$

Note that "simplifying" is an inexact term because any exponential term can be written in an infinite number of ways. For example, 2^5 could be written as any of the following:

$$2^2 \cdot 2^3 \qquad 2^{29} \cdot 2^{-24} \qquad \left(2^{30}\right)^{\frac{1}{6}} \qquad \frac{1}{2^{-5}} \qquad \text{etc...}$$

Simplifying exponential terms, as we use it, refers to rewriting the expressions in a way that is useful in solving any particular problem on the test. Take the questions on a case by case basis. As long as you have a good understanding of the rules, anything is possible, but some options will be clearly more advantageous.

Additional Problems

1 6.2

$$\sqrt[3]{8x^9}$$

If $x > 0$, which of the following is equivalent to the given expression?

A) $\frac{8}{3}x^3$

B) $2x^2$

C) $2x^3$

D) $8x^3$

2 6.3

Which of the following is equivalent to $8^{\frac{5}{6}}$?

A) $\sqrt{2}$

B) $\sqrt[5]{8}$

C) $4\sqrt{2}$

D) $5\sqrt{2}$

3 6.2

Which of the following is equal to $a^{\frac{3}{4}}$, for all values of a ?

A) $\sqrt[4]{a^3}$

B) $\sqrt[4]{a^{\frac{1}{3}}}$

C) $\sqrt[3]{a^4}$

D) $\sqrt[3]{a^{\frac{1}{4}}}$

4 6.2

Which of the following is equivalent to $r^{\frac{3}{4}} \cdot \sqrt[3]{r}$, where $r > 0$?

A) $r^{\frac{1}{4}}$

B) $r^{\frac{1}{3}}$

C) $r^{\frac{4}{7}}$

D) $r^{\frac{13}{12}}$

5 6.2

Which of the following is an equivalent form of $\sqrt[4]{f^{8a}k}$, where $f > 0$ and $k > 0$?

A) $f^{4a}k^{-3}$

B) $f^{2a}k^{\frac{1}{4}}$

C) $f^{\frac{1}{2a}}k^{-3}$

D) $f^{\frac{1}{4a}}k^4$

6 6.2

Which of the following expressions is equivalent to $5a^4(a+2)$?

A) $7a^5$

B) $15a^5$

C) $5a^5 + 2$

D) $5a^5 + 10a^4$

7 1600.io 6.3

If $a^{-\frac{1}{6}} = x$, where $a > 0$, what is a in terms of x ?

A) $-\sqrt[6]{x}$

B) $\sqrt[6]{x}$

C) $-\frac{1}{x^6}$

D) $\frac{1}{x^6}$

8 1600.io 6.2

Which of the following expressions is equivalent to $\left(16x^4\right)^{\frac{1}{4}}$?

A) $\sqrt[4]{4x}$

B) $2|x|$

C) $4|x|$

D) $16x$

9 1600.io 6.2

An exponential function f is defined by $f(t) = b^t$, where b is a constant greater than 1. If $f(9) = 64 \cdot f(6)$, what is the value of b ?

10 1600.io 6.2

Which of the following expressions is equivalent to $\left(27x^8y^4\right)^{\frac{1}{3}}$, where $x \geq 0$ and $y \geq 0$?

A) $3x^2y^{\frac{4}{3}}$

B) $3x^{\frac{8}{3}}y^{\frac{4}{3}}$

C) $9x^2y^4$

D) $9x^{\frac{8}{3}}y^4$

11 1600.io 6.3

If $a^{\frac{b}{3}} = 27$ for positive integers a and b, what is one possible value of b ?

12 1600.io 6.3

Which of the following expressions is equivalent to $\left(-9x^3\right)^{\frac{2}{3}}$?

A) $-3x^2 \cdot \sqrt[3]{3}$

B) $-x^2 \cdot \sqrt[3]{81}$

C) $3x^2 \cdot \sqrt[3]{3}$

D) $3x^2 \cdot \sqrt[3]{81}$

Answer Key

SkillDrill 6.1-1

1. 27
2. 16
3. 1
4. 81
5. 0
6. 1
7. -125
8. 17
9. 12
10. 11
11. 1
12. 32
13. x^2
14. $16y^2$
15. $2x$
16. x^3y
17. $3a^2$
18. $b^2 - b^3$
19. $2xy$
20. $x^2y + xy^2$
21. $a^2b^2c^2$
22. $4x^2y$
23. $dx + d^3$
24. $2x^2$

SkillDrill 6.2-1

1. x^4
2. $64y^7$
3. $2x^5$
4. $x^{14}y^5$
5. a^{11}
6. $b^4 - b^5$
7. x^5y^7
8. 1
9. $x^8y + xy^5$
10. $64a^6b^6c^2$
11. $12d^7x^3$
12. 0

SkillDrill 6.2-2

1. x^6
2. 64
3. a^{18}
4. $x^{14}y^{35}$
5. $15b^{16}$
6. $x^6y^{10} + x^5y^{10}$
7. $8x^{15}$
8. $\left(x^8 + y^{10}\right)^2$

SkillDrill 6.2-3

1. $a^{\frac{1}{2}}$
2. $a^{\frac{2}{3}}$
3. $2h$
4. $x^{\frac{1}{3}}$
5. $4x^2$
6. $a^{\frac{3}{4}}$
7. $2x^{\frac{3}{4}}$
8. $x^{\frac{2}{5}}y^2$
9. $1 + \frac{1}{3}$
10. $1 + \frac{2}{5}$
11. $2 + \frac{1}{2}$
12. $1 + \frac{3}{10}$
13. $1 + \frac{1}{2}$
14. $2 + \frac{1}{5}$
15. $2 + \frac{1}{2}$
16. $4 + \frac{3}{5}$

SkillDrill 6.2-4

1. $4 \cdot 6$
2. $4 \cdot 3$
3. $9 \cdot 5$
4. $25 \cdot 2$
5. $4 \cdot 8$ or $16 \cdot 2$
6. $49 \cdot 2$
7. $9 \cdot 8$ or $36 \cdot 2$
8. $4 \cdot 12$ or $16 \cdot 3$
9. $8 \cdot 4$
10. $8 \cdot 10$
11. $27 \cdot 2$
12. $125 \cdot 2$
13. $2\sqrt{6}$
14. $2\sqrt{3}$
15. $3\sqrt{5}$
16. $5\sqrt{2}$
17. $4\sqrt{2}$
18. $7\sqrt{2}$
19. $6\sqrt{2}$
20. $4\sqrt{3}$
21. $\sqrt{x}$
22. $\sqrt[3]{y^2}$
23. $a\sqrt{a}$
24. $b^3\sqrt[3]{b^2}$
25. $x\sqrt[3]{x}$
26. $a^3\sqrt{a}$
27. $3x^2\sqrt{3x}$
28. $2b^2\sqrt[3]{2b^2}$

SkillDrill 6.2-5

1. x^2
2. y^5
3. $4a^2b^3$
4. a^8
5. $3^{\frac{1}{2}}x^{\frac{3}{2}}$
6. $y^{\frac{1}{4}}$
7. $a^{\frac{1}{6}}b^{\frac{1}{2}}$
8. $x^3y^{\frac{1}{10}}$

SkillDrill 6.2-6

1. $\frac{1}{x^2}$
2. y^3
3. $\frac{y^3}{3x^2}$
4. $\frac{1}{r^7}$
5. $x^{\frac{5}{2}}$
6. $\frac{1}{x^{10}y^{\frac{1}{5}}}$
7. $\frac{b}{a^3}$
8. $\frac{9}{x^6y^{\frac{4}{3}}}$

Additional Problems

1. C
2. C
3. A
4. D
5. B
6. D
7. D
8. B
9. 4
10. B
11. 1, 3, or 9
12. C

7 Introduction to Polynomials

7.1 What are Polynomials?

Let's talk about polynomials. **A polynomial is a mathematical expression that consists of a set of terms added together, where each term contains a variable raised to a power**. Each term can have a numerical coefficient (multiplier) in front of it; if there's no explicit coefficient shown, the coefficient is just 1.

We'll limit our discussion to polynomials that only have one variable, such as x, in each term. These happen to be called univariate polynomials, but you don't need to memorize that unless you want to be shunned at social gatherings. The **degree** of a polynomial is the highest power that the variable is raised to in any term in the expression.

We've previously discussed one simple flavor of polynomial: the linear expression, which can be written in the form $mx + b$. For example:

$$2x + 6$$

This polynomial expression has two terms. You might think that it doesn't qualify as a polynomial, because though the first term has a variable (x) and a coefficient (m, which is 2 in this example), it doesn't show x raised to any power; furthermore, the second term, b (which is 6 in this example), doesn't even have x in it anywhere. But if you recall that a number raised to the first power, such as x^1, is the same as just the base (here, x), you'll realize that the expression could be written as $mx^1 + b$. For our specific example:

$$2x^1 + 6$$

But what about that constant term (represented here by 6)? Well, another fact we've discussed is that a number raised to the zeroth power is equal to 1, so $x^0 = 1$, which means that we could write the same expression as $2x^1 + 6x^0$.

When we write the polynomial this way, we can see that the second term is in exactly the same general form as the first term, complete with coefficient (6), variable (x), and exponent (0). Now our expression is more obviously a single-variable polynomial, with a series of terms that have that variable raised to some power. (Note that we conventionally place the terms in order of decreasing degree, so here, the term of degree 1 comes first, followed by the term of degree 0; this keeps things neat and organized.) Just for completeness, let's consider the ultra-simple constant expression b (for example, -24). Believe it or not, this does qualify as a single-variable polynomial, because it could be thought of as bx^0 (for example: $-24x^0$).

This fact is not terribly useful, though it might help you understand how constants, variables, and variables raised to powers can all relate to polynomials. Specifically, you should understand that a term that has a variable with no exponent isn't really any different from a term that has an exponent—we just leave off the exponent if it's 1. Similarly, a term that doesn't have a variable at all (a constant by itself) might appear to be of a different type than the other terms in a polynomial, but in a univariate polynomial, it's really just a coefficient for the x^0 term.

Let's quickly look at another example, just to be sure this principle is clear:

$$x^2 + 2x - 24$$

Here, we see there are three terms, but they all look different; what's with polynomials and their seemingly endless unique term formats? The first term has no coefficient, the second one has no exponent, and the third one has no variable! Well, we now know that this is simply the following super-consistent series of terms, but with a few math-writing shorthand rules applied:

$$1x^2 + 2x^1 - 24x^0$$

Ah, order has been restored: each term has a coefficient, the variable, and an exponent, with those exponents obediently marching down 2, 1, 0 (writing the terms in order of descending degree is the **Standard Form** for polynomials—weirdly, when it comes to linear polynomials in this form, we refer to it as Slope-Intercept Form and call something entirely different Standard Form). It just so happens that when we apply some conventions, each term in this three-term univariate polynomial—also known as a **quadratic**—takes on a different form:

1. We drop the coefficient of 1 from the first term, because doing so doesn't change the value of the term (anything multiplied by 1 remains unchanged)
2. We drop the exponent of 1 from the second term's variable, because any base raised to the first power is just the base
3. We drop the whole variable component from the third term, because anything raised to the zeroth power is 1, so we don't need to keep that extraneous stuff either; that leaves just the numerical coefficient, which we happen to refer to as a constant

You should be able to see now that polynomials can be built out of terms that consist of a coefficient and a variable raised to some power, though we might not need to explicitly write some of those components with every term.

Standard Form Polynomials

A polynomial is simply a mathematical expression that consists of a set of terms added together, where each term contains a variable raised to a power. When written in Standard Form, they are expressed in decreasing order of the power of the x terms.

The Standard Form of a quadratic polynomial (the highest power of x is 2) takes the form

$$ax^2 + bx + c$$

where a, b, and c are constants.

The Standard Form of a cubic polynomial (the highest power of x is 3) takes the form

$$ax^3 + bx^2 + cx + d$$

where a, b, c, and d are constants.

The same pattern continues for higher degree polynomials (where the highest power of x is more than 3).

Combining Like Terms

As we've already seen, terms of the same variable (same base, same exponent) can be added together. In the simplest case, we know that $x + x = 2x$. In the last chapter, we briefly discussed how in expressions with multiple different variable terms, the terms of the same variables can be added together. For example, we can add the expressions $x^3 + 3x^2 - x - 7$ and $5x^3 + 8x^2 + 9$ by **combining the like terms**: add x^3 and $5x^3$; add $3x^2$ and $8x^2$; there is no x term in the second expression, so the $-x$ from the first expression stands alone; add the constants -7 and 9.

$$(x^3 + 3x^2 - x - 7) + (5x^3 + 8x^2 + 9)$$

$$\boxed{x^3 + 5x^3} + \boxed{3x^2 + 8x^2} - x\boxed{-7 + 9}$$

$$6x^3 + 11x^2 - x + 2$$

Some problems on the test are just a simple matter of adding (or subtracting) expressions by combining like terms.

Example 7.1-1

1 7.1

Which expression is equivalent to
$(5x^2 - 4) - (-6x^2 + 3x - 5)$?

A) $11x^2 + 3x - 1$

B) $11x^2 - 3x + 1$

C) $-x^2 + 3x - 9$

D) $-x^2 - 3x - 9$

Solution

1. Drop the parentheses around the first expression and distribute the negative sign through the second expression (be careful about which terms have negative coefficients).

$$(5x^2 - 4) - (-6x^2 + 3x - 5)$$
$$5x^2 - 4 + 6x^2 - 3x + 5$$

2. Group and combine like terms.

$$5x^2 - 4 + 6x^2 - 3x + 5$$
$$\boxed{5x^2 + 6x^2} - 3x \boxed{-4 + 5}$$
$$11x^2 - 3x + 1$$

3. The answer is B.

View related real-test problems at 1600.io/p/smtex?topic=7.1

7.2 Multiplying Polynomials

Polynomials can be multiplied by each other to produce new, higher degree polynomials, and we will need to build on the knowledge of exponent rules (established in the previous chapter) in order to multiply variable terms and combine like terms.

We already know how to multiply a numerical value and an expression with multiple terms by distributing the value across the terms. For example:

$$3(x^2 - 4x + 2)$$
$$3\left(x^2\right) - 3(4x) + 3(2)$$
$$3x^2 - 12x + 6$$

By the same principle, we can also distribute variable terms across multiple terms (we saw this in a few examples in the last chapter), applying exponent rules when terms with the same base variable x are multiplied by each other. For example, let's replace the 3 in the previous example with an x (or x^1) term, and find the resulting expression. We'll also rewrite the terms inside the parentheses as x-based variable terms:

$$x(x^2 - 4x + 2)$$
$$x^1(x^2 - 4x^1 + 2x^0)$$
$$x^1(x^2) - x^1(4x^1) + x^1(2x^0)$$
$$x^{1+2} - 4x^{1+1} + 2x^{1+0}$$
$$x^3 - 4x^2 + 2x$$

You want to get comfortable multiplying variable terms of polynomials so that you don't always have to write the intermediate steps (writing x-terms as x^1, for example).

Example 7.2-1

1 1600.io 7.2

$$x(x^2 - 1) + (3x^2 - x)$$

Which of the following expressions is equivalent to the expression above?

A) $4x^2 - 2x$

B) $4x^2$

C) $x^3 + 3x^2$

D) $x^3 + 3x^2 - 2x$

Solution

1. Distribute the x to both terms in the first parenthetical expression, and combine multiplied variable terms using exponent rules. The parentheses can be removed from around the second parenthetical expression because no multipliers need to be distributed.

$$x(x^2 - 1) + (3x^2 - x)$$

$$x(x^2) - x(1) + 3x^2 - x$$

$$x^3 - x + 3x^2 - x$$

2. Combine like terms and write the variable terms in descending order of degree to simplify the expression to match the format of the answer choices.

$$x^3 - x + 3x^2 - x$$

$$x^3 + 3x^2 - x - x$$

$$x^3 + 3x^2 - 2x$$

3. The answer is D.

Polynomial expressions with multiple terms can also be multiplied by multi-term polynomials (instead of by just a single variable term as in the previous example). For example, what if we wanted to write the product of $2x + 3$ and $x + 2$ as a polynomial in Standard Form (in terms of descending degree variable terms)? When we want to carry out the multiplication of polynomial expressions, **each term in the first expression has to be distributed to all the terms in the the second expression**.

For example, if we want to multiply $2x + 3$ and $x + 2$, we need to distribute $2x$ to both terms in the expression $x + 2$ and distribute 3 to both terms in the expression $x + 2$.

$$(2x + 3)(x + 2) = 2x(x + 2) + 3(x + 2)$$
$$(2x + 3)(x + 2) = 2x(x) + 2x(2) + 3(x) + 3(2)$$
$$(2x + 3)(x + 2) = 2x^2 + 4x + 3x + 6$$
$$(2x + 3)(x + 2) = 2x^2 + 7x + 6$$

Example 7.2-2

2 7.2

$$(x + 4)(4x - 2)$$

Which of the following is equivalent to the expression above?

A) $x^2 + 20x + 2$

B) $5x^2 + 14x + 2$

C) $4x^2 + 14x - 8$

D) $4x^2 + 16x - 8$

Solution

1. Distribute the x from the first expression to both terms in the second expression, and then distribute the 4 from the first expression to both terms in the second expression.

$$(x + 4)(4x - 2) = x(4x) - x(2) + 4(4x) - 4(2)$$
$$(x + 4)(4x - 2) = 4x^2 - 2x + 16x - 8$$
$$(x + 4)(4x - 2) = 4x^2 + 14x - 8$$

2. The answer is C.

SkillDrill 7.2-1

Directions: Multiply the polynomials and write the resulting expression in Standard Polynomial Form.

Challenge problems are boxed.

1. $x(x - 3)$ **2.** $(x + 1)(x + 2)$ **3.** $(x - 4)(x - 5)$ **4.** $(x - 1)(x + 2)$

5. $(x - 3)(x - 9)$ **6.** $\boxed{(2x + 10)(x + 7)}$ **7.** $\boxed{(x^2 + 1)(x^2 + 2)}$ **8.** $\boxed{(x^2 + 2x + 1)(3x + 4)}$

Two-term expressions like $a + b$ can be squared (or raised to any power, though squaring is particularly relevant to this test), and there is a shortcut to finding the resulting expanded Standard Form polynomial that is particularly useful on this test (and which comes in handy when factoring polynomials, covered in the next chapter). Before we get to that, remember that squaring an expression just means that we will multiply the expression by itself, so $(a + b)^2$ can also be written as $(a + b)(a + b)$.

$$(a + b)^2 = (a + b)(a + b)$$
$$(a + b)^2 = a(a) + a(b) + b(a) + b(b)$$
$$(a + b)^2 = a^2 + ab + ab + b^2$$
$$(a + b)^2 = a^2 + 2ab + b^2$$

We can use the result that $(a + b)^2 = a^2 + 2ab + b^2$ to devise a general rule for squaring two-term expressions. For example, in the expression $(x + 2)^2$, where x is in the same position as a was in the previous example, and 2 is in the same position as b was in the previous example, we should be able to shortcut the process of distributing all the terms step-by-step and just say that $(x + 2)^2$ is equal to $x^2 + 2(x)(2) + 2^2$, which simplifies to $x^2 + 4x + 4$. Let's quickly verify that result by simplifying this expression the long way.

$$(x + 2)^2 = (x + 2)(x + 2)$$
$$(x + 2)^2 = x(x) + x(2) + 2(x) + 2(2)$$
$$(x + 2)^2 = x^2 + 2x + 2x + 2^2$$
$$(x + 2)^2 = x^2 + 4x + 4$$

Perfect Square Binomials

Any expression (including just a simple value) that can be produced by squaring another expression is called a **perfect square**. For example, 9 is a perfect square because it can be produced by squaring 3, and x^2 is a perfect square because it's the result of squaring x. More relevantly for the current discussion, a polynomial can be a perfect square when it can be formed by squaring another expression; let's look at the perfect square produced by squaring a binomial (two-term polynomial).

When a binomial expression, $a + b$ is squared, the result is equal to $a^2 + 2ab + b^2$ (as was just shown).

$$(a + b)^2 = a^2 + 2ab + b^2$$

Though the following is consistent with the "formula" above (and does not need its own rule), it is helpful to show that, similarly, when $a - b$ is squared, the result is equal to $a^2 - 2ab + b^2$.

$$(a - b)^2 = (a - b)(a - b)$$
$$(a - b)^2 = a(a) + a(-b) - b(a) - b(-b)$$
$$(a - b)^2 = a^2 - ab - ab + b^2$$
$$(a - b)^2 = a^2 - 2ab + b^2$$

SkillDrill 7.2-2

Directions: Square the expressions—either by multiplying the expression by itself or by using the fact that $(a + b)^2 = a^2 + 2ab + b^2$—in order to write the resulting expression in Standard Polynomial Form.

Challenge problems are boxed.

1. $(x + 3)^2$

2. $(x + 1)^2$

3. $(x - 4)^2$

4. $(x - 1)^2$

5. $\boxed{(2x + 10)^2}$

6. $\boxed{\left(x - \frac{3}{2}\right)^2}$

7. $\boxed{(x^2 + 1)^2}$

8. $\boxed{\left(\frac{1}{5}x - \frac{1}{4}\right)^2}$

There is another useful shortcut when multiplying a binomial by its **conjugate**. The conjugate of a binomial is formed by negating the second term of the original binomial. For example, let's see what happens when we multiply $a + b$ by its conjugate, $a - b$ (notice that this expression differs from the first in that the second term, b, was negated to form the conjugate).

$$(a + b)(a - b) = a(a) + a(-b) + b(a) + b(-b)$$
$$(a + b)(a - b) = a^2 - ab + ab - b^2$$
$$(a + b)(a - b) = a^2 - b^2$$

Notice that the two middle terms in the expansion canceled each other, leaving us with an arrangement called the **Difference of Squares**, which just means that one square is subtracted from another.

Once again, we can generalize this to a pattern we can use as a shortcut when multiplying a binomial by its conjugate. For example, we can predict that $(x + 2)(x - 2)$—where x is in the same position as a was in the previous example, and 2 is in the same position as b was in the previous example—will result in the polynomial $x^2 - 4$ (because 4 is 2^2). Indeed, if we multiply the expressions the long way, we will find that our prediction is correct.

$$(x+2)(x-2) = x(x) + x(-2) + 2(x) + 2(-2)$$
$$(x+2)(x-2) = x^2 - 2x + 2x - 2^2$$
$$(x+2)(x-2) = x^2 - 4$$

Note, importantly, that it doesn't matter whether the original binomial used addition or subtraction; the conjugate will always use the opposite operation, so the results of the multiplication will be the same: $(a+b)(a-b) = (a-b)(a+b)$. Also, note that the operation in the final difference of squares binomial will **always** be subtraction regardless of the operation in the original binomial due to the reason given above.

Difference of Squares

When a binomial expression $a + b$ is multiplied by its conjugate, $(a - b)$, the result is equal to $a^2 - b^2$ (as was just shown).

$$(a+b)(a-b) = a^2 - b^2$$

SkillDrill 7.2-3

Directions: Find the product of the binomial conjugates, either by multiplying the expressions or by using the fact that $(a+b)(a-b) = a^2 - b^2$, and write the resulting expression in Standard Polynomial Form.
Challenge problems are boxed.

1. $(x+3)(x-3)$

2. $(x+1)(x-1)$

3. $(x-4)(x+4)$

4. $(x-2)(x+2)$

5. $\boxed{\left(x+\frac{1}{2}\right)\left(x-\frac{1}{2}\right)}$

6. $\boxed{\left(2x-\frac{3}{5}\right)\left(2x+\frac{3}{5}\right)}$

7. $\boxed{(3x^3+\sqrt{6})(3x^3-\sqrt{6})}$

8. $\boxed{\left(\frac{1}{5}x^2-\frac{1}{4}x\right)\left(\frac{1}{5}x^2+\frac{1}{4}x\right)}$

Example 7.2-3

3 1600.io 7.2

Which of the following is equivalent to $(3x+9)^2 - 9x^2$?

A) $9(3x+9)$

B) $27(2x+3)$

C) $54(x+1)$

D) $81(x+1)$

Solution

1. Using the "shortcut" for squaring binomials, we can quickly rewrite the given expression in order to match Standard Form for polynomials.

$$(3x+9)^2 - 9x^2 = (3x^2) + 2(3x)(9) + (9)^2 - 9x^2$$
$$(3x+9)^2 - 9x^2 = 9x^2 + 54x + 81 - 9x^2$$
$$(3x+9)^2 - 9x^2 = 54x + 81$$

2. The given expression simplifies to $54x + 81$. If you are comfortable factoring numbers from terms, you can factor 27 from both $54x$ and 81 in order to match the format of the answer choices, or, alternatively, you can multiply out each of the answer choices to see which one yields $54x + 81$.

$$54x + 81 = 27(2x+3)$$

3. The answer is B.

View related real-test problems at 1600.io/p/smtex?topic=7.2

7.3 Polynomial Equations and Functions

Polynomial expressions can also be found in equations. First, a reminder: an expression is not the same thing as an equation. This is an expression, which is a series of terms that are added to (or subtracted from) each other:

$$x^2 + 2x - 24$$

This is an equation which has the above expression on one side of the equals sign:

$$x^2 + 2x - 24 = 0$$

In some polynomial equation problems, you may have Standard Form polynomials on both sides of the equation, as in the following equation:

$$x^2 + 2x - 24 = ax^2 + bx + c$$

If you are told that an equation is true for all values of x, then the two sides of the polynomial equation must be the same, so we can simply match the coefficients of the terms of the same degree to find the values of a, b, and c. In the example above, a must be equal to 1 because the coefficient of the x^2 term on the other side of the equation is 1; b must be equal to 2 because the coefficient of the x term on the other side is 2; and c must be equal to -24 because the constant term on the other side of the equation is -24.

Sometimes you may need to take steps to write both sides of a polynomial equation in standard form. Place all terms with numerical coefficients on one side of the equation and all terms with unknown coefficients on the other side of the equation. Once both sides of the equation are in the same form, all you have to do is match the coefficients of each term.

Example 7.3-1

1 1600.io 7.3

$$-2x(5x+1)+6(5x+1)=ax^2+bx+c$$

In the equation above, a, b, and c are constants. If the equation is true for all values of x, what is the value of b ?

Solution

1. Distribute the $-2x$ to both terms in the first set of parentheses, and then distribute the 6 to both terms in the second set of parentheses. Combine any like terms on the left side of the equation.

$$-2x(5x+1)+6(5x+1)=ax^2+bx+c$$
$$-10x^2-2x+30x+6=ax^2+bx+c$$
$$-10x^2+28x+6=ax^2+bx+c$$

2. Since b is the coefficient of the x term on the right side of the equation, it must be the same as the coefficient of the x term on the left side of the equation. Therefore, $b=28$.
3. The answer is 28.

Notes

If you are comfortable that this is simply a coefficient-matching problem, you can ignore any of the terms on the left side that will not be x (or x^1) terms, only multiplying -2 by 1 (which would give us the coefficient of x from the first distribution) and 6 by 5 (which would give us the coefficient of x from the second distribution) giving you $-2(1)+6(5)=-2+30=28$.

Evaluating quadratic functions is the same as evaluating any function. Remember that for any function $f(x)$, you can substitute (replace) every x with whatever is put into the function, and the result is the y-value. For example, the value of $f(4)$ would be the y-value of the point on the graph of the function when the x-value is 4.

Example 7.3-2

2 1600.io 7.3

In the xy-plane, the point $(6,-11)$ lies on the graph of the function f. If $f(x)=k-x^2$, where k is a constant, what is the value of k ?

Solution

1. Plug in 6 for x.

$$f(x)=k-x^2$$
$$f(6)=k-(6)^2$$
$$f(6)=k-36$$

2. We know that $f(6) = -11$ because the point $(6, -11)$ is on the graph of the function. Therefore, the y-value (or $f(x)$ value) is -11 when the x-value is 6. Replace $f(6)$ with -11, then solve for k.

$$\begin{aligned} f(6) &= k - 36 \\ -11 &= k - 36 \\ 25 &= k \end{aligned}$$

3. The answer is 25.

Section 7.3 Suggested Problems from Real Tests

View related real-test problems at 1600.io/p/smtex?topic=7.3

CHAPTER 7 RECAP

- The Standard Form for a univariate (single variable) polynomial puts the terms in order from highest to lowest power, so the Standard Form of a quadratic (second-degree polynomial) equation is $y = ax^2 + bx + c$, where a, b, and c are constants.
- When adding or subtracting expressions, group and combine like terms of the same variable (same base and exponent).
- When multiplying expressions, distribute all terms in the first expression to all terms in the second expression.
- When a binomial (two-term polynomial) expression $a + b$ is squared, the result is equal to $a^2 + 2ab + b^2$.

  $$(a + b)^2 = a^2 + 2ab + b^2$$

  Similarly, when $a - b$ is squared, the result is equal to $a^2 - 2ab + b^2$.

  $$(a - b)^2 = a^2 - 2ab + b^2$$

- When a binomial expression $(a + b)$ is multiplied by its conjugate, $(a - b)$, the result is equal to the difference of squares $a^2 - b^2$.

  $$(a + b)(a - b) = a^2 - b^2$$

- If the two sides of an equation are polynomials written in Standard Form, and you are told that the equation is true for all values of the variable (that is, the polynomials are **equivalent**), you can match the coefficients of corresponding terms to find the values of any unknown coefficients.
- Evaluating polynomial functions is the same as evaluating any function: substitute (replace) each instance of x (or whatever the parameter variable is) with the value for which you want to evaluate the function.

Additional Problems

1 7.3

In the xy-plane, the point $(2, 0)$ lies on the graph of the function $f(x) = 2x^2 - bx + 15$. What is the value of b ?

2 7.2

Which of the following expressions is equivalent to $x^2 + 13x + 42$?

A) $(x+6)(x+7)+4$

B) $(x+6)(x+7)+4x$

C) $(x+5)(x+8)+2$

D) $(x+5)(x+8)+2x$

3 7.2

$$(5x+5)(ax-2) - x^2 + 10$$

In the expression above, a is a constant. If the expression is equivalent to bx, where b is a constant, what is the value of b ?

A) -11

B) -10

C) -9

D) -5

4 7.3

$$-3(x+a) + 5(x^2 - a) = 5x^2 - 3x - 6$$

In the equation above, a is a constant. If the equation is true for all values of x, what is the value of a ?

5 7.2

$$(5x^4 + 6x)(x^4 - 3x)$$

Which of the following is equivalent to the expression above?

A) $4x^4 + 9x$

B) $6x^4 + 3x$

C) $5x^8 - 9x^5 - 18x^2$

D) $6x^8 - 9x^5 - 18x^2$

6 7.2

Which of the following is an equivalent form of $(2.5x - 1.8)^2 - (3.8x^2 - 4.3)$?

A) $1.2x^2 + 0.7$

B) $1.2x^2 + 7.9$

C) $2.45x^2 - 9x + 1.06$

D) $2.45x^2 - 9x + 7.54$

7 1600.io 7.2

$$7x^2 - 4(2 - x) - 3x(x + 2)$$

Which of the following polynomials is equivalent to the expression above?

A) $4x^2 + 2x - 8$

B) $4x^2 - 2x - 8$

C) $7x^2 + x - 8$

D) $7x^2 - 5x - 8$

8 1600.io 7.3

$$(ax - 5)(2x^2 + bx + 3) = 4x^3 - 4x^2 - 9x - 15$$

The equation above is true for all x, where a and b are constants. What is the value of ab ?

A) -14

B) -4

C) 4

D) 6

9 1600.io 7.3

In the xy-plane, the point $(3, 30)$ lies on the graph of the function f. If $f(x) = k + 2x^2$, where k is a constant, what is the value of k ?

10 1600.io 7.3

The function f is defined by $f(x) = x^2 + 4x + 7$. What is the value of $f(-2)$?

A) -5

B) 3

C) 11

D) 13

11 1600.io 7.2

$$2(3x + 2)(5x + 2)$$

Which of the following is equivalent to the expression above?

A) $70x$

B) $16x^2 + 8$

C) $30x^2 + 8$

D) $30x^2 + 32x + 8$

12 1600.io 7.3

$$-5x(x - 3) + 3(x - 2) = ax^2 + bx + c$$

In the equation above, a, b, and c are constants. If the equation is true for all values of x, what is the value of $a + b + c$?

A) 7

B) 11

C) 12

D) 13

13 7.3

If $y = x^2 + ax - a$, where a is constant, and $y = 7$ when $x = 3$, what is the value of a ?

A) -8

B) -1

C) 1

D) 8

14 7.2

If $y = x + \frac{3}{2}$ and $z = 4x - 3$, which of the following is equivalent to $y + yz$?

A) $4x^2 + 3x - \frac{9}{2}$

B) $4x^2 + 3x + 3$

C) $4x^2 + 4x - 3$

D) $4x^2 + 4x + 4$

15 7.3

$$-2zw^2 + 2w + 15 = -4z$$

In the equation above, what is the value of z when $w = -3$?

16 7.2

Which of the following is equivalent to $\left(a - \frac{b}{2}\right)^2$?

A) $a^2 - \frac{b^2}{2}$

B) $a^2 - \frac{b^2}{4}$

C) $a^2 - \frac{ab}{2} + \frac{b^2}{4}$

D) $a^2 - ab + \frac{b^2}{4}$

17 7.1

Which of the following is equivalent to the sum of $5x^5 + 2x^4$ and $3x^5 + 4x^4$?

A) $14x^5$

B) $8x^{10} + 6x^8$

C) $15x^5 + 8x^4$

D) $8x^5 + 6x^4$

18 7.1

Which of the following expressions is equivalent to $2q^2 + r^2 + 6r - 3q + 4(q^2 - r)$?

A) $6r^2 + 3q^2$

B) $r^2 + 6q^2 - qr$

C) $r^2 + 6q^2 - 3q + 2r$

D) $r^2 + 6q^2 - 3q + 5r$

Answer Key

SkillDrill 7.2-1

1. $x^2 - 3x$
2. $x^2 + 3x + 2$
3. $x^2 - 9x + 20$
4. $x^2 + x - 2$
5. $x^2 - 12x + 27$
6. $2x^2 + 24x + 70$
7. $x^4 + 3x^2 + 2$
8. $3x^3 + 10x^2 + 11x + 4$

SkillDrill 7.2-2

1. $x^2 + 6x + 9$
2. $x^2 + 2x + 1$
3. $x^2 - 8x + 16$
4. $x^2 - 2x + 1$
5. $4x^2 + 40x + 100$
6. $x^2 - 3x + \frac{9}{4}$
7. $x^4 + 2x^2 + 1$
8. $\frac{1}{25}x^2 - \frac{1}{10}x + \frac{1}{16}$

SkillDrill 7.2-3

1. $x^2 - 9$
2. $x^2 - 1$
3. $x^2 - 16$
4. $x^2 - 4$
5. $x^2 - \frac{1}{4}$
6. $4x^2 - \frac{9}{25}$
7. $9x^6 - 6$
8. $\frac{1}{25}x^4 - \frac{1}{16}x^2$

Additional Problems

1. $\frac{23}{2}$ or 11.5
2. C
3. C
4. $\frac{3}{4}$ or 0.75
5. C
6. D
7. B
8. D
9. 12
10. B
11. D
12. A
13. B
14. C
15. $\frac{9}{14}$, .642, or .643
16. D
17. D
18. C

8 Solving Quadratic Equations

On the test, you will often need to find the solutions to a quadratic equation. There are several techniques that you can use for this; each has strengths and weaknesses associated with the characteristics of the problem you are faced with, but it is important to understand that any method can solve any problem—it might just be difficult or exceedingly time-consuming if the problem is a bad fit for the selected method. Here's a table that summarizes the solving methods we'll go on to explain in detail:

Method	Form(s) of Most Susceptible Expressions	Other Clues	Strengths	Weaknesses
Simple Factoring	$x^2 + bx + c = 0$	Answer choices are whole numbers, do not contain $\sqrt{\ }$	Simple, fast, low error risk	Requires some guesswork, very difficult for some values of b and c
Product-Sum (ac) Factoring	$ax^2 + bx + c = 0$	Answer choices are whole or rational numbers, do not contain $\sqrt{\ }$	Simple, fairly fast, fairly low error risk	Requires some guesswork, very difficult for some values of a, b and c
Completing the Square	$x^2 + bx + c = 0$ or $ax^2 + bx + c = 0$	$a \neq 1$; Answer choices contain $\sqrt{\ }$	Directly solves any quadratic	Somewhat time-consuming, moderate error risk
Quadratic Formula	$x^2 + bx + c = 0$ or $ax^2 + bx + c = 0$	Answer choices contain $\sqrt{\ }$	Directly solves any quadratic	Time-consuming, relatively high error risk

8.1 What is Factoring?

A very important technique that can be used in manipulating expressions and solving equations is called **factoring**. When we factor, we convert an expression, or a part of an expression, into a set of terms, called factors, that are multiplied; this set of multiplied terms is equivalent to the expression being replaced.

For example, here's one way we could factor 10:

$$10 = 2 \cdot 5$$

Here, 2 and 5 are factors of 10.

Here's an example with some variables:

$$4x + 4y = 4(x + y)$$

Here, we've factored $4x + 4y$ into two factors: 4 and $(x + y)$. You can see that if we multiply out (distribute) the 4 on the right hand side of this equation, we'll get the left hand side:

$$4(x + y)$$
$$4(x) + 4(y)$$
$$4x + 4y$$

You can see that **factoring is really just the inverse operation of distribution**. We're just dividing each term by some expression (here, just the constant 4), then multiplying the whole thing by that constant so its value is unchanged.

Notice that in the previous example, we "factored out" the number 4 because it was a coefficient of both the x-term and the y-term. However, the factor doesn't need to be explicitly shown for it to be factored out. For example, if we had

$$4x + 8y$$

we can still factor out 4 by dividing both terms by 4, and then multiplying what remains by 4:

$$4x + 8y$$
$$4\left(\frac{4x}{4} + \frac{8y}{4}\right)$$
$$4(x + 2y)$$

The terms in the expression being factored don't even need to be evenly divisible by the factor being pulled out. We could factor

$$4x + 3y$$

as

$$4\left(x + \frac{3y}{4}\right)$$

if that would be useful—such as when we need to isolate the variable x with no coefficient. Speaking of x, we can factor out a variable, too; if we start with

$$4x + 7xy$$

that can be factored as

$$x(4 + 7y)$$

Importantly, note that if the variable has no coefficient, that's really an implied coefficient of 1, so

$$x + 7xy$$

can be factored as

$$x(1 + 7y)$$

This is sometimes confusing for students, because they wonder where that 1 comes from. This is likely because the implicit coefficient of 1 is, well, implicit—it's not shown, so it has to be imagined when factoring. That is, the first expression should be thought of as

$$1x + 7xy$$

which should make it much more obvious how we factor that and obtain

$$x(1 + 7y)$$

A factor doesn't need to be a single term; it can be an expression. This should already be apparent from the above examples, where the second term is an expression, but here's another example. Let's start with

$$(x - 3)(x + y) - (x - 3)(z)$$

Notice that there are two terms here, with the second being subtracted from the first, and each term has $(x - 3)$ as a factor. We can factor out $(x - 3)$ from both terms to get

$$(x - 3)[(x + y) - z]$$

As a reminder, factors are a set of expressions that, when multiplied, yield the original expression.

Factors Help Us Find Solutions

Factoring has many uses, but one of the most important is that if we are presented with an equation we need to solve, we can move all the terms to one side of the equation (leaving 0 on the other side), and then we can try to factor the resulting expression. Then, **if we can figure out the values of the variable(s) that would make any of the factors equal 0, we know the whole expression will equal 0 (because 0 times anything is 0)**, and we will have solved the equation (which, remember, has a 0 on the other side). We're going to explore the applications of this principle that apply to the math section of the test in what follows, but first, let's dig into a few more essential concepts.

An expression is not the same thing as an equation. This is a **quadratic expression**, which is a univariate (single variable) polynomial expression consisting of a series of terms being added to (or subtracted from) each other, where the degree of the polynomial is 2:

$$x^2 + 2x - 24$$

This is a **quadratic equation** which has the above expression on one side of the equals sign:

$$x^2 + 2x - 24 = 0$$

You solve equations, not expressions. Expressions merely have a value, not a truth or falsity; equations are solved by finding the value(s) of any variable(s) that make the equation true.

Solving polynomial equations of degree zero is... meaningless! Polynomials of degree zero only have a term in the following form:

$$ax^0$$

Because $x^0 = 1$, as discussed above, this is equivalent to just a, and that's a constant. Therefore, an equation with such a sad little polynomial would be something like $3 = 3$. There's no variable at all here, so there's nothing to solve; the equation is either true or false, all the time.

For something with a little more substance, let's look at a polynomial of degree 1:

$$2x^1 - 24x^0$$

By now, you'll know we can write this more compactly by applying a couple of those exponent rules, so we'll drop the exponent of 1 and the variable raised to the zeroth power:

$$2x - 24$$

Let's set up a simple equation using this first-degree polynomial:

$$2x - 24 = 0$$

Now, let's solve this using simple algebra. There are several ways we could proceed; for example, we could isolate the x term on one side as our first step, and, it's true, that would ordinarily be the most straightforward way to begin. However, because we want to illustrate a specific principle, we'll take a different approach. First, we'll get an x term with no coefficient by factoring out that coefficient of 2:

$$2\left(x - \frac{24}{2}\right) = 0$$

$$2(x - 12) = 0$$

At this point, we have a multiplication of two terms, which are 2 and $(x - 12)$. As we explained earlier, each term involved in a multiplication is a factor of the result of that multiplication. The equations tells us that the product of these two factors equals 0. Here's the most important consequence of the factoring: if the product of the factors equals 0, it means that if either factor is 0, the equation is true, because 0 times anything is still 0. Obviously, 2 doesn't equal zero, but $(x - 12)$ will equal zero when $x = 12$, so $x = 12$ is the solution to the equation.

More generally, we can see that once we get to a setup where we have an equation with a fully factored form on one side and 0 on the other side...

$$a(x - z) = 0$$

...we know that $x = z$, because that will make the second factor $(x - z)$ equal 0, which will make the whole left side equal 0.

The same principle applies if we end up with addition in the expression on the left, effectively changing the sign of the constant term; we just change the sign in the solution:

$$a(x + z) = 0$$

...which means that $x = -z$ is a zero. Simple enough.

Note that, importantly, this simple technique relies completely on arranging the equation so that 0 is on one side; whenever we can get just a series of multiplications (factored form) on one side and a 0 on the other side of an equation, we can exploit this, because **if any one of the terms (factors) involved in the multiplication evaluates to 0, the equation will be true**.

Expressions vs. Equations

Let's introduce and clarify some terms. It should already be clear that **an expression (as contrasted with an equation) doesn't have solutions, because it doesn't make any claims to be equal to anything in particular.** However, we do say that an **expression or a function can have zeros, which are the solutions that would exist if the expression or function were set equal to zero**, thus creating an equation. We also call these solutions **roots**.

Of course, **if we're presented with an equation with zero on one side, the zeros or roots of the expression on the other side are the solutions of the whole equation, and, more casually, we can just refer to the zeros or roots of the whole equation.** If we have an **equation that has something other than zero on one side, it can certainly have solutions (which can also be called roots in this situation, confusingly enough), but the equation as a whole cannot properly be said to have zeros** (though the polynomial expression on the other side of the equation can have zeros).

One final terminological note: **be careful not to mix up the term roots as used in this context with the word as used in terms such as "square root," "cube root," and so on.**

We could solve the generic form of a first-degree polynomial equation, which would give us a formula that would apply to any such equation. Let's try making that formula, starting with the simple equation setup above, where the right side is zero:

$$ax + b = 0$$

We'll factor out that a by simply dividing each term on the left by a, and multiplying the entire original expression by a to counter that division:

$$a\left(x + \frac{b}{a}\right) = 0$$

From what we learned above, we know that if the factor $x + \frac{b}{a} = 0$, the equation is true, and therefore this means

$$x = \frac{-b}{a}$$

That's pretty simple. Let's test it with the example we've been developing, which we solved earlier to find $x = 12$:

$$2x - 24 = 0$$

Here, $a = 2$ and $b = -24$. Our formula says $x = \frac{-b}{a}$. Substituting gives us the following result:

$$x = \frac{-(-24)}{2} = \frac{24}{2} = 12$$

That checks out, thank goodness. Now, we're not suggesting that you memorize this formula; it's not necessary to know it when solving simple equations of the form shown here, which you were probably already able to dispatch with little difficulty using a bit of simple algebra. However, we did want to step through its derivation to lay some groundwork for what is to follow.

Now, let's take a look at second-degree univariate polynomial (quadratic) expressions and equations. Remember, second-degree polynomials are just like the first-degree expressions we've been working with, except they will have one more term at the beginning that contains a variable raised to the second power, so second-degree polynomials will look like this when written in Standard Form:

$$ax^2 + bx^1 + cx^0$$

Again, by convention, we'll always be writing this by dropping the extraneous bits:

$$ax^2 + bx + c$$

The simplest equation we can make just has zero on the right, which will help us when it comes to solving (this should give you an idea of where we are going with this!):

$$ax^2 + bx + c = 0$$

Of course, any equation that has just zeroth-, first-, and second-degree terms in any order and on either side can be put into the form shown above simply by combining all the like terms on one side of the equation and placing them in decreasing order of degree.

For example, if you're presented with some mathematical jambalaya such as...

$$-8 + 4x - 2 + 3x^2 = 14 - 3x + x^2 + 5x$$

...just let out a big sigh and start collecting like terms and herding them over to one side in descending degree order, leaving nothing but zero on the other side:

$$3x^2 - x^2 + 4x + 3x - 5x - 8 - 2 - 14 = 0$$
$$2x^2 + 2x - 24 = 0$$

Standard Form Quadratic Equation

The Standard Form of a quadratic equation, where a, b, and c are constants, is the following:

$$y = ax^2 + bx + c$$

Most often the value of a is 1 in problems on the test. For example, in the quadratic equation $y = x^2 + 3x + 2$, the value of a is 1 because the x^2 term has a coefficient of 1 (which is why there is no number shown in front of the x^2).

Usually, in the course of solving quadratic problems on the test, we will set the y-value equal to 0 (or make one side of the quadratic equation equal to 0) because it enables us to find the zeros or solutions of the quadratic equation using the most common techniques. If the y-value is already set equal to 0, the problem may ask you for solutions to the equation, which, as previously noted, are the same as the zeros in this situation. Though solution is not an interchangeable term for zero, the most frequently utilized setup for solving quadratics involves a quadratic expression on one side of the equation and a value of 0 on the other side of the equation.

Just as we discovered that there's a formula for solving a first-degree polynomial (linear) equation (remember that the solution of $0 = ax + b$ is $x = \frac{-b}{a}$), there's also a formula for second-degree equations: it's commonly referred to as the **Quadratic Formula**, and you've probably heard of it.

Quadratic Formula

For a quadratic equation in Standard Form, $0 = ax^2 + bx + c$, the solutions can be found with the following formula:

$$x = \frac{-b \pm \sqrt{b^2 - 4ac}}{2a}$$

which we choose to split into two fractions as below (the expression $\frac{-b}{2a}$ helps reinforce an important feature of quadratic graphs, the x-value of the vertex, which will be discussed later):

$$x = \frac{-b}{2a} \pm \frac{\sqrt{b^2 - 4ac}}{2a}$$

Note, importantly, that this formula can produce not just one but two different values due to the presence of the $\pm$ symbol, which indicates that both the positive and negative square roots must be separately determined.

Though the Quadratic Formula can be used to solve any quadratic equation by substituting the values of a, b, and c, there is a fair amount of work involved to evaluate the formula, and that means it can be time-consuming, and the procedure is susceptible to errors due to the number of steps needed, the presence of the square root operation, and the nesting of operations. On the test, time and accuracy are precious, and the use of the Quadratic Formula can use up a lot of time and introduce errors.

All of this brings us to the question: are there simpler methods for finding the solutions to a quadratic equation?

There are. The Quadratic Formula is a valid solving method, and it does have some strengths in certain situations, so we will discuss it in depth later on, but first, we're going to explain easier, more streamlined methods for solving quadratics.

Let's start with the one called **factoring**, which is by far the most frequently applicable technique when it comes to the test. This method relies on the fact that just as a first-degree expression can be expressed as the product of a constant and a simple two-term (binomial) expression of the form $(x + p)$, a quadratic expression can be expressed as the product of a constant and two simple first-degree expressions.

First-degree expression:

$$a(x+p)$$

Second-degree (quadratic) expression:

$$a(x+p)(x+q)$$

Let's multiply out that factored expression just to show that it results in a quadratic (second-degree univariate polynomial):

$$a(x+p)(x+q)$$
$$a(x)(x)+a(p)(x)+a(q)(x)+apq$$
$$ax^2+a(p+q)x+apq$$

That's definitely a quadratic expression, as it has a term ax^2 with an exponent of 2, a term $a(p+q)x$ with an implied exponent of 1, and a final term with an exponent of 0, represented by the constant term apq.

In the overwhelming majority of cases, quadratic expressions that appear on the test don't have any a coefficient on the second-degree term, so they correspond to the simpler Factored Form

$$(x+p)(x+q)$$

which, when multiplied out into Standard Form, gives

$$(x)(x)+qx+px+pq$$
$$x^2+(p+q)x+pq$$

Now we are prepared to solve quadratic equations using factoring. If we have—or can get—a quadratic equation into the factored form

$$(x+p)(x+q)=0$$

then we can determine a value of x that makes either of the factors equal 0. **If any one of the factors is equal to 0, then the whole expression will evaluate to 0, making the equation true**; put another way, we will have found a solution.

Here, we can see that $x=-p$ will make the first factor, $(x+p)$, equal to 0, so the whole left side will be 0, and thus the equation will be true. Similarly, $x=-q$ will make the second factor, $(x+q)$, equal to 0, and the equation will again be true. Therefore, there are, in the general case, two solutions to quadratic equations in the above factored form (if p and q happen to be the same, there will be just one solution, sometimes called a "double root"):

$$x=-p$$
$$x=-q$$

It should be noted that p and q can be negative numbers themselves, in which case the solutions would be positive values.

Note also that either p or q (or both) could be equal to 0, in which case the factor that corresponds to that solution is $(x-0)$, which is the same as a factor of x, so $x=0$ is one solution. **When quadratics have a factor of x (p or q is equal to 0), there is no constant term (the value of c is 0) in the Standard Form representation of that expression**. For example, an expression with factors x and $x-4$ would be the following in Standard Form (as a result of distributing x to both terms in the factor $x-4$).

$$x(x-4)=x^2-4x$$

Note once again that in the expression x^2-4x (which is in Standard Form for quadratics, ax^2+bx+c) the value of c is 0 (there is no constant term written after the x-term).

If both p and q are 0, then both factors are simply x, and the resulting quadratic expression is $x \cdot x$ or x^2, for which there is no x-term or constant term (the values of b and c for this Standard Form expression are both 0). In this scenario, the quadratic equation degenerates to $x^2=0$, and the one solution is $x=0$.

When we want to solve quadratic equations using the factoring method, our goal is to have the quadratic expression written as the product of two binomials, which are just expressions with two terms that have the same variable (or a constant).

For example, the quadratic equation $y = x^2 + 3x + 2$ can also be written as $y = (x + 2)(x + 1)$. We will learn how to produce the Factored Form shortly, but for now, you can verify that the two equations are the same by multiplying the two factors and seeing that the result will be the same Standard Form equation.

Factored Form of Quadratic Equation

In general, the Factored Form of a quadratic equation, where a, p, and q are constants, is the following:

$$0 = a(x + p)(x + q)$$

Most often on this test, the value of a will be 1 (most of the time when factoring is a good solution method, the value of the x^2 coefficient in the Standard Form of the quadratic is 1).

When we are asked to find the **solutions** of a quadratic equation, we want to have all of the individual terms for each degree of the variable including the constant term (if the equation is still in Standard Form) or the factors (if the equation is in Factored Form) on one side of the equation and a 0 on the other side of the equation. Once the equation has a 0 on one side of the equation and a polynomial written in Factored Form on the other side of the equation, we know that the product of the factors is 0 and, therefore, this equation will be true whenever any one of the factors is equal to 0 (any number times 0 equals 0).

Given the equation $0 = a(x + p)(x + q)$, where the factors of the quadratic equation are $(x + p)$ and $(x + q)$, we know that $-p$ and $-q$ are the solutions to the equation because the factor $(x + p)$ will be equal to 0 when $x = -p$, and the factor $(x + q)$ will be equal to 0 when $x = -q$.

Note that if 0 is one of the solutions (because either p or q is 0), then x, which is the same as the factor $(x - 0)$, is one of the factors.

All of these ideas extend beyond quadratics to other polynomials with more than two factors. For example, in the polynomial equation, $0 = (x + j)(x + k)(x + \ell)$, the right side of the equation has factors $(x + j)$, $(x + k)$, and $(x + \ell)$. Therefore, $-j$, $-k$, and $-\ell$ are all solutions to the equation because each of those values of x would cause one of the factors to be equal to 0, and thus the entire expression would equal 0.

At this point, you should be able to easily solve any equation that has a quadratic expression in Factored Form set equal to 0. Let's look at a quick example:

$$(x + 6)(x - 4) = 0$$

Here, the solutions should be immediately apparent because of the Factored Form; we can see right away that $x = -6$ or $x = 4$ will make the equation true, because either value of x will produce a value of 0 for one of the factors, and if any factor is 0, the whole expression will be 0, and the equation will be valid.

You might encounter an expression that doesn't exactly match the Factored Form, but which nonetheless consists of a series of factors. The central principle of finding the roots still applies; set each factor equal to 0 and solve for the variable to find one of the solutions. For example, if you are given

$$(4x - 12)(x + 3)^3 = 0$$

set the first factor, $4x - 12$, equal to 0 and solve for x:

$$4x - 12 = 0$$
$$4x = 12$$
$$x = 3$$

Then, set the second factor equal to 0 and solve for x:

$$(x+3)^3 = 0$$
$$x+3 = 0$$
$$x = -3$$

Don't let such a variation throw you off; just keep in mind the principle that if any factor is 0, the equation is valid, so just find those values of the variable that make each factor equal 0.

Example 8.1-1

 8.1

What is the sum of the solutions to $(x-4)(x+0.3)=0$?

A) -4.3
B) -3.7
C) 3.7
D) 4.3

Solution

1. We need to find values of x that make each factor equal to 0 in order to find both solutions.
2. The first factor, $(x-4)$, will be equal to 0 when x is 4. To determine this, set the factor equal to 0 and solve for x.

$$x-4=0$$
$$x=4$$

3. The first solution is 4 since the factor $x-4$ is equal to 0 when $x=4$.
4. The second factor, $(x+0.3)$, will be equal to 0 when x is -0.3, so the second solution is -0.3.

$$x+0.3=0$$
$$x=-0.3$$

5. The sum of the two solutions is $4+(-0.3)$.

$$4+(-0.3)=4-0.3=3.7$$

6. The answer is C.

View related real-test problems at 1600.io/p/smtex?topic=8.1

Section 8.1 Practice Problems

1 1600.io 8.1

$$7(x+1)(x-8)=0$$

What positive value of x satisfies the equation above?

2 1600.io 8.1

$$(3x-2)(x+4)^2=0$$

What is the solution set to the equation above?

A) $\left\{-\frac{2}{3}, 4\right\}$

B) $\left\{\frac{2}{3}, -4\right\}$

C) $\left\{-\frac{2}{3}, -4, 4\right\}$

D) $\left\{\frac{2}{3}, -4, 4\right\}$

8.2 How to Factor

On the test, we are not usually provided with a quadratic polynomial in Factored Form. We need to learn to factor quadratic polynomials that are written in Standard Form, $y = ax^2 + bx + c$. This is easiest when the value of a is 1.

Let's pick back up with our example from the previous section:

$$(x+6)(x-4)=0$$

Clearly, we already know the solutions to this equation (based on Factored Form), but let's put this same equation into Standard Form, and work forward from there. We can multiply out the above example to put it into Standard Form:

$$\begin{aligned}(x+6)(x-4)&=0\\(x)(x)-4x+6x+6(-4)&=0\\x^2+2x-24&=0\end{aligned}$$

Of course, the solutions are the same ($x=-6$ or $x=4$), because we've only transformed the quadratic expression from Factored Form into Standard Form (the two are equivalent even though they look different). But what if we had to start with the equation in Standard Form, where the solutions aren't so obvious? What would we do if we were presented with this at the outset?

$$x^2+2x-24=0$$

We know that there's a Quadratic Formula for finding the solutions, but it's time-consuming and somewhat complicated. If we could simply convert the quadratic expression to Factored Form, the solutions would be at hand, so let's take a look at that procedure.

Remember, when we multiply out a factored quadratic

$$(x+p)(x+q)$$

we get

$$x^2+(p+q)x+pq$$

This means that when we consider the Standard Form of a quadratic expression to be $x^2 + bx + c$ (where the value of the x^2 coefficient is 1), we see that $p + q = b$ and $pq = c$ (match the terms that occupy the same positions in this example expression and the Standard Form expression).

We know that if we can determine p and q, we can get the solutions easily because $x = -p$ and $x = -q$. Though the Standard Form shown above doesn't directly isolate p and q like the Factored Form does, we do have some valuable information: **the sum of p and q equals the b coefficient**, and **the product of p and q equals the constant term c**. Therefore, if we can figure out two numbers that add up to b and that multiply to yield c, we can solve a quadratic equation where the polynomial is in Standard Form. In our current example, $x^2 + 2x - 24 = 0$, the b coefficient is 2, and c is -24, so that means if we can figure out the two numbers that add up to 2 and that multiply to -24, we will have identified the p and q that we need to create the factored form, and thus to solve the equation.

In this case, we won't yet show the generalized, exhaustive procedure for finding all the candidates for p and q and testing them, but we'll observe that $6 + (-4) = 2$, and $6(-4) = -24$. That means that our p and q are 6 and -4 (it doesn't matter which is which), and we can rewrite our quadratic equation in Factored Form as $(x + 6)(x - 4) = 0$.

From our previous discussion, you should be able to see right away that this means $x = -6$ is a solution (because it makes the first factor equal 0), and also that $x = 4$ is a solution (same, but for the second factor).

The key to solving a quadratic equation by factoring the expression is this process of figuring out those two numbers that add to make the b coefficient while also multiplying to equal the c coefficient (again, assuming that the x^2 coefficient is 1).

For example, to find the factors of the quadratic expression in the equation $y = x^2 + 3x + 2$, we need to find two numbers that add to 3 and multiply to 2. The numbers 1 and 2 add to 3 (we know that $1 + 2 = 3$) and multiply to 2 (we know that $1(2) = 2$), so the factors are $(x + 1)$ and $(x + 2)$.

$$y = x^2 + 3x + 2$$
$$y = (x + 1)(x + 2)$$

Remember that the main purpose we have for factoring quadratics on this test is to find solutions to a quadratic equation, and our goal is to have 0 on one side of the equation and factors on the other (again, if the product of the factors is equal to 0, then the solutions are the values of x that make any of the individual factors equal to 0).

Generally, the reason we'd like to factor the quadratic expression in an equation is to find the zeros of the expression; recall that the zeros are the values of the variable that result in a value of 0 for the entire expression. We can set up an equation that expresses this by replacing y with 0.

$$y = (x + 1)(x + 2)$$
$$0 = (x + 1)(x + 2)$$

The factor $(x + 1)$ tells us that -1 is a solution, because when $x = -1$, $(x + 1) = 0$. We can check by substituting -1 for x in the original equation and verifying that y is equal to 0.

$$y = x^2 + 3x + 2$$
$$y = (-1)^2 + 3(-1) + 2$$
$$y = 1 - 3 + 2$$
$$y = 0$$

The factor $(x + 2)$ tells us that -2 is a solution, because when $x = -2$, $(x + 2) = 0$. We can check by substituting -2 for x in the original equation and verifying that y is equal to 0.

$$y = x^2 + 3x + 2$$
$$y = (-2)^2 + 3(-2) + 2$$
$$y = 4 - 6 + 2$$
$$y = 0$$

Factoring Quadratic Equations

The Standard Form of a quadratic equation, where a, b, and c are constants, is the following:

$$y = ax^2 + bx + c$$

On the test, when the coefficient of the x^2 term in a quadratic polynomial is 1, such as in the equation $y = x^2 + bx + c$, it is usually easy to factor (we will examine other solution methods later in the chapter to see what to do when this is not the case). **You need to determine the two numbers, p and q, whose sum is b and whose product is c.**

When the values of p and q are found, the quadratic expression can be rewritten as $y = (x + p)(x + q)$.

If we are trying to find zeros of the quadratic, we should substitute 0 for y and find the values that would make each factor equal to zero (because if any factor is 0, the entire expression has a value of 0). If the factors are $(x + p)$ and $(x + q)$, then the zeros are $x = -p$ and $x = -q$, respectively.

If you are using the factoring method to find solutions, you don't need to actually write out the Factored Form of the quadratic; once you determine the values of p and q, you know that the solutions are $-p$ and $-q$.

One tip for making finding the factors easier is to look at the signs of the b and c terms. If the c term is positive, both signs for p and q will be the same as each other (either both positive or both negative) because a positive times a positive is positive, and a negative times a negative is also positive. To determine whether both signs should be positive, look to the b term: if the b term is positive, both p and q should have positive signs, because adding two negative numbers can't produce a positive result; if the b term is negative, both p and q should have negative signs.

If the c term is negative, then p and q should have opposite signs (one being positive, and the other negative). If the signs for p and q are mixed, the sign of the b term will determine which of p and q should have the negative sign. If b is positive, then the larger value of p and q should be positive (and the smaller should thus be negative) because adding a larger positive number and a smaller negative number yields a positive result; if b is negative, then the larger value of p and q should be negative (and the smaller should therefore be positive) because adding a smaller positive number and a larger negative number yields a negative result.

When a quadratic expression in Standard Form has no constant term written at the end (it consists of only an x^2-term and x-term), factoring is actually simpler, but this throws off students who are expecting three terms in factorable quadratic expressions. For example, let's look at the quadratic expression $x^2 - 4x$. The most straightforward way to approach factoring this expression is to recognize that both terms, x^2 and $-4x$, share a common factor of x, so we can factor x out from both terms.

$$x^2 - 4x$$
$$(x)(x) - 4(x)$$
$$x(x - 4)$$

However, even if you fail to recognize this simplified factoring method available with these two-term quadratics, the good news is that the more generalized factoring method explained previously still works as long as you understand that the absence of a constant term just means that you can consider the constant term to be 0.

Let's again look at the quadratic expression $x^2 - 4x$, which is in Standard Form where $a = 1$, $b = -4$, and $c = 0$ (remember, the constant term appears not to be there, but that just means its value is 0). Based on how we factored other quadratic expressions above, in order to find the factors of this equation, we need two numbers that add to -4 and multiply to 0. In order to multiply to 0, one of the two number must be 0, so $(x + 0)$ is a factor. Since 0 and -4 add to -4, then -4 must be the other number, meaning that $(x + (-4))$, or $(x - 4)$, is a factor.

$$x^2 - 4x$$
$$(x + 0)(x - 4)$$

Since $(x + 0)$ is the same as x, the expression $x^2 - 4x$ in Factored Form is $x(x - 4)$.

Hopefully, you will not freeze up if you encounter one of these on the test because you could apply these generalized principles. However, it's considerably simpler to just factor out the variable as explained.

SkillDrill 8.2-1

Directions: Find two numbers whose sum is S and whose product is P.

Challenge questions are boxed.

1. $S = 7, P = 10$ **2.** $S = -7, P = 10$ **3.** $S = -4, P = -12$ **4.** $S = 1, P = -12$

5. $S = 13, P = 40$ **6.** $S = 4, P = -77$ **7.** $\boxed{S = -9, P = -52}$ **8.** $\boxed{S = -20, P = 96}$

Directions: Write each of the following polynomial expressions in Factored Form.

Challenge questions are boxed.

9. $x^2 + 3x - 4$ **10.** $x^2 - 10x + 21$ **11.** $a^2 + 18a + 80$ **12.** $b^2 - b - 30$

13. $a^2 - 3a$ **14.** $x^2 + x$ **15.** $\boxed{x^4 + 18x^2 + 80}$ **16.** $\boxed{x^5 + 18x^3 + 80x}$

Directions: Find the solutions to the polynomial equations below by factoring.

Challenge problems are boxed.

17. $x^2 + 3x - 4 = 0$ **18.** $x^2 - 8x + 7 = 0$ **19.** $x^2 + 9x + 20 = 0$ **20.** $x^2 - 10x + 16 = 0$

21. $x^2 - x - 12 = 0$ **22.** $x^2 + x - 2 = 0$ **23.** $a^2 + 3a - 28 = 0$ **24.** $b^2 - 14b + 48 = 0$

25. $\boxed{a^2 - 2a + 8 = 16}$ **26.** $\boxed{b^2 + 4b - 6 = 5b}$ **27.** $\boxed{x^2 + 22x + 140 = 20}$ **28.** $\boxed{x^2 - x - 12 = 3x}$

Example 8.2-1

1 1600.io 8.2

$$x^2 + 5x - 24 = 0$$

If a is a solution of the equation above and $a > 0$, what is the value of a?

Solution 1

1. In order to factor this equation to find the solutions, we need to start by finding two numbers that add to 5 and multiply to -24.

2. The numbers 8 and -3 add to 5 and multiply to -24. Therefore, one of the factors is $(x+8)$ and the other factor is $(x-3)$.

$$x^2 + 5x - 24 = 0$$
$$(x + 8)(x - 3) = 0$$

3. Since $(x + 8)$ is a factor, the equation will be true when $x + 8 = 0$, so $x = -8$ is a solution, but the question tells us that the solution a must be greater than 0 (a positive number). Since $(x - 3)$ is also a factor, the equation will be true when $x - 3 = 0$. Therefore, $x = 3$ is also a solution. The value of the solution a must be 3 since 3 is the only solution that is greater than 0.

4. The answer is 3.

Solution 2

1. Use the Quadratic Formula to find the solutions. For this equation, $a = 1$, $b = 5$, and $c = -24$.

$$x = \frac{-b}{2a} \pm \frac{\sqrt{b^2 - 4ac}}{2a}$$

$$x = \frac{-(5)}{2(1)} \pm \frac{\sqrt{(5)^2 - 4(1)(-24)}}{2(1)}$$

$$x = \frac{-5}{2} \pm \frac{\sqrt{25 + 96}}{2}$$

$$x = \frac{-5}{2} \pm \frac{\sqrt{121}}{2}$$

$$x = \frac{-5}{2} \pm \frac{11}{2}$$

2. The two possible solutions are $x = \frac{-5}{2} + \frac{11}{2}$ and $x = \frac{-5}{2} - \frac{11}{2}$, but only the first one will be a positive value, so we can ignore the second one since we are told that we are looking for a solution that is greater than 0. Therefore, the only solution that answers the questions is $x = \frac{-5}{2} + \frac{11}{2} = \frac{6}{2} = 3$.

3. The answer is 3.

Notes

Hopefully this example helps show why it is good to know conventional factoring. Overreliance on the Quadratic Formula is a time killer.

View related real-test problems at 1600.io/p/smtex?topic=8.2

Section 8.2 Practice Problems

1 8.2

$$x^2 + 2x - 15 = 0$$

If a is a solution of the equation above and $a > 0$, what is the value of a?

2 8.2

A bricklayer is designing a rectangular patio. The length of the patio is to be 4 feet longer than the width. If the area of the patio will be 192 square feet, what will be the length, in feet, of the patio?

8.3 Other Methods of Finding Roots

Not all quadratic expressions are easily factorable, so we need other tools to deal with those situations. We have already seen the Quadratic Formula being used to find solutions, and that option is always on the table, but if the only tool you have is a hammer, then every problem will look like a nail. In reality, there are subtle differences between quadratics problems, and you really want to use the appropriate tools in order to minimize the time needed for solving while also minimizing the chances of an error creeping in.

Divide Through and Factor when $a \neq 1$

Sometimes the coefficient of the x^2 term is not 1, but you might find that all of the coefficients in the equation share a common factor that can be divided out, making it easy to factor the quadratic expression (it's important that we are dividing both sides by a constant, not a variable—dividing by a variable can have greater ramifications that are discussed in a later chapter).

Example 8.3-1

1 1600.io 8.3

What are the solutions of the quadratic equation $3x^2 - 12x - 15 = 0$?

A) $x = -1$ and $x = 5$

B) $x = -1$ and $x = -5$

C) $x = 1$ and $x = 5$

D) $x = 1$ and $x = -5$

Solution 1

1. Divide both sides of the equation by 3 (or multiply by $\frac{1}{3}$ if you prefer to think of it that way) to make the x^2 coefficient equal to 1. Remember to divide all three terms on the left side (distribute the $\frac{1}{3}$ to all of the terms).

$$3x^2 - 12x - 15 = 0$$

$$\frac{3x^2 - 12x - 15}{3} = \frac{0}{3}$$

$$x^2 - 4x - 5 = 0$$

2. In order to factor the equation, we need to find two numbers that add to −4 and multiply to −5.

3. The numbers −5 and 1 add to −4 and multiply to −5, so one of the factors is $(x - 5)$ and the other factor is $(x + 1)$.

$$x^2 - 4x - 5 = 0$$
$$(x - 5)(x + 1) = 0$$

4. Since $(x - 5)$ is a factor, the equation will be true when $x - 5 = 0$. Therefore, we know that $x = 5$ is a solution to the quadratic equation.

5. Since $(x + 1)$ is a factor, the equation will also be true when $x + 1 = 0$. Therefore, we know that $x = -1$ is a solution to the quadratic equation.

6. The two solutions are $x = -1$ and $x = 5$.

7. The answer is A.

Solution 2

Step 1 is the same as in Solution 1.

2. In the Quadratic Formula (which you really shouldn't need for this problem because the expression should be easily factorable after we divided by 3), plug in 1 for a, -4 for b, and -5 for c.

$$x = \frac{-b}{2a} \pm \frac{\sqrt{b^2 - 4ac}}{2a}$$

$$x = \frac{-(-4)}{2(1)} \pm \frac{\sqrt{(-4)^2 - 4(1)(-5)}}{2(1)}$$

$$x = \frac{4}{2} \pm \frac{\sqrt{16 + 20}}{2}$$

$$x = 2 \pm \frac{\sqrt{36}}{2}$$

$$x = 2 \pm \frac{6}{2}$$

$$x = 2 \pm 3$$

3. The two solutions are $x = 2 - 3 = -1$ and $x = 2 + 3 = 5$.

4. The answer is A.

Notes

In Solution 1, you could have stopped writing after Step 3: once you find the numbers p and q that sum to b and multiply to c, you know that the solutions must be $-p$ and $-q$, which are -1 and 5 in this example.

In Solution 2, you do not have to start by factoring out 3, but it makes evaluating the Quadratic Formula easier because the numbers are smaller and more manageable. In practice, after dividing through by 3, you would check if conventional factoring seems like a viable option (which of course it is in this case).

You could do this problem by plugging in each set of answer choices and making sure that both values of x in a choice will make the left side of the equation equal to 0 (weak).

Product Sum (ac) Method when $a \neq 1$

Another method for finding the roots of quadratics is the **Product Sum (ac) Method**, which is particularly useful when the x^2 coefficient, a, is not equal to 1 and dividing all of the terms by a will not produce an easily factorable expression. This method is simply the generalized factoring procedure that can be applied when the a coefficient is not 1; in fact, you'll see that when $a = 1$, this method degenerates to the simpler factoring process that we explained previously.

When factoring a quadratic equation $ax^2 + bx + c = 0$ using the Product Sum (ac) Method, we need to find a product number and a sum number, just as with the somewhat simpler task of factoring a quadratic expression where the a-coefficient is 1.

As we saw, when the a-coefficient is 1, we factor by finding the two numbers whose sum is equal to b and whose product is equal to c. **In the situation where the a-coefficient isn't 1, the sum must still be b, but the product needs to be a times c (that is, ac, which is where the method gets its nickname)**. As with the simpler factoring procedure, you need to find the two values that add up to the sum number and multiply to the product number.

For example, in the equation $0 = 8x^2 - 2x - 15$, the sum number is -2, and the product number is $8(-15)$, or -120. The two numbers that add up to -2 and multiply to -120 are -12 and 10.

Once we have the two values that satisfy the product and sum constraints, the solutions are just the negatives of those values divided by a.

Here, once you've found -12 and 10, the roots are $-\left(\frac{-12}{a}\right) = -\left(\frac{-12}{8}\right)$, which simplifies to $\frac{3}{2}$, and $-\left(\frac{10}{a}\right) = -\left(\frac{10}{8}\right)$, which simplifies to $\frac{-5}{4}$, and you're done (you can plug these back in to the original to check that they are indeed zeros).

Product Sum (ac) Method

Here's a concise description of the procedure for finding roots using this method (we call this the ac method because that serves as a reminder of the most critical step):

1. Find two numbers r and s that add up to b and that multiply to ac.
2. The roots are $\frac{-r}{a}$ and $\frac{-s}{a}$.

If you need to construct the complete Factored Form (which is not necessary for solving), it's

$$a\left(x + \frac{r}{a}\right)\left(x + \frac{s}{a}\right)$$

Alternatively, the Factored Form can be written as

$$a(x+p)(x+q)$$

where $p = \frac{r}{a}$ and $q = \frac{s}{a}$.

It should again be noted that this is just factoring, generalized to the case where $a \neq 1$.

SkillDrill 8.3-1

Directions: Divide out a common factor from all of the coefficients or use the Product Sum (ac) Method to find the solutions to the following polynomial equations. Beware the frumious bandersnatch (non-zero right-hand side).

1. $4x^2 + 12x + 8 = 0$

2. $3x^2 - 15x + 18 = 0$

3. $-5x^2 + 15x + 22 = 2$

4. $-2x^2 - 10x + 25 = -3$

5. $4x^2 - x - 3 = 0$

6. $6x^2 + 7x + 2 = 0$

7. $8x^2 - 15x - 2 = 0$

8. $2x^2 + 17x + 22 = 1$

Generalized Quadratic Solving Methods

There are equations that have solutions that are not whole numbers or even rational numbers (fractions in which the numerator and denominator are whole numbers)—for example, they may contain square roots—which makes finding factors nearly impossible with simple factoring or the Product Sum (ac) Method. The test rarely includes these kinds of equations, but, for such situations, there are other methods available for solving quadratic equations when conventional factoring is too difficult.

Completing the Square

We've already discussed one such method: the Quadratic Formula. This method is very popular, and you most likely knew about it already. However, if you can't factor a quadratic equation easily, there is yet another option besides the Quadratic Formula called **Completing the Square**. This method is based around creating perfect square expressions like the ones we talked about earlier in this chapter. This method often seems rather mysterious at first, but it is very formulaic and easy to repeat once you get used to it.

In fact, like the more familiar Quadratic Formula (which is, in fact, derived from Completing the Square), Completing the Square can be used to find solutions to any quadratic equation, regardless of the coefficients and whether or not we can find numbers p and q that sum to b and multiply to ac.

As mentioned earlier, sometimes it is too difficult or even impossible to come up with two whole numbers whose sum is equal to b and whose product is equal to ac (there could be no solutions, which will be discussed in the coming chapters, or the solutions may not be whole numbers or even fractions). Also, when the coefficient of the x^2 term is not 1, factoring could be a tricky option (even if it is viable through the Product Sum (ac) Method). The goal of Completing the Square is to use the typical unwrapping solving approach—keep peeling apart an expression until the variable is isolated. There's one special move here when there are two x-terms of different degree, so an operation is used that can eliminate that mix of variables of differing degree, leaving just one variable term of degree 1; everything else is boring algebra. It should be noted again that the Quadratic Formula is derived from this technique, so they are equivalent in theory, but in practice, this method can be quicker and can involve fewer simplification steps than using the Quadratic Formula (not to mention it can be a good way to find the Vertex Form of quadratic equations and to find the equations of circles, both of which are discussed in later chapters).

Let's walk through the method using a simple equation (one that can be factored conventionally, as we saw in Example 8.3-1): $3x^2 - 12x - 15 = 0$.

1. Divide both sides of the equation by the a coefficient to eliminate the coefficient of the x^2 term.

$$3x^2 - 12x - 15 = 0$$
$$x^2 - 4x - 5 = 0$$

2. Move the constant c to other side to isolate the x terms.

$$x^2 - 4x - 5 = 0$$
$$x^2 - 4x = 5$$

3. Replace the left side of the equation with $\left(x + \frac{b}{2}\right)^2$ (where b is the coefficient of the x term) and balance the extra constant $\left(\frac{b}{2}\right)^2$ produced by this perfect square by adding $\left(\frac{b}{2}\right)^2$ to the right side of the equation (this step seems like magic now, but if you're interested in seeing an explanation, ask George to make a video about it or sneak a peek at the appendix to this chapter).

   Because the term $\frac{b}{2}$ is used twice, it pays to simplify and reduce it first before deploying it so you don't have to do that twice; here, $\frac{b}{2} = \frac{-4}{2}$ and it reduces to -2. Note that this balancing constant $\left(\frac{b}{2}\right)^2$ will always be positive because squares of real numbers are always positive, so you don't need to think about what sign to use when you put this value on the right side, but we'll show it with the correct sign so you're not confused. From this point forward, it's straightforward algebra to solve for the variable now that it only appears as a first-degree term. Start that process by combining the constant terms on the right side (creating a common denominator as necessary if you've got a fraction or two there so you can complete the addition).

$$x^2 - 4x = 5$$
$$\left(x + \frac{b}{2}\right)^2 = 5 + \left(\frac{b}{2}\right)^2 \quad \text{where} \quad \frac{b}{2} = \frac{-4}{2} = -2$$
$$(x-2)^2 = 5 + (-2)^2$$
$$(x-2)^2 = 5 + 4$$
$$(x-2)^2 = 9$$

4. Take the square root of both sides, being careful to include both positive and negative square roots.

$$(x-2)^2 = 9$$
$$x - 2 = \pm\sqrt{9}$$
$$x - 2 = \pm 3$$

5. Move the constant to right side of the equation to isolate and solve for x.

$$x - 2 = \pm 3$$
$$x = 2 \pm 3$$

6. Enumerate the solutions.

$$x = 2 \pm 3$$
$$x = 2 + 3, \quad x = 2 - 3$$
$$x = 5, \quad x = -1$$

As you can see, there are just six steps needed to get to the solutions with no guesswork required. Though our example could also have been solved by using factoring, the value of Completing the Square is that it can be used on *any* quadratic equation regardless of whether it can be easily factored, and it works just as well when a quadratic expression has an a coefficient that does not divide neatly into the b and c coefficients. For example, here's a problem that's a bit messier, but the solving steps are exactly the same; Completing the Square doesn't care about a coefficients or fractions.

For this walkthrough, let's use the same example equation that we used for the Product Sum (ac) Method: $8x^2 - 2x - 15 = 0$.

1. Divide both sides of the equation by the a coefficient to eliminate the coefficient of the x^2 term; don't be put off by the appearance of a couple of fractions; you're in high school.

$$8x^2 - 2x - 15 = 0$$

$$x^2 - \frac{2}{8}x - \frac{15}{8} = 0$$

$$x^2 - \frac{1}{4}x - \frac{15}{8} = 0$$

2. Move the constant to other side to isolate the x terms.

$$x^2 - \frac{1}{4}x - \frac{15}{8} = 0$$

$$x^2 - \frac{1}{4}x = \frac{15}{8}$$

3. Replace the left side of the equation with $\left(x + \frac{b}{2}\right)^2$ (where b is the coefficient of the x term) and balance the extra constant that expression produces by adding $\left(\frac{b}{2}\right)^2$ to the right side of the equation; you'll be using the term $\frac{b}{2} = \frac{\frac{-1}{4}}{2}$ in two places in the equation, and it can be simplified to $\frac{-1}{8}$, so take care of that before deploying it in both locations—there's no need to do that math twice. Complete this phase by combining the constants on the right side; this time, you'll need to form a common denominator.

$$x^2 - \frac{1}{4}x = \frac{15}{8}$$

$$\left(x + \frac{b}{2}\right)^2 = \frac{15}{8} + \left(\frac{b}{2}\right)^2 \quad \text{where} \quad \frac{b}{2} = \frac{\frac{-1}{4}}{2} = \frac{-1}{8}$$

$$\left(x - \frac{1}{8}\right)^2 = \frac{15}{8} + \left(\frac{-1}{8}\right)^2$$

$$\left(x - \frac{1}{8}\right)^2 = \frac{15}{8} + \frac{1}{64}$$

$$\left(x - \frac{1}{8}\right)^2 = \frac{120}{64} + \frac{1}{64}$$

$$\left(x - \frac{1}{8}\right)^2 = \frac{121}{64}$$

4. Take the square root of both sides, being careful to include both positive and negative square roots.

$$\left(x - \frac{1}{8}\right)^2 = \frac{121}{64}$$

$$x - \frac{1}{8} = \pm\sqrt{\frac{121}{64}}$$

$$x - \frac{1}{8} = \pm\frac{11}{8}$$

5. Move the constant to right side of the equation to isolate and solve for x.

$$x - \frac{1}{8} = \pm\frac{11}{8}$$

$$x = \frac{1}{8} \pm \frac{11}{8}$$

6. Enumerate the solutions.

$$x = \frac{1}{8} \pm \frac{11}{8}$$

$$x = \frac{1}{8} - \frac{11}{8}, \quad x = \frac{1}{8} + \frac{11}{8}$$

$$x = \frac{-10}{8}, \quad x = \frac{12}{8}$$

$$x = \frac{-5}{4}, \quad x = \frac{3}{2}$$

This method works just as well when the solutions will involve radicals; you just need to follow the steps and the solutions will emerge.

Completing the Square

1. Divide both sides of the equation by the a coefficient to eliminate the coefficient of the x^2 term.
2. Move the constant to other side to isolate the x terms.
3. Replace the left side of the equation with $\left(x + \frac{b}{2}\right)^2$ (where b is the coefficient of the x term) and balance the extra constant by adding $\left(\frac{b}{2}\right)^2$ to the right side of the equation; combine constants.
4. Take the square root of both sides, being careful to include both positive and negative square roots.
5. Move the constant to right side of the equation to isolate and solve for x.
6. Enumerate the solutions.

Quadratic Formula

If you are having trouble factoring a quadratic equation by any of the previously outlined methods (or if you are weak), you may want to make use of the **Quadratic Formula** presented in Section 8.1 of this chapter (some people prefer to use it all the time, and while it will work, it is often inefficient and error-prone, so we recommend not relying on it as the only tool in your quadratic-solving toolkit). It has an advantage over conventional factoring and the Product Sum (ac) Method in that, like Completing the Square, the Quadratic Formula will always help you find the solutions to a quadratic equation (as long as you don't mess up any plugging in, square-rooting, multiplying, dividing, or simplifying steps).

SkillDrill 8.3-2

Directions: Use Completing the Square or the Quadratic Formula (weak) to find the solutions to the following polynomial equations.

Challenge problems are boxed.

1. $x^2 + 4x - 4 = 0$

2. $x^2 + x - 1 = 0$

3. $x^2 - 3x + 5 = 8$

4. $x^2 - 6x + 9 = 8$

5. $2x^2 - 8x - 6 = 6$

6. $\boxed{3x^2 + 3x - 2 = 0}$

7. $2a^2 + 10a + 5 = 0$

8. $\boxed{4b^2 - 9b - 2 = 0}$

Example 8.3-2

2 8.3

Which of the following is a solution to the equation $3x^2 - 4x - 4 = 0$?

A) -2

B) $-\frac{2}{3}$

C) $\frac{1}{3}$

D) 4

Solution 1

This solution makes use of Product Sum (ac) Method.

1. The product number, which is equal to ac for a quadratic expression in Standard Form, is equal to $3(-4)$ or -12. The sum number, which is equal to b for a quadratic expression in Standard Form, is -4. We need to find values, r and s, that add to -4 and multiply to -12.

2. The values −6 and 2 add to −4 and multiply to −12, so $r = -6$ and $s = 2$ (it doesn't matter which is which). We can speed our way to this determination by observing that because the product target of −12 is a negative number, we know that one of the two numbers will be positive and the other will be negative; because the sum number is negative, we know that the number with the larger absolute value must be the negative number because we want to subtract a larger number from a smaller one to get a negative result.
3. At this point we are done because the roots are equal to $\frac{-r}{a}$ and $\frac{-s}{a}$ (we don't need to write the equation in Factored Form).
4. Since $r = -6$ and $a = 3$, then one of the solutions is $x = \frac{-(-6)}{3}$, which reduces to $x = 2$. This does not match any answer choices.
5. Since $s = 2$ and $a = 3$, then the other solution is $x = \frac{-2}{3}$. This matches answer choice B.
6. The answer is B.

Solution 2

This solution makes use of Completing the Square.

1. Divide both sides of the equation by 3 in order to eliminate the coefficient of the x^2 term.

$$3x^2 - 4x - 4 = 0$$

$$x^2 - \frac{4}{3}x - \frac{4}{3} = 0$$

2. Move the constant term to the other side of the equation in order to isolate the x terms: add $\frac{4}{3}$ to both sides of the equation.

$$x^2 - \frac{4}{3}x - \frac{4}{3} = 0$$

$$x^2 - \frac{4}{3}x = \frac{4}{3}$$

3. Replace the left side of the equation with $\left(x - \frac{4}{3(2)}\right)^2$ and balance the extra constant on the other side by adding $\left(\frac{4}{2(3)}\right)^2$ to the right side of the equation.

$$x^2 - \frac{4}{3}x = \frac{4}{3}$$

$$\left(x - \frac{4}{3(2)}\right)^2 = \left(\frac{4}{2(3)}\right)^2 + \frac{4}{3}$$

$$\left(x - \frac{2}{3}\right)^2 = \left(\frac{2}{3}\right)^2 + \frac{4}{3}$$

$$\left(x - \frac{2}{3}\right)^2 = \frac{4}{9} + \frac{4}{3}$$

4. Combine the constants on the right side of the equation (make a common denominator of 9).

$$\left(x-\frac{2}{3}\right)^2=\frac{4}{9}+\frac{4}{3}$$

$$\left(x-\frac{2}{3}\right)^2=\frac{4}{9}+\frac{12}{9}$$

$$\left(x-\frac{2}{3}\right)^2=\frac{16}{9}$$

5. Take the square root of both sides, being careful to include both positive and negative square roots.

$$\left(x-\frac{2}{3}\right)^2=\frac{16}{9}$$

$$x-\frac{2}{3}=\pm\sqrt{\frac{16}{9}}$$

$$x-\frac{2}{3}=\pm\frac{4}{3}$$

6. Move the constant to right side of the equation (add $\frac{2}{3}$ to both sides of the equation) to isolate and solve for x.

$$x-\frac{2}{3}=\pm\frac{4}{3}$$

$$x=\frac{2}{3}\pm\frac{4}{3}$$

$$x=\frac{2}{3}+\frac{4}{3},\quad x=\frac{2}{3}-\frac{4}{3}$$

$$x=\frac{6}{3},\quad x=\frac{-2}{3}$$

$$x=2,\quad x=\frac{-2}{3}$$

7. The two solutions are $x=2$ and $x=\frac{-2}{3}$, but only $\frac{-2}{3}$ is available as an answer choice.

8. The answer is B.

Solution 3

This solution makes use of Quadratic Formula.

1. There is no real value in dividing by 3 to start this problem, because it does not help simplify the terms that will be plugged into the Quadratic Formula. Substitute 3 for a, −4 for b, and −4 for c, then chug away.

$$x = \frac{-b}{2a} \pm \frac{\sqrt{b^2 - 4ac}}{2a}$$

$$x = \frac{-(-4)}{2(3)} \pm \frac{\sqrt{(-4)^2 - 4(3)(-4)}}{2(3)}$$

$$x = \frac{4}{6} \pm \frac{\sqrt{16+48}}{6}$$

$$x = \frac{2}{3} \pm \frac{\sqrt{64}}{6}$$

$$x = \frac{2}{3} \pm \frac{8}{6}$$

$$x = \frac{2}{3} \pm \frac{4}{3}$$

$$x = \frac{2}{3} + \frac{4}{3},\ x = \frac{2}{3} - \frac{4}{3}$$

$$x = \frac{6}{3},\ x = \frac{-2}{3}$$

$$x = 2,\ x = \frac{-2}{3}$$

2. The two solutions are $x = 2$ and $x = \frac{-2}{3}$, but only $\frac{-2}{3}$ is available as an answer choice.
3. The answer is B.

Notes

Alternatively, you could just plug in each answer choice to see which one makes the equation true (still weak).

All roads lead to Rome, but the roads are not always equal. If it's unfamiliar to you, Completing the Square may seem like a worse option for this problem than Quadratic Formula, but if you get good at Completing the Square, all of the steps can be performed in your head, and, again, ultimately Completing the Square not only forms the basis of the Quadratic Formula, but also has uses outside of these factoring problems.

Example 8.3-3

3 1600.io 8.3

$$x^2 - 6x + 4 = 0$$

Which of the following is a solution to the equation above?

A) $x = -3 + \sqrt{5}$

B) $x = -3 + \sqrt{11}$

C) $x = 3 + \sqrt{5}$

D) $x = 3 + \sqrt{11}$

Solution 1

Since we cannot find whole numbers that add to -6 and multiply to 4, we should use the Completing the Square or the Quadratic Formula to factor this equation and find solutions. In this problem, you don't even need to try to factor, because if you examine the answer choices, you'll see that all the options are expressions, not single whole number values, and they all have a square root term, so the correct answer will have a square root term. That would mean that at least one of the factors would be of the form $x - (r + \sqrt{s})$, so $r + \sqrt{s}$ would need to be one of the values you'd need to find if you use factoring, but it's impractical to search for anything other than whole numbers. More to the point, whenever you see a problem where the answer choices are of the form $d + \sqrt{e}$ (or $d - \sqrt{e}$), you should probably use Completing the Square or the Quadratic Formula to find the solution(s), not factoring. This is a great example of why it can be extremely informative to examine the answer choices before commencing work.

First, we'll use Completing the Square.

1. Move the constant term to the other side of the equation by subtracting 4 from both sides of the equation.

$$x^2 - 6x + 4 = 0$$
$$x^2 - 6x = -4$$

2. Replace $x^2 - 6x$ with $(x-3)^2$ and add 3^2 to the other side of the equation to neutralize the unwanted constant generated by the squaring operation.

$$x^2 - 6x = -4$$
$$(x-3)^2 = -4 + 3^2$$
$$(x-3)^2 = -4 + 9$$
$$(x-3)^2 = 5$$

3. Take the square root of both sides of the equation, being careful to retain both the positive and negative square roots on the right side.

$$(x-3)^2 = 5$$
$$x - 3 = \pm\sqrt{5}$$

4. Add 3 to both sides of the equation in order to isolate x.

$$x - 3 = \pm\sqrt{5}$$
$$x = 3 \pm \sqrt{5}$$
$$x = 3 + \sqrt{5}, \quad x = 3 - \sqrt{5}$$

5. Out of the two solutions, only $x = 3 + \sqrt{5}$ appears as an answer choice.

6. The answer is C.

Solution 2

As stated in Solution 1, based on the answer choices, there is no point in searching for factors, so for this solution, we will use the Quadratic Formula.

1. The value of a is 1; the value of b is -6; the value of c is 4.

$$x = \frac{-b}{2a} \pm \frac{\sqrt{b^2 - 4ac}}{2a}$$

$$x = \frac{-(-6)}{2(1)} \pm \frac{\sqrt{(-6)^2 - 4(1)(4)}}{2(1)}$$

$$x = \frac{6}{2} \pm \frac{\sqrt{36 - 16}}{2}$$

$$x = 3 \pm \frac{\sqrt{20}}{2}$$

2. The radical can be simplified since $\sqrt{20} = \sqrt{4(5)} = \sqrt{4}\sqrt{5} = 2\sqrt{5}$.

$$x = 3 \pm \frac{\sqrt{20}}{2}$$

$$x = 3 \pm \frac{\sqrt{4}\sqrt{5}}{2}$$

$$x = 3 \pm \frac{2\sqrt{5}}{2}$$

$$x = 3 \pm \sqrt{5}$$

3. The two solutions are $x = 3 + \sqrt{5}$, which is choice C, and $x = 3 - \sqrt{5}$.

4. The answer is C.

Notes

While many people like to have a formula to fall back on, it is undeniable that the numbers are much easier to work with in Solution 1, using Completing the Square. You WILL accept Completing the Square as your primary method of finding solutions to Quadratic Equations that aren't easily factorable.

Section 8.3 Suggested Problems from Real Tests

View related real-test problems at 1600.io/p/smtex?topic=8.3

Section 8.3 Practice Problems

1 8.3

What are the solutions to $3x^2 + 18x + 9 = 0$?

A) $x = -3 \pm \sqrt{6}$

B) $x = -3 \pm 2\sqrt{3}$

C) $x = -6 \pm \sqrt{6}$

D) $x = -6 \pm 2\sqrt{3}$

2 8.3

$$y = -16t^2 + 48t + 160$$

The equation above gives the height of an object above the ground, y in feet, t seconds after it is launched from the roof of a building. How many seconds after it is launched does the object reach the ground?

3 8.3

$$6w^2 + 10w + 1 = 0$$

Which of the following values is a solution to the equation above?

A) $\dfrac{-5 + \sqrt{19}}{6}$

B) $\dfrac{-5 + \sqrt{31}}{6}$

C) $\dfrac{5 + \sqrt{19}}{6}$

D) $\dfrac{5 + \sqrt{31}}{6}$

4 8.3

$$2x^3 - 13x^2 - 7x$$

Which of the following is NOT a factor of the polynomial above?

A) x

B) $x - 7$

C) $2x - 7$

D) $2x + 1$

8.4 Simplified Factoring Situations

There are some patterns that appear often on the test in quadratic equations. If you learn to spot these patterns, you can save a lot of time.

Difference of Squares

A common form of quadratic equation on this test is **the Difference of Squares**. Learning to spot quadratic equations in this form will save time and effort because you will immediately know how to factor them.

Generally, when multiplying a pair of binomials of the form $(x + a)$ and $(x + b)$, we end up with a three-term quadratic expression:

$$(x + a)(x + b)$$
$$x^2 + ax + bx + ab$$
$$x^2 + (a + b)x + ab$$

Notice that the middle (x) term's coefficient is $(a + b)$. If that term evaluates to 0, there will be no middle (x) term at all. That will happen when $b = -a$, because $(a + (-a)) = 0$.

Let's substitute $-a$ for b to show this:

$$(x + a)(x - a)$$
$$x^2 + ax - ax - a^2$$

You should be able to see where this is leading already. Here's the final step after those two middle terms cancel out:

$$x^2 - a^2$$

What this means is that any expressions in the form $x^2 - a^2$ can be factored as $(x + a)(x - a)$

Factoring the Difference of Squares

Any expression of the form $a^2 - b^2$, which is the difference of two squares, can be factored as $(a + b)(a - b)$.

In the following example, we will see that both terms are perfect squares:

$$x^2 - 9 = (x)^2 - (3)^2$$

Since this equation fits the difference of squares pattern, we know that the factors must be $(x + 3)$ and $(x - 3)$.

$$x^2 - 9 = (x + 3)(x - 3)$$

In this example, we will see that the we can use any number as the second term, and the situation works the same even when the constant is not a perfect square:

$$x^2 - 6$$
$$(x)^2 - (\sqrt{6})^2$$
$$(x + \sqrt{6})(x - \sqrt{6})$$

In this final example, we will see that this pattern is true for the difference of any two squares (even cases where the exponents of x terms are are greater than 2):

$$x^4 - 81 = (x^2)^2 - 9^2 = (x^2 + 9)(x^2 - 9)$$

Did you notice that one of these factors, $(x^2 - 9)$, is also a difference of two squares expression? We can factor this expression further. The other factor, $(x^2 + 9)$, is not a difference of squares (the terms within it are being added, not subtracted), and we cannot factor it any further (it does not have any real solutions).

$$x^4 - 81$$
$$(x^2 + 9)(x^2 - 9)$$
$$(x^2 + 9)(x + 3)(x - 3)$$

SkillDrill 8.4-1

Directions: Write the following difference of squares polynomials as the product of factors. If a factor is itself a difference of squares, decompose it further.

Challenge questions are boxed.

1. $x^2 - 4$ **2.** $x^2 - 81$ **3.** $a^2 - b^2$ **4.** $a^2 - 25$

5. $\boxed{9a^2 - 4b^2}$ **6.** $\boxed{x^4 - 81}$

Example 8.4-1

 1 8.4

If $x + y = 12$ and $x - y = 4$, what is the value of $x^2 - y^2$?

A) 4

B) 8

C) 48

D) 196

Solution 1

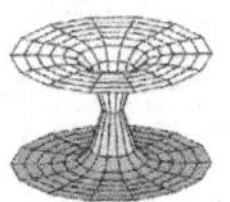

1. Since $x^2 - y^2$ is in a difference of squares pattern, it can be factored as $(x + y)(x - y)$. You can set the expression $x^2 - y^2$ equal to $(x + y)(x - y)$.

$$x^2 - y^2 = (x + y)(x - y)$$

2. Because we are told that $x + y = 12$ and $x - y = 4$, we can substitute 12 in for $(x + y)$ and 4 in for $(x - y)$.

$$x^2 - y^2 = (x + y)(x - y)$$
$$x^2 - y^2 = (12)(4)$$
$$x^2 - y^2 = 48$$

3. The answer is C.

Solution 2

This is a slower solution that does not make use of the difference of two squares. The problem can simply be looked at as a system of linear equations.

1. Add the two given equations, $x + y = 12$ and $x - y = 4$, in order to eliminate y and solve for x.

$$\begin{array}{rl} & x + y = 12 \\ + & x - y = 4 \\ \hline & 2x \quad = 16 \\ & \Downarrow \\ & x \quad = 8 \end{array}$$

2. Substitute 8 in for x in the first equation, $x + y = 12$, to solve for y.

$$x + y = 12$$
$$(8) + y = 12$$
$$y = 4$$

3. Since $x = 8$ and $y = 4$, we can solve for the value of $x^2 - y^2$ by replacing x with 8 and y with 4.

$$x^2 - y^2 = 8^2 - 4^2$$
$$x^2 - y^2 = 64 - 16$$
$$x^2 - y^2 = 48$$

4. The answer is C.

Perfect Square Expressions

For some factorable quadratic expressions, the two factors are actually the same. For example, if we factor the the expression $x^2 + 8x + 16$, we need to find two numbers that add to 8 and multiply to 16. Those numbers are 4 and 4 (the same number), so the two factors are $(x+4)$ and $(x+4)$, which means that $x^2 + 8x + 16 = (x+4)(x+4)$. Written another way, the expression $x^2 + 8x + 16$ is a perfect square that is equivalent to $(x+4)^2$.

Since $(x+a)^2 = x^2 + 2ax + a^2$ (as we saw in the previous chapter), **any expressions in the form $x^2 + 2ax + a^2$ can be factored as $(x+a)^2$.**

Note that the particular letters are not important, and any of the letters can represent either a variable or a constant; don't conclude that x must be matched by a variable or that c must represent a constant. In fact, we could define the pattern with any letters we choose; for example:

$$(g+h)^2 = g^2 + 2gh + h^2$$

Note that the order of the letters g and h in the middle term $2gh$ is reversed from what we saw in the middle term of the previous expansion of $(x+a)^2$, where the middle term was written as $2ax$. Due to the commutative property of multiplication, $2ax$ is equal to $2xa$, just as $2gh$ is equal to $2hg$. In the first example, since we assumed x was a variable and a was a constant (as will be the case in many factoring problems), by convention, we wrote the constant first. In the second example, since we assumed both g and h are constants, we wrote the constants in alphabetical order.

Don't let the simple reordering of constants and variables get in the way of spotting this pattern. You can check for a match by seeing if the middle term of the expansion is equal to the product of 2, the square root of the first term, and the square root of the last term.

Another expression that fits the pattern is as follows:

$$x + 2\sqrt{x}\sqrt{a} + a$$
$$(\sqrt{x} + \sqrt{a})^2$$

Or, equivalently (because it doesn't matter what letters we pick),

$$g + 2\sqrt{g}\sqrt{h} + h$$
$$(\sqrt{g} + \sqrt{h})^2$$

This form might seem scarier with those radicals in the middle term, but it's actually rather useful when trying to determine if certain expressions qualify as perfect squares, such as those that don't have first or last terms with explicit exponents of 2. The key here is to see if the middle term is the product of 2 and the square roots of each of the other two terms.

Sometimes, when either x or a has a known value or includes a coefficient, it is harder to see that the middle term fits the pattern. For example, the expression $x^2 + 6x + 9$ fits the pattern, where $x = x$ and $a = 3$, which means that the middle term is equal to $2ax$ (in this case $2ax$ should equal $2(3)(x)$ or $6x$ based on the values of x and a). Using the first version of the pattern,

$$x^2 + 6x + 9$$
$$(x)^2 + 2(3)(x) + (3)^2$$
$$(x+3)^2$$

It might be easier to see how we could determine that the expression matches the pattern by using the second version.

$$x^2 + 6x + 9$$

$$x^2 + 2(\sqrt{x^2})(\sqrt{9}) + 9$$

$$x^2 + 2(x)(3) + 9$$

$$\left(\sqrt{x^2} + \sqrt{9}\right)^2$$

$$(x + 3)^2$$

The pattern can be disguised fairly well if you are aren't looking for it. In the pattern $x^2 + 2ax + a^2$, the values of x and a might be entire expressions with coefficients and unknown constants.

For example the expression $4p^4 + 12p^2q^2 + 9q^4$ also fits the pattern $x^2 + 2ax + a^2$ even though it looks vastly more complicated. If we take the value of x to be $2p^2$, which, when squared, equals $4p^4$, and we take the value of a to be $3q^2$, which, when squared, equals $9q^4$, then we can see that it does fit the pattern, where the middle term is equal to $2ax$ (which in this case is $2\left(2p^2\right)\left(3q^2\right)$ or $12p^2q^2$ based on the values of a and x), and can be factored as $\left(2p^2 + 3q^2\right)^2$.

$$4p^4 + 12p^2q^2 + 9q^4$$

$$\left(2p^2\right)^2 + 2\left(2p^2\right)\left(3q^2\right) + \left(3q^2\right)^2$$

$$\left(2p^2 + 3q^2\right)^2$$

This is another case where you might find it helpful to use the second form of the pattern to determine if the expression is a perfect square and exactly what the components would be.

Using the pattern

$$g + 2\sqrt{g}\sqrt{h} + h$$

we identify $4p^4$ as g and $9q^4$ as h, giving us

$$4p^4 + 2\left(\sqrt{4p^4}\right)\left(\sqrt{9q^4}\right) + 9q^4$$

$$4p^4 + 2\left(2p^2\right)\left(3q^2\right) + 9q^4$$

$$4p^4 + 12p^2q^2 + 9q^4$$

$$\left(\sqrt{4p^4} + \sqrt{9q^4}\right)^2$$

$$\left(2p^2 + 3q^2\right)^2$$

The following is actually a result of the same pattern as above, where the value of a happens to be negative. Nonetheless, for completeness, we will demonstrate the following recurring pattern.

Since $(x - a)^2 = x^2 - 2ax + a^2$, **any expressions in the form $x^2 - 2ax + a^2$ can be factored as $(x - a)^2$.**

For example, the expression $x^2 - 2xy + y^2$ fits the pattern $x^2 - 2ax + a^2$, so it can be factored as $(x - y)^2$.

$$x^2 - 2xy + y^2$$
$$(x)^2 - 2(x)(y) + (y)^2$$
$$(x - y)^2$$

Similar to the above pattern, these expressions can be well disguised if you aren't aware of them. For example the expression $4p^4 - 12p^2q^2 + 9q^4$ also fits the pattern $x^2 - 2ax + a^2$, where $x = 2p^2$ and $a = 3q^2$ (or, alternatively, the pattern $x - 2\sqrt{x}\sqrt{a} + a$, where $x = 4p^4$ and $a = 9q^4$).

$$4p^4 - 12p^2q^2 + 9q^4$$
$$\left(2p^2\right)^2 - 2\left(2p^2\right)\left(3q^2\right) + \left(3q^2\right)^2$$
$$\left(2p^2 - 3q^2\right)^2$$

Factoring Perfect Square Expressions

Any expression of the form $a^2 + 2ab + b^2$ can be factored as $(a + b)^2$.

Any expression of the form $a^2 - 2ab + b^2$ can be factored as $(a - b)^2$.

SkillDrill 8.4-2

Directions: Write the following perfect square polynomial expressions in Factored Form.

1. $x^2 + 2x + 1$

2. $p^2 - 6p + 9$

3. $y^2 + 8y + 16$

4. $9x^2 - 18x + 9$

5. $4a^2 + 16ab + 16b^2$

6. $b^4 + 2b^2 + 1$

Example 8.4-2

2 8.4

If $a^2 + b^2 = z$ and $ab = y$, which of the following is equivalent to $9z + 18y$?

A) $(a + 3b)^2$

B) $(3a + 3b)^2$

C) $(9a + 9b)^2$

D) $(9a + 18b)^2$

Solution 1

1. To find the value of $9z + 18y$, substitute $a^2 + b^2$ for z and ab for y.

$$9z + 18y = 9(a^2 + b^2) + 18(ab)$$
$$9z + 18y = 9a^2 + 9b^2 + 18ab$$

2. It might be tempting to factor out 9 at some point in this process, as the alert student is always on the lookout for ways to factor and simplify expressions in the course of solving a problem, but an examination of the form of all the answer choices shows that there is no factored-out constant in any of them, so this temptation must be resisted in this situation. We should reorder the expression on the right side of the equation, in order to "polarize" the expression such that the squared terms, $9a^2$ and $9b^2$, are separated by the term $18ab$, in order to match the general structure of squaring binomials (after all, all of the answer choices tell us that the value of $9z + 18y$ must be the result of squaring a binomial).

$$9z + 18y = 9a^2 + 9b^2 + 18ab$$
$$9z + 18y = 9a^2 + 18ab + 9b^2$$

3. The expression on the right side is a perfect square expression and can be factored easily. Even though it looks intimidating, it matches the form of the perfect square expression $g^2 + 2gh + h^2$, where g in the template corresponds to $3a$ in the expression we have, and h corresponds to $3b$, so we know how to factor it.

$$9z + 18y = 9a^2 + 18ab + 9b^2$$
$$9z + 18y = (3a)^2 + 2(3a)(3b) + (3b)^2$$
$$9z + 18y = (3a + 3b)^2$$

4. The answer is B.

Solution 2

This is a slower solution that does not make use of factoring perfect square expressions; instead, it expands each answer choice and tests it.

1. To find the value of $9z + 18y$, substitute $a^2 + b^2$ in for z and ab in for y.

$$9z + 18y = 9(a^2 + b^2) + 18(ab)$$
$$9z + 18y = 9a^2 + 18ab + 9b^2$$

2. Expand (multiply out) each answer choice to see which one evaluates to $9a^2 + 18ab + 9b^2$.

3. Start with choice A, $(a + 3b)^2$.

$$(a + 3b)^2 = (a + 3b)(a + 3b)$$
$$(a + 3b)^2 = a^2 + 3ab + 3ab + 9b^2$$
$$(a + 3b)^2 = a^2 + 6ab + 9b^2$$

4. Since choice A does not evaluate to $9a^2 + 18ab + 9b^2$, we can eliminate answer choice A, and move on to choice B, $(3a + 3b)^2$.

$$(3a + 3b)^2 = (3a + 3b)(3a + 3b)$$
$$(3a + 3b)^2 = 9a^2 + 9ab + 9ab + 9b^2$$
$$(3a + 3b)^2 = 9a^2 + 18ab + 9b^2$$

5. Choice B does evaluate to $9a^2 + 18ab + 9b^2$, so this is the correct choice.

6. The answer is B.

Notes

After Step 1 in either solution, we could have taken a shortcut by noticing that the first term in the expanded expression we need to find is $9a^2$. Looking at just the a terms in the answer choices, it is clear that only choice B would expand such that $9a^2$ would be the first term.

View related real-test problems at 1600.io/p/smtex?topic=8.4

Section 8.4 Practice Problems

1 8.4

$$x^4 - 18x^2 + 81$$

Which of the following is equivalent to the expression above?

A) $(x - 9)^4$
B) $(x - 3)^4$
C) $(x^2 + 9)(x + 3)(x - 3)$
D) $(x - 3)^2(x + 3)^2$

2 8.4

If $t > 0$ and $t^2 - 36 = 0$, what is the value of t ?

3 8.4

$$36x^2 - 16 = (px + t)(px - t)$$

In the equation above, p and t are constants. Which of the following could be the value of p ?

A) 4
B) 6
C) 16
D) 36

4 8.4

In the equations $a = x + 3$ and $b = x - 3$, a and b are constants. When the product ab is written in the form $x^2 - c$, where c is a constant, what is the value of c ?

8.5 Systems of Quadratic Equations and Linear Equations

Just like linear equations, quadratic equations can be represented in graphs, and when the graph of a quadratic equation intersects the graph of another equation, the intersection points are called solutions to the system; these points represent values of the x and y variables that make all the equations true. For now we will not need to see the graphs of quadratic equations because, just as with systems of linear equations, systems of quadratic equations can be solved without the graphs by using some of the same techniques we used to solve systems of linear equations. However, these quadratic systems will be more frequently solved using substitution (or setting the polynomials equal to each other if the equations are already solved in terms of the same variable) rather than by using the elimination method often preferred for solving systems of linear equations.

If you are given a system of equations consisting of one linear equation and one quadratic equation, or less commonly, two quadratic equations, you can use substitution to collapse the system of two equations into one quadratic equation which you can then solve. Often, the two equations are already solved for y in terms of x, so you can just set the expressions containing the x-variables equal to each other. Once you have one equation, you can write it in Standard Form so that one side of the equation is only 0 and the other side of the equation is a quadratic expression. Once the quadratic equation is in Standard Form, you can proceed to find the solutions using your technique of choice.

It is possible that there are no values of x and y that satisfy both the linear equation and the quadratic equation, or, put into graphical terms, the graph of a line does not intersect the graph of a quadratic equation (a case that will be discussed in the coming chapters) and it is also possible to to solve systems of two quadratic equations by similar methods (again, this is discussed in later chapters as there are more possibilities for the number of solutions). In this chapter, we are only presenting systems with one linear and one polynomial equation and which are solvable by this method.

Example 8.5-1

1 1600.io 8.5

$$y = x^2$$
$$y = 8x + 20$$

The system of equations above is graphed in the xy-plane. The graphs of the equations intersect at a point (x, y) where $x > 0$ and $y > 0$. What is the y-coordinate of this point of intersection?

A) 2

B) 10

C) 36

D) 100

Solution

1. Set the two polynomials equal to each other because they are both already solved for x in terms of y.

$$x^2 = 8x + 20$$

2. Bring all the terms to the left side of the equation so that we have a standard form of a quadratic on the left side that we can factor.

$$x^2 - 8x - 20 = 0$$

3. We'll attempt simple factoring, so we need to find two numbers that add to -8 and multiply to -20.

4. The values -10 and 2 add to -8 and multiply to -20, so the factors are $(x - 10)$ and $(x + 2)$.

$$x^2 - 8x - 20 = 0$$
$$(x - 10)(x + 2) = 0$$

5. Since $(x - 10)$ is a factor, then $x = 10$ is a solution. Because $(x + 2)$ is also a factor, $x = -2$ is also a solution, but since we only care about the solution where $x > 0$, it is irrelevant that $x = -2$ is also a solution. Note that we didn't need to actually write out the factors to arrive at the solutions; once we determine that -10 and 2 satisfied the factoring constraints, we can conclude that the negatives of those numbers, 10 and -2, are the solutions.

6. It is important to be absolutely sure of what the question is asking for; wrongly assuming that it is the positive solution for x that is being sought will cause the student to select choice B, which the test-maker has thoughtfully supplied to avoid tipping off students that the are not yet done solving the problem, but the problem asks for the y-coordinate of the solution point. Since the solution occurs when $x = 10$, plug in 10 for x in either one of the two given equation to find the value of y. We will use the first equation, $y = x^2$.

$$y = 10^2$$
$$y = 100$$

7. The answer is D.

View related real-test problems at 1600.io/p/smtex?topic=8.5

Section 8.5 Practice Problems

1 8.5

$$y = -6$$
$$y + 22 = x^2$$

If (x_1, y_1) and (x_2, y_2) are solutions to the system of equations above, what are the values of x_1 and x_2 ?

A) $-2\sqrt{7}$ and $2\sqrt{7}$

B) $-\sqrt{22}$ and $\sqrt{22}$

C) -4 and 4

D) -6 and 6

2 8.5

$$y = 2x + 4$$
$$y = x^2 + 6x + 8$$

What is the y-coordinate of the point of intersection, in the xy-plane, of the graphs of the equations above?

A) -2

B) 0

C) 2

D) 8

3 1600.io 8.5

$$y = x^2 - 12x + 12$$
$$y = 12 - x$$

If the ordered pair (x, y) satisfies the system of equations above, what is one possible value of x ?

4 1600.io 8.5

$$x^2 + y = 16$$
$$x - y = 4$$

Which value is a y-coordinate of a solution to the system of equations above?

A) -9

B) -8

C) -5

D) -4

8.6 Extra Tools for Factoring and Quadratics Problems

If a question asks you to find the sum or product of the solutions (or zeros, x-coordinates of points of intersection, "values that satisfy," or roots) of a quadratic expression, equation, function, or a system of equations that includes a quadratic equation, you don't necessarily need to find the individual solutions to answer the question. If the quadratic expression or equation is given to you in (or is easily converted into) Standard Form, then there are useful shortcuts that can help you answer sum and product of solutions questions very easily.

Remember, a quadratic *equation* of the form $ax^2 + bx + c = 0$ has solutions or roots; a quadratic *equation* of the form $y = ax^2 + bx + c$ has roots or zeros; a quadratic *function* of the form $f(x) = ax^2 + bx + c$ has roots or zeros; and a quadratic *expression* of the form $ax^2 + bx + c$ has roots or zeros. These formulas apply to any of those characteristics, so generalize the summaries below accordingly. We empathize with the confusion this terminology can elicit, but we are not responsible for the proliferation of these overlapping terms.

Sum of Solutions

For quadratic equations in the form $ax^2 + bx + c = 0$, where a, b, and c are constants, the **sum of the solutions** is equal to $\frac{-b}{a}$.

$$\text{Sum of Solutions} = \frac{-b}{a}$$

Product of Solutions

For quadratic equations in the form $ax^2 + bx + c = 0$, where a, b, and c are constants, the **product of the solutions** is equal to $\frac{c}{a}$.

$$\text{Product of Solutions} = \frac{c}{a}$$

SkillDrill 8.6-1

Directions: Find the sum s and product p of the solutions or roots for each of the following quadratics. Use the formulas above instead of finding the individual solutions.

1. $x^2 + 4x + 3 = y$ **2.** $x^2 + 12x + 32 = 0$ **3.** $x^2 - 8x + 6 = 1$ **4.** $2x^2 - 18x + 9 = 0$

5. $3x^2 + 2x - 5 = y$ **6.** $x^2 - x + 17 = -3$ **7.** $5x^2 + 8x - 30 = 0$ **8.** $9x^2 - 81x + 9 = 0$

Quadratics Not in x and U-Substitution

In most cases, quadratic expressions will be based in a simple variable such as x. It's important (and interesting) to understand that as long as the *structure* of a quadratic expression is maintained, you can have a quadratic in a more complicated term, such as a variable with a coefficient, an exponentiated variable, or even an expression. For example, just as $y = x^2 + 5x + 6$ is a quadratic equation in x, so too is $y = (7x)^2 + 5(7x) + 6$ a quadratic equation in $7x$. The equation $y = \left(x^4\right)^2 + 5\left(x^4\right) + 6$ is a quadratic in x^4, and the equation $y = (x - 3)^2 + 5(x - 3) + 6$ is a quadratic equation in $(x - 3)$.

Because these are all quadratic equations, they are all susceptible to the solving methods that apply to quadratic equations as long as the term that serves as the basis for the quadratic expression is used wherever you'd use the simple variable. Be on the lookout for complicated-seeming equations that are really just quadratics in something other than a simple variable; they are easily solved when recognized.

We have looked at factoring with respect to single variable terms, but when certain expressions occur multiple times in an equation on this test, you can probably shortcut the problem by factoring with respect to that expression rather than a single variable. For example, if we encounter the equation $(x - 4)^2 + 2(x - 4) - 15 = 0$, one method of finding solutions is to expand all the terms and rewrite the equation in Standard Form in terms of x.

$$\begin{aligned} (x - 4)^2 + 2(x - 4) - 15 &= 0 \\ x^2 - 8x + 16 + 2x - 8 - 15 &= 0 \\ x^2 - 6x - 7 &= 0 \\ (x - 7)(x + 1) &= 0 \\ x = 7,\quad x &= -1 \end{aligned}$$

However, we could reduce the number of steps if we realize that the equation $(x - 4)^2 + 2(x - 4) - 15 = 0$ is already in Standard Form in terms of the expression $x - 4$ instead of just x. The process is the same as factoring when a single variable like x is the repeated term, but we are using $(x - 4)$ as the term we are factoring in terms of. We still need to find two numbers that add to 2 (the b-coefficient) and multiply to -15 (the constant term c). These numbers are -3 and 5, so our factors will be $[(x - 4) - 3]$ and $[(x - 4) + 5]$.

$$\begin{aligned} (x - 4)^2 + 2(x - 4) - 15 &= 0 \\ [(x - 4) - 3][(x - 4) + 5] &= 0 \\ (x - 7)(x + 1) &= 0 \\ x = 7,\quad x &= -1 \end{aligned}$$

Notice that we ended up with the same factors (as we must), but we skipped the steps of expanding out the multiplied expressions and combining like terms, which would be an avoidable source of error and a waste of time.

For some people, it can be easier to temporarily replace the repeated expression with a variable. By custom, u is generally used for this purpose, and that gives the name **U-Substitution** to this technique. This makes the equation more approachable because the equation is transformed to look like a familiar quadratic equation in terms of a single variable rather than an expression. Once u is substituted for the repeated expression, factor the equation normally and then replace the value of u (reverse the substitution) at the end.

For example, in the equation above, we could say that $u = x - 4$, and we'd then substitute u for the repeated expression $x - 4$, allowing us to factor with respect to a single variable without having to expand and recombine terms. To reiterate, you do have to substitute $x - 4$ back in for u at the end in order to find solution values of x (and not for our temporary placeholder value u, which is equal to $x - 4$).

$$(x-4)^2 + 2(x-4) - 15 = 0$$
$$u^2 + 2u - 15 = 0$$
$$(u-3)(u+5) = 0$$
$$u = 3, \quad u = -5$$

We've now solved for u, but ultimately, we need to solve for x. Remember that $u = x - 4$, so if we want to find the solution values of x, we need to replace u with $x - 4$.

$$u = 3, \quad u = -5$$
$$x - 4 = 3, \quad x - 4 = -5$$
$$x = 7, \quad x = -1$$

The key to identifying equations that are susceptible to this streamlined technique is to see if there's an expression that appears with an exponent of 2 in one term and that also appears with no exponent (that is, with an implied exponent of 1) in a second term. The following example should clarify how to factor in terms of an expression rather than a single variable and how to use U-Substitution to find the solutions of a quadratic equation.

There is an additional discussion of these quadratics in non-simple terms in the "Wormholes" chapter, if you're interested in a deeper dive.

Example 8.6-1

1 1600.io 8.6

If $(x+5)^2 - 4(x+5) + 4 = 0$, what is the value of x?

A) -5

B) -3

C) 2

D) 5

Solution 1

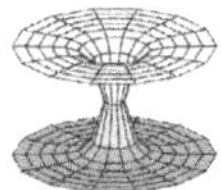

1. Factor the equation with respect to the expression $x + 5$ instead of just a single variable term like x. This is a perfect square expression (matches the form $p^2 - 2pq + q^2 = (p - q)^2$, where $p = x + 5$ and $q = 2$), so we can factor it easily.

$$\begin{aligned}(x+5)^2 - 4(x+5) + 4 &= 0\\(x+5)^2 - 2(x+5)(2) + (2)^2 &= 0\\[(x+5) - 2]^2 &= 0\\(x+3)^2 &= 0\end{aligned}$$

2. Since $(x + 3)$ is a factor, $x = -3$ is a solution.

3. The answer is B.

Solution 2

In this solution, we substitute u for the expression $x + 5$ so that the factoring step is more reminiscent of factoring in terms of a single variable.

1. Since the expression $x+5$ shows up as both a squared term and (with a coefficient) as a first-degree term, we can declare a new variable u, and say that $u = x + 5$. Now we can replace $(x + 5)$ with u in the original equation in order to avoid distributing and combining many terms.

$$\begin{aligned}(x+5)^2 - 4(x+5) + 4 &= 0\\u^2 - 4u + 4 &= 0\end{aligned}$$

2. This is a perfect square expression (matches the form $p^2 - 2pq + q^2$ where $p = u$ and $q = 2$) that can be factored easily.

$$\begin{aligned}u^2 - 4u + 4 &= 0\\(u)^2 - 2(u)(2) + (2)^2 &= 0\\(u-2)^2 &= 0\end{aligned}$$

3. Since $(u - 2)$ is a factor, $u = 2$ is a solution.

4. This is the crucial step with U-Substitution. After you solve for u, **you must never forget to rewrite u in terms of the original variable used**, thus reversing the substitution. Since $u = x + 5$, replace u with $x + 5$ in order to solve for x.

$$\begin{aligned}u &= 2\\x + 5 &= 2\\x &= -3\end{aligned}$$

5. The answer is B.

Solution 3

This is a solution that does not make use of U-Substitution. It is not necessarily slower, but is possibly more error prone since you have to expand and combine many more terms in the early steps.

1. Expand and simplify the original equation.

$$(x+5)^2 - 4(x+5) + 4 = 0$$
$$x^2 + 10x + 25 - 4x - 20 + 4 = 0$$
$$x^2 + 6x + 9 = 0$$

2. This is a perfect square expression that can be factored easily.

$$x^2 + 6x + 9 = 0$$
$$(x+3)^2 = 0$$

3. Since $(x+3)$ is a factor, $x = -3$ is a solution.

4. The answer is B.

Notes

If you do not recognize the perfect square pattern in Solution 3, you can factor the quadratic expression (or any other perfect square quadratic expression) by conventional factoring. You just need to look for numbers that multiply to 9 and add to 6, which happen to be 3 and 3. Notice that this will still get you the factors $x + 3$ and $x + 3$, but with a tiny bit of extra thought. Ultimately, factoring perfect square expressions is just a minor extension to conventional factoring, and offers a small time savings on may problems.

Alternatively, you could plug in each answer choice and see what value of x makes the equation true. Generally, plugging in answer choices can be used to solve many problems on the test, but we DO NOT recommend it because it does not help you gain any understanding of the topics at hand, and it usually wastes time and leads to more errors.

Factoring by Grouping

Factoring by Grouping is a method of factoring that is used to help factor certain types of equations in which the degree is greater than 2. You can break a Standard Form polynomial into sets of expressions that all share a common factor, forming subsets of terms that make the polynomial easier to factor and solve. For example, in the equation $x^5 - 3x^4 + 3x - 9 = 0$, we can break the polynomial expression into two subsets for which the terms in each of the subsets share a common factor. We can factor x^4 from both of the first two terms.

$$x^5 - 3x^4 + 3x - 9 = 0$$
$$x^4(x-3) + 3x - 9 = 0$$

From the third and fourth original terms, we can factor out a 3.

$$x^4(x-3) + 3x - 9 = 0$$
$$x^4(x-3) + 3(x-3) = 0$$

Now, we discover that we have had some good fortune bestowed on us by the omnipotent powers that craft these problems so that mortals can solve them: because both expression share a common factor of $(x - 3)$, we can factor $(x - 3)$ from both subsets, showing us that $x = 3$ must be one of the solutions.

$$x^4(x - 3) + 3(x - 3) = 0$$
$$(x - 3)(x^4 + 3) = 0$$

Note that the factor $x^4 + 3$ provides no more real number solutions because it will never equal 0 (because x^4 cannot be equal to -3, as no real number raised to an even power will ever be negative). Non-real (complex) solutions are discussed elsewhere in this text, if you're curious about that.

The fact that $(x - 3)$ was a factor of both of the subsets may seem like a coincidence, but as alluded to earlier, the problems on the test are very well designed, and the way that this problem was solvable with factoring by grouping was not an accident. If you are asked to find solutions to a higher-degree polynomial on the test, you should be able to solve the problem by factoring by grouping, but you can, in a moment of weakness, also find the solutions graphically on your calculator (*only* if it is on the calculator section: NO CHEATING!!—we'll discuss the graphs of polynomials in another chapter), or simply plug in answer choices and see which one makes the equation true.

Take it under advisement that the only time factoring by grouping has been required on the test is for polynomials where the leading x-term has an exponent greater than 2 (that is, for polynomials of degree 3 or higher), and there are four terms in the polynomial expression. If you encounter this setup, factor anything you can from the first set of two terms (the two highest-degree terms) and factor anything you can from the second set of two terms (the two lowest-degree terms). What should happen is that you will discover that both pairs of terms have a common factor, allowing you to factor the entire expression and thus to find the roots. These problems will be specifically constructed so they have that characteristic.

Example 8.6-2

2 8.6

$$x^3 - 4x^2 + 2x - 8 = 0$$

For what real value of x is the equation above true?

Solution

1. Group the first two terms as one expression (the two highest-degree terms) and group the third and fourth terms as another expression (the two lowest-degree terms).

$$x^3 - 4x^2 + 2x - 8 = 0$$
$$(x^3 - 4x^2) + (2x - 8) = 0$$

2. We can factor x^2 out of the first set of two terms.

$$(x^3 - 4x^2) + (2x - 8) = 0$$
$$x^2(x - 4) + (2x - 8) = 0$$

3. We can factor 2 out of the second set of two terms.

$$x^2(x - 4) + (2x - 8) = 0$$
$$x^2(x - 4) + 2(x - 4) = 0$$

4. We have found that $(x-4)$ is a factor of both sets of terms. Factor $(x-4)$ from both sets of terms.

$$x^2(x-4)+2(x-4)=0$$
$$(x-4)(x^2+2)=0$$

5. Since $(x-4)$ is a factor, then $x=4$ is a solution.

6. The factor (x^2+2) produces no real solutions. Set the expression equal to 0 and try to solve for x.

$$x^2+2=0$$
$$x^2=-2$$

Since no real number squared can be equal to a negative number, there are no more real solutions. We will talk more about real roots and other types of roots in the coming chapters. The only real solution is $x=4$.

7. The answer is 4.

View related real-test problems at 1600.io/p/smtex?topic=8.6

Section 8.6 Practice Problems

1 1600.io 8.6

What is the sum of all values of m that satisfy $3m^2-18m+9=0$?

A) -6

B) $-2\sqrt{6}$

C) $2\sqrt{6}$

D) 6

2 1600.io 8.6

$$x(x+4)=21$$

What is the product of the solutions to the given equation?

A) 21

B) 10

C) -4

D) -21

3 1600.io 8.6

If $t>0$ and $(2t)^2-2(2t)-48=0$, what is the value of t ?

4 1600.io 8.6

Which of the following is an equivalent form of the expression $(4x-3)^2-4(4x-3)$?

A) $(4x-3)(4x-3)$

B) $(4x-3)(4x-7)$

C) $4x^2-28x+21$

D) $16x^2-40x-3$

CHAPTER 8 RECAP

- Factoring is the inverse operation of distribution.
- When factoring a quadratic expression in Standard Form where the coefficient of the x^2 term is 1, $x^2 + bx + c = 0$, we need to find two numbers, p and q, such that $p + q = b$ (the sum of the numbers is b) and $pq = c$ (the product of the numbers is c). The solutions to the equation are $-p$ and $-q$, and we can rewrite the expression in Factored Form. One of the factors is $(x + p)$ and the other factor is $(x + q)$.

$$(x + p)(x + q) = 0$$

- When the coefficient of the x^2 term is NOT 1 (when $a \neq 1$), first try dividing all of the terms by a to see if the resulting expression is easily factorable.
- Sometimes, when the coefficient of the x^2 term is NOT 1 (when $a \neq 1$), you can use the Product Sum (ac) Method, which is a generalized form of factoring.

  When factoring a quadratic expression in Standard Form $ax^2 + bx + c = 0$ using the Product Sum (ac) Method, we need to find two numbers, r and s, such that $r + s = b$ (the sum of the numbers is b) and $rs = ac$ (the product of the numbers is ac). The solutions to the equation are $\frac{-r}{a}$ and $\frac{-s}{a}$, and we can rewrite the expression in Factored Form. One of the factors is $\left(x + \frac{r}{a}\right)$ and the other factor is $\left(x + \frac{s}{a}\right)$.

$$a\left(x + \frac{r}{a}\right)\left(x + \frac{s}{a}\right) = 0$$

- If you cannot find numbers that satisfy the conditions for factoring, you can always use Completing the Square:
  1. Divide both sides of the equation by the a coefficient to eliminate the coefficient of the x^2 term.
  2. Move the constant to other side to isolate the x terms.
  3. Replace the left side of the equation with $\left(x + \frac{b}{2}\right)^2$ (where b is the coefficient of the x term) and balance the extra constant on the other side by adding $\left(\frac{b}{2}\right)^2$ to the right side of the equation, pre-calculating $\frac{b}{2}$ so you don't have to do that twice.
  4. Take the square root of both sides, being careful to include both positive and negative square roots.
  5. Move the constant to right side of the equation to isolate and solve for x.
  6. Enumerate the solutions.
- The Quadratic Formula is constructed by using Completing the Square, and both methods can be used to find the solutions of any quadratic equation.
- The Quadratic Formula can be used to find the solutions of quadratic equations in Standard Form, $0 = ax^2 + bx + c$.

$$x = \frac{-b \pm \sqrt{b^2 - 4ac}}{2a}$$

  or, as we prefer,

$$x = \frac{-b}{2a} \pm \frac{\sqrt{b^2 - 4ac}}{2a}$$

- The Difference of Squares $x^2 - a^2$ can be quickly factored as $(x - a)(x + a)$.

- Perfect square quadratics of the form $x^2 + 2ax + a^2$ can be quickly factored as $(x + a)^2$.
- Perfect square quadratics of the form $x^2 - 2ax + a^2$ can be quickly factored as $(x - a)^2$.
- If you are given a system of equations consisting of one linear equation and one quadratic equation, or less commonly, two quadratic equations, you can use substitution to collapse the system of two equations into one quadratic equation which you can then solve.
- The sum of the solutions of a quadratic equation in Standard Form, $ax^2 + bx + c = 0$, is equal to $\frac{-b}{a}$.
- The product of the solutions of a quadratic equation in Standard Form, $ax^2 + bx + c = 0$, is equal to $\frac{c}{a}$.
- When an expression appears multiple times in a quadratic equation, you can probably shortcut the problem by factoring with respect to that expression rather than a single variable via U-Substitution, replacing the expression with the variable u, and then factoring normally with respect to u. Don't forget to finish up by solving for the original variable.
- Factoring by grouping is extremely rarely necessary on the test. The dead giveaway will be that the polynomial you are asked to solve has more than three terms (it probably would be four terms, just as a practical matter). If this is the case, find a factor that is common to the first set of two terms and the second set of two terms.

Additional Problems

1 8.5

$$(x-2)^2 = 3x - 2$$

What is one possible solution to the equation above?

2 8.2

$$x(x-3) = 4$$

Which of the following lists all solutions to the quadratic equation above?

A) $\sqrt{7}$

B) -1 and 4

C) 1 and -4

D) 4 and 7

3 8.2

If $(ax+4)(bx+5) = 14x^2 + cx + 20$ for all values of x, and $a+b=9$, what are the two possible values for c ?

A) 2 and 7

B) 8 and 35

C) 10 and 28

D) 38 and 43

4 8.4

If $4x - 12y = 8z$, which of the following expressions is equivalent to $x^2 - 6xy + 9y^2$?

A) $8z$

B) $2z^2$

C) $4z^2$

D) $64z^2$

5 8.4

The expression $\frac{1}{5}x^2 - 3$ can be rewritten as $\frac{1}{5}(x-k)(x+k)$, where k is a positive constant. What is the value of k ?

A) 3

B) 15

C) $\sqrt{3}$

D) $\sqrt{15}$

6 8.6

$$x^2 - 12x + 27 = 3x + 1$$

What is the sum of the solutions to the given equation?

A) -15

B) -12

C) 12

D) 15

7 1600.io 8.1

$$(x-7)^6 = 0$$

What value of x makes the equation above true?

8 1600.io 8.4

If $u + t = -3$ and $u - t = 2$, what is the value of $(u+t)(u^2 - t^2)$?

9 1600.io 8.5

In the xy-plane, the graph of the equation $y = -4x + 5$ intersects the graph of the equation $y = x^2$ at two points. What is the sum of the x-coordinates of the two points?

A) -6

B) -4

C) 4

D) 6

10 1600.io 8.5

In the xy-plane, the graph of $y = 5x^2 - 6x$ intersects the graph of $y = x$ at the points $(0, 0)$ and (a, a). What is the value of a ?

11 1600.io 8.5

$$x^2 - 9x + 26 = y$$
$$x = y - 2$$

The system of equations above is graphed in the xy-plane. Which of the following is the y-coordinate of an intersection point (x, y) of the graphs of the two equations?

A) -6

B) -4

C) 4

D) 6

12 1600.io 8.3

$$x^2 - \frac{k}{2}x = 4p$$

In the quadratic equation above, k and p are constants. What are the solutions for x ?

A) $x = \frac{k}{2} \pm \frac{\sqrt{k^2 + 64p}}{2}$

B) $x = \frac{k}{2} \pm \frac{\sqrt{k^2 + 4p}}{2}$

C) $x = \frac{k}{4} \pm \frac{\sqrt{k^2 + 64p}}{4}$

D) $x = \frac{k}{4} \pm \frac{\sqrt{k^2 + 4p}}{4}$

13 8.5

$$y = x^2$$
$$5y + 20 = 5(x + 4)$$

If (x, y) is a solution of the system of equations above and $x > 0$, what is the value of xy ?

A) 1

B) 4

C) 5

D) 16

14 8.2

$$x^3(x^2 - 13) = -36x$$

If $x > 0$, what is one possible solution to the equation above?

15 8.5

$$y = 3x + 6$$
$$y = (x + 4)(x + 2)$$

The system of equations above is graphed in the xy-plane, At which of the following points do the graphs of the equations intersect?

A) $(-4, -6)$

B) $(-4, 0)$

C) $(-1, -2)$

D) $(-1, 3)$

16 8.4

If $x^4 - y^4 = -26$ and $x^2 - y^2 = -2$, what is the value of $x^2 + y^2$?

A) 1

B) 2

C) 13

D) 16

17 8.5

$$x - y = 1$$
$$x + y = x^2 - 5$$

Which ordered pair is a solution to the system of equations above?

A) $\left(1 + \sqrt{7}, \sqrt{7}\right)$

B) $\left(\sqrt{7}, -1 + \sqrt{7}\right)$

C) $\left(\sqrt{5}, -\sqrt{5}\right)$

D) $\left(1 + \sqrt{5}, \sqrt{5}\right)$

18 8.5

$$(x + 4)^2 + (y - 3)^2 = 51$$
$$y = -4x + 4$$

Which of the following could be the x-coordinate of a solution to the system of equations above?

A) $\sqrt{2}$

B) $\dfrac{\sqrt{34}}{4}$

C) $\dfrac{8 + \sqrt{642}}{17}$

D) $\dfrac{20 + \sqrt{723}}{17}$

19 1600.io 8.4

Which of the following is equivalent to $\sqrt[4]{x^2 - 6x + 9}$, where $x > 0$?

A) $(x-3)^2$

B) $(x-3)$

C) $(x-3)^{\frac{1}{2}}$

D) $(x-3)^{\frac{1}{4}}$

20 1600.io 8.3

In the equation $(ax - 2)^2 = 16$, a is a constant. If $x = -2$ is one solution to the equation, what is a possible value of a ?

A) -9

B) -3

C) -1

D) 6

21 1600.io 8.4

If $\frac{x^{a^2}}{x^{b^2}} = x^8$, $x > 1$, and $a + b = 2$, what is the value of $a - b$?

A) 4

B) 6

C) 8

D) 10

22 1600.io 8.2

$$h = -4.9t^2 + 30t$$

The equation above expresses the approximate height h, in meters, of a ball t seconds after it is launched vertically upward from the ground with an initial velocity of 30 meters per second. After approximately how many seconds will the ball hit the ground?

A) 5.5

B) 6.0

C) 6.5

D) 7.0

23 1600.io 8.1

$$P(x) = x^2 - 7x + k$$

In the function above, k is a constant. If 3 is a zero of the function, what is the value of k ?

A) -12

B) -3

C) 4

D) 12

Answer Key

Section 8.1 Practice Problems

1. 8
2. B

SkillDrill 8.2-1

1. 5 and 2
2. −5 and −2
3. −6 and 2
4. −3 and 4
5. 5 and 8
6. −7 and 11
7. −13 and 4
8. −12 and −8
9. $(x-1)(x+4)$
10. $(x-7)(x-3)$
11. $(a+8)(a+10)$
12. $(b-6)(b+5)$
13. $a(a-3)$
14. $x(x+1)$
15. $(x^2+8)(x^2+10)$
16. $x(x^2+8)(x^2+10)$
17. $x=-4$ and $x=1$
18. $x=1$ and $x=7$
19. $x=-5$ and $x=-4$
20. $x=2$ and $x=8$
21. $x=-3$ and $x=4$
22. $x=-2$ and $x=1$
23. $a=-7$ and $a=4$
24. $b=6$ and $b=8$
25. $a=-2$ and $a=4$
26. $b=-2$ and $b=3$
27. $x=-12$ and $x=-10$
28. $x=-2$ and $x=6$

Section 8.2 Practice Problems

1. 3
2. 16

SkillDrill 8.3-1

1. $x=-2, x=-1$
2. $x=2, x=3$
3. $x=-1, x=4$
4. $x=-7, x=2$
5. $x=\frac{-3}{4}, x=1$
6. $x=\frac{-1}{2}, x=\frac{-2}{3}$
7. $x=\frac{-1}{8}, x=2$
8. $x=-7, x=\frac{-3}{2}$

SkillDrill 8.3-2

1. $x=-2\pm 2\sqrt{2}$
   or $x=-4.828, x=0.828$
2. $x=\frac{-1}{2}\pm\frac{\sqrt{5}}{2}$
   or $x=-1.618, x=0.618$
3. $x=\frac{3}{2}\pm\frac{\sqrt{21}}{2}$
   or $x=-0.791, x=3.791$
4. $x=3\pm 2\sqrt{2}$
   or $x=0.172, x=5.828$
5. $x=2\pm\sqrt{10}$
   or $x=-1.162, x=5.162$
6. $x=\frac{-1}{2}\pm\frac{\sqrt{33}}{6}$
   or $x=-1.457, x=0.457$
7. $a=\frac{-5}{2}\pm\frac{\sqrt{15}}{2}$
   or $a=-4.436, a=-0.564$
8. $b=\frac{9}{8}\pm\frac{\sqrt{113}}{8}$
   or $b=-0.203, b=2.454$

Section 8.3 Practice Problems

1. A
2. 5
3. A
4. C

SkillDrill 8.4-1

1. $(x-2)(x+2)$
2. $(x-9)(x+9)$
3. $(a-b)(a+b)$
4. $(a-5)(a+5)$
5. $(3a-2b)(3a+2b)$
   or $9\left(a-\frac{2}{3}b\right)\left(a+\frac{2}{3}b\right)$
6. $(x-3)(x+3)(x^2+9)$

SkillDrill 8.4-2

1. $(x+1)^2$
2. $(p-3)^2$
3. $(y+4)^2$
4. $(3x-3)^2$ or $9(x-1)^2$
5. $(2a+4b)^2$ or $4(a+2b)^2$
6. $(b^2+1)^2$

Section 8.4 Practice Problems

1. D
2. 6
3. B
4. 9

Section 8.5 Practice Problems

1. C
2. B
3. 0 or 11
4. A

SkillDrill 8.6-1

1. $s=-4, p=3$
2. $s=-12, p=32$
3. $s=8, p=5$
4. $s=9, p=\frac{9}{2}$
5. $s=\frac{-2}{3}, p=\frac{-5}{3}$
6. $s=1, p=20$
7. $s=\frac{-8}{5}, p=-6$
8. $s=9, p=1$

Section 8.6 Practice Problems

1. D
2. D
3. 4
4. B

Additional Problems

1. 1 or 6
2. B
3. D
4. C
5. D
6. D
7. 7
8. 18
9. B
10. $\frac{7}{5}$ or 1.4
11. D
12. C
13. A
14. 2 or 3
15. D
16. C
17. D
18. A
19. C
20. B
21. A
22. B
23. D

Appendix: Proofs and Alternative Reasoning

Explanation of Product Sum (ac) Method

Note: In the discussion that follows, we assume that the coefficients a, b, and c are integers (or can be converted into integers by multiplication or reducing).

We've seen that when the a coefficient is 1 in a quadratic equation in Standard Form $0 = ax^2 + bx + c$, we can express the quadratic expression in Factored Form as follows:

$$(x + p)(x + q)$$

This leads to the zeros being $x = -p$ and $x = -q$.

When expanded, this Factored Form produces the following Standard Form expression:

$$x^2 + qx + px + pq$$
$$x^2 + (p + q)x + pq$$

We see that $p + q = b$, and $pq = c$. Therefore, to determine the values of p and q, we need to find two numbers that sum to b and whose product is c.

Here's a compact example:

$$0 = x^2 - 2x - 15$$
$$a = 1,\ b = -2,\ c = -15$$

$$x^2 - 2x - 15 = (x + p)(x + q)$$
$$x^2 - 2x - 15 = x^2 + qx + px + pq$$
$$x^2 - 2x - 15 = x^2 + (p + q)x + pq$$
$$\Downarrow$$
$$p + q = b = -2$$
$$pq = c = -15$$
$$\Downarrow$$
$$p = 3,\ q = -5$$ (or $p = -5, q = 3$; the assignment is arbitrary)
$$\Downarrow$$
$$x^2 - 2x - 15 = (x + 3)(x - 5)$$
$$\text{Zeros: } x = -3,\ x = 5$$

When the a coefficient is *not* one, but the b and c coefficients are evenly divisible by a, we can simply divide through by a to end up with a quadratic expression whose a coefficient is 1, and we can still use the above procedure to find the zeros. Example:

$$0 = 3x^2 - 6x - 45$$
$$\frac{0}{3} = \frac{x^2 - 2x - 15}{3}$$
$$0 = x^2 - 2x - 15$$

At this point, we have the same equation as we did above, and the solving proceeds the same way.

The situation in which this procedure usually becomes too difficult to employ occurs when dividing through by the a coefficient does *not* produce integer b and c coefficients, but instead produces irreducible fractions, making the determination of p and q much harder; directly finding two values (one or both of which must also be a fraction for their sum and/or product to be a fraction) that sum to b and whose product is c is usually far too time-consuming. Here's an example, shown symbolically and with specific values:

$$0 = ax^2 + bx + c \qquad\qquad 0 = 8x^2 - 2x - 15$$

We can certainly eliminate the a coefficient (that is, have it become 1) by dividing through by a, which is 8:

$$\frac{0}{a} = \frac{ax^2 + bx + c}{a} \qquad\qquad \frac{0}{3} = \frac{8x^2 - 2x - 15}{8}$$

$$0 = x^2 + \frac{b}{a}x + \frac{c}{a} \qquad\qquad 0 = x^2 - \frac{2}{8}x - \frac{15}{8}$$

Now, the coefficient of the x^2 term is 1 (which is good), but the x coefficient is $\frac{b}{a} = \frac{-2}{8}$ and the constant is $\frac{c}{a} = \frac{15}{8}$, which is not at all good, because they're fractions; how are we to go about finding the two values p and q that sum to $\frac{-2}{8}$ and that multiply to $\frac{15}{8}$?

Though it is of course *possible* to determine those two values given enough time, it would be far easier if we only had to deal with integers for the sum and product goals, as we can use the same methodology we'd use when we have a simpler quadratic factoring task. We can accomplish exactly that by using two fractions, but they will both have the same denominator, a (which in our example is 8), as that is the denominator of the fractional coefficients, and so we only need to concern ourselves with the integer numerators, so we'll only be working with integers. We'll use r and s to denote those numerators, so the two fractions we'll use instead of p and q are $\frac{r}{a}$ and $\frac{s}{a}$.

To elaborate, rather than use p and q, which yield the following Factored Form and equivalent Standard form,

$$(x + p)(x + q) = x^2 + (p + q)x + q$$

we'll use $\frac{r}{a}$ and $\frac{s}{a}$, so we'll have this Factored Form and Standard Form:

$$\left(x + \frac{r}{a}\right)\left(x + \frac{s}{a}\right) = x^2 + \left(\frac{r + s}{a}\right)x + \frac{rs}{a^2}$$

Remember, when we divided through by a, here's what we got:

$$0 = x^2 + \frac{b}{a}x + \frac{c}{a} \qquad\qquad 0 = x^2 - \frac{2}{8}x - \frac{15}{8}$$

Matching coefficients with our new Standard Form, $x^2 + \left(\frac{r+s}{a}\right)x + \frac{rs}{a^2}$, we see

x coefficient:

$$\frac{r+s}{a} = \frac{b}{a}$$

$$r + s = b \qquad \Rightarrow \qquad r + s = -2$$

Constant:

$$\frac{rs}{a^2} = \frac{c}{a}$$

$$rs = \frac{a^2c}{a}$$

$$rs = ac \qquad \Rightarrow \qquad rs = 8(-15) = -120$$

We now have our product and sum goal values: **the sum of r and s must be b** (-2 in our example), and **the product of r and s must be ac** (which is -120 in our example) (this is where this method gets its name, by the way).

For our example, we can satisfy these constraints with the values 10 and -12, which we can assign arbitrarily to the two variables; we'll set $r = 10$ and $s = -12$. We can now substitute those values in our Factored Form equation:

$$0 = \left(x + \frac{r}{a}\right)\left(x + \frac{s}{a}\right)$$

$$0 = \left(x + \frac{10}{8}\right)\left(x - \frac{12}{8}\right)$$

$$0 = \left(x + \frac{5}{4}\right)\left(x - \frac{3}{2}\right)$$

Solving,

$$x + \frac{5}{4} = 0, x - \frac{3}{2} = 0$$

$$x = \frac{-5}{4}, x = \frac{3}{2}$$

As always when using factoring, if you don't actually need the Factored Form (or any of the constituent factors), you can skip writing that out and just go right to the solutions; when using p and q, the solutions are $-p$ and $-q$, but here, we have to remember that r and s are the numerators of fractions where the denominators are a, so the solutions are $-\left(\frac{r}{a}\right)$ and $-\left(\frac{s}{a}\right)$.

Detailed Walkthrough of Completing the Square

We will find the solutions of the equation $3x^2 - 12x - 15 = 0$, using Completing the Square, but with a little more explanation of each step. You don't need to look at this if you are willing to accept the "magic" step where we replace $x^2 + bx$ with $\left(x + \frac{b}{2}\right)^2$ and add $\left(\frac{b}{2}\right)^2$ to the other side of the equation.

We are starting with the following equation:

$$3x^2 - 12x - 15 = 0$$

Divide by the a coefficient (which is 3 in this example) to eliminate coefficient of x^2 term:

$$x^2 - 4x - 5 = 0$$

Now we have a normal quadratic equation of the form

$$x^2 + bx + c = 0$$

where $b = -4$ and $c = -5$.

Move the constant c (which is -5 in this example) to other side to isolate the x terms:

$$x^2 - 4x = 5$$

At this point, all the x terms are on one side, and there are no other terms on that side, so we need to replace the remaining expression with one that has only one x term of degree 1 (that is, it has an exponent of 1, which does not need to be written because it's implied when no exponent is shown) so we can eventually isolate and thus solve for x.

How can we craft a term that only has a first-degree x term but that will be equivalent to a second-degree binomial? Here's one way: we know from squaring binomials of the form $x + d$ that these operations will produce quadratic expressions, which have both first- and second-degree variable terms:

$$(x + d)^2 = x^2 + 2dx + d^2$$

Notice that the b coefficient of the resulting quadratic expression is equal to $2d$; put another way, $d = \frac{b}{2}$. Also, note that the c coefficient is equal to d^2, and because $d = \frac{b}{2}$, the c coefficient is equal to $\left(\frac{b}{2}\right)^2$. Therefore, here's another way we could write this equation:

$$(x + d)^2 = x^2 + 2dx + d^2$$

$$\left(x + \frac{b}{2}\right)^2 = x^2 + bx + \left(\frac{b}{2}\right)^2$$

So back to our example. We have

$$x^2 - 4x = 5$$

We're just looking at the simple quadratic expression $x^2 - 4x$ on the left side for now; it's in the form

$$x^2 + bx$$

where $b = -4$. Looking at our earlier work, we know we can get a quadratic from an expression of the form

$$\left(x + \frac{b}{2}\right)^2$$

Here, that would be

$$\left(x + \frac{-4}{2}\right)^2$$

$$\left(x - \frac{4}{2}\right)^2$$

$$(x - 2)^2$$

Let's perform that squaring operation to see if we get what we're looking for—the two-term quadratic $x^2 - 4x$:

$$(x - 2)^2$$

$$x^2 - 4x + 4$$

So close...we have produced the desired expression $x^2 - 4x$, but we also ended up with a third term. You might have had a feeling that was coming! We didn't account for the fact that there would be an extra, constant term, representing $\left(\frac{b}{2}\right)^2$ (here evaluating to $\left(\frac{-4}{2}\right)^2 = (-2)^2 = 4$), but we don't want that constant, and it messes up our brilliant plan. However, there is a simple solution: instead of replacing

$$x^2 - 4x$$

with just

$$(x-2)^2$$

which produces that extra constant 4, we'll counteract that unwanted effect by simply subtracting that same unwanted value. Therefore, instead of replacing $x^2 - 4x$ with $(x-2)^2$, we'll replace it with

$$(x-2)^2 - 4$$

That is, we know we're going to get an extra 4, so we neutralize that by also subtracting 4.

As a check, let's multiply things out and combine like terms to see if our fix has had the desired effect:

$$\begin{gathered}(x-2)^2 - 4\\ x^2 - 4x + 4 - 4\\ x^2 - 4x\end{gathered}$$

Success! We now have an expression we can use as a replacement for the two-term quadratic on the left side of the equation, and it will leave us with only a single x term with no exponent, which sets us up to continue our quest for the value of x.

Let's go ahead and perform that substitution on our original equation:

$$\begin{aligned}x^2 - 4x &= 5\\ (x-2)^2 - 4 &= 5\end{aligned}$$

Because we're trying to have only x terms on the left side, we'll move that correcting constant -4 to the other side by adding 4 to both sides:

$$\begin{aligned}(x-2)^2 - 4 &= 5\\ (x-2)^2 &= 4 + 5\end{aligned}$$

Because we're always going to perform the previous step, we can streamline the procedure by combine the last two steps when performing this substitution by simply adding the unwanted constant $\left(\frac{b}{2}\right)^2 = 4$ to the other side of the equation directly, so we can go right from

$$x^2 - 4x = 5$$

to

$$(x-2)^2 = 5 + 4$$

Let's look at what we did in the last few steps with the symbolic representation alongside. We started with a quadratic equation

$$x^2 - 4x - 5 = 0 \qquad\qquad x^2 + bx + c = 0$$

We moved c to the other side:

$$x^2 - 4x = 5 \qquad\qquad x^2 + bx = -c$$

We replaced the second-degree binomial on the left side with a term having only a first-degree variable, and we balanced the unwanted constant that's generated by adding it to the other side of the equation:

$$(x-2)^2 = 4+5 \qquad \left(x+\frac{b}{2}\right)^2 = \left(\frac{b}{2}\right)^2 - c$$

Proceeding with our example, let's combine those constants on the right side

$$(x-2)^2 = 4+5$$
$$(x-2)^2 = 9$$

To further unwrap the left side where the jewel we seek, x, is nestled, we'll take the square root of both sides, being careful to include both positive and negative square roots:

$$(x-2)^2 = 9$$
$$x-2 = \pm\sqrt{9}$$
$$x-2 = \pm 3$$

Move that remaining constant over to the right side to isolate and thus solve for x:

$$x-2 = \pm 3$$
$$x = 2 \pm 3$$
$$x = 2+3,\ x = 2-3$$
$$x = 5,\ x = -1$$

Proof of the Quadratic Formula based on Completing the Square

The derivation of this formula comes by following the steps of Completing the Square for a Standard Form quadratic equation: $ax^2 + bx + c = 0$.

1. Divide both sides of the equation by a in order to eliminate the coefficient of the x^2 term.

$$ax^2 + bx + c = 0$$

$$x^2 + \frac{b}{a}x + \frac{c}{a} = 0$$

2. Move the constant term to the other side of the equation in order to isolate the x terms.

$$x^2 + \frac{b}{a}x + \frac{c}{a} = 0$$

$$x^2 + \frac{b}{a}x = -\frac{c}{a}$$

3. Replace the left side of the equation with $\left(x+\frac{b}{2a}\right)^2$ and balance the extra constant on the other side by adding $\left(\frac{b}{2a}\right)^2$ to the right side of the equation.

$$x^2+\frac{b}{a}x=-\frac{c}{a}$$

$$\left(x+\frac{b}{2a}x\right)^2=\left(\frac{b}{2a}\right)^2-\frac{c}{a}$$

$$\left(x+\frac{b}{2a}x\right)^2=\frac{b^2}{4a^2}-\frac{c}{a}$$

4. Combine the constants on the right side of the equation by making a common denominator of $4a^2$.

$$\left(x+\frac{b}{2a}x\right)^2=\frac{b^2}{4a^2}-\frac{c}{a}$$

$$\left(x+\frac{b}{2a}x\right)^2=\frac{b^2}{4a^2}-\left(\frac{c}{a}\right)\left(\frac{4a}{4a}\right)$$

$$\left(x+\frac{b}{2a}x\right)^2=\frac{b^2}{4a^2}-\frac{4ac}{4a^2}$$

$$\left(x+\frac{b}{2a}x\right)^2=\frac{b^2-4ac}{4a^2}$$

5. Take the square root of both sides, being careful to include both positive and negative square roots.

$$\left(x+\frac{b}{2a}x\right)^2=\frac{b^2-4ac}{4a^2}$$

$$x+\frac{b}{2a}=\pm\sqrt{\frac{b^2-4ac}{4a^2}}$$

$$x+\frac{b}{2a}=\pm\frac{\sqrt{b^2-4ac}}{2a}$$

6. Move the constant to right side of the equation to isolate and solve for x.

$$x+\frac{b}{2a}=\pm\frac{\sqrt{b^2-4ac}}{2a}$$

$$x=\frac{-b}{2a}\pm\frac{\sqrt{b^2-4ac}}{2a}$$

It is done!

Proof of the Sum and Product of Roots

We can verify that the sum of the roots is equal to $\frac{-b}{a}$ by considering the Factored Form of a polynomial expression.

A polynomial expression in Standard Form, $ax^2 + bx + c$ can be factored as

$$ax^2 + bx + c = a(x - p)(x - q)$$

where p and q are the zeros or roots. When we distribute the Factored Form, we can see how the Standard Form of the equation takes shape based on the values of the roots (which we will use to prove the Sum of the Roots Formula).

$$ax^2 + bx + c = ax^2 - apx - aqx + apq$$

We can factor out a and x from both of the x terms on the right side of the equation in order to rewrite the expression in a way that matches Standard Form (and then we can match the coefficients to find the sum of the roots in terms of the Standard Form coefficients).

$$ax^2 + bx + c = ax^2 - a(p + q)x + apq$$

The quadratic expression on the right side of the equation is now in Standard Form, and the coefficient of the x term, denoted as b on the other side of the equation, must be equal to $-a(p + q)$.

$$b = -a(p + q)$$

Remember that p and q are the roots of the expression, so $p + q$ is the sum of the roots, and we can find the value of the sum of the roots by dividing both sides of the equation by $-a$.

$$\frac{-b}{a} = p + q$$

Thus, we have shown that the sum of the roots is equal to $\frac{-b}{a}$.

Another proof of this formula comes if we accept the Quadratic Formula as our starting point. The two root values, x, can be found with the equation below:

$$x = \frac{-b}{2a} \pm \frac{\sqrt{b^2 - 4ac}}{2a}$$

One of the roots is equal to $\frac{-b}{2a} + \frac{\sqrt{b^2 - 4ac}}{2a}$ and the other root is equal to $\frac{-b}{2a} - \frac{\sqrt{b^2 - 4ac}}{2a}$. If we add these two roots, we will find that the sum of the roots is $\frac{-b}{a}$.

$$\left(\frac{-b}{2a} + \frac{\sqrt{b^2 - 4ac}}{2a}\right) + \left(\frac{-b}{2a} - \frac{\sqrt{b^2 - 4ac}}{2a}\right)$$

$$\frac{-b}{2a} + \cancel{\frac{\sqrt{b^2 - 4ac}}{2a}} - \frac{b}{2a} - \cancel{\frac{\sqrt{b^2 - 4ac}}{2a}}$$

$$\frac{-b}{2a} - \frac{b}{2a}$$

$$\frac{-2b}{2a}$$

$$\frac{-b}{a}$$

Similar to the proof above, based on expanding the Factored Form into Standard Form, we know that

$$ax^2 + bx + c = ax^2 - a(p+q)x + apq$$

By matching coefficients, we can see that the constant terms must be equal:

$$c = apq$$

Remember that since p and q are the roots of the expression, the product of the roots is pq, and we can find the value of the product of the roots by dividing both sides of the equation by a.

$$\frac{c}{a} = pq$$

Thus, we have shown that the product of the roots is equal to $\frac{c}{a}$.

Similar to the above proof of the sum of roots, we can start with the two root values provided by the Quadratic Formula. The two roots happen to be conjugates of one another, so their product can be calculated more quickly using the Difference of Squares.

$$\left(\frac{-b}{2a} + \frac{\sqrt{b^2-4ac}}{2a}\right)\left(\frac{-b}{2a} - \frac{\sqrt{b^2-4ac}}{2a}\right)$$

$$\left(\frac{-b}{2a}\right)^2 - \left(\frac{\sqrt{b^2-4ac}}{2a}\right)^2$$

$$\frac{b^2}{4a^2} - \frac{b^2-4ac}{4a^2}$$

$$\frac{b^2-b^2+4ac}{4a^2}$$

$$\frac{4ac}{4a^2}$$

$$\frac{c}{a}$$

Extraneous Solutions and Dividing Polynomials

9

9.1 Phantom Equations and Extraneous Solutions

In the exponents chapter, we saw that we could solve some equations by raising both sides of the equation to a power. For example, if we wanted to find the value of x given the equation $\sqrt[5]{x} = 2$, we could raise both sides to the fifth power to solve for x.

$$\sqrt[5]{x} = 2$$
$$\left(\sqrt[5]{x}\right)^5 = (2)^5$$
$$x = 32$$

Example 9.1-1

1 9.1

If $a = 3\sqrt{6}$ and $3a = \sqrt{6x}$, what is the value of x ?

Solution

1. Since $a = 3\sqrt{6}$, substitute $3\sqrt{6}$ for a in the second equation.

$$3a = \sqrt{6x}$$
$$3(3\sqrt{6}) = \sqrt{6x}$$
$$9\sqrt{6} = \sqrt{6x}$$

2. Square both sides of the equation to get rid of the radical. Make sure to distribute the exponent on the left side of the equation.

$$(9\sqrt{6})^2 = (\sqrt{6x})^2$$
$$9^2(\sqrt{6})^2 = 6x$$
$$81(6) = 6x$$

3. Instead of multiplying 81 by 6, divide both sides of the equation by 6 to solve for x.

$$81(6) = 6x$$
$$81 = x$$

4. The answer is 81.

Notes

In Step 2 (or at the end of Step 1), we could have split the right side of the equation into $\sqrt{6}\sqrt{x}$ and canceled the $\sqrt{6}$ on both sides of the equation before squaring both sides.

When there are x terms on both sides of an equation with a radical expression, however, the situation can be a bit more tricky because invalid solutions arise in the process of solving these equations. Specifically, let's limit ourselves to square root equations like $\sqrt{x} = -x$. We can solve this algebraically by squaring both sides of the equation.

$$\sqrt{x} = -x$$
$$\left(\sqrt{x}\right)^2 = (-x)^2$$
$$x = x^2$$

By squaring both sides of the original equation, we created a quadratic equation that can be solved as shown in the last chapter; however, as we will see, one of the solutions to this new equation does not actually satisfy the original equation. Let's solve the equation by getting all the x terms on one side and factoring.

$$x = x^2$$
$$0 = x^2 - x$$
$$0 = x(x - 1)$$
$$x = 0,\ x = 1$$

It would seem that both $x = 0$ and $x = 1$ are solutions, but if we substitute 1 for x in the original equation, $\sqrt{x} = -x$, we will arrive at the equation $\sqrt{1} = -1$, which is not true. Remember that by definition, a symbolic reference to a square root (e.g. $\sqrt{x}$ or $x^{\frac{1}{2}}$) indicates only the non-negative (principal) root. This also applies to any other even-numbered root, such as $\sqrt[4]{x}$ or $x^{\frac{1}{4}}$. Therefore, the solution $x = 1$ is invalid.

These invalid solutions are called **extraneous solutions**. As a result of squaring, we sometimes come up with values that violate the starting conditions; **specifically, we might find values of x that cause the square root to be set equal to a negative number or result in an invalid equation**, such as $5 = 1$ (as seen in the example that follows). The square root of a positive number (or of 0) can't be negative, and 5 clearly isn't equal to 1, so if solutions to these equations violate these restrictions, then they are extraneous.

Why does this happen? Other algebraic manipulations we use don't have this weird side-effect. It's because the squaring operation (or, in fact, raising to any even power) can produce **the same result for two different values**: the number being squared, and also the *negative* of that number, because both produce the same positive result when squared. This means that from that point forward in the solving process, you're actually solving not *just* for the original equation, *but also for a second equation where the value you squared has the opposite sign*. Therefore, you might get two solutions, but one of them is for this phantom equation, NOT for the real equation you're trying to solve.

In the example above, we started with this sequence:

$$\sqrt{x} = -x$$

Squaring both sides,

$$\left(\sqrt{x}\right)^2 = (-x)^2$$
$$x = x^2$$

The complication that has now appeared is that the x^2 on the right side could have been produced by squaring either $-x$ **or** x:

$$(-x)^2 = x^2$$

and

$$(x)^2 = x^2$$

That means that when we proceed with solving $x = x^2$, we're actually solving for not only the original equation

$$\sqrt{x} = -x$$

but *also* for the phantom equation

$$\sqrt{x} = x$$

Indeed, if you plug the extraneous solution we found ($x = 1$) into the phantom equation ($\sqrt{x} = x$) we see that it is a solution:

$$\sqrt{1} = 1$$

In general, if you see there is a radical sign in the original equation and that the question is asking you about the **solution set** of the equation, then you should **just plug in the possible solutions from the answer choices and see which ones are extraneous**. You can solve these equations by squaring both sides and finding solutions algebraically, but for this test, it is rarely worth the time and effort. If you solve for the possible solutions algebraically, you will have to plug back in any of the possible solutions to check if they are extraneous, so you might as well just plug in the possibilities offered to you in the answer choices.

You may see new notation for solution sets that you don't recognize. When you see $\{3, 4\}$, that means that the solution set includes $x = 3$ and $x = 4$ (that is, both 3 and 4 are solutions).

Example 9.1-2

2 9.1

$$\sqrt{2x-2} + 3 = x - 2$$

What is the solution set of the equation above?

A) $\{3\}$

B) $\{9\}$

C) $\{3, 9\}$

D) $\{0, 3, 9\}$

Solution 1

Instead of solving the equation, just plug in the values 3, 9, and 0 to see if any violate the initial conditions of the problem.

1. Plug in 3 for x.

$$\sqrt{2x-2}+3=x-2$$
$$\sqrt{2(3)-2}+3=(3)-2$$
$$\sqrt{6-2}+3=1$$
$$\sqrt{4}+3=1$$
$$✗ \qquad 2+3=1$$
$$5\neq 1$$

2. It is clear that 5 does not equal 1, so 3 is not a valid solution (though if you solved this algebraically you would find that it appears to be). Eliminate choices A, C, and D because all of those solution sets include 3.

3. By process of elimination, choice B is the only one left, but you probably should check the other numbers included in the solution sets (9 and 0) to be sure (9 will work out but 0 will not because the number in the radical will be negative).

4. The answer is B.

Solution 2

1. Subtract 3 from both sides of the equation.

$$\sqrt{2x-2}+3=x-2$$
$$\sqrt{2x-2}=x-5$$

2. Square both sides of the equation in order to eliminate the radical. Be aware that this step is where the phantom equation $\sqrt{2x-2}=-(x-5)$ is injected into the problem and this is why we have to check for extraneous solutions at the end.

$$\left(\sqrt{2x-2}\right)^2=(x-5)^2$$
$$2x-2=x^2-10x+25$$

3. Group all of the terms on the right side of the equation.

$$2x-2=x^2-10x+25$$
$$0=x^2-12x+27$$

4. Factor the expression on the right side of the equation in order to find the possible solutions.

$$0=x^2-12x+27$$
$$0=(x-9)(x-3)$$

5. Since $(x-9)$ is a factor, $x=9$ is a possible solution. Since $(x-3)$ is a factor, $x=3$ is a possible solution.

6. Because this problem started with a radical, we need to check both solutions to see if either is extraneous. In the meantime, we can eliminate choice D because 0 is not even a possible solution.

7. Plug in 9 for x to see if it is an extraneous solution. When doing this step, remember that $\sqrt{16}$ is equal to 4 but is not equal to -4.

$$\sqrt{2x-2}+3=x-2$$
$$\sqrt{2(9)-2}+3=(9)-2$$
$$\sqrt{18-2}+3=7$$
$$\sqrt{16}+3=7$$
$$4+3=7$$
$$\checkmark \quad 7=7$$

8. We have found that 9 is a valid solution, so we can eliminate choice A, which does not include 9 in the solution set.

9. Plug in 3 for x to see if it is an extraneous solution. When doing this step, remember that $\sqrt{4}$ is equal to 2 but is not equal to -2 (this is the most common mistake people make when using this method to solve this problem).

$$\sqrt{2x-2}+3=x-2$$
$$\sqrt{2(3)-2}+3=(3)-2$$
$$\sqrt{6-2}+3=1$$
$$\sqrt{4}+3=1$$
$$\text{✗} \quad 2+3=1$$
$$5\neq 1$$

10. We have found that 3 is an extraneous solution. Therefore, the only valid solution is 9.

11. The answer is B.

Notes

Notice that Solution 2 takes longer, and in the end, we still had to plug in the possible solutions to check for any extraneous solutions.

Because $x=3$ was found to be an extraneous solution to the original equation, it follows that 3 must be a solution to the phantom equation $\sqrt{2x-2}=-(x-5)$ injected into the problem when we squared both sides of an equation during the solving process (to reiterate, 3 is still not a valid solution to the original equation). To prove that, we can plug in 3 for x in that phantom equation:

$$\sqrt{2x-2}=-(x-5)$$
$$\sqrt{2(3)-2}=-(3-5)$$
$$\sqrt{6-2}=-3+5$$
$$\sqrt{4}=2$$
$$2=2$$

If you are not given choices to plug in because the question is a free response question, make sure to **check any solutions you do find because those solutions may be extraneous**.

If you're wondering if there is a method for dealing with solving equations with radicals without having to test all the possible solutions to see if any are extraneous, the answer is yes. You can preserve the radical throughout the solving process and terminate any branch of the solving path if the radical would be negative (radicals cannot be negative). This framework prohibits the injection of the phantom equation.

Let's look at the previous example problem and solve it using this method. Though it is not strictly necessary, it's most convenient to bottle up the radical using U-Substitution so the terms remain compact throughout the solving procedure. Here's the equation we're asked to solve:

$$\sqrt{2x-2}+3=x-2$$

Substitute the radical term, $\sqrt{2x-2}$, with u. Because u represents a radical, it can never be negative, and that will be used to filter out any invalid solution path.

$$u=\sqrt{2x-2}$$

Solve for x in preparation for substituting for x on the right side of the equation so the only variable in the equation is u.

$$u=\sqrt{2x-2}$$
$$u^2=2x-2$$
$$u^2+2=2x$$
$$\frac{u^2+2}{2}=x$$

Now that we have expressions in terms of u for both the radical and for x, we can substitute for $\sqrt{2x-2}$ and x in the original equation.

$$\sqrt{2x-2}+3=x-2$$
$$u+3=\frac{u^2+2}{2}-2$$

Rearrange to get a quadratic equation in u in Standard Form in preparation for factoring.

$$u+3=\frac{u^2+2}{2}-2$$
$$0=\frac{u^2+2}{2}-2-u-3$$
$$0=\frac{u^2+2}{2}-u-5$$
$$0=(u^2+2)-2(u)-2(5)$$
$$0=u^2+2-2u-10$$
$$0=u^2-2u-8$$

Factor.

$$0=(u+2)(u-4)$$

Solve for u. First let's find the solution that we get from the factor $(u+2)$.

$$u+2=0$$
$$u=-2$$

Remember, u **cannot** be negative, so this solution path is terminated. This is where a potential extraneous solution is squashed before it can weasel its way into our solution set. Proceed with the second solution.

$$u - 4 = 0$$
$$u = 4$$

Reverse the U-Substitution to find the value of x, using the equation for x in terms of u that we made at the start.

$$\frac{u^2 + 2}{2} = x$$
$$\frac{4^2 + 2}{2} = x$$
$$\frac{16 + 2}{2} = x$$
$$\frac{18}{2} = x$$
$$9 = x$$

We do not need to test this solution to see if it is extraneous, because this method only produces correct solutions. Therefore, the solution set is $\{9\}$.

Section 9.1 Suggested Problems from Real Tests

View related real-test problems at 1600.io/p/smtex?topic=9.1

Section 9.1 Practice Problems

1 9.1

$$\sqrt{x - 3} = 12$$

What value of x satisfies the equation above?

2 9.1

$$\sqrt{k + 4} - x = 0$$

In the equation above, k is a constant. If $x = 5$, what is the value of k ?

A) 1

B) 3

C) 9

D) 21

3 1600.io 9.1

$$\left(12-2\sqrt{x}\right)^2=\left(3+\sqrt{x}\right)^2$$

Which of the following is a solution to the equation above?

A) $x = 81$

B) $x = 25$

C) $x = 9$

D) $x = 3$

4 1600.io 9.1

$$\sqrt{x+a}=x-5$$

If $a = 1$, what is the solution set of the equation above?

A) $\{3, 8\}$

B) $\{-1\}$

C) $\{3\}$

D) $\{8\}$

9.2 Rational Functions

Operations that are performed on constants or variables can also be performed on entire polynomial expressions. We can add or subtract two polynomials, $f(x)$ and $g(x)$, combining like terms to produce a new polynomial $h(x)$. For example, if $f(x) = 2x^2 + 3x$ and $g(x) = x^2 - 12$, then the sum of $f(x)$ and $g(x)$ is found as follows:

$$h(x) = f(x) + g(x)$$
$$h(x) = (2x^2 + 3x) + (x^2 - 12)$$
$$h(x) = 2x^2 + 3x + x^2 - 12$$
$$h(x) = 3x^2 + 3x - 12$$

As we saw in the last chapter, we can also multiply two polynomials. For example, we know that $x + 2$ and $x - 4$ are both first-degree polynomials, and we showed how two first-degree polynomials could be multiplied to produce a second-degree polynomial.

$$(x + 2)(x - 4)$$
$$x^2 - 2x - 8$$

In this chapter, we are going to look at the division of polynomials, sometimes called **Rational Functions**. Terms in math are said to be **rational** when they can be expressed as a *ratio* (they're "ratio-nal") or, equivalently, as a fraction. Note that this has nothing to do with whether the number or expression is capable of logical thinking. A **rational number** can be expressed as a ratio or fraction of two integers, such as 3/5 or 23/1. A **rational function** can be expressed as a fraction where both the numerator and the denominator are polynomials, such as

$$\frac{x^2+2x+3}{x+1} \qquad \frac{x+1}{x-5} \qquad \frac{1}{3x^3}$$

A number that can't be expressed as a fraction with integer numerator and denominator is said to be **irrational**. Some examples of irrational numbers are $\sqrt{2}$ and π.

In a way, factoring has prepared us for the task of polynomial division (factoring is akin to dividing out a factor), though the two processes are not exactly the same, as true division carries some implications that were not present when we factored. We will discuss these implications in more detail later in the chapter, but for now, we just need to get comfortable rewriting (simplifying, if you like, though again, this is an inexact term) rational expressions to match answer choices.

One necessary skill is the ability to make common denominators in order to combine terms. We know how to do this for numerical fractions. For example, we can write the sum $2+\frac{3}{5}$ as an improper fraction by multiplying 2 by the fraction $\frac{5}{5}$, which is the same as multiplying by 1 (because $\frac{5}{5}=1$), allowing us to represent 2 as a fraction with 5 in the denominator without changing its value.

$$2+\frac{3}{5}$$

$$2\left(\frac{5}{5}\right)+\frac{3}{5}$$

$$\frac{10}{5}+\frac{3}{5}$$

$$\frac{13}{5}$$

The process of finding a common denominator is no different when the fractions involve polynomials. For example, we can turn the sum $2+\frac{3}{x+5}$ into a single fraction if we multiply 2 by $\frac{x+5}{x+5}$ (by exactly the same reasoning as that used in the previous example).

$$2+\frac{3}{x+5}$$

$$2\left(\frac{x+5}{x+5}\right)+\frac{3}{x+5}$$

$$\frac{2x+10}{x+5}+\frac{3}{x+5}$$

$$\frac{2x+13}{x+5}$$

Example 9.2-3

3 9.2

$$\frac{1}{3x+2}+6$$

Which of the following expressions is equivalent to the expression above, for $x>0$?

A) $\frac{3x+12}{3x+2}$

B) $\frac{3x+13}{3x+2}$

C) $\frac{18x+12}{3x+2}$

D) $\frac{18x+13}{3x+2}$

Solution

1. Since all of the answer choices are a single fraction, write the terms with a common denominator by multiplying 6 by $\frac{3x+2}{3x+2}$, and then combine the two fractions.

$$\frac{1}{3x+2} + 6$$

$$\frac{1}{3x+2} + 6\left(\frac{3x+2}{3x+2}\right)$$

$$\frac{1}{3x+2} + \frac{18x+12}{3x+2}$$

$$\frac{18x+13}{3x+2}$$

2. The answer is D.

Notes

The information that $x > 0$ was not necessary to know in order to answer this problem. It is a necessary restriction to eliminate the one value of x for which this equation would not be true, which is when $x = \frac{-2}{3}$. This value of x would cause the denominator to be equal to 0, which is a situation we will discuss a little more later on in this chapter.

In general, if limits are put on the values of variables, the limits exist to ensure that the conclusions drawn are mathematically accurate for all considered cases, but they do not affect the solution method and should simply be checked once solutions are found to verify consistency with the limits placed on the problem.

If you find that you do have to make a common denominator, multiply the numerator and denominator of each fraction by the denominator of the other fraction, just as you would if the denominators were numbers.

For example, if you had to simplify $\frac{1}{x+2} + \frac{1}{x+3}$, multiply the first fraction by $\frac{x+3}{x+3}$ and multiply the second fraction by $\frac{x+2}{x+2}$.

$$\frac{1}{x+2} + \frac{1}{x+3}$$

$$\frac{1}{x+2}\left(\frac{x+3}{x+3}\right) + \frac{1}{x+3}\left(\frac{x+2}{x+2}\right)$$

$$\frac{x+3}{(x+2)(x+3)} + \frac{x+2}{(x+3)(x+2)}$$

$$\frac{2x+5}{(x+2)(x+3)}$$

Most of the time when we are working with equations rather than standalone expressions, we are given the freedom to completely avoid dealing with common denominators by **getting rid of all fractions. Multiply both sides of the equation by all of the denominators** (make sure to cancel any expressions before multiplying when possible).

In the following example, instead of making common denominators on the right side of the equation, our first step will be to combine terms with the same denominator, and then multiply both sides of the equation by that denominator in order to eliminate the fractions.

Example 9.2-4

4 9.2

$$\frac{4(x-3)}{x+2} = 3 - \frac{1}{x+2}$$

What is the solution to the equation above?

A) 13

B) 15

C) 17

D) 19

Solution 1

1. Instead of trying to make a common denominator on the right side of the equation, combine the terms with the same denominator by adding $\frac{1}{x+2}$ to both sides of the equation. Since we are combining the fraction terms, we should also distribute the 4 to the expression $x - 3$ in order to combine the terms in the numerator expression.

$$\frac{4(x-3)}{x+2} = 3 - \frac{1}{x+2}$$

$$\frac{4x-12}{x+2} + \frac{1}{x+2} = 3$$

$$\frac{4x-12+1}{x+2} = 3$$

$$\frac{4x-11}{x+2} = 3$$

2. Multiply both sides of the equation by $x + 2$ in order to eliminate the fraction.

$$\frac{4x-11}{x+2} = 3$$

$$\frac{4x-11}{\cancel{x+2}}(\cancel{x+2}) = 3(x+2)$$

$$4x - 11 = 3x + 6$$

3. Collect and combine the x terms on the left side of the equation by subtracting $3x$ from both sides of the equation, and collect and combine the constant terms on the right side of the equation by adding 11 to both sides of the equation.

$$4x - 11 = 3x + 6$$

$$4x - 3x = 6 + 11$$

$$x = 17$$

4. The answer is C.

Solution 2

In this solution, we opt to make a common denominator in the first step. This method is not necessarily longer, but is perhaps more elaborate, leaving room for errors.

1. Make the two fractions on the right side of the equation have common denominators (which will also match the denominator of the fraction on the left side of the equation). Multiply 3 by $\frac{x+2}{x+2}$ in order to write it in terms of a common denominator, $x + 2$, without changing its value.

$$\frac{4(x-3)}{x+2} = 3 - \frac{1}{x+2}$$

$$\frac{4x-12}{x+2} = 3\left(\frac{x+2}{x+2}\right) - \frac{1}{x+2}$$

$$\frac{4x-12}{x+2} = \frac{3x+6}{x+2} - \frac{1}{x+2}$$

$$\frac{4x-12}{x+2} = \frac{3x+6-1}{x+2}$$

$$\frac{4x-12}{x+2} = \frac{3x+5}{x+2}$$

2. Both sides of the equation are written in the same form, so we can simply match equivalent terms (or you can now choose to eliminate the fractions by multiplying both sides by $x+2$, which will cancel both denominators). The two numerators must be the same.

$$4x - 12 = 3x + 5$$

3. Combine the x terms on the left side of the equation by subtracting $3x$ from both sides of the equation, and combine the constant terms on the right side of the equation by adding 12 to both sides of the equation.

$$4x - 12 = 3x + 5$$
$$4x - 3x = 5 + 12$$
$$x = 17$$

4. The answer is C.

The following example is very similar to the previous example. We could solve this problem by making common denominators, but since there are more terms (none of which have the same denominator), it is more evident how getting rid of the fractions instead of working with them simplifies the work (the more terms you have to copy down line by line, the more potential there is for errors).

Example 9.2-5

5 9.2

$$\frac{2}{x-4}+\frac{1}{x+4}=\frac{rx+t}{(x-4)(x+4)}$$

The equation above is true for all $x > 4$, where r and t are positive constants. What is the value of rt ?

A) -12

B) 0

C) 8

D) 12

Solution 1

1. Instead of trying to make a common denominator, simply get rid of all fractions by multiplying both sides of the equation by $(x-4)(x+4)$. Even though all three fractions have different denominators, multiplying by $(x-4)(x+4)$ will cancel all three of the denominators (the denominator of the fraction on the right side is the product of the other two denominators). Remember to distribute.

$$\frac{2}{x-4}+\frac{1}{x+4}=\frac{rx+t}{(x-4)(x+4)}$$

$$(x-4)(x+4)\left(\frac{2}{x-4}+\frac{1}{x+4}\right)=\cancel{(x-4)(x+4)}\left(\frac{rx+t}{\cancel{(x-4)(x+4)}}\right)$$

$$\cancel{(x-4)}(x+4)\left(\frac{2}{\cancel{x-4}}\right)+(x-4)\cancel{(x+4)}\left(\frac{1}{\cancel{x+4}}\right)=rx+t$$

$$(x+4)(2)+(x-4)(1)=rx+t$$

$$2x+8+x-4=rx+t$$

$$3x+4=rx+t$$

2. Based on matching coefficients, the value of r is 3 and the value of t is 4. Therefore, the value of rt is equal to 3(4) or 12.

3. The answer is D.

Solution 2

1. Make the two fractions on the left side of the equation have common denominators. Multiply the first fraction by $\frac{x+4}{x+4}$, and multiply the second fraction by $\frac{x-4}{x-4}$. When simplifying, don't expand the expressions in the denominators.

$$\frac{x+4}{x+4}\left(\frac{2}{x-4}\right)+\frac{x-4}{x-4}\left(\frac{1}{x+4}\right)=\frac{rx+t}{(x-4)(x+4)}$$

$$\frac{2(x+4)}{(x+4)(x-4)}+\frac{x-4}{(x+4)(x-4)}=\frac{rx+t}{(x-4)(x+4)}$$

$$\frac{2x+8}{(x+4)(x-4)}+\frac{x-4}{(x+4)(x-4)}=\frac{rx+t}{(x-4)(x+4)}$$

2. Since the fractions have the same denominator, we can combine the numerators.

$$\frac{2x+8}{(x+4)(x-4)}+\frac{x-4}{(x+4)(x-4)}=\frac{rx+t}{(x-4)(x+4)}$$

$$\frac{2x+8+x-4}{(x+4)(x-4)}=\frac{rx+t}{(x-4)(x+4)}$$

$$\frac{3x+4}{(x+4)(x-4)}=\frac{rx+t}{(x-4)(x+4)}$$

3. Both sides of the equation are written in the same form, so we can simply match equivalent terms. The two numerators must be the same.

$$3x+4=rx+t$$

4. The x-coefficients must match, so $r=3$. Similarly, the constant terms must match, so $t=4$.
5. Since $r=3$ and $t=4$, then rt is equal to $3(4)$, or 12.
6. The answer is D.

View related real-test problems at 1600.io/p/smtex?topic=9.2

Section 9.2 Practice Problems

1 1600.io 9.2

$$x-3=\frac{6}{x-3}$$

In the equation above, which of the following is a possible value of $x-3$?

A) $\sqrt{6}$

B) 3

C) $2\sqrt{3}$

D) $3+\sqrt{6}$

2 1600.io 9.2

$$\frac{5x+23}{(x+4)^2}-\frac{5}{x+4}$$

The expression above is equivalent to $\frac{a}{(x+4)^2}$, where a is a positive constant and $x \neq -4$. What is the value of a ?

9.3 Undefined Values and Extraneous Solutions for Rational Functions

As we stated earlier, dividing polynomials is not quite the same as factoring because there are added restrictions (this was also alluded to in Example 9.2-3). We already know that fractions with 0 as the denominator are undefined (you can't divide by 0). So, if you are given a rational function and asked for what values of x the function is undefined, you need to find the zeros of the polynomial expression in the denominator; remember, the zeros of a polynomial are simply the values of the variable that make the whole polynomial equal to zero.

Example 9.3-6

6 9.3

Which of the following is a value of x for which the expression $\frac{-7}{x^2 + 12x - 13}$ is undefined?

A) -7

B) -1

C) 0

D) 1

Solution

1. Set the quadratic expression in the denominator equal to 0 so that we can factor it and find the zeros.

$$x^2 + 12x - 13 = 0$$

2. Two numbers that add to 12 and multiply to -13 are 13 and -1, so the factors are $(x + 13)$ and $(x - 1)$.

$$x^2 + 12x - 13 = 0$$
$$(x + 13)(x - 1) = 0$$

3. Since $(x + 13)$ is a factor, $x = -13$ is a zero of the denominator (which would cause the denominator to be 0, producing an undefined value for the fraction), but it is not one of the choices.

4. Since $(x - 1)$ is a factor, $x = 1$ is a zero of the polynomial in the denominator. When the value of x is 1, the denominator will be 0, making the expression undefined.

5. The answer is D.

When there are terms with common denominators on both sides of the equation, you can solve for x algebraically by grouping those terms with common denominators together on one side of the equation and then cross multiplying in order to eliminate denominators. We used this procedure with no complications in earlier examples in this chapter in order to solve certain problems.

However, when we do multiply both sides of the equation by expressions that were in the denominators, we disguise and lose sight of the added restrictions on possible values of x; since these expressions are no longer in the denominator, it is not clear that the zeros of those expressions could cause undefined values. When we multiply the expressions, we create new polynomials that do not obviously have the same restrictions.

Occasionally, in the process of solving rational function equations algebraically, we arrive at extraneous solutions for x which satisfy the new polynomials we created as a result of multiplying, but, when they are plugged back into the original equation, will cause denominators in the original equation to be equal to 0, thus producing undefined values.

As with problems involving radical equations, if you are presented with possible solution sets as answer choices, there is a good chance that some of the values in those sets are values that you would find if you were to solve the problem algebraically but which don't truly satisfy the original equation. This is because they would cause a denominator to be equal to 0, leading to undefined values. **Rational function questions with solution sets for answer choices are often easiest to solve by plugging in the answer choices.**

We have to stress that the questions in this chapter represent some of the *ONLY* cases on the test where plugging in answer choices is the best solving method. This strategy makes sense for these questions because even if you take the time to solve the problem algebraically, you still have to check for extraneous solutions by plugging those solutions back into the original equation.

Example 9.3-7

7 1600.io 9.3

$$\frac{x-2}{x-4}=\frac{1}{x}+\frac{2}{x-4}$$

What is the solution set of the equation above?

A) $\{1\}$

B) $\{0,4\}$

C) $\{1,4\}$

D) $\{2,4\}$

Solution 1

1. Since this is a rational function problem where we are asked about the solution set of the equation, we should start by plugging in possible solutions from the answer choices. In general, you want to start with any possible solution values that appear frequently in the answer choices because if you can eliminate those values, you'll substantially narrow the set of possible answer choices. In this case, 4 is a possible solution in three of the answer choices, so we should start by plugging in 4 for x. It should be immediately apparent that plugging in 4 will produce undefined values because the denominator of two of the expressions is $x-4$. (It should be noted that 0 also should not be in the answer set because x is a denominator that would be equal to 0 when $x=0$.)

$$\frac{x-2}{x-4}=\frac{1}{x}+\frac{2}{x-4}$$

$$\frac{4-2}{4-4}=\frac{1}{4}+\frac{2}{4-4}$$

$$\frac{2}{0}=\frac{1}{4}+\frac{2}{0}$$

2. Since choices B, C, and D include 4 as a possible solution, all of these choices can be eliminated (though you can check what happens when x equals 0, 1, or 2 to see which ones are valid solutions—0 will also produce an undefined value, and 2 is not even an extraneous solution—1 will work of course).

3. The answer is A.

Solution 2

1. Combine the two terms with a denominator of $x - 4$ by subtracting $\frac{2}{x-4}$ from both sides of the equation.

$$\frac{x-2}{x-4} = \frac{1}{x} + \frac{2}{x-4}$$

$$\frac{x-2}{x-4} - \frac{2}{x-4} = \frac{1}{x}$$

$$\frac{x-4}{x-4} = \frac{1}{x}$$

2. On the left side of the equation, the numerator and the denominator are the same, so the fraction reduces to 1. Noticing this now actually helps eliminate an extraneous solution that would arise from cross multiplying and distributing terms (which we will see in Solution 3).

$$\frac{\cancel{x-4}}{\cancel{x-4}} = \frac{1}{x}$$

$$1 = \frac{1}{x}$$

3. Multiply both sides of the equation by x to get x out from the denominator and solve for x.

$$1 = \frac{1}{x}$$

$$x = 1$$

4. Check that 1 is a valid solution by plugging 1 in for x.

$$\frac{x-2}{x-4} = \frac{1}{x} + \frac{2}{x-4}$$

$$\frac{1-2}{1-4} = \frac{1}{1} + \frac{2}{1-4}$$

$$\frac{-1}{-3} = 1 + \frac{2}{-3}$$

$$\frac{1}{3} = 1 - \frac{2}{3}$$

$$\frac{1}{3} + \frac{2}{3} = 1$$

$$\frac{3}{3} = 1$$

$$\checkmark \quad 1 = 1$$

5. When $x = 1$, no initial constraints of the problem are violated, so 1 is a valid solution. Only choices A and C contain 1 as part of the solution set; however, we did not find that 4 was a valid solution by this method (as we said earlier, we luckily avoid solving for this extraneous solution by reducing the fraction in the previous step). Choice C is questionable, and we should double check that $x = 4$ is not also a solution (these extra checks are why we advocate plugging in right away on this particular type of problem).

6. If we tried to test $x = 4$, we would see that plugging in 4 would cause the denominators of the fractions in the given equation to be equal to 0, so 4 should not be included in the solution set. Eliminate choice C.

7. The answer is A.

Solution 3

In Step 2 of Solution 2, suppose we had not reduced the fraction to 1 when we saw $\frac{x-4}{x-4}$. This is the step where we will introduce an extraneous solution to the problem because by multiplying by $x - 4$, we disguise the fact that there will be undefined values if $x = 4$.

1. Combine the two terms with a denominator of $x - 4$ by subtracting $\frac{2}{x-4}$ from both sides of the equation.

$$\frac{x-2}{x-4} = \frac{1}{x} + \frac{2}{x-4}$$

$$\frac{x-2}{x-4} - \frac{2}{x-4} = \frac{1}{x}$$

$$\frac{x-4}{x-4} = \frac{1}{x}$$

2. Multiply both sides of the equation by each of the denominators (cross multiply) in order to eliminate fractions.

$$\frac{x-4}{x-4} = \frac{1}{x}$$

$$(x-4)(x) = (1)(x-4)$$

$$x^2 - 4x = x - 4$$

3. Bring all the terms to the left side of the equation so that we have a quadratic expression set equal to 0 (which we need to do in order to find solutions).

$$x^2 - 4x = x - 4$$

$$x^2 - 4x - x + 4 = 0$$

$$x^2 - 5x + 4 = 0$$

4. Factor the quadratic expression in order to find the solutions (zeros). In case you still aren't comfortable factoring, we'll remind you that we need to find two numbers that add to -5 and multiply to 4 (alternatively, you could use your solving technique of choice, of course). Those numbers are -1 and -4, so the factors are $(x - 1)$ and $(x - 4)$.

$$x^2 - 5x + 4 = 0$$

$$(x-1)(x-4) = 0$$

5. Since $x - 4$ and $x - 1$ are factors, then $x = 4$ and $x = 1$ are possible solutions, but we need to verify that they are not extraneous.

6. If we try to plug 4 into the original equation, we will see that it would cause the denominators of two of the fractions to be equal to 0.

$$\frac{x-2}{x-4} = \frac{1}{x} + \frac{2}{x-4}$$

$$\frac{4-2}{4-4} = \frac{1}{4} + \frac{2}{4-4}$$

$$\frac{2}{0} = \frac{1}{4} + \frac{2}{0}$$

7. Since $x = 4$ would result in undefined values in the original equation, 4 is an extraneous solution, and should not be included in the solution set. You can eliminate choices B, C, and D (which all include 4 in the solution set), leaving only choice A as a possibility. To be safe, you should verify that 1 (the only value in the solution set in choice A) is actually a valid solution.

8. Check that 1 is a valid solution by plugging 1 in for x in the original equation.

$$\frac{x-2}{x-4} = \frac{1}{x} + \frac{2}{x-4}$$

$$\frac{1-2}{1-4} = \frac{1}{1} + \frac{2}{1-4}$$

$$\frac{-1}{-3} = 1 + \frac{2}{-3}$$

$$\frac{1}{3} = 1 - \frac{2}{3}$$

$$\frac{1}{3} + \frac{2}{3} = 1$$

$$\frac{3}{3} = 1$$

$$\checkmark \quad 1 = 1$$

9. When $x = 1$, no initial constraints of the problem are violated, so 1 is a valid solution.

10. The answer is A.

Section 9.3 Suggested Problems from Real Tests

View related real-test problems at 1600.io/p/smtex?topic=9.3

Section 9.3 Practice Problems

1 1600.io 9.3

$$\frac{x^2-4}{x-2}=-2$$

What are all the values of x that satisfy the equation above?

A) -4

B) -2

C) 2

D) -4 and 2

2 1600.io 9.3

$$\frac{4x^2}{x^2-16}-\frac{2x}{x+4}=\frac{3}{x-4}$$

What value of x satisfies the equation above?

A) -4

B) $-\frac{3}{2}$

C) $\frac{3}{2}$

D) 4

9.4 Polynomial Long Division, Polynomial Remainder Theorem, and Matching Coefficients

When faced with dividing one polynomial by another, the first thing you should try is factoring. If you find a common factor to both the numerator and the denominator, you can cancel those factors to simplify the fraction.

Example 9.4-8

8 1600.io 9.4

$$f(x)=x^3-4x$$

$$g(x)=x^2+5x+6$$

Which of the following expressions is equivalent to $\frac{f(x)}{g(x)}$, for $x>-2$?

A) $\frac{1}{x+3}$

B) $\frac{x-2}{x+3}$

C) $\frac{x(x-2)}{x+3}$

D) $\frac{x(x+2)}{x+3}$

Solution

1. Since $f(x) = x^3 - 4x$ and $g(x) = x^2 + 5x + 6$, then we can write the following equation:

$$\frac{f(x)}{g(x)} = \frac{x^3 - 4x}{x^2 + 5x + 6}$$

2. Factor the numerator and denominator to see if there are any common factors that can be canceled in order to simplify; notice that after we factor x from the numerator in the first step below, the difference of squares term $(x^2 - 4)$ appears in the numerator, so we factor that further.

$$\frac{f(x)}{g(x)} = \frac{x^3 - 4x}{x^2 + 5x + 6}$$

$$\frac{f(x)}{g(x)} = \frac{x(x^2 - 4)}{(x + 2)(x + 3)}$$

$$\frac{f(x)}{g(x)} = \frac{x(x + 2)(x - 2)}{(x + 2)(x + 3)}$$

3. The numerator and denominator both have a factor of $(x + 2)$, so we can cancel $(x + 2)$.

$$\frac{f(x)}{g(x)} = \frac{x\cancel{(x + 2)}(x - 2)}{\cancel{(x + 2)}(x + 3)}$$

$$\frac{f(x)}{g(x)} = \frac{x(x - 2)}{x + 3}$$

4. The answer is C.

Polynomial Long Division

In the previous example, we did not have to divide any further in order to match an answer choice, so we didn't need to know any other ways to perform division. While polynomial long division is not a necessary skill to succeed on the test, it can be useful, and it is helpful in explaining why certain other viable solution methods are valid.

Polynomial division can be accomplished by using long division (for cases when factoring isn't easy to do). The process works much like long division of numbers. Though as noted, polynomial long division has never been a necessary technique for the test, it is useful to know, and it makes it easier to understand the Remainder Theorem (we'll get to it) and the associated techniques for dealing with factoring and dividing polynomials.

Here's how the long division operation looks symbolically, with the names of each of the components:

$$\text{divisor}\overline{\big)\ \text{dividend}}^{\ \text{quotient}} \quad + \frac{\text{remainder}}{\text{divisor}}$$

Written using fraction notation, this would be

$$\frac{\text{dividend}}{\text{divisor}} = \text{quotient} + \frac{\text{remainder}}{\text{divisor}}$$

For example, a simple numerical long division might look like this:

$$4\overline{\big)\ 11}^{\ 2} \quad + \frac{3}{4}$$

Written using fraction notation, this would be

$$\frac{11}{4} = 2 + \frac{3}{4}$$

which indicates that 4 goes into 11 twice (the quotient is 2) with a remainder of 3, or, put another way, 4 goes into 11 two and three-quarter times.

Polynomial long division uses the same framework as numerical long division. For now, let's walk through the process of long division by dividing $x^3 - 2x + 4$ by $x + 2$ (most of the time on the test, long division and the Remainder Theorem will be applicable when dividing by binomial first degree polynomials like $x + 2$, which play an important role in factoring and finding zeros).

In order to start the process, let's place the **divisor**, $x + 2$, outside of the division bracket, and the **dividend**, $x^3 - 2x + 4$, inside of the division bracket. When you are performing long division with a dividend that has any degree of x missing, you should hold its place inside the division bracket by adding the term with a coefficient of 0 or by leaving extra space to indicate the position of the zero term so you can line up the quotient (answer) terms with those of the same degree in the dividend. For example, since the dividend is $x^3 - 2x + 4$, you should also include the term $0x^2$ and write the dividend polynomial as $x^3 + 0x^2 - 2x + 4$.

$$x+2 \enclose{longdiv}{\;x^3 + 0x^2 - 2x + 4}$$

The first step is seeing how many times the leading term, x, of the divisor, $x + 2$, goes into the first term of the dividend, $x^3 + 0x^2 - 2x + 4$. Since x goes into the leading term, x^3, x^2 times (since x times x^2 equals x^3), write x^2 above the x^2 term of the dividend; the placeholder term $0x^2$ that we inserted into the dividend keeps things aligned and minimizes the chances of an error.

$$\begin{array}{rl} & \quad\;\;\;\; \mathbf{x^2} \\ x+2 & \overline{)\; x^3 + 0x^2 - 2x + 4} \end{array}$$

Multiply the divisor, $x + 2$, by x^2, then subtract the product from the dividend, $x^3 + 0x^2 - 2x + 4$, carrying down only the result of the subtraction and the subsequent term from the dividend. Note that because you chose the quotient term x^2 so that when multiplied by x, it would equal the first term, x^3, of the dividend, it's therefore not strictly necessary to perform that part of the multiplication and subsequent subtraction, because you already know that the first term will drop out ($x^3 - x^3 = 0$); nonetheless, those redundant steps do serve as a useful double-check on your work.

$$\begin{array}{rl} & \quad\;\;\;\; x^2 \\ x+2 & \overline{)\; x^3 + 0x^2 \;\; - 2x + 4} \\ & \underline{\mathbf{-(x^3 + 2x^2)}} \;\Downarrow \\ & \quad\;\; \mathbf{-2x^2 \;\; -2x} \end{array}$$

Next, see how many times x (again, the leading term of the divisor) goes into $-2x^2$ (the result of the subtraction). Since x goes into $-2x^2$ exactly $-2x$ times, write $-2x$ above the x term of the dividend.

$$\begin{array}{rl} & \quad\;\;\;\; x^2 \;\; \mathbf{-2x} \\ x+2 & \overline{)\; x^3 + 0x^2 \;\; - 2x \;\; + 4} \\ & \underline{-(x^3 + 2x^2)} \\ & \quad\;\; -2x^2 \;\; -2x \end{array}$$

Multiply the divisor, $x + 2$, by $-2x$ then subtract the result from $-2x^2 - 2x$ (be very careful about distributing the negative sign) and carry down the next (and final) term from the dividend.

$$\begin{array}{rl} & \quad\;\;\;\;\;\;\; x^2 \;\; -2x \\ x+2 & \overline{)\; x^3 \;\; + 0x^2 \;\; - 2x \;\; + 4} \\ & \underline{-(x^3 \;\; + 2x^2)} \qquad\quad \Downarrow \\ & \qquad\quad -2x^2 \;\; -2x \;\; \Downarrow \\ & \qquad \underline{\mathbf{-(-2x^2 \;\; -4x)}} \;\Downarrow \\ & \qquad\qquad\qquad\; \mathbf{2x \;\; +4} \end{array}$$

Since x goes into $2x$ twice, write +2 above the constant term of the dividend.

$$
\begin{array}{rrrrr}
 & & x^2 & -2x & +\mathbf{2} \\
\cline{2-5}
x+2 \,\big) & x^3 & +0x^2 & -2x & +4 \\
 & -(x^3 & +2x^2) & & \\
\cline{2-3}
 & & -2x^2 & -2x & \\
 & & -(-2x^2 & -4x) & \\
\cline{3-4}
 & & & 2x & +4
\end{array}
$$

Multiply $x + 2$ by 2 and subtract the product from $2x + 4$.

$$
\begin{array}{rrrrr}
 & & x^2 & -2x & +2 \\
\cline{2-5}
x+2 \,\big) & x^3 & +0x^2 & -2x & +4 \\
 & -(x^3 & +2x^2) & & \\
\cline{2-3}
 & & -2x^2 & -2x & \\
 & & -(-2x^2 & -4x) & \\
\cline{3-4}
 & & & 2x & +4 \\
 & & & -(\mathbf{2x} & \mathbf{+4}) \\
\cline{4-5}
 & & & & \mathbf{0}
\end{array}
$$

Notice that this final subtraction results in a 0. This 0 indicates that there is no remainder, which means that $x + 2$ divides evenly into $x^3 - 2x + 4$. Here's how this division operation looks when written using fraction notation:

$$\frac{x^3 - 2x + 4}{x + 2} = x^2 - 2x + 2$$

This means that both the divisor $x + 2$ and the quotient $x^2 - 2x + 2$ are factors of $x^3 - 2x + 4$. This can be made more obvious by multiplying both sides of the above equation by the divisor $x + 2$, yielding

$$x^3 - 2x + 4 = (x + 2)(x^2 - 2x + 2)$$

To verify this, we can multiply these two factors to show that their product is $x^3 - 2x + 4$.

$$
\begin{gathered}
(x + 2)(x^2 - 2x + 2) \\
x\left(x^2\right) + x(-2x) + x(2) + 2\left(x^2\right) + 2(-2x) + 2(2) \\
x^3 - 2x^2 + 2x + 2x^2 - 4x + 4 \\
x^3 \cancel{- 2x^2} + 2x + \cancel{2x^2} - 4x + 4 \\
x^3 + 2x - 4x + 4 \\
x^3 - 2x + 4
\end{gathered}
$$

To reiterate: when the division was complete, the remainder was 0 because $x + 2$ was a factor of $x^3 - 2x + 4$; that is, when a polynomial is divided by one of its factors, the result is just another factor—no remainder is produced.

The Steps of Polynomial Long Division

1. See how many times the leading term of the divisor goes into the x-term of the greatest remaining power in the dividend.
2. Write that term on top of the division symbol directly above the dividend term of matching degree as part of the resulting quotient.
3. Multiply the divisor by that term and subtract it from the dividend (remember to distribute the negative sign).
4. Carry down the next term in the dividend.
5. Repeat the process seeing how many times the leading term of the divisor goes into the first term of what remains of the dividend as a result of the previous subtraction step.
6. Stop when only a constant is left. That constant is the remainder.

Before you practice this skill, walk yourself through the same steps on the following long divisions (all of which also have no remainder (the remaining constant is 0). The repeated process is always the same:

$$\frac{x^2+8x+15}{x+3}$$

$$\begin{array}{r|lll}
 & x & +5 & \\
\hline
x+3 & x^2 & +8x & +15 \\
 & -(x^2 & +3x) & \Downarrow \\
\hline
 & & 5x & +15 \\
 & & -(5x & +15) \\
\hline
 & & & 0
\end{array}$$

So

$$x^2+8x+15=(x+3)(x+5)$$

$$\frac{2x^2-7x-4}{2x+1}$$

$$\begin{array}{r|lll}
 & & x & -4 \\
\hline
2x+1 & 2x^2 & -7x & -4 \\
 & -(2x^2 & +x) & \Downarrow \\
\hline
 & & -8x & -4 \\
 & & -(-8x & -4) \\
\hline
 & & & 0
\end{array}$$

So

$$2x^2-7x-4=(2x+1)(x-4)$$

$$\frac{9x^3+23x-18}{3x-2}$$

$$\begin{array}{r|llll}
 & 3x^2 & +2x & +9 & \\
\hline
3x-2 & 9x^3 & +0x^2 & +23x & -18 \\
 & -(9x^3 & -6x^2) & \Downarrow & \Downarrow \\
\hline
 & & 6x^2 & +23x & \Downarrow \\
 & & -(6x^2 & -4x) & \Downarrow \\
\hline
 & & & 27x & -18 \\
 & & & -(27x & -18) \\
\hline
 & & & & 0
\end{array}$$

So

$$9x^3+23x-18=(3x-2)(3x^2+2x+9)$$

SkillDrill 9.4-1

Directions: Perform Polynomial Long Division in order to find the quotient of the following 0-remainder divisions. Remember to insert placeholder terms into the dividend as needed.

1. $\dfrac{x^2 - 7x + 12}{x - 3}$

2. $\dfrac{x^2 + 3x - 10}{x - 2}$

3. $\dfrac{x^3 + 6x^2 - 2x - 7}{x + 1}$

4. $\dfrac{x^3 - 5x - 12}{x - 3}$

5. $\dfrac{x^4 - 4x^3 - 2x^2 + 12x - 16}{x - 4}$

6. $\dfrac{4x^3 + 6x^2 + 8x + 12}{2x + 3}$

Polynomial Division with a Remainder

Remember that factoring polynomials allowed us to find zeros of those polynomials. Let's look back to our previous example: we divided $x^3 - 2x + 4$ by $x + 2$ and found that the remainder was 0, which also means that $x + 2$ is a factor of $x^3 - 2x + 4$. The fact that $x + 2$ is a factor of $x^3 - 2x + 4$ indicates that $x = -2$ is a zero of the polynomial because when $x = -2$, $x + 2 = 0$, and therefore the entire polynomial will equal 0.

If we plug -2 in for x in the equation $y = x^3 - 2x + 4$, we can verify that the y-value is 0 (this is obvious if we write $x^3 - 2x + 4$ in Factored Form, $y = (x + 2)(x^2 - 2x + 2)$, because the factor $x + 2$ would be equal to 0).

$$y = x^3 - 2x + 4$$
$$y = (-2)^3 - 2(-2) + 4$$
$$y = -8 + 4 + 4$$
$$y = 0$$

Let's try dividing $x^3 - 2x + 4$ by another binomial, $x - 1$, to see what happens and what to do with nonzero remainders. The process is exactly the same as the one above, but there will be a nonzero constant left over once we run out of x-terms in the dividend.

$$\begin{array}{r|llll} & x^2 & +x & -1 & \\ \hline x-1 & x^3+0x^2 & -2x & +4 & \\ & -(x^3 \ -x^2) & \Downarrow & \Downarrow & \\ \hline & x^2 & -2x & \Downarrow & \\ & -(x^2 & -x) & \Downarrow & \\ \hline & & -x & +4 & \\ & & -(-x & +1) & \\ \hline & & & 3 & \end{array}$$

When we arrive at this step, we cannot proceed any further as the x-term from the divisor does not divide evenly into 3 (technically, x goes into 3 a total of $\frac{3}{x}$ times, but that is not helpful to us), so 3 is the remainder, and we can represent the division in fraction form.

$$\frac{\text{dividend}}{\text{divisor}} = \text{quotient} + \frac{\text{remainder}}{\text{divisor}}$$

$$\frac{x^3 - 2x + 4}{x - 1} = x^2 + x - 1 + \frac{3}{x - 1}$$

SkillDrill 9.4-2

Directions: Perform Polynomial Long Division in order to write the result of the divisions in the form

$$\text{quotient} + \frac{\text{remainder}}{\text{divisor}}$$

1. $\frac{x^2 + 3x + 5}{x + 2}$

2. $\frac{x^2 - x - 7}{x + 2}$

3. $\frac{x^2 - 7x + 13}{x - 3}$

4. $\frac{3x^2 + 11x - 9}{3x - 1}$

5. $\frac{x^3 - 5x^2 + 10x - 17}{x - 3}$

6. $\frac{2x^3 - x^2 - 7x - 1}{2x + 1}$

Polynomial Remainder Theorem

Let's look at polynomial division symbolically alongside the example we used above.

Remember, this is the symbolic representation of long division:

$$\text{divisor}\overset{\text{quotient}}{\overline{\big)\ \text{dividend}}} + \frac{\text{remainder}}{\text{divisor}}$$

In our example, here's how that looks:

$$x-1\overset{x^2+x-1}{\overline{\big)\ x^3+0x^2-2x+4}} + \frac{3}{x-1}$$

There's nothing fancy going on here; it's just division with a remainder.

Let's rewrite those two representations as equations using fraction notation for the division operation so that we can do a little algebra:

$$\frac{\text{dividend}}{\text{divisor}} = \text{quotient} + \frac{\text{remainder}}{\text{divisor}}$$

$$\frac{x^3-2x+4}{x-1} = x^2+x-1+\frac{3}{x-1}$$

Now, let's rearrange things so the dividend is isolated; we'll simply multiply both sides by the divisor, which is $x-1$:

$$\text{dividend} = (\text{divisor})(\text{quotient}) + \text{remainder}$$
$$x^3-2x+4 = (x-1)(x^2+x-1)+3$$

At this point, we can observe that **if the divisor equals 0, the dividend will equal the remainder**, because the first term on the right side will drop out:

$$\text{dividend} = (0)(\text{quotient}) + \text{remainder} = \text{remainder}$$
$$x^3-2x+4 = (0)(x^2+x-1)+3 \qquad = 3$$

This means that **we can easily find the remainder of a division operation by simply finding the value of the variable that makes the divisor equal 0**. In our example, the divisor $x-1$ will equal 0 when $x=1$ because $1-1=0$. That means that if we plug in 1 for x in the dividend (represented here as a function), it should evaluate to 3; let's try it:

$$f(x) = x^3-2x+4$$
$$f(1) = (1)^3-2(1)+4$$
$$f(1) = 1-2+4$$
$$f(1) = 3$$

Generalizing, we can say that if we have a polynomial function $f(x)$ divided by a binomial $x-r$, $f(r)$ will evaluate to the remainder of the division. Symbolically, that means if we have a division of the form

$$\frac{f(x)}{x-r}$$

then

$$f(r) = \text{remainder}$$

In our example, we have our dividend as

$$f(x) = x^3 - 2x + 4$$

and our divisor is the binomial

$$x - 1$$

so

$$r = 1$$

Therefore, the remainder of

$$\frac{f(x)}{x - 1}$$

is equal to $f(1)$, meaning

$$f(1) = \text{remainder} = 3$$

This represents the **Polynomial Remainder Theorem**, which is an exotic-sounding term for the principle explained above: **if we have a polynomial function $f(x)$ divided by a binomial $x - r$, $f(r)$ will evaluate to the remainder of the division.**

Polynomial Remainder Theorem

When a polynomial $f(x)$ is divided by a binomial, $x - r$, the remainder is equal to $f(r)$.

This shows that **when $x - r$ is a factor of $f(x)$, then $x = r$ is a zero of $f(x)$.**

For example, if you are told that $x - 4$ is a factor of a polynomial, then you know that $x = 4$ is a zero of that polynomial.

Similarly, **if $f(r) = 0$** ($x = r$ is a zero of the function), **then $x - r$ is a factor of $f(x)$.**

For example, if you are told that $f(4) = 0$, then you know that $x - 4$ is a factor of the polynomial.

In a more general sense, **if you are told that the remainder of dividing $f(x)$ by $x - r$ is R, then you know that $f(r) = R$.**

For example, if dividing $f(x)$ by $x + 5$ results in a remainder of -7, then you know that $f(-5) = -7$.

Similarly, **if you are told that $f(r) = R$, then you know that the remainder of dividing $f(x)$ by $x - r$ is R.**

For example, if you are told that $f(-5) = -7$, then you know that the remainder of dividing $f(x)$ by $x + 5$ is -7.

On the test, the above definition is all you need to equip yourself to quickly answer the problems that are susceptible to rapid solving via the Remainder Theorem. For completeness, we will also explain the more general case where this theorem can be applied, though knowledge of this is not especially important for the test as presently constructed, as alternative solving methods, such as polynomial long division or factoring, are typically as good or better in situations where this more general version of the theorem applies.

When a polynomial $f(x)$ is divided by a binomial, $ax - r$, the remainder is equal to $f\left(\frac{r}{a}\right)$.

This shows that **when $ax - r$ is a factor of $f(x)$, then $x = \frac{r}{a}$ is a zero of $f(x)$.** Note that this means that $f(x)$ will equal the remainder for the value of x that makes the divisor $ax - r$ evaluate to 0; when $a = 1$, as in all the previous examples and discussions, we can simply use r as the value of x that makes the binomial evaluate to 0, but more generally, we need to use $\frac{r}{a}$.

For example, if you are told that $2x - 1$ is a factor of a polynomial, then you know that $x = \frac{1}{2}$ is a zero of that polynomial.

Similarly, **if $f\left(\frac{r}{a}\right) = 0$** ($x = \frac{r}{a}$ is a zero of the function), **then $ax - r$ is a factor of $f(x)$.**

For example, if you are told that $f\left(\frac{-2}{3}\right) = 0$, then you know that $3x + 2$ is a factor of the polynomial.

In a more general sense, **if you are told that the remainder of dividing $f(x)$ by $ax - r$ is R, then you know that $f\left(\frac{r}{a}\right) = R$.**

For example, if dividing $f(x)$ by $3x + 5$ results in a remainder of -7, then you know that $f\left(\frac{-5}{3}\right) = -7$.

Similarly, **if you are told that $f\left(\frac{r}{a}\right) = R$, then you know that the remainder of dividing $f(x)$ by $ax - r$ is R.**

For example, if you are told that $f\left(\frac{-5}{3}\right) = -7$, then you know that the remainder of dividing $f(x)$ by $3x + 5$ is -7.

Awareness of the Polynomial Remainder Theorem allows you to handle questions that deal with polynomial long division and remainders by plugging values into functions rather than actually performing long division.

SkillDrill 9.4-3

Directions: Use the Polynomial Remainder Theorem to find the remainder when $f(x)$ is divided by $x - r$. The theorem states that the remainder will be $f(r)$.

Challenge problems are boxed.

1. $\frac{x^2 + 3x + 6}{x + 1}$ **2.** $\frac{x^2 - 2x + 1}{x - 4}$ **3.** $\frac{x^2 - 3x - 5}{x - 5}$ **4.** $\frac{x^2 + x - 6}{x - 2}$

5. $\frac{x^3 - 2x^2 + 3}{x - 2}$ **6.** $\frac{x^3 - 5x - 3}{x + 2}$ **7.** $\frac{x^2 + 3x - 20}{x - 1}$ **8.** $\boxed{\frac{x^2 + 4x + 2}{2x + 1}}$

For the following example, we will use two different solutions. The first solution makes use of Polynomial Remainder Theorem; the second solution employs long division.

Example 9.4-9

9 1600.io 9.4

Which of the following expressions is equivalent to

$$\frac{x^2 - 3x - 10}{x - 4}?$$

A) $x - 7 - \frac{38}{x - 4}$

B) $x - 7 - \frac{18}{x - 4}$

C) $x + 1 - \frac{14}{x - 4}$

D) $x + 1 - \frac{6}{x - 4}$

Solution 1

This solution requires some thought up front, but by far has the fewest steps involving copying down terms correctly, making it the most efficient method for this problem.

1. For this solution, we will use the truths related to the Polynomial Remainder Theorem to choose the answer choice that shows the correct remainder. Notice that this problem involves dividing a polynomial $f(x)$, where $f(x) = x^2 - 3x - 10$, by a polynomial of the form $x - r$, where $r = 4$, and all of the answer choices are written in the form

$$\text{quotient} + \frac{\text{remainder}}{\text{divisor}}$$

   where **the value of the remainder is different in each answer choice, so if we can simply determine the remainder, we can select the correct answer choice**—we don't even need to figure out what the quotient is.

   We know from Polynomial Remainder Theorem that $f(r)$ is equal to the remainder, so if we plug in 4 for x in the expression $x^2 - 3x - 10$, we will get the correct value of the remainder.

2. Plug in 4 for x in the expression $x^2 - 3x - 10$.

$$f(x) = x^2 - 3x - 10$$
$$f(4) = (4)^2 - 3(4) - 10$$
$$f(4) = 16 - 12 - 10$$
$$f(4) = -6$$

3. Since for $f(x) = x^2 - 3x - 10$, the value of $f(4)$ is -6, we know that the remainder when we divide $x^2 - 3x - 10$ by $x - 4$ will be -6, which is only found in one of the answer choices.

4. The answer is D.

Solution 2

1. Use polynomial long division to find the result of dividing $x^2 - 3x - 10$ by $x - 4$.

$$\begin{array}{r|l} & x \quad +1 \\ \hline x-4 & x^2 - 3x - 10 \\ & -(x^2 - 4x) \quad \Downarrow \\ \hline & x - 10 \\ & -(x \quad - 4) \\ \hline & -6 \end{array}$$

2. Since the result is $x + 1$ (shown above the division bracket) with a remainder of -6, we know that the following equation is true.

$$\frac{x^2 - 3x - 10}{x - 4} = x + 1 - \frac{6}{x - 4}$$

3. The answer is D.

Long division and Polynomial Remainder Theorem are not always the best ways to do polynomial division problems. The following is an example of yet another variation on the idea of matching coefficients. Simply group terms based on common denominators, and then cross multiply. Match the coefficients once both sides of the equation are in the same form.

Example 9.4-10

10 9.4

The equation $\dfrac{-12x^2 + 28x - 44}{ax - 4} = -6x + 2 - \dfrac{36}{ax - 4}$ is

true for all values of $x \neq \dfrac{4}{a}$, where a is a constant. What

is the value of a ?

A) -6

B) -2

C) 2

D) 6

Solution 1

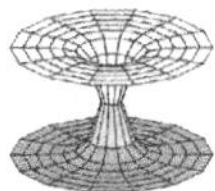

1. In order for the first term of the quotient to be $-6x$, which is the result of dividing $-12x^2$ (the first term of the dividend) by ax (the first term of the divisor), the value of a must be 2.

$$\frac{-12x^2}{ax} = -6x$$
$$-12x^2 = (-6x)(ax)$$
$$-12\cancel{x^2} = -6a\cancel{x^2}$$
$$\frac{-12}{-6} = a$$
$$2 = a$$

2. The answer is C.

Solution 2

1. Group the terms with the denominator $ax - 4$ on the left side of the equation.

$$\frac{-12x^2 + 28x - 44}{ax - 4} = -6x + 2 - \frac{36}{ax - 4}$$
$$\frac{-12x^2 + 28x - 44}{ax - 4} + \frac{36}{ax - 4} = -6x + 2$$
$$\frac{-12x^2 + 28x - 8}{ax - 4} = -6x + 2$$

2. Multiply both sides of the equation by $ax - 4$.

$$\frac{-12x^2 + 28x - 8}{ax - 4} = -6x + 2$$
$$-12x^2 + 28x - 8 = (-6x - 2)(ax - 4)$$

3. You can distribute if you like, but really we are only concerned about the coefficients of the x^2 terms. Since $-6x$ times ax has to be equal to $-12x^2$, the value of a must be 2.

$$-12x^2 = (-6x)(ax)$$
$$-12x^2 = -6ax^2$$
$$-12 = -6a$$
$$2 = a$$

4. The answer is C.

Notes

The more comfortable you get with the topics covered in this chapter, the easier it is to think of faster and faster methods for handling these problems, most of which can be done in quite a number of ways.

View related real-test problems at 1600.io/p/smtex?topic=9.4

Section 9.4 Practice Problems

1 9.4

$$\frac{x^2 + 20x + 99}{x + 11}$$

If the expression above is equivalent to an expression of the form $x + a$, where $x \neq -11$, what will be the value of a ?

2 9.4

The expression $\frac{4x - 1}{x + 6}$ is equivalent to which of the following?

A) $\frac{4 - 1}{6}$

B) $4 - \frac{1}{6}$

C) $4 - \frac{1}{x + 6}$

D) $4 - \frac{25}{x + 6}$

9.5 Solving in Terms of Variables

This section covers problems that involve solving equations with multiple variables or unknown constants for one variable or unknown constant in terms of the others. The equations in these problems can be of any form (not just linear or quadratic) and may involve squaring or taking square roots of both sides in scientific equations. Essentially, this boils down to performing algebraic steps in the correct order to rearrange a provided equation as required, but you will not be bothered with the properties of numbers or polynomials at all, and you don't have to worry about plugging anything in or evaluating numbers. These problems are much easier than anything else in this chapter as long as you simply unwrap the equations one step at a time.

The equation $p = \frac{2}{3}t$ contains two unknowns and is currently solved for p in terms of t. If we want to solve for t in terms of p we would just multiply both sides of the equation by $\frac{3}{2}$ in order to isolate t: $\frac{3}{2}p = t$. Just to be sure you understand what just happened, we could have multiplied both sides by the reciprocal of $\frac{2}{3}$ (as we did), we could have divided both sides by $\frac{3}{2}$, or we could have performed the two separate steps of multiplying both sides by 3 and dividing both sides by 2 (in either order); these are all equivalent in their effect.

Let's look at a slightly more complicated equation with multiple unknown values.

$$A = \frac{B + 3C + D}{5}$$

If we wanted to solve for C in terms of the other unknowns (A, B, and D), we should start by multiplying both sides of the equation by 5 because the C is currently grouped into the numerator and this step would allow us to isolate the numerator group first.

$$5A = B + 3C + D$$

Now that the numerator group is isolated, the term $3C$ is the next grouping that C belongs to, so subtract B and D from both sides of the equation.

$$5A - B - D = 3C$$

Finally, we can solve for C in terms of the other unknowns by dividing both sides of the equation by 3.

$$\frac{5A - B - D}{3} = C$$

Similarly, we can solve an equation for an *expression* rather than a single term as in the example below.

Example 9.5-11

11 1600.io 9.5

$$\text{James's formula: } A = \frac{\sqrt{\ell w}}{10}$$

$$\text{McNeil's formula: } A = \frac{8 + w}{5}$$

The formulas above are used by cobblers to estimate the body surface area A, in square feet, of snakes whose weight w ranges between 10 and 40 pounds and whose length ℓ is measured in inches.

If James's and McNeil's formulas give the same estimate for A, which of the following expressions is equivalent to $\sqrt{\ell w}$?

A) $\frac{8 + w}{2}$

B) $\frac{8 + w}{50}$

C) $\frac{(8 + w)^2}{2}$

D) $2(8 + w)$

Solution

Take note that we are looking to isolate the entire expression $\sqrt{\ell w}$, so be sure to stop when that expression is isolated.

1. The problem states that the two formulas give the same value of A for a certain length and width, so set the two expressions from the right sides of the formulas equal to each other.

$$\frac{\sqrt{\ell w}}{10} = \frac{8 + w}{5}$$

2. Multiply both sides of the equation by 10 in order to isolate the expression $\sqrt{\ell w}$ on the left side of the equation and reduce the fraction.

$$\frac{\sqrt{\ell w}}{10} = \frac{8+w}{5}$$

$$\sqrt{\ell w} = 10\left(\frac{8+w}{5}\right)$$

$$\sqrt{\ell w} = 2(8+w)$$

3. The answer is D.

Notes

Notice that we did not distribute the 2 in Step 2 because we already had a match to an answer choice.

If the term you need to solve for is "trapped" in a radical, you will need to raise both sides to a power (usually squaring both sides).

Example 9.5-12

12 1600.io 9.5

$$T = \sqrt{\frac{4\pi^2 L}{g}}$$

The formula above is used to calculate the period, T, of a pendulum given the length, L, of the pendulum and the acceleration due to gravity, g. Which of the following correctly expresses the acceleration due to gravity in terms of the other variables?

A) $g = \sqrt{\frac{4\pi^2 L}{T}}$

B) $g = \frac{\sqrt{4\pi^2 L}}{T}$

C) $g = \frac{4\pi^2 L}{T^2}$

D) $g = \frac{T^2}{4\pi^2 L}$

Solution

1. We need to isolate the term g, the acceleration due to gravity, which is in the radical sign. Our first step should be to square both sides of the equation in order to "free the g from the radical prison."

$$T = \sqrt{\frac{4\pi^2 L}{g}}$$

$$T^2 = \frac{4\pi^2 L}{g}$$

2. Multiply both sides of the equation by g in order to get g out from the denominator.

$$T^2 = \frac{4\pi^2 L}{g}$$

$$gT^2 = 4\pi^2 L$$

3. Divide both sides of the equation by T^2 in order to solve for g in terms of the other variables.

$$gT^2 = 4\pi^2 L$$

$$g = \frac{4\pi^2 L}{T^2}$$

4. The answer is C.

In other cases, the term you want to solve for is raised to a power in the initial equation, so you will end up taking a root of both sides of the equation in order to solve for that term.

Example 9.5-13

13 1600.io 9.5

The volume of a cone is given by the formula $V = \frac{1}{3}hr^2$, where r is the radius of the base of the cone and h is the height of the cone. Which of the following gives the radius of the base of the cone in terms of the volume of the cone and the height of the cone?

A) $\frac{3V}{h}$

B) $\frac{h}{3V}$

C) $\sqrt{\frac{3V}{h}}$

D) $\sqrt{\frac{h}{3V}}$

Solution

1. We need to isolate the term r, the radius of the base of the cone, which is a squared term in the original equation. First we need to isolate the term r^2 on one side of the equation by itself. Start by multiplying both sides of the equation by 3 in order to get rid of the fraction.

$$V = \frac{1}{3}hr^2$$

$$3V = hr^2$$

2. Divide both sides of the equation by h in order to isolate r^2.

$$3V = hr^2$$

$$\frac{3V}{h} = r^2$$

3. Finally, in order to solve for r (which is currently raised to the second power), take the square root of both sides of the equation.

$$\frac{3V}{h} = r^2$$

$$\sqrt{\frac{3V}{h}} = r$$

4. The answer is C.

If the variable or unknown constant is found in multiple terms, you will need to **group those terms and then factor the variable or constant out of those terms**. For example, we can solve the equation $wx + wy = zy$ for w in terms of x, y, and z. First factor the w from both terms on the left side of the equation: $w(x + y) = zy$. All we have to do now is divide both sides of the equation by the expression $x + y$ in order to isolate w: $w = \frac{zy}{x + y}$.

If the variable or unknown constant you need to isolate is "trapped" in the denominator of a fraction, you should **multiply both sides of the equation by the denominator** in order to get rid of the fractions.

In the example below, there are multiple terms that contain the constant we want to solve for, and we have to multiply by a denominator in order to put all the terms on the same level.

Example 9.5-14

 14 9.5

$$R = \frac{U}{D + U}$$

James McNeil uses the formula above to calculate a snake photo's rating, R, based on the number of upvotes, U, and downvotes, D, the photo gets on social media. Which of the following expresses the number of upvotes in terms of the other variables?

A) $U = \frac{RD}{1 - R}$

B) $U = \frac{RD}{R - 1}$

C) $U = \frac{D}{1 - R}$

D) $U = \frac{D}{R - 1}$

Solution

1. Multiply both sides of the equation by the expression $D+U$ from the denominator of the fraction on the right side of the equation in order to free the variable U from the denominator and get rid of fractions.

$$R = \frac{U}{D+U}$$
$$R(D+U) = U$$

2. Distribute R on the left side of the equation.

$$R(D+U) = U$$
$$RD + RU = U$$

3. Subtract RU from both sides of the equation in order to group the terms with U.

$$RD + RU = U$$
$$RD = U - RU$$

4. Factor U from both terms on the right side of the equation in order to isolate U.

$$RD = U - RU$$
$$RD = U(1-R)$$

5. Divide both sides of the equation by $1-R$ in order to isolate and solve for U in terms of the other variables.

$$RD = U(1-R)$$
$$\frac{RD}{1-R} = U$$

6. The answer is A.

Section 9.5 Suggested Problems from Real Tests

View related real-test problems at 1600.io/p/smtex?topic=9.5

Section 9.5 Practice Problems

1 9.5

$$\frac{1}{r}mv^2 = ma$$

Uniform circular motion is represented by the equation above, where m represents mass, r represents the radius, v represents the velocity, and a represents the acceleration. According to the equation for uniform circular motion, which of the following is equivalent to the velocity, v ?

A) ra

B) $\frac{1}{r}am^2$

C) $\sqrt{ra}$

D) $\sqrt{\frac{1}{r}ma}$

2 9.5

James McNeil uses the formula $n = 10\ell w$ to estimate the number of snakes, n, needed to fill a snakepit that is ℓ feet long and w feet wide. Which of the following correctly expresses w in terms of n and ℓ ?

A) $w = \frac{10}{n\ell}$

B) $w = \frac{n}{10\ell}$

C) $w = \frac{\ell}{10n}$

D) $w = \frac{n}{10 + \ell}$

3 9.5

$$A = 6s^2$$

The formula above gives the surface area, A, of a cube in terms of the length of its sides, s. Which of the following gives the length of the sides of the cube in terms of its surface area?

A) $s = \sqrt{\frac{A}{6}}$

B) $s = \sqrt{\frac{6}{A}}$

C) $s = \frac{\sqrt{A}}{6}$

D) $s = \frac{\sqrt{6}}{A}$

4 9.5

Sludge volume, V_S, in a pond can be determined using the equation $V_S = \frac{V_P}{1 - W}$, where V_P is the poison volume and W is the hydrocrit (the fraction of sludge volume that is water). Which of the following correctly expresses the hydrocrit in terms of the sludge volume and the poison volume?

A) $W = V_S - V_P$

B) $W = \frac{V_P}{V_S}$

C) $W = 1 + \frac{V_P}{V_S}$

D) $W = 1 - \frac{V_P}{V_S}$

CHAPTER 9 RECAP

- Most of the problems that are covered in this chapter have several completely valid solution methods, and any one method will not be the fastest in all cases. It is important to note the benefits and drawbacks of each, and it is better to use a method in which you're confident over one that may be faster but that requires a greater "leap of faith" for you.
- When a given equation has an expression in a radical sign, move everything to the other side of the equation before squaring both sides of the equation to eliminate the radical.
- When squaring both sides of an equation, extraneous solutions are often created. Remember that even though both $x = 2$ and $x = -2$ are valid solutions to the equation $x^2 = 4$, when an equation is given to you with an existing square root, the value of that square root, by definition, is non-negative (this is also true for all other even roots).
- For questions that ask you to pick the correct solution set for an equation containing a radical, you will need to double check any solutions you find algebraically by plugging those solutions back into the equation (unless you are using the sophisticated U-Substitution solving approach). Because of this need to check answers on these problems, you are usually better off not working algebraically on these problems. You will save time by checking the answer choices right away (it is rare that plugging in is the preferred solution method, so revel in it).
- Rational expressions consist of one polynomial being divided by another. For some questions, you may need to combine terms through addition or subtraction. To do so, you may need to write terms so that they have common denominators.
- In equations with rational functions, you may be able to make quick assessments based on the Polynomial Remainder Theorem to determine what the remainder would be. If the remainders in the answer choices are not unique or if the leading coefficient of the divisor is not known, you may be able to discern based on the first term of the quotient what the coefficient of the divisor must be.

  If you are not comfortable with these methods, you should combine any terms that share a common denominator before doing anything else. After that, instead of making common denominators on terms that don't already share them, simply multiply both sides of the equations by the different denominators of individual expressions in order to eliminate fractions. In this process, you may end up finding solutions that would have caused the denominator of one or more of the terms in the given equation to be equal to 0 (causing an undefined value), so make sure to double check that any solutions you find will not cause this problem.
- The value of a rational function is undefined when the denominator is equal to 0. Use factoring skills to determine what values of x will cause the denominator to be 0.
- Polynomial Long Division is rarely necessary (there are always multiple routes through a problem), but you should have a handle on the process just in case. In part, we presented Polynomial Long Division to set up the explanation of the Polynomial Remainder Theorem, a tool that can often be used to solve problems more easily than can long division. Another technique for performing polynomial division is called Synthetic Division, which we have not presented herein, but if you're interested, you can easily find explanations of it through the Google machine.
- The Polynomial Remainder Theorem states that when a polynomial $f(x)$ is divided by a binomial $x - r$, the remainder of the division, R, is equal to $f(r)$. Therefore, when $f(r) = 0$, $f(x)$ is divisible by $x - r$. For example, if we wanted to check if $f(x)$ is divisible by $x - 4$, we could plug 4 into $f(x)$. If $f(4) = 0$, then $f(x)$ is divisible by $x - 4$.

  In cases where the divisor is of the form $ax - r$, the Polynomial Remainder Theorem states that when a polynomial $f(x)$ is divided by a binomial $ax - r$, the remainder of the division, R, is equal to $f\left(\frac{r}{a}\right)$. Therefore, when $f\left(\frac{r}{a}\right) = 0$, $f(x)$ is divisible by $ax - r$. For example, if we wanted to check if $f(x)$ is divisible by $2x - 3$, we could plug $\frac{3}{2}$ into $f(x)$. If $f\left(\frac{3}{2}\right) = 0$, then $f(x)$ is divisible by $2x - 3$.

- In science or geometry equations, you often need to solve for one variable in terms of the others.

  If the variable you need to solve for is "trapped" in a radical sign, start by moving everything outside of the radical to the other side of the equation before you raise both sides of the equation to any power to eliminate the radical. Luckily, you do not need to worry about extraneous solutions to these when you square both sides of an equation.

  Similarly, if the variable you are solving for is raised to a power in the given equation, move everything else to the other side of the equation before taking a root of both sides.

  If there are multiple terms containing the variable you need to solve for, group those terms and factor the variable out from those terms.

  If the variable you are solving for is in the denominator, multiply both sides of the equation by the denominator to "free" the variable from the denominator.

Additional Problems

1 1600.io 9.1

$$\sqrt{9x} = x - 4$$

What are all values of x that satisfy the equation above?

I. 1

II. 16

A) I only

B) II only

C) I and II

D) Neither I nor II

2 1600.io 9.1

$$\sqrt{x+62} - 4\sqrt{x+2} = 0$$

What value of x satisfies the equation above?

A) 2

B) 4

C) 18

D) 20

3 1600.io 9.1

What is the set of all solutions to the equation $\sqrt{x+42} = -x$?

A) $\{-6, 7\}$

B) $\{-6\}$

C) $\{7\}$

D) There are no solutions to the given equation.

4 1600.io 9.4

In the xy-plane, what is the y-coordinate of the y-intercept of the graph of the equation $y = \dfrac{5x+20}{x-4}$?

A) -5

B) -4

C) -1

D) 4

5 9.2

$$\frac{x}{x-10} = \frac{4x}{4}$$

Which of the following represents all the possible values of x that satisfy the equation above?

A) 0 and 9

B) 0 and 11

C) 9 and 11

D) 11

6 9.1

$$x - 3 = \sqrt{x-1}$$

Which of the following values of x is a solution to the equation above?

A) −2

B) 2

C) 5

D) 9

7 9.2

If $x > 7$, which of the following is equivalent to $\dfrac{1}{\dfrac{1}{x+5} + \dfrac{1}{x+7}}$?

A) $2x + 12$

B) $x^2 + 12x + 35$

C) $\dfrac{2x+12}{x^2+12x+35}$

D) $\dfrac{x^2+12x+35}{2x+12}$

8 9.3

$$h(x) = \frac{1}{(x-3)^2 + 6(x-3) + 9}$$

For what value of x is the function h above undefined?

9 1600.io 9.1

$$\sqrt{3k^2+4}-x=0$$

If $k>0$ and $x=4$ in the equation above, what is the value of k ?

A) 0

B) 2

C) 4

D) 6

10 1600.io 9.4

Which of the following is equivalent to $\dfrac{5x^2+9x}{5x+4}$?

A) x

B) $x+5$

C) $x-\dfrac{4}{5x+4}$

D) $x+1-\dfrac{4}{5x+4}$

11 1600.io 9.1

$$\sqrt{x}+3=10$$

Which of the following is the solution to the equation above?

A) 7

B) 13

C) 49

D) 97

12 1600.io 9.4

$$f(x)=4x^3+10x^2+6x$$
$$g(x)=2x^2+5x+3$$

The polynomials $f(x)$ and $g(x)$ are defined above. Which of the following polynomials is divisible by $2x+5$?

A) $h(x)=f(x)+g(x)$

B) $k(x)=f(x)+5g(x)$

C) $m(x)=2f(x)+5g(x)$

D) $p(x)=5f(x)+2g(x)$

13 9.4

For a polynomial $p(x)$, the value of $p(6)$ is 4. Which of the following must be true about $p(x)$?

A) $x - 4$ is a factor of $p(x)$.

B) $x - 2$ is a factor of $p(x)$.

C) $x + 4$ is a factor of $p(x)$.

D) The remainder when $p(x)$ is divided by $x - 6$ is 4.

14 9.1

$$\sqrt[4]{x^4} = x$$

Which of the following values of x is NOT a solution to the equation above?

A) -2

B) 0

C) 1

D) 2

15 9.1

If $r > 0$ and $\sqrt[3]{\dfrac{25r}{2}} = \dfrac{1}{2}r$, what is the value of r ?

16 9.4

$$\frac{x^2 - 2c}{x - b}$$

In the expression above, b and c are positive integers. If the expression is equivalent to $x + b$ and $x \neq b$, which of the following could be the value of c ?

A) 1

B) 2

C) 4

D) 16

17 1600.io 9.1

If $\sqrt{3x} = 6$, what is the value of x ?

A) 2
B) 6
C) 12
D) 36

18 1600.io 9.1

Which of the following is a solution to the equation $\sqrt{22 + 2x} + 1 = x$?

I. -3

II. 5

III. 7

A) I only
B) II only
C) III only
D) I and III

19 1600.io 9.1

If $\sqrt{x - 3} = 9$, what is the value of x ?

20 1600.io 9.5

$$W = \frac{288x^2}{2}$$

In the equation above, the potential energy, W, of a spring with a spring constant of 288 units is given in terms of the distance the spring is stretched, x. If the equation is rewritten in the form $x = a\sqrt{W}$, where a is a positive constant, what is the value of a ?

21 9.1

$$\sqrt{x-7} = 7 - \sqrt{x}$$

If x is the solution to the equation above, what is the value of $\sqrt{x-7}$?

A) $\sqrt{7}$

B) 3

C) 7

D) 16

22 9.2

$$\frac{1}{x^2 - 18x + 81} = 9$$

If x is a solution to the given equation, which of the following is a possible value of $x - 9$?

A) $\frac{1}{3}$

B) $\frac{10}{3}$

C) $\frac{26}{3}$

D) $\frac{28}{3}$

23 9.1

$$x - 3\sqrt{x} - 4 = 0$$

What value of x satisfies the equation above?

24 9.4

$$\frac{x-5}{(x-5)^2}$$

Which of the following expressions is equivalent to the given expression, where $x \neq 5$?

A) $x - 5$

B) $x^2 - 10x + 25$

C) $\frac{1}{x-5}$

D) $\frac{1}{x^2 - 10x + 25}$

25 1600.io 9.1

If $\sqrt{x} + \sqrt{16} = \sqrt{49}$, what is the value of x ?

A) $\sqrt{3}$

B) 3

C) 9

D) 33

26 1600.io 9.2

A group of coworkers decided to divide the \$300 cost of a team-building retreat equally among themselves. When one of the coworkers decided not to go on the retreat, those remaining still divided the \$300 cost equally, but each coworker's share of the cost increased by \$10. How many coworkers were in the group originally?

27 1600.io 9.5

$$x = a\sqrt{1 - \frac{y^2}{b^2}}$$

For an ellipse centered at the origin with half-width a and half-height b, the x-coordinate, x, of a point on the ellipse can be determined with the formula above, where y is the y-coordinate of that point. The formula above expresses x in terms of a, b, and y. Which of the following gives the y-coordinate of the point in terms of the other quantities?

A) $y = b\sqrt{1 + \frac{x^2}{a^2}}$

B) $y = b\sqrt{1 - \frac{x^2}{a^2}}$

C) $y = b^2\left(1 + \frac{x^2}{a^2}\right)^2$

D) $y = b^2\left(1 - \frac{x^2}{a^2}\right)^2$

28 1600.io 9.5

$$abd + bcd = bc - cd$$

In the equation above, a, b, and c are each greater than 1. Which of the following is equivalent to d ?

A) $ab + c$

B) $\frac{1}{a + 2c}$

C) $\frac{1}{abc}$

D) $\frac{bc}{ab + bc + c}$

Answer Key

Section 9.1 Practice Problems

1. 147
2. D
3. C
4. D

Section 9.2 Practice Problems

1. A
2. 3

Section 9.3 Practice Problems

1. A
2. C

SkillDrill 9.4-1

1. $x-4$
2. $x+5$
3. x^2+5x-7
4. x^2+3x+4
5. x^3-2x+4
6. $2x^2+4$

SkillDrill 9.4-2

1. $x+1+\frac{3}{x+2}$
2. $x-3-\frac{1}{x+2}$
3. $x-4+\frac{1}{x-3}$
4. $x+4-\frac{5}{3x-1}$
5. $x^2-2x+4-\frac{5}{x-3}$
6. $x^2-x-3+\frac{2}{2x+1}$

SkillDrill 9.4-3

1. 4
2. 9
3. 5
4. 0
5. 3
6. -1
7. -16
8. $\frac{1}{4}$ or 0.25

Section 9.4 Practice Problems

1. 9
2. D

Section 9.5 Practice Problems

1. C
2. B
3. A
4. D

Additional Problems

1. B
2. A
3. B
4. A
5. B
6. C
7. D
8. 0
9. B
10. D
11. C
12. B
13. D
14. A
15. 10
16. B
17. C
18. C
19. 84
20. $\frac{1}{12}$ or .083
21. B
22. A
23. 16
24. C
25. C
26. 6
27. B
28. D

The Graphs of Quadratic Equations and Polynomials 10

10.1 Standard Form: General Shape of Graphs

The graphs of quadratic equations (or functions) are called **parabolas**, and they are U-shaped graphs that have a maximum or minimum point. The **range** of a function is the set of all possible y-values that can be produced by a function (we'll see a different definition for range when we discuss statistics in a later chapter). For quadratics, the range is bounded on one end by the maximum or minimum y-value of the function at its vertex, and is unbounded (goes to infinity) on the other end.

Let's consider the quadratic functions $f(x) = x^2 + 2x + 2$ and $g(x) = -2x^2 + 8x - 8$. The tables below show the function values for several values of x. We will use the points given in the table to construct the graphs of these functions.

x	$y = f(x)$	$y = g(x)$
−4	10	−72
−3	5	−50
−2	2	−32
−1	1	−18
0	2	−8
1	5	−2
2	10	0
3	17	−2
4	26	−8
5	37	−18

You may notice that the series of values for each function shows a pattern in which the y-values reach a maximum or minimum and then begin repeating in reverse order. This is due to the fact that **parabolas are symmetric about their maximum or minimum points** (the maximum and minimum points for each function do appear in the table, as these two functions were chosen because their maximum and minimum points both have integer x-values), and we will learn more about this symmetry in the coming parts of this chapter when we discuss Factored Form and especially Vertex Form. This maximum or minimum point is called the **vertex** of the parabola because it's where the "axis of symmetry" line meets the parabola, just as the point in a triangle or other figure at which two lines meet is called a vertex. All parabolas are symmetrical—the graph on one side of the axis of symmetry is the mirror image of the graph on the other side.

To see what the graphs of these equations look like, let's graph some of the points on each function. For $f(x)$ let's use the following points: $(-4, 10)$, $(-3, 5)$, $(-2, 2)$, $(-1, 1)$, $(0, 2)$, $(1, 5)$, and $(2, 10)$.

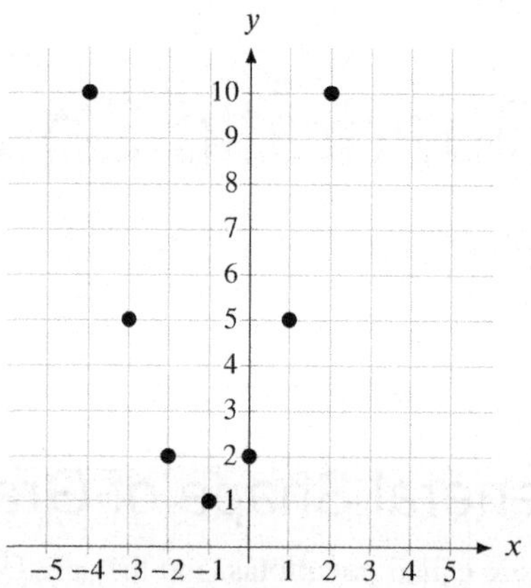

When we connect the points, we should use a smooth curve instead of a bunch of straight lines between the points, thus forming a U-shaped graph for $f(x)$. You should notice that the y-value reaches its lowest value at the point $(-1, 1)$, which is the vertex of the parabola, the point where the graph of $f(x)$ intersects the line of the axis of symmetry, $x = -1$ (notice that the graph is mirrored over this line). We will discuss later in this chapter methods of finding the lowest (or highest) points of the graphs of parabolas, but we would say that the **range** of this function is $y \geq 1$ because the vertex, at which the y-value is 1, is the lowest point on the graph, and there is no highest point because the y-values increase infinitely.

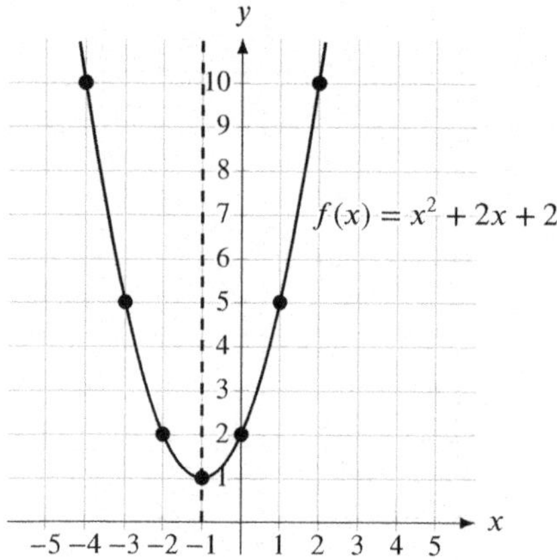

Let's do the same for $g(x)$ by graphing, and then connecting with a smooth curve, the following points: $(-1, -18)$, $(0, -8)$, $(1, -2)$, $(2, 0)$, $(3, -2)$, $(4, -8)$, and $(5, -18)$. (Note that the y-axis is on a different scale than the x-axis to keep the diagram compact.)

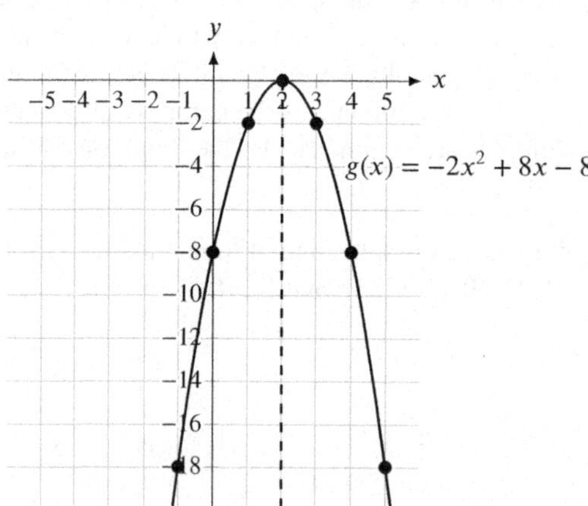

Once again, we see a U-shaped graph called a parabola, but in this case, the graph is pointed in the opposite direction, so that the vertex point, $(2, 0)$, represents the maximum y-value of the equation (the range is $y \leq 0$); again, the vertex point is where the graph of $g(x)$ intersects the line of the axis of symmetry, $x = 2$.

There are three main forms of quadratic equations that will be discussed in this chapter, and each one can be used to easily find key features of the graphs (and, conversely, the graphs can be used to easily form these equations based on which features and points are evident in the graph), but for now we are only interested in the Standard Form.

When quadratics are written in Standard Form, $y = ax^2 + bx + c$, each of the terms in the quadratic expression can be used to tell us some information about what the graph looks like. There are problems on the test that probe exactly this knowledge, and a solid grasp on these principles helps you make simple, rapid assessments about what a graph for a given quadratic equation will look like in general terms and what attributes the equation that models a particular graph will have.

Let's start with the leading x^2 terms of quadratic equations. Whether the graph opens upward or downward depends on the coefficient of the x^2 term. **Positive coefficients of the x^2 term make the graph open upwards, and negative coefficients of the x^2 term make the graph open downwards** (we saw this with our previous examples of $f(x) = x^2 + 2x + 2$ and $g(x) = -2x^2 + 8x - 8$).

This is because x^2 alone is always positive (or zero), so as x becomes larger in absolute value (that is, more positive or more negative), x^2 becomes larger, too. Because x^2, or x to the second power, literally has more "power" than the other terms of lower degree (smaller exponents), it is the x^2 term's value that dominates the value of the whole polynomial as x gets sufficiently large in absolute value (very positive or very negative).

When the coefficient of the x^2 term is positive, this means that the quadratic expression's value, which represents y when graphing, will become greater and greater as the value of x increases on the right side of the vertex, and it *also* means that the value of the expression (the y-value) will become larger and larger as the value of x decreases on the left side of that same vertex point. The result is that the graph of the parabola opens upwards and the vertex represents the minimum point.

The converse is true when the coefficient of the x^2 term is negative; that ensures that the value of the x^2 term is always negative (or zero), and the y-value will decrease on both sides of the vertex point, which produces a parabola that opens downward with the vertex representing the maximum point.

Similarly, the same x^2 coefficient determines how wide or narrow the graph looks. Coefficients with higher absolute values (bigger numbers, whether positive or negative) will make the graph stretch vertically (look narrower) because the y-values are changing more rapidly as the x-values change. Conversely, coefficients with lower absolute values will make the graph flatten vertically (look wider) because the y-values are changing more slowly as the x-values change.

Direction of Parabola

For a quadratic equation in Standard Form, $y = ax^2 + bx + c$, where a, b, and c are constants, the coefficient of the x^2 term, a, dictates the direction and elongation of the parabola.

Positive values of a make the graph open upwards; negative values of a make the graph open downwards. Note that when, as is frequently the case, there is no a coefficient (or negative sign) explicitly shown, that simply means that $a = 1$; in that case, the parabola opens upwards, because 1 is positive. In the less-common case that the quadratic has a negative sign in front of the x^2 term, the implied a coefficient is -1, and therefore, the parabola opens downwards.

$y = x^2$

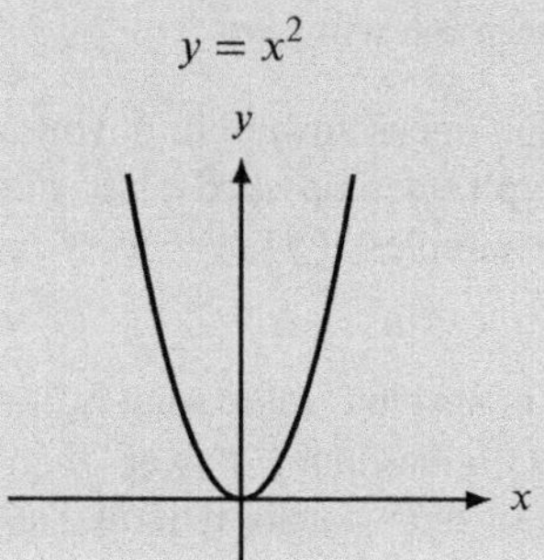

$y = -x^2$

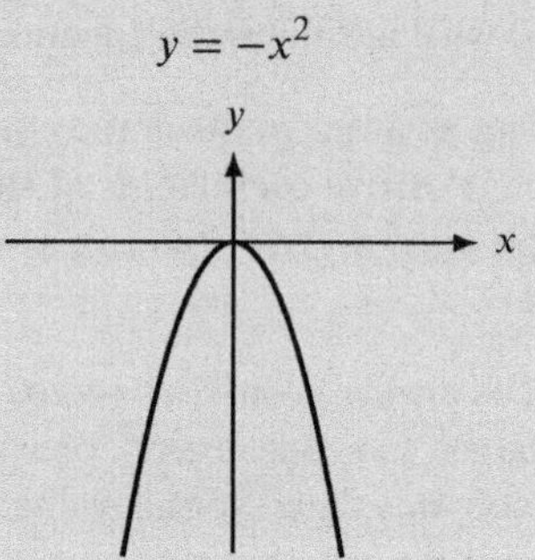

As the absolute values of a decreases, the parabola gets flatter because the x^2 term grows more slowly, which in turn slows the absolute value growth of y-values. As the absolute value of a increases, the parabola gets narrower (more pointy looking) because the x^2 term grows more rapidly, which in turn accelerates the absolute value growth of y-values.

$y = \frac{1}{4}x^2$

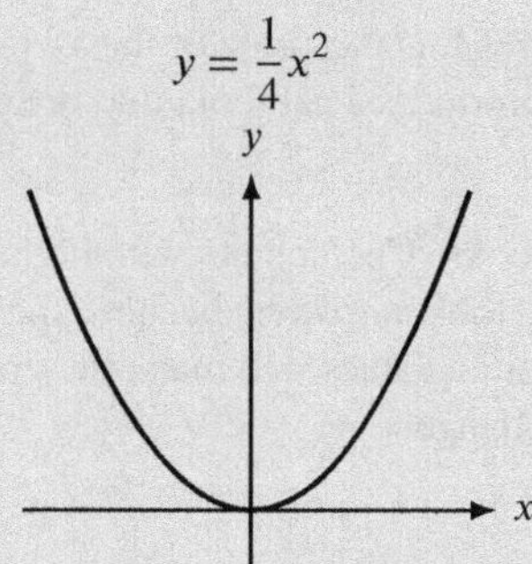

$y = -4x^2$

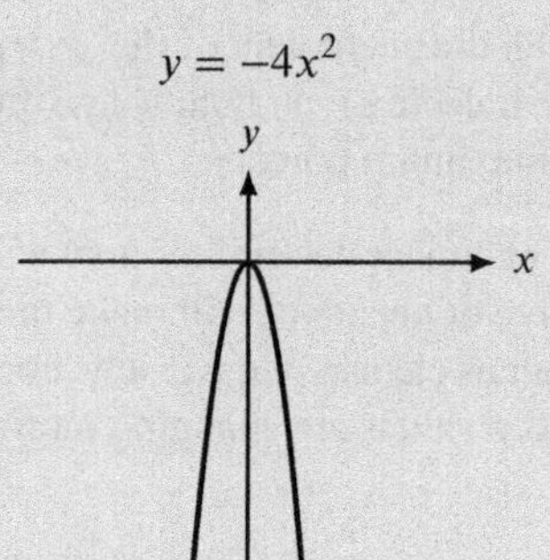

Notice that the graph of the equation $y = -4x^2$ is narrower than the graph of $y = \frac{1}{4}x^2$ because $|-4| > \left|\frac{1}{4}\right|$; that is, the y-value changes more rapidly due to the x^2 term's coefficient having a higher absolute value.

The attribute of a quadratic equation in Standard Form that is easiest to determine is the value of the y-intercept. The y-intercept is the value of the equation when the x-value is 0. **The constant term, c, is the y-intercept of a quadratic equation in Standard Form** (just as the constant term showed us the y-intercept of lines in Slope-Intercept Form) because the other terms, which have x in them, become 0 when x is 0.

For example, the y-intercept of $y = x^2 + 2x + 3$ is found by setting $x = 0$: $y = 0^2 + 2(0) + 3 = 3$. As you can see, when the x-coordinate is 0, as it is at the y-intercept, the value of the y-coordinate will always equal the constant c.

The value of b, the coefficient of the x term, can also be useful when sketching the graph of a quadratic equation. From Standard Form, we can already determine which way a parabola opens and what its y-intercept is, but we do not necessarily know which side of the y-axis the maximum or minimum point of the graph (the vertex) should be on.

The b value tells you the slope of the graph as it passes through the y-intercept (the slope of a parabola is constantly changing, unlike that of a line, which has a constant slope). You can draw a **tangent line** (a line that just touches the graph at one point) through the y-intercept to help visualize this. For a parabola $y = ax^2 + bx + c$, the equation of the tangent line at the y-intercept is simply $y = bx + c$ (as if the x^2 term has gone to zero).

For now, you will have to accept this fact without explanation because it is most easily demonstrated with Calculus, though the upcoming discussion on the Vertex Form of a parabola could shed some light on how the value of the x coefficient determines the position of the vertex.

Once you know the slope of the graph at the y-intercept, you can tell what the graph looks like as it crosses the y-axis and which side the maximum or minimum point (the vertex) is on, though later we will discuss other methods of locating the vertex (again, once you understand the Vertex Form, it is clear how the value of b is linked to the position of the vertex).

y-intercept from Standard Form

For a quadratic equation in Standard Form, $y = ax^2 + bx + c$, where a, b, and c are constants, the constant term, c, gives the value of the y-intercept, and the x coefficient, b, gives the slope of the graph (the slope of a line tangent to the graph) as it goes through the y-intercept.

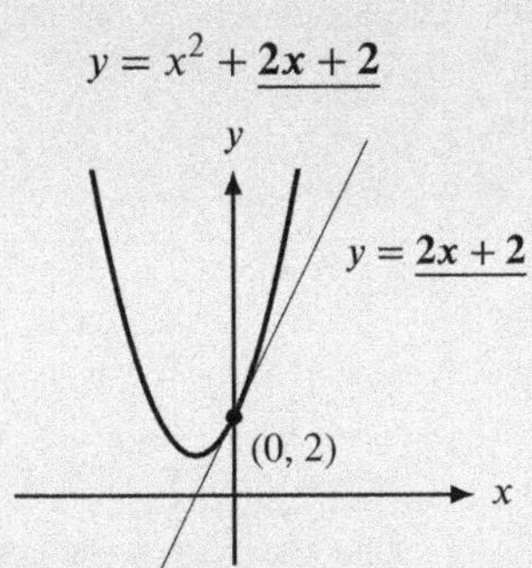

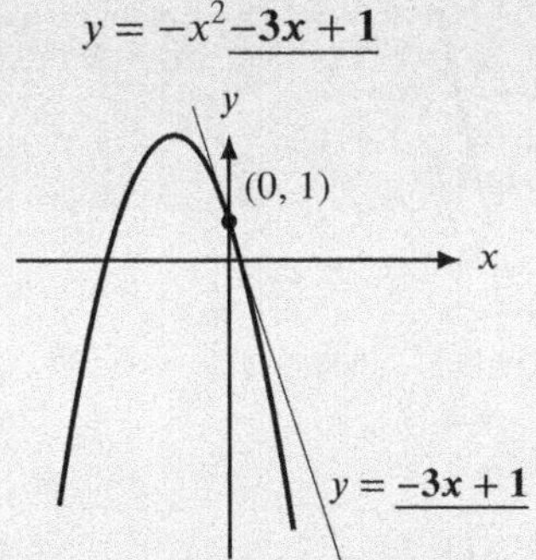

As you can see, knowing the sign of the b coefficient (which gives the sign of the slope of the tangent line at the y-intercept) in conjunction with the sign of the a coefficient (which determines whether the parabola opens up or down) lets you determine the sign of the x coefficient of the vertex; put another way, the b coefficient tells you which side of the y-axis the vertex lies on.

If the parabola opens upwards (the a coefficient is positive) and the slope of the tangent line is positive (the b coefficient is positive), the vertex's x coefficient is negative (the figure above on the left shows this situation). More generally, the sign of the x-coordinate of the vertex is opposite the sign of the product ab; as another example, in the figure above on the right, the product ab is positive (it's $-1(-3) = 3$), so the x-coordinate of the vertex is negative. Note that if there is no middle term, the effective value of b is 0, and the product ab is therefore 0; this means that the vertex lies directly on the y-axis.

SkillDrill 10.1-1

Directions: Based on the Standard Form quadratic equations given below, identify the direction the parabola opens (up or down), on which side of the y-axis the vertex lies (right, left, or 0), and the y-intercept.

For example, given the equation $y = x^2 - x + 3$, your answer should be "up, right, 3" (you can use shorthand such as ↑ and ↓ for the direction the parabola opens and +, 0, or − for which side of the y-axis the vertex is on).

1. $y = x^2 + 3x - 6$ **2.** $y = -2x^2 - 2x + 1$ **3.** $y = 3x^2 - 3x + 5$ **4.** $y = -x^2 - 8$

5. $y = 4x^2 - 2x - 4$ **6.** $y = -10x^2 + 5x - 3$ **7.** $y = x^2 + 20$ **8.** $y = -x^2 - 4x + 2$

Example 10.1-1

1 1600.io 10.1

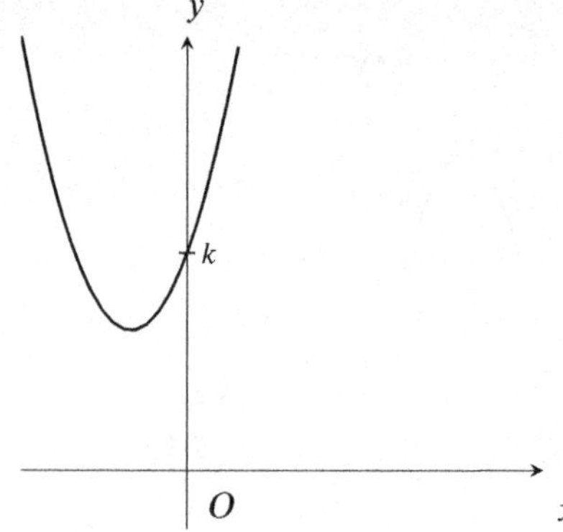

The graph of $y = 3x^2 + 8x + 15$ is shown. If the graph crosses the y-axis at the point $(0, k)$, what is the value of k?

A) 3

B) 5

C) 8

D) 15

Solution 1

1. Since k is the y-value of the equation when $x = 0$, k is the y-intercept of the equation.
2. The constant in the equation is also the y-intercept, so the value of k is 15.
3. The answer is 15.

Solution 2

1. Plug in 0 for x to find the value of the y-intercept, which is the point on the graph where the x-value is 0.

$$y = 3x^2 + 8x + 15$$
$$y = 3(0)^2 + 8(0) + 15$$
$$y = 15$$

2. The answer is 15.

Example 10.1-2

2 10.1

The scatterplot below shows the amount of electric energy generated, in megawatt-hours, by watermills over a 10-year period.

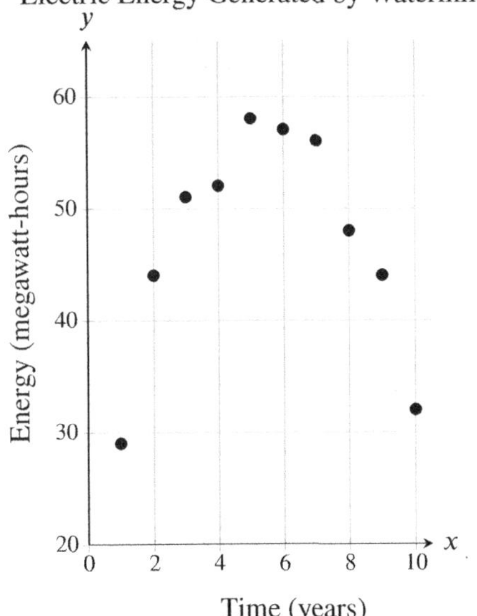

Of the following, which best models the data in the scatterplot?

A) $y = 1.234x^2 + 13.57x - 20.67$

B) $y = -1.234x^2 - 13.57x - 20.67$

C) $y = 1.234x^2 + 13.57x + 20.67$

D) $y = -1.234x^2 + 13.57x + 20.67$

Solution

1. The scatterplot points can clearly be modeled by a parabola—not to mention that all of the choices are quadratic equations. If you want to, you can sketch in a parabola to approximate the curve of best fit. Scatterplots have a whole chapter dedicated to them later, but the main idea is that the points shown roughly fit the shape of a graph, in this case a parabola, and the curve will go through the cluster of points, with some points above the curve of best fit and some points below the curve of best fit as shown in the picture below.

Electric Energy Generated by Watermills

y

60
50
40
30
20

Energy (megawatt-hours)

0 2 4 6 8 10 x

Time (years)

2. The parabola opens downward, so the x^2 coefficient must be negative. Eliminate choices A and C.

3. We can tell for sure that the graph will have a positive slope as it passes through the y-intercept, meaning that the x coefficient must be positive. Choice B can be eliminated.

4. The answer is D.

Notes

The y-axis in this picture starts at 20 and not at 0. Students who do not notice the actual starting point of the y-axis often think that a y-intercept of 20.67 would be too high because at first glance, it appears that the parabola of best fit intersects the "origin" of the graph. For this reason, they will then immediately jump to choices A and B based on the y-intercept alone (even though -20.67 is just as far away from the origin as is 20.67).

For this problem, it might be easier to make a decision based on the x^2 and x coefficients alone, but if you correctly read the axis, you will realize that 20.67 is a much better estimate than -20.67 for the value of the y-intercept.

View related real-test problems at 1600.io/p/smtex?topic=10.1

Section 10.1 Practice Problems

1 10.1

$$h(t) = -9t^2 + 90t + 31$$

The function above models the height h, in centimeters, of an object above ground t seconds after being thrown straight up in the air. What does the number 31 represent in the function?

A) The initial speed, in centimeters per second, of the object

B) The maximum speed, in centimeters per second, of the object

C) The initial height, in centimeters, of the object

D) The maximum height, in centimeters, of the object

2 10.1

If $y = 4x^2 + 8x + 3$ is graphed in the xy-plane, which of the following characteristics of the graph is displayed as a constant or coefficient in the equation?

A) y-coordinate of the vertex

B) y-intercept

C) x-intercept of the line of symmetry

D) x-intercept(s)

10.2 Factored Form: Zeros of the Quadratic

We have seen quadratic equations (or functions) in Standard Form and Factored Form, and both can tell us certain things about what the graphs of these equations will look like.

Not all quadratic equations are easily factorable, and not all parabolas intersect the x-axis (have real zeros or x-intercepts). But when quadratics can be factored, they will definitely have x-intercepts, and the Factored Form makes it easy to visualize the graph of a quadratic equation because when a quadratic equation is written in Factored Form, $y = a(x+p)(x+q)$, we know that its zeros are $-p$ and $-q$ (it has x-intercepts at $(-p, 0)$ and $(-q, 0)$).

Remember, the main utility of factoring is in finding the values of x that make the y-value equal to 0. Once we know the factors, we know the zeros because the values of x that make the factors equal to 0 will cause the y-value to be equal to 0.

The zeros correspond to points on the graph where the y-value is 0 (these are x-intercepts). **If we know that $(x+p)$ is a factor of a polynomial, then we know that $-p$ is a zero of the polynomial**. For example, if we know that $x-4$ is a factor of a quadratic, then we know that $x = 4$ is a zero of the function because plugging in 4 for x would make that factor equal to 0. Therefore, the graph intersects the x-axis at $x = 4$.

The reverse is also true: **if we see that the graph of a polynomial touches the x-axis when $x = z$ (or are told in words that z is a zero of the function), then we know that $x - z$ is a factor of the quadratic**.

Zeros from Factored Form

For a quadratic equation in Factored Form, $y = a(x+p)(x+q)$, where a, p, and q are constants, the zeros of the equation are $-p$ and $-q$. That means that when $x = -p$ or $x = -q$, the quadratic expression will evaluate to zero, and therefore y will equal zero.

If $x = -p$,

$$y = a(x+p)(x+q)$$
$$y = a(-p+p)(-p+q)$$
$$y = a(0)(-p+q)$$
$$y = 0$$

On the xy-plane, we can represent this zero of this equation with the xy-coordinate pair (also known as a point) $(-p, 0)$ because $x = -p$ and $y = 0$.

If $x = -q$,

$$y = a(x + p)(x + q)$$
$$y = a(-q + p)(-q + q)$$
$$y = a(-q + p)(0)$$
$$y = 0$$

On the xy-plane, we can represent this zero of this equation with the xy-coordinate pair (also known as a point) $(-q, 0)$ because $x = -q$ and $y = 0$.

In summary, when $x = -p$ or $x = -q$, y is zero, so we say that $-p$ and $-q$ are zeros of the quadratic expression. Graphically, when a point satisfying an equation has $y = 0$, the point lies on the x-axis, so the graph of the equation will intersect the x-axis at that point.

Note that we can still tell the direction the parabola opens from Factored Form. **If a is positive, the graph will open upwards, and if a is negative, the graph will open downwards**. Recall that when a quadratic expression is in Standard Form, the coefficient a of the x^2 term tells us which way the parabola opens. You can see that when the Factored Form is expanded to Standard Form, a is again the coefficient of the x^2 term and thus indicates which way the parabola opens:

$$y = a(x + p)(x + q)$$
$$y = \boldsymbol{ax^2} + aqx + apx + apq$$

Note that when, as is frequently the case, there is no a coefficient (or negative sign) explicitly shown, that simply means that $a = 1$; in that case, the parabola opens upwards, because 1 is positive. In the case that the quadratic has a negative sign in front of the x^2 term, the implied a coefficient is -1, and therefore, the parabola opens downwards.

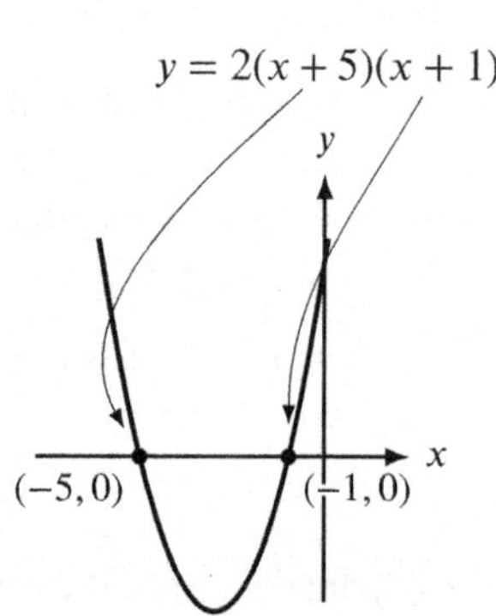

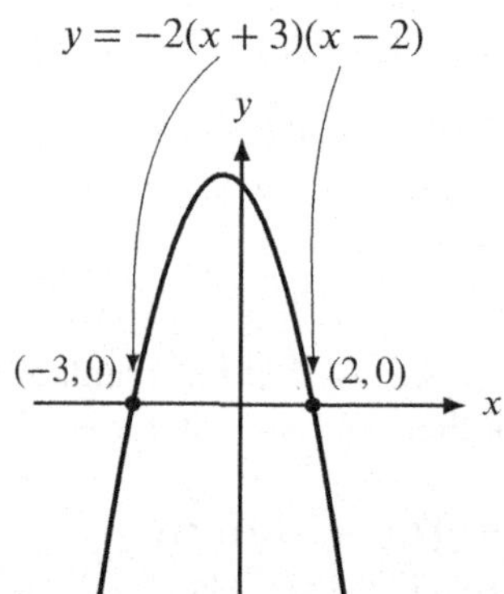

It should also be noted that **values of a with larger absolute values will stretch the parabola more, meaning that the vertex is farther from the x-axis for Factored Form quadratics with larger absolute values of the a coefficient** (unless the vertex is actually on the x-axis, meaning the y-coordinate of the vertex is 0, in which case the parabola will stretch with larger a-values, but the vertex will remain on the x-axis because the y-coordinate value of 0 will not change regardless of what value of a it's multiplied by).

SkillDrill 10.2-1

Directions: Based on the Factored Form quadratic equations given below, identify the zeros. For example, given the equation $y = (x-1)(2x+3)$, your answers should be 1 and $\frac{-3}{2}$.

1. $y = (x-4)(x+2)$

2. $y = (x+3)(x+5)$

3. $y = (x-1)(x-3)$

4. $y = (3x-1)(2x-5)$

5. $y = (x+24)^2$

6. $y = 2x(x+10)$

7. $y = 3(x-4)^2$

8. $y = -4(x+2)(4x+7)$

Example 10.2-1

1 10.2

$$f(x) = (x+2)(x-k)$$

The function f is defined above. If k is a positive integer, which of the following could represent the graph of $y = f(x)$ in the xy-plane?

A)

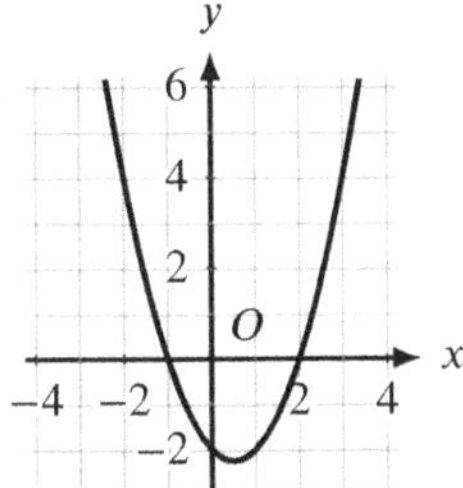

B)

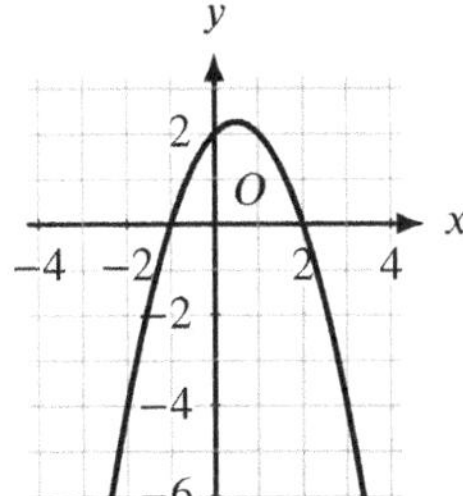

C)

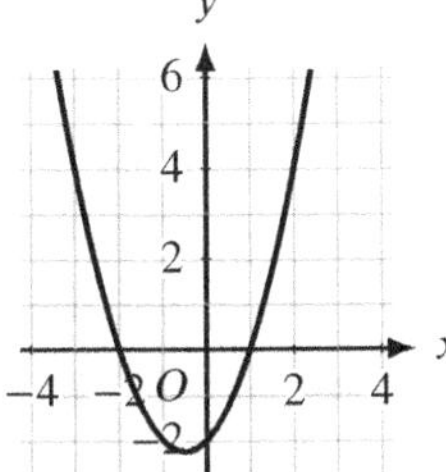

D)

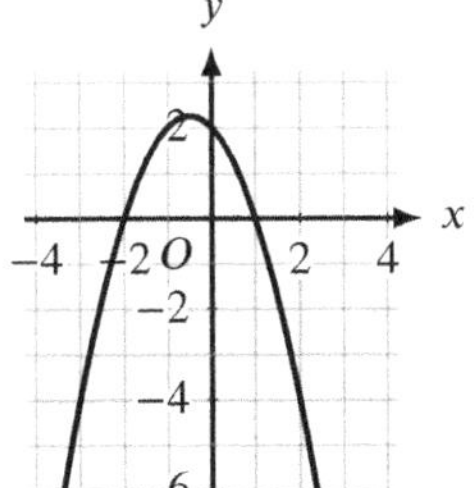

Solution

1. Since there is an implied leading constant of 1, which is positive, the graph must open upwards, so we can eliminate choices B and D.

2. Since $(x+2)$ is a factor, -2 is a zero of the function, the graph must pass through the point $(-2, 0)$. Choice A does not pass through the point $(-2, 0)$, so choice A can be eliminated.

3. The answer is C.

The same relationship between factors and zeros holds true for all other polynomials (not just quadratics) as well, like linear x^1 functions, cubic x^3 functions, and quartic x^4 functions. The factors of *any* polynomial tell you the zeros of the function.

The Factor Theorem

For any polynomial, if you are told that $(x + p)$ is a factor, then $-p$ is a zero of the function (the y-value is 0 when $x = -p$), and you can plug in $-p$ for x and set the y-value equal to 0.

Similarly, if you are told that z is a zero of the function (the y-value is 0 when $x = z$), then $(x - z)$ is a factor, and you can rewrite the function with $(x - z)$ as one of the factors.

The proof of this is closely linked to the Polynomial Remainder Theorem which was discussed in the previous chapter (not to mention all of our previous work with factoring polynomials).

If $x - r$ is a factor (r is a zero of the function) and $x - s$ is another factor (s is also a zero of the same function), then the product of those factors, $(x - r)(x - s)$, is also a factor.

Example 10.2-2

2 1600.io 10.2

$$f(x) = (x + 2)(x - 3)(5x + 4)$$

The function f is defined above. Which of the following is NOT an x-intercept of the graph of the function in the xy-plane?

A) $(-2, 0)$

B) $\left(\frac{-5}{4}, 0\right)$

C) $\left(\frac{-4}{5}, 0\right)$

D) $(3, 0)$

Solution

1. An x-intercept means a point where the y-value is 0, which means that x-intercepts represent zeros of the function by definition. Since $(x + 2)$ is a factor, then $x = -2$ is a zero of the function, so the graph must pass through the point $(-2, 0)$, which is choice A, so choice A can be eliminated.
2. Since $(x - 3)$ is another factor, $x = 3$ is also a zero of the function, so the graph must pass through the point $(3, 0)$, which is choice D, so we can eliminate choice D.
3. Since $(5x + 4)$ is the last factor, $x = \frac{-4}{5}$ is the third and final zero of the function (if you're unsure why this is, simply set $5x + 4$ equal to 0 and solve for x), so the graph must pass through the point $\left(\frac{-4}{5}, 0\right)$; that's choice C, so we can eliminate that as well.
4. Because we've eliminated the choices corresponding to all three of the zeros, only choice B remains, so it must be the answer.
5. The answer is B.

We've factored perfect square quadratics in previous chapters, finding that they had one squared factor, indicating that there was only one distinct zero for the quadratic, not two as we see in the general case. What are the implications of this for the graph of such a function?

If we started with an upward-opening parabola with two zeros and then gradually shifted the graph upwards, the two zeros of a quadratic would get closer and closer together until the two points actually are the same (when the vertex is on the x-axis). Since the two zeros, and thus the two factors, would be the same, the equation is a perfect square. For example, the quadratic equation $y = x^2 - 4x + 4$ can be written as $y = (x-2)^2$ or as $y = (x-2)(x-2)$, so the equation has one "double zero" at $x = 2$, and the graph looks like it "bounces" off of the point $(2, 0)$.

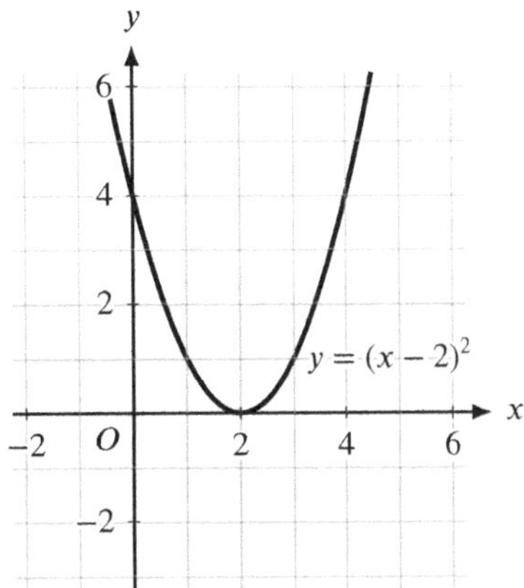

Odd and Even Degree Factors

For any polynomial, when a factor, $x - z$, is raised to an **odd** power, the graph goes through the point $(z, 0)$. That is, the curve goes from above the x-axis to below it, or it goes from below the x-axis to above it, through the point $(z, 0)$.

When a factor, $x - z$, is raised to an **even** power, the graph "bounces" off of the x-axis at the point $(z, 0)$ instead of passing through. That is, the curve remains above or below the x-axis on both sides of that point.

This behavior is explained by the fact that raising a value to an even power always produces a non-negative number regardless of the sign of the original value (e.g. $5^2 = 25$, and $(-5)^2 = 25$). Conversely, raising a value to an odd power preserves the sign of the original value (e.g. $5^3 = 125$, but $(-5)^3 = -125$).

For example, the polynomial $f(x) = x(x-1)^2(x+3)^3$ has three factors: x, $x-1$, and $x+3$. Since the factor x (which corresponds to a zero at $x = 0$) is raised to the first power (an **odd** degree), the graph will **cross** the x-axis point $(0, 0)$. Since the factor $x - 1$ (which means there's a zero at $x = 1$) is raised to the second power (an **even** degree) the graph will **bounce off** the x-axis at the point $(1, 0)$. Finally, since the factor $x + 3$ (giving a zero at $x = -3$) is raised to the third power (an **odd** degree), the graph will **cross** the x-axis at the point $(-3, 0)$.

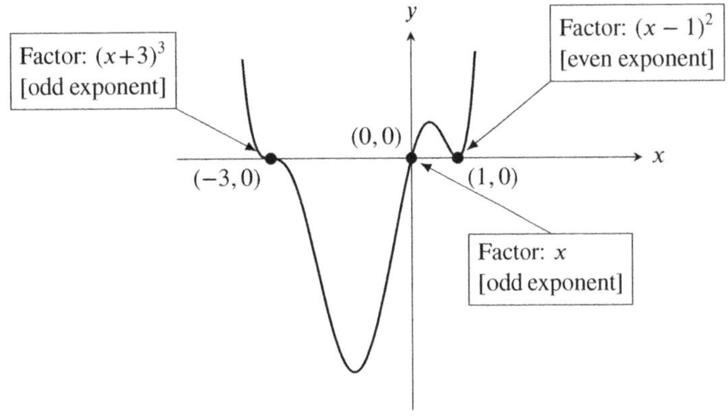

Example 10.2-3

3 1600.io 10.2

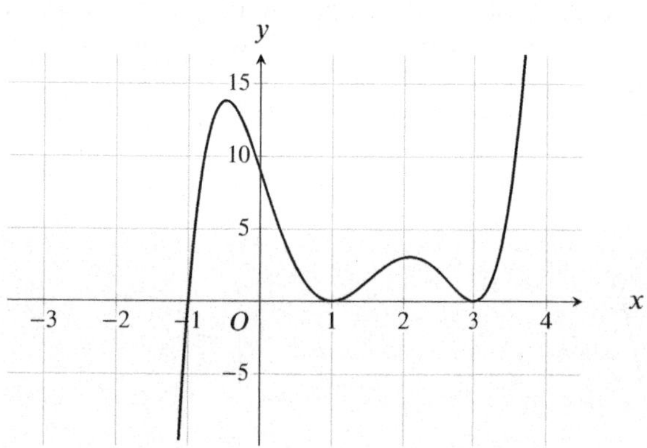

The graph of the function f is shown in the xy-plane above, where $y = f(x)$. Which of the following functions could define f ?

A) $f(x) = (x+3)(x+1)(x-1)^2$

B) $f(x) = (x+3)^2(x+1)^2(x-1)$

C) $f(x) = (x-3)(x-1)(x+1)^2$

D) $f(x) = (x-3)^2(x-1)^2(x+1)$

Solution

1. Since the zeros of the function are $x = -1$, $x = 1$, and $x = 3$, the factors of the function must include $(x+1)$, $(x-1)$, and $(x-3)$. Eliminate choices A and B.
2. The graph bounces off the x-axis when $x = 1$ and $x = 3$, so the factors $(x-1)$ and $(x-3)$ must have even exponents. This condition is true in choice D, but not in choice C.
3. The answer is D.

Section 10.2 Suggested Problems from Real Tests

View related real-test problems at 1600.io/p/smtex?topic=10.2

Section 10.2 Practice Problems

1 10.2

In the xy-plane, the graph of the function $f(x) = x^2 + 6x + 5$ has two x-intercepts. What is the distance between the x-intercepts?

A) 2

B) 4

C) 5

D) 6

2 10.2

$$ax^3 + bx^2 + cx + d = 0$$

In the equation above, a, b, c, and d are constants. If the equation has roots -3, -2, and 4, which of the following is a factor of $ax^3 + bx^2 + cx + d$?

A) $x - 3$

B) $x - 2$

C) $x + 2$

D) $x + 4$

3 10.2

$$h(x) = -9x^2 + 90x + 31$$

The quadratic function above models the height above the ground h, in centimeters, of a ball x seconds after it had been thrown vertically. If $y = h(x)$ is graphed in the xy-plane, which of the following represents the real-life meaning of the positive x-intercept of the graph?

A) The time at which the ball hits the ground

B) The time at which the ball reaches its maximum height

C) The maximum height of the ball

D) The initial height of the ball

4 10.2

$$h(x) = x^3 + ax^2 + bx + c$$

The function h is defined above, where a, b, and c are integer constants. If the zeros of the function are -3, 1, and 4, what is the value of c ?

10.3 Vertex Form: Maximums and Minimums

Another form of quadratic equation is the **Vertex Form**. The **vertex of a parabola is the maximum or minimum point on the parabola, and the Vertex Form displays the x- and y-coordinates of the vertex as constants in the equation**. We will discuss how to find the Vertex Form shortly; for now, let's just see what it looks like and what it tells us.

Vertex Form

For any quadratic of the form $y = a(x - h)^2 + k$, where a, h, and k are constants, the vertex of the parabola is located at the point (h, k), and the value of a dictates the direction and elongation of the parabola. Positive values of a make the graph open upward, and negative values make the graph open downward.

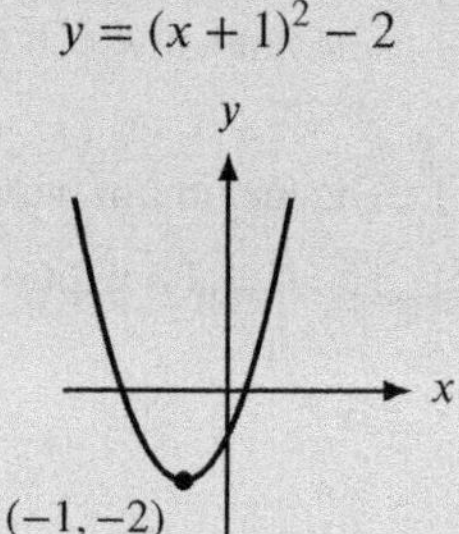

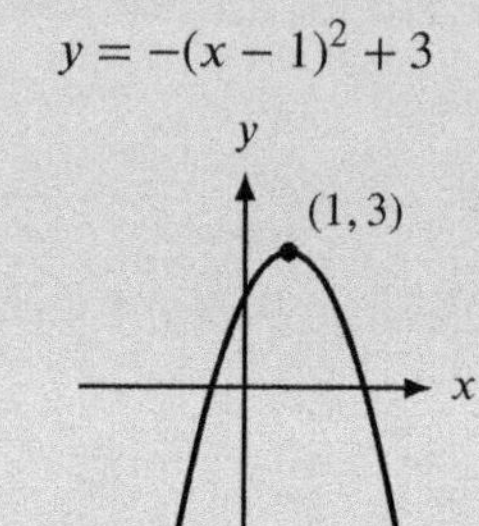

Notice that the x-coordinate, h, is the opposite of the sign shown in the parentheses. In the graphs above, $(x + 1)^2$ tells us that the x-value of the vertex is -1; $(x - 1)^2$ tells us that the x-value of the vertex is 1.

Also notice that the constant term in this form is NOT the y-intercept (as it is in Standard Form), but instead is the y-value of the vertex. This is easy to understand if you simply substitute h (the x-coordinate of the vertex) for x; then, the equation becomes $y = a(h - h)^2 + k$, or simply $y = k$, so k is the y-coordinate of the vertex. Though the y-intercept does not appear directly in the Vertex Form, you can always determine it by simply substituting $x = 0$ and evaluating the expression to find the y-value, which represents the y-intercept.

It should be noted that the range of a quadratic in Vertex Form is easy to determine. If the parabola opens upward, it has a minimum point, and the range of the function is $y \geq k$. If the parabola opens downward, it has a maximum point, and the range of the function is $y \leq k$.

In a way, you can think of the Vertex Form as a quadratic equation written in terms of a double zero, $(x - h)(x - h)$, which is shifted up or down depending on the value of k and then elongated or flattened based on the value of a.

When Standard Form quadratics have no x-term (because the b coefficient is 0), they are simultaneously written in Vertex Form already. The x-value of the vertex is 0, and the y-value of the vertex is equal to the constant term (which is also the y-intercept for these particular cases).

SkillDrill 10.3-1

Directions: Based on the Vertex Form quadratic equations given below, identify the vertex point, state whether the vertex is a maximum or minimum (max or min), and find the y-intercept by plugging in 0 for x.

For example, given the equation $y = (x + 2)^2 + 4$, your answer should be "(−2, 4), min, 8."

1. $y = (x - 1)^2 - 3$ **2.** $y = -(x + 5)^2 + 10$ **3.** $y = (x + 2)^2 + 3$ **4.** $y = (x - 3)^2$

5. $y = -2(x - 1)^2 + 1$ **6.** $y = x^2 + 5$ **7.** $y = -3x^2$ **8.** $y = -2(x - 2)^2 - 5$

Example 10.3-1

 10.3

$$y = 3(x + 4)^2 + a$$

In the equation above, a is a constant. The graph of the equation in the xy-plane is a parabola. Which of the following is true about the parabola?

A) Its minimum occurs at $(-4, a)$.

B) Its minimum occurs at $(4, a)$.

C) Its maximum occurs at $(-4, a)$.

D) Its maximum occurs at $(4, a)$.

Solution

1. The quadratic equation is given in Vertex Form. The positive constant 3 tells us that the graph opens upward, so the parabola will have a minimum value, but no maximum value. Therefore, we can eliminate choices C and D.
2. The expression $(x+4)^2$ tells us that the x-coordinate of the vertex is −4, and the constant term a tells us that y-coordinate of the vertex is a, so the minimum occurs at the point $(-4, a)$.
3. The answer is A.

Notes

By convention, we write the Vertex Form symbolically as $y = a(x - h)^2 + k$, so we refer to the coefficient of the first term as the a coefficient; here, that's 3. Don't be confused by the use of the letter a as the constant term in this particular problem, which is represented symbolically in the Vertex Form as the letter k.

Vertex Form to Standard Form and Factored Form

We can find the Standard Form from the Vertex Form by simply distributing and expanding. For example, given the following quadratic equation in Vertex Form

$$y = (x - 3)^2 - 4$$

we can square the expression $(x - 3)$ in order to expand it into more terms and then combine like terms to end up with the Standard Form of the same equation.

$$y = (x - 3)^2 - 4$$
$$y = x^2 - 6x + 9 - 4$$
$$y = x^2 - 6x + 5$$

We can use the Vertex Form to find zeros of the function (though the zeros aren't immediately apparent as they are in Factored Form), and we can convert from Vertex Form to Factored Form (when real number factors exist) as well.

One way to find zeros or to find the Factored Form would be to convert from Vertex Form to Standard Form and then factor the expression.

Let's expand the Vertex Form equation $y = 2(x - 2)^2 - 72$ into Standard Form so that we can then factor the expression and use it to find the zeros.

$$y = 2(x - 2)^2 - 72$$
$$y = 2(x^2 - 4x + 4) - 72$$
$$y = 2x^2 - 8x + 8 - 72$$
$$y = 2x^2 - 8x - 64$$

Since all of the constants and coefficients are even, we can factor out a 2 to make factoring easier.

$$y = 2x^2 - 8x - 64$$
$$y = 2(x^2 - 4x - 32)$$

In order to factor the quadratic expression in parentheses, we need numbers that sum to -4 and multiply to -32. Those numbers are -8 and 4, so the factors are $(x - 8)$ and $(x + 4)$.

$$y = 2(x^2 - 4x - 32)$$
$$y = 2(x - 8)(x + 4)$$

Setting $y = 0$, we will see that the zeros are $x = -4$ and $x = 8$ based on the factors. This is a bit of a roundabout way to find zeros from Vertex Form.

However, we can take a more direct route if we use the Vertex Form to find the zeros of the quadratic equation (we did this a few chapters ago when we solved quadratic equations by Completing the Square), and, if desired, we can then write the Factored Form based on the factors that correspond to those zeros. Solving a Vertex Form quadratic equation just involves some straightforward algebra.

Again using the equation $y = 2(x - 2)^2 - 72$, which is in Vertex Form ($y = a(x - h)^2 + k$), we can find the zeros of the equation, p and q, and use those to write the equation in Factored Form, $y = a(x + p)(x + q)$.

Set the y-value to zero.

$$0 = 2(x-2)^2 - 72$$

Add 72 to both sides of the equation.

$$72 = 2(x-2)^2$$

Divide both sides of the equation by 2.

$$36 = (x-2)^2$$

Take the square root of both sides, remembering to account for both the positive and negative square roots.

$$\pm 6 = x - 2$$

Add 2 to both sides of the equation.

$$2 \pm 6 = x$$

Enumerate the solutions.

$$x = 2+6, \quad x = 2-6$$
$$x = 8, \quad x = -4$$

Since 8 is one of the zeros, $x-8$ is a factor, and since -4 is one of the zeros, $x+4$ is factor. Remembering to account for the value of a, which is 2, we can rewrite the equation in Factored Form: $y = 2(x-8)(x+4)$.

Once again, the primary point of discussion in this chapter is about the Vertex Form's utility as a representation of a quadratic equation that displays the coordinates of the vertex point as constants in the expression. That said, when you need to find zeros of a quadratic equation in Vertex Form (or, less commonly, rewrite the equation in Factored Form), there is no need to take a roundabout approach.

SkillDrill 10.3-2

Directions: Convert the following Vertex Form quadratic equations to Standard Form by expanding the squared term and combining like terms.

1. $y = (x-1)^2 - 3$ **2.** $y = -(x+5)^2 + 10$ **3.** $y = -2(x-1)^2 + 1$ **4.** $y = x^2 + 5$

Directions: Use the Vertex Form directly (without converting to Standard Form first) to find the zeros of the quadratic.

5. $y = (x-1)^2 - 4$ **6.** $y = -(x+5)^2 + 9$ **7.** $y = -2(x-1)^2 + 32$ **8.** $y = x^2 - 5$

9. $y = (x-1)^2 - 3$ **10.** $y = -(x+5)^2 + 10$ **11.** $y = -4(x+1)^2 + 1$ **12.** $y = 5(x-6)^2 - 3$

Example 10.3-2

2 1600.io 10.3

$$h(x) = 3(x-3)^2 - 27$$

The quadratic function h is defined as shown. In the xy-plane, the graph of $y = h(x)$ intersects the x-axis at the points $(0,0)$ and $(t,0)$, where t is a constant. What is the value of t ?

A) 1

B) 3

C) 6

D) 9

Solution 1

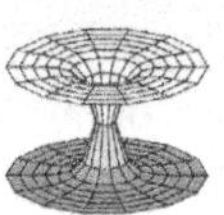

1. We know that the vertex, which has an x-value of 3 based on the Vertex Form equation given, lies on the axis of symmetry (the line $x = 3$). The two zeros must be equidistant from the axis of symmetry.

   One zero exists when $x = 0$ (shown by the point $(0,0)$), and that point is a distance of 3 units to the left of the axis of symmetry. Therefore, the other zero, the point $(t,0)$, must be a distance of 3 units to the right of the axis of symmetry. That means that $t = 6$.

2. The answer is C.

Solution 2

1. Based on the fact that the graph of $h(x)$ intersects the x-axis at the point $(t,0)$, we know that $x = t$ is one of the zeros of the function. Set $h(x)$ equal to 0 and substitute t for x, then solve for t.

$$\begin{aligned} h(x) &= 3(x-3)^2 - 27 \\ 0 &= 3(t-3)^2 - 27 \\ 27 &= 3(t-3)^2 \\ 9 &= (t-3)^2 \\ \pm 3 &= t - 3 \\ 3 \pm 3 &= t \\ 3+3 = t,&\ \ 3-3 = t \\ 6 = t,&\ \ 0 = t \end{aligned}$$

2. The solution $t = 0$ is already shown when we are told that $(0,0)$ is one of the x-intercepts (and 0 is not an answer choice). Therefore $t = 6$ is the zero of the equation that will give us the other x-intercept.

3. The answer is C.

View related real-test problems at 1600.io/p/smtex?topic=10.3

Section 10.3 Practice Problems

1 10.3

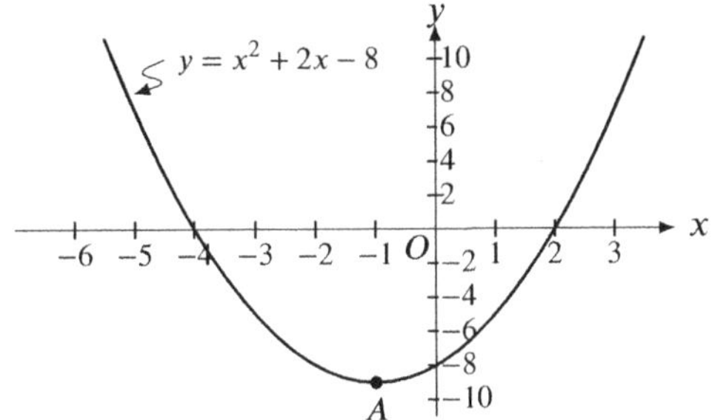

Which of the following is an equivalent form of the equation of the graph shown in the xy-plane above, from which the y-coordinate of vertex A can be identified as a constant in the equation?

A) $y = (x + 1)^2 - 9$

B) $y = x(x + 2) - 8$

C) $y = (x - 4)(x + 2)$

D) $y = (x + 4)(x - 2)$

2 10.3

The expressions $x^2 + bx + 14$ and $(x - 4)^2 + c$, where b and c are constants, are equivalent. What is the value of $b + c$?

A) 10

B) 4

C) −6

D) −10

10.4 Vertex Form from Factored Form

If you are given a quadratic equation in Factored Form, it is easy to find the vertex because **the x-coordinate of the vertex is exactly halfway between the two roots**. In fact, all parabolas are symmetrical—the graph on one side of the vertex is the mirror image of the graph on the other side. The vertex is the one and only point on the parabola that lies on the axis of symmetry; both x-intercepts (which correspond to the roots) are equidistant from the axis of symmetry. In fact, any two points on the parabola that have the same y-coordinate are equidistant from the axis of symmetry (thus the name!).

For example, the x-coordinate of the vertex of the parabola $y = (x - 2)(x + 4)$ is -1 because -1 is exactly halfway between the two roots, $x = -4$ and $x = 2$, so the axis of symmetry is at $x = -1$, and, as explained, the vertex lies on that axis of symmetry. You can average the two roots' values (add the roots and divide by 2) to find the value that is midway between them:

$$x_{vertex} = \frac{-4+2}{2} = \frac{-2}{2} = -1$$

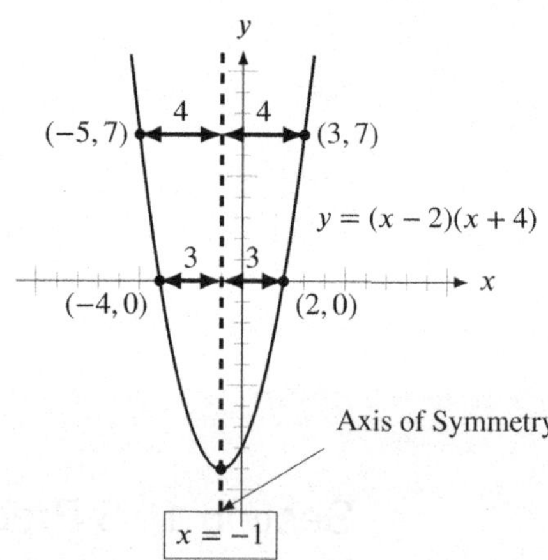

If you need to know the y-coordinate of the vertex, you can just plug the x-value of the vertex into the Factored Form. There is no need to expand the Factored Form into the Standard Form. In this example, we would plug -1 in for x in order to find the y-value of the vertex.

$$y_{vertex} = (x-2)(x+4)$$
$$y_{vertex} = (-1-2)(-1+4)$$
$$y_{vertex} = (-3)(3)$$
$$y_{vertex} = -9$$

Once you have the coordinates of the vertex, you can write the equation in Vertex Form. Since the x-value of the vertex is -1 and the y-value of the vertex is -9, the Vertex Form of this parabola is $y = (x+1)^2 - 9$.

Remember to account for the value of a. In our example, the value of a was 1, so we didn't have to worry about it. However, if the Standard Form has any other value of a, you need to include it as the coefficient of the $(x-h)^2$ term when writing the Vertex Form.

x-value of the Vertex Based on Roots

For any quadratic function $y = f(x)$, the x-value of the vertex is exactly halfway between the two zeros and can be found by averaging the two zeros of the function (add the roots and divide by 2). Recall that when we're talking about functions, the terms "zero" and "root" mean the same thing and thus are interchangeable; we're using both terms here to make sure you're paying attention. Also, eat your vegetables.

For example, for the equation $y = (x+3)(x+7)$, the roots are -3 and -7, the x-value of the vertex (denoted below as h) is -5 because the average of -3 and -7 is -5.

$$h = \frac{-3+(-7)}{2}$$
$$h = \frac{-3-7}{2}$$
$$h = \frac{-10}{2}$$
$$h = -5$$

y-value of the Vertex Based on Roots

Once you have the x-value of the vertex, you can simply plug it into the quadratic equation to find the y-value of the vertex.

The x-value of the vertex (denoted as h) of the equation $y = (x + 3)(x + 7)$ is -5, as we found above. Plug -5 in for x in order to find the y-value of the vertex (denoted as k below).

$$y = (x + 3)(x + 7)$$
$$k = (h + 3)(h + 7)$$
$$k = (-5 + 3)(-5 + 7)$$
$$k = (-2)(2)$$
$$k = -4$$

SkillDrill 10.4-1

Directions: Use the Factored Form to find the coordinates of the vertex of the parabola, and convert the quadratic equation to Vertex Form.

Challenge problems are boxed.

1. $y = (x - 4)(x + 2)$ **2.** $y = (x + 3)(x + 5)$ **3.** $y = -(x - 1)(x - 3)$ **4.** $y = (x + 6)^2$

5. $y = 2x(x + 10)$ **6.** $y = 3(x - 4)^2$

7. $\boxed{y = 4\left(x - \frac{1}{2}\right)\left(x - \frac{5}{2}\right)}$ **8.** $\boxed{y = -8(x + 1)\left(x + \frac{1}{2}\right)}$

Which Form to Use For Particular Information

There is a particular style of question on the test that asks us to rewrite quadratic equations in different forms. Usually, several of the choices will be different forms of the same quadratic equation; however, the questions require that you pick one particular form based on the type of information that each form shows.

Choosing the Correct Form of Quadratic Equation or Function

When asked to pick an equivalent form of a quadratic equation or function, you must choose an answer that is not only equivalent, but that also shows the features as stated in the question.

- **Roots, Zeros, or x-Intercepts**
  If you are asked for an equivalent form of the equation or function that displays the roots, zeros, or x-intercepts of the function as constants or coefficients, you want to pick a choice that is in Factored Form. For a quadratic equation in Factored Form $y = a(x+p)(x+q)$, $-p$ and $-q$ are the zeros/roots/x-intercepts (note that "root," "zero," and "x-intercept" all mean the same thing in this context).

- **Maximum, Minimum, or Vertex**
  If you are asked for an equivalent form of the equation or function that displays the maximum or minimum of the graph (or the coordinates of the vertex) as constants or coefficients, you want to pick an answer choice that is in Vertex Form. For a quadratic equation in Vertex Form $y = a(x-h)^2+k$, (h, k) is the vertex; it will represent the maximum or minimum point of the parabola.

- ***y*-intercept**
  If you are asked for an equivalent form of the equation or function that displays the y-intercept of the parabola as a constant or coefficient, you want to pick a choice that is in Standard Form. For a quadratic equation in Standard Form $y = ax^2 + bx + c$, the constant c is the y-intercept, because when $x = 0$, the other terms drop out.

Example 10.4-1

 1600.io 10.4

$$f(x) = (x + 2)(x - 8)$$

Which of the following is an equivalent form of the function f above in which the minimum value of f appears as a constant or coefficient?

A) $f(x) = x^2 - 16$

B) $f(x) = x^2 - 6x - 16$

C) $f(x) = (x + 3)^2 + 11$

D) $f(x) = (x - 3)^2 - 25$

Solution

1. Since we want an equivalent form that shows the minimum value, we need to select a choice that is in Vertex Form. Eliminate choices A and B.

   Note that we don't have to worry about whether the function has a minimum value or a maximum value, because it must have only one of those, and if the problem asks for a minimum, the function has a minimum at the vertex. The same principle applies if the problem asks for a maximum—the function will have one at the vertex. Here, you can verify that the function has a minimum because the parabola opens up as indicated by the (implied) a coefficient of 1, which is positive.

2. The two roots of the function are −2 and 8. The value halfway between the two (the average of the two values) is 3, so the x-value of the vertex is 3.

$$h = \frac{-2 + 8}{2}$$

$$h = \frac{6}{2}$$

$$h = 3$$

3. Substitute 3 in for x to find the y-value of the vertex, which will be the minimum value of the function f (remember that $f(x)$ is equal to the y-value for a given value of x).

$$
\begin{aligned}
f(x) &= (x+2)(x-8) \\
k = f(h) &= (h+2)(h-8) \\
k = f(3) &= (3+2)(3-8) \\
k &= (5)(-5) \\
k &= -25
\end{aligned}
$$

4. We must choose the answer in which the y-value of the vertex (the minimum value of the function), -25, appears as a constant or coefficient. Choice D is the only choice that shows -25 as a constant.

5. The answer is D.

Notes

We could have eliminated choice C (leaving only choice D) as soon as we found that the x-value of the vertex is 3 because choice C, which is in Vertex Form, indicates that the x-value of the vertex would be -3.

Section 10.4 Suggested Problems from Real Tests

- Test 2-C-7
- Test 3-NC-12
- Test 4-C-28
- Test 7-NC-12

View related real-test problems at 1600.io/p/smtex?topic=10.4

Section 10.4 Practice Problems

1 10.4

The function f is defined by $f(x) = (x+6)(x+2)$. The graph of f in the xy-plane is a parabola. Which of the following intervals contains the x-coordinate of the vertex of the graph of f ?

A) $-7 < x < -6$

B) $-7 < x < -5$

C) $-6 < x < 2$

D) $2 < x < 6$

2 10.4

$$y = a(x-3)(x+5)$$

In the quadratic equation above, a is a nonzero constant. The graph of the equation in the xy-plane is a parabola with vertex (c, d). Which of the following is equal to d ?

A) $-16a$

B) $-15a$

C) $-12a$

D) $-2a$

10.5 Finding the Vertex from Standard Form

If you are given a quadratic equation in Standard Form, it is easy to find the vertex using a simple method.

x-value of the Vertex Based on Standard Form

For any quadratic in Standard Form, $y = ax^2 + bx + c$, where a, b, and c are constants, the x-value of the vertex (denoted as h below) is equal to $\frac{-b}{2a}$.

$$h = \frac{-b}{2a}$$

For example, for the quadratic $y = -2x^2 + 4x - 8$, the x-value of the vertex is equal to 1.

$$h = \frac{-4}{2(-2)}$$

$$h = \frac{-4}{-4}$$

$$h = 1$$

You might recall that $\frac{-b}{a}$ represents the sum of the zeros, so it makes sense that the x-coordinate of the vertex, which represents the *average* of the zeros, would be $\frac{-b}{2a}$.

y-value of the Vertex Based on Standard Form

Once you have the x-value of the vertex, you can plug that value into the equation to find the y-value of the vertex.

For example, for the quadratic $y = -2x^2 + 4x - 8$, plug in 1, which is the x-value of the vertex (denoted as h), in order to find the y-value of the vertex (denoted as k).

$$y = -2x^2 + 4x - 8$$
$$k = -2h^2 + 4h - 8$$
$$k = -2(1)^2 + 4(1) - 8$$
$$k = -2 + 4 - 8$$
$$k = -6$$

Vertex Form Based on Standard Form

Once you have found the values of h and k (and you already know the value of a from the Standard Form equation), you can plug those values into the general Vertex Form equation, which is $y = a(x - h)^2 + k$.

In our example, $y = -2x^2 + 4x - 8$, we know that $a = -2$, $h = 1$, and $k = -6$, so the Vertex Form is as follows:

$$y = a(x - h)^2 + k$$
$$y = -2(x - 1)^2 - 6$$

Vertex Form by Completing the Square

There is a streamlined method for converting directly from Standard Form to Vertex form without having to first find the x-coordinate of the vertex, then plug that x-value into the quadratic equation and evaluate it to determine the y-coordinate, then construct the Vertex Form once the x- and y-values are in hand. The direct method relies on the same principles used in the Completing the Square quadratic solving method discussed elsewhere, and it's both rapid and has the benefit of producing both the x- and y-coordinates of the vertex at the same time.

Here's the procedure that applies when there is no a coefficient (that is, when there is an implied a coefficient of 1):

1. Replace the first two terms (the x^2 term and the bx term) with

$$\left(x + \frac{b}{2}\right)^2 - \left(\frac{b}{2}\right)^2$$

The purpose of subtracting the second term is to eliminate the unwanted constant $\left(\frac{b}{2}\right)^2$ that's created when squaring the first term. (You might observe that this correcting term could be simplified as $\frac{b^2}{4}$, but you'll already have the term $\frac{b}{2}$ evaluated in the first term, so it's simpler to just square that value, and it's also easier to remember that the second term is just the negative of the constant term generated by expanding the first term.)

2. Combine like terms.

To demonstrate the simplicity of this new method, we will first find the vertex of an example function by separately determining the x- and y-coordinates so you can see how much more efficient the streamlined method is when later applied to the same problem.

$$y = x^2 - 6x - 16$$

Here, $a = 1$, $b = -6$, and $c = 16$.

The x-coordinate, h, of the vertex is $\frac{-b}{2a}$.

$$h = \frac{-b}{2a}$$

$$h = \frac{-(-6)}{2(1)}$$

$$h = \frac{6}{2}$$

$$h = 3$$

Plug in $x = 3$ to find the y-coordinate, k, of the vertex.

$$k = (3)^2 - 6(3) - 16$$
$$k = 9 - 18 - 16$$
$$k = -25$$

The vertex (h, k) is $(3, -25)$. Now we can construct the Vertex Form.

$$y = a(x - h)^2 + k$$
$$y = (x - 3)^2 - 25$$

Now, let's use the streamlined Completing the Square procedure for comparison.

1. Replace the first two terms with $\left(x + \frac{b}{2}\right)^2 - \left(\frac{b}{2}\right)^2$. Recall that for the equation $y = x^2 - 6x - 16$, the value of b is -6, so $\frac{b}{2} = \frac{-6}{2} = -3$.

$$y = \mathbf{x^2 - 6x} - 16$$
$$y = \mathbf{(x - 3)^2 - (-3)^2} - 16$$
$$y = \mathbf{(x - 3)^2 - 9} - 16$$

2. Combine like terms.

$$y = (x - 3)^2 - 25$$

Voilà! The equation is now in Vertex Form $y = a(x - h)^2 + k$; here, $h = 3$ and $k = -25$, so the vertex is at $(3, -25)$. Notice how rapidly we were able to reach our goal.

The same principle can also be used when a is not 1. Here's the more general procedure:

Vertex Form by Completing the Square when $a \neq 1$

1. Replace the first two terms (the ax^2 term and the bx term) with

$$a\left(x + \frac{b}{2a}\right)^2 - a\left(\frac{b}{2a}\right)^2$$

Again, the purpose of subtracting the second term is to eliminate the unwanted constant $a\left(\frac{b}{2a}\right)^2$ that's created when expanding the first term. (You could simplify the second term symbolically to $\frac{b^2}{4a}$, though you'll already have the value of $\frac{b}{2a}$ in hand and it might be simpler to just square that and multiply it by a; it's also easier to remember that the second term is just the negative of the constant term generated by expanding the first term.)

2. Combine like terms.

Let's demonstrate this using the example shown above when we explained how to find the vertex's x- and y-coordinates separately.

$$y = -2x^2 + 4x - 8$$

Here, $a = -2$, $b = 4$, and $c = 8$.

1. Replace the first two terms with $a\left(x + \frac{b}{2a}\right)^2 - a\left(\frac{b}{2a}\right)^2$. Recall that for the equation $y = -2x^2 + 4x - 8$, $a = -2$ and $b = 4$, so $\frac{b}{2a} = \frac{4}{2(-2)} = \frac{4}{-4} = -1$.

$$y = \mathbf{-2x^2 + 4x} - 8$$
$$y = \mathbf{-2(x-1)^2 - [-2(-1)^2]} - 8$$
$$y = \mathbf{-2(x-1)^2 + 2} - 8$$

2. Combine like terms.

$$y = -2(x-1)^2 - 6$$

The equation is now in Vertex Form $y = a(x-h)^2 + k$; here, $h = 1$ and $k = -6$, so the vertex is at $(1, -6)$.

SkillDrill 10.5-1

Directions: Convert the Standard Form quadratic to Vertex Form. You can first find the x-coordinate then plug in to find the y-coordinate and assemble the equation, or you can try to use the streamlined direct Completing the Square procedure.

Challenge problems are boxed.

1. $y = x^2 + 2x - 4$ **2.** $y = x^2 - 6x + 20$ **3.** $y = x^2 + 10x - 15$ **4.** $y = x^2 - 4x - 7$

5. $y = x^2 - 8x + 3$ **6.** $y = x^2 + 20x + 100$ **7.** $y = x^2 + 14x + 32$ **8.** $y = x^2 - 10$

9. $\boxed{y = x^2 + 5x - 1}$ **10.** $\boxed{y = x^2 - 3x + 2}$ **11.** $\boxed{y = 2x^2 + 8x + 10}$ **12.** $\boxed{y = -3x^2 + 12x + 12}$

Example 10.5-1

1 10.5

The fuel economy $M(s)$, in kilometers per liter, of a moped traveling s kilometers per hour is modeled by the function below, where $30 \le s \le 100$.

$$M(s) = -\frac{1}{20}s^2 + 6s + 230$$

According to the model, at what speed, in kilometers per hour, does the moped obtain its greatest fuel economy?

A) 30

B) 60

C) 75

D) 90

Solution

1. The moped will achieve its greatest fuel economy at the vertex (maximum) of the graph of the function. We need to find the speed (the s-value) of the moped at the vertex.
2. The s-value of the vertex (remember that s is acting like the x-variable here), denoted as h, can be found using the formula $h = \frac{-b}{2a}$, where b is the coefficient of the s-term, 6, and a is the coefficient of the s^2-term, $-\frac{1}{20}$.

$$h = \frac{-b}{2a}$$
$$h = \frac{-6}{2\left(-\frac{1}{20}\right)}$$
$$h = \frac{-6}{-\frac{2}{20}}$$
$$h = \frac{-6}{-\frac{1}{10}}$$
$$h = -6(-10)$$
$$h = 60$$

3. The answer is B.

Notes

If we needed to know the maximum fuel economy, achieved at that optimal speed of 60 $\frac{\text{km}}{\text{h}}$, we would plug in 60 for s and solve for $M(60)$.

$$M(s) = -\frac{1}{20}s^2 + 6s + 230$$
$$M(60) = -\frac{1}{20}(60)^2 + 6(60) + 230$$
$$M(60) = -\frac{3600}{20} + 360 + 230$$
$$M(60) = -180 + 590$$
$$M(60) = 410$$

Consequently, knowing that the vertex point is $(60, 410)$, we could, if desired, rewrite the equation in Vertex Form:

$$M(s) = -\frac{1}{20}(s-60)^2 + 410$$

In the next example, it is not obvious that we need the Vertex Form to get the correct answer. Earlier in this chapter, we talked about what we can tell about the graph of a quadratic equation in Standard Form, which is good for quick visualizations of the general direction and location of the parabola. However, in the following question, that knowledge gets us down to two choices, but we will need to know about the position of the vertex in order to make a final decision.

Example 10.5-2

2 10.5

Which of the following could be the graph of $y = x^2 + 4x + 6$?

A)

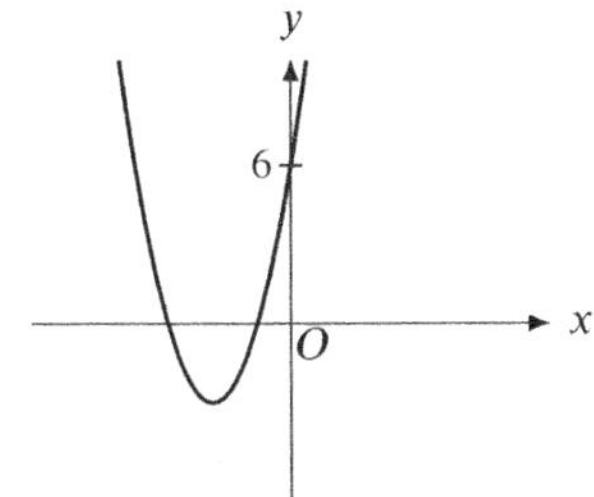

B)

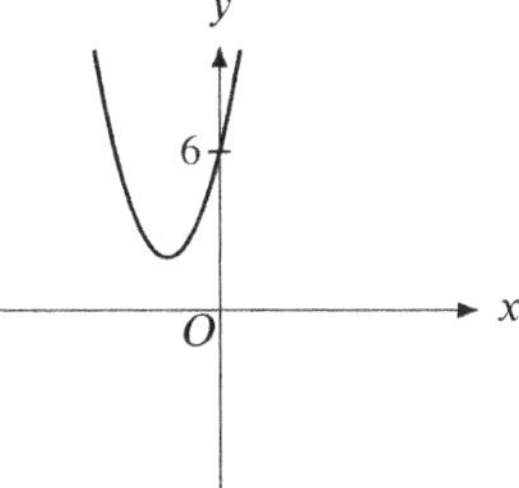

C)

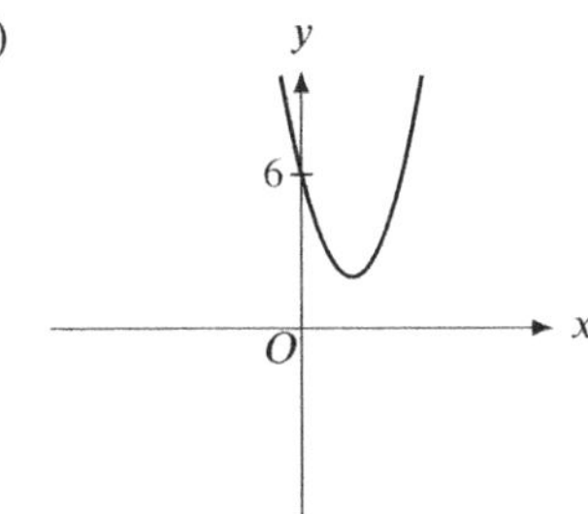

D)

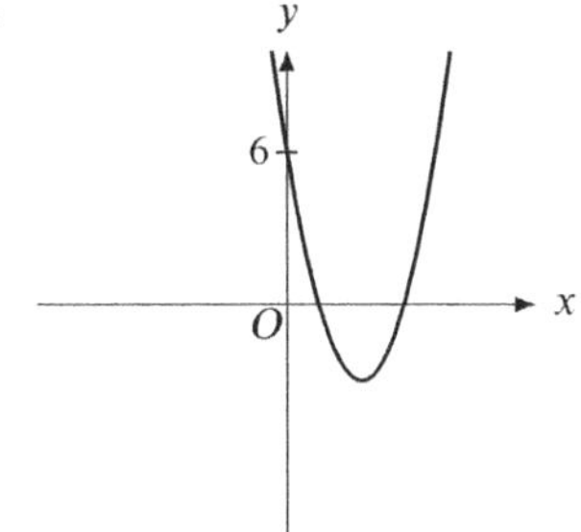

Solution 1

The Standard Form of the provided equation tells us that the parabola opens upwards due to the positive (implied) a-coefficient, and that the y-intercept (the c constant) is 6, but all the answer choices satisfy those constraints, so we need to use another approach to identifying the correct graph. Notice that the vertex of each parabola is in a different quadrant of the xy-coordinate plane; that means if we can determine the vertex, we can select the proper graph. Because finding the vertex would lead directly to the correct answer choice, we can use the streamlined procedure for converting from Standard Form directly to Vertex Form to rapidly solve this problem without even needing to eliminate any answer choices at the outset.

1. Replace the first two terms of the Standard Form quadratic with $\left(x + \frac{b}{2}\right)^2 - \left(\frac{b}{2}\right)^2$. In the equation $y = x^2 + 4x + 6$, the value of b is 4, so $\frac{b}{2} = 2$.

$$y = \mathbf{x^2 + 4x} + 6$$
$$y = \mathbf{(x + 2)^2 - 2^2} + 6$$
$$y = \mathbf{(x + 2)^2 - 4} + 6$$

2. Combine like terms.

$$y = (x+2)^2 - 4 + 6$$
$$y = (x+2)^2 + 2$$

3. This Vertex Form of the quadratic tells us that the vertex is at $(-2, 2)$, and only choice B matches that constraint.
4. The answer is B.

Solution 2

1. Based on Standard Form, we know that the y-intercept must be 6 (the constant term is 6), which is shown in every choice, and thus does not help us eliminate any choices.
2. Based on Standard Form, we know that the vertex of the parabola must be on the left side of the y-axis because the parabola opens up due to the (implied) a coefficient of 1, and the coefficient of the x term is 4, which is positive (the line that is tangent to the parabola at the y-intercept has a slope of 4). We can eliminate choices C and D based on this information, but we cannot adequately decide between choices A and B. For one thing, we don't know the scale of the axes and we don't know if this quadratic has zeros (because we cannot easily factor the equation).
3. We can find the coordinates of the vertex to help decide between choices A and B. The x-value of the vertex, denoted h, is equal to $\frac{-b}{2a}$, where $b = 4$ and $a = 1$.

$$h = \frac{-b}{2a}$$
$$h = \frac{-4}{2(1)}$$
$$h = -2$$

4. We know that the x-value of the vertex is -2, but this is still insufficient to decide between choices A and B. Since we have no indication of the scale of the x-axis, we cannot tell which one of the vertices of these graphs has an x-coordinate of -2. Therefore, we should substitute -2 for x in order to find the y-value of the vertex.

$$y = x^2 + 4x + 6$$
$$y = (-2)^2 + 4(-2) + 6$$
$$y = 4 - 8 + 6$$
$$y = 2$$

5. The vertex is the point $(-2, 2)$, which is above the x-axis, eliminating choice A (in which the vertex is clearly below the x-axis) and leaving us with only choice B (in which the vertex is clearly above the x-axis, and also to the left of the y-axis).
6. The answer is B.

View related real-test problems at 1600.io/p/smtex?topic=10.5

Section 10.5 Practice Problems

1 10.5

$$y = x^2 + 4x + 16$$

The graph of the equation above in the xy-plane is a parabola. Which of the following equivalent forms of the equation includes the x- and y-coordinates of the vertex as constants?

A) $y = x(x + 4) + 16$

B) $y - 16 = x(x + 4)$

C) $y = (x + 2)^2 + 12$

D) $y = x^2 + 4(x + 3)$

2 10.5

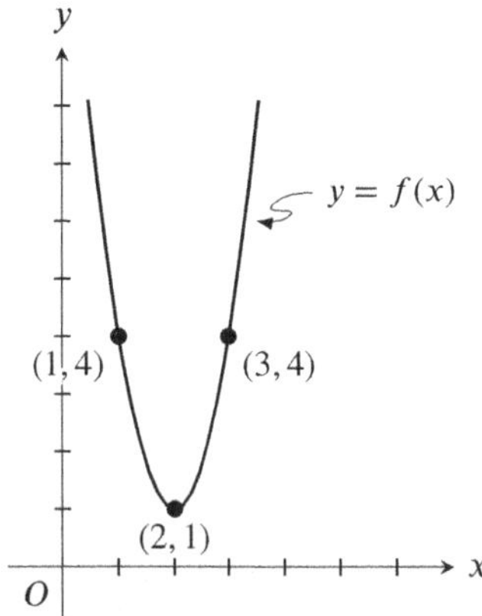

The graph of the function f in the xy-plane above is a parabola. Which of the following defines f ?

A) $f(x) = 2(x + 2)^2 + 1$

B) $f(x) = (x - 2)^2 + 1$

C) $f(x) = 3(x + 2)^2 + 1$

D) $f(x) = 3(x - 2)^2 + 1$

10.6 Number of Intersections = Number of Solutions

We already have talked about Systems of Linear Equations and Systems of Quadratic and Linear Equations. We know that the solutions to systems consist of the intersection points of all of the equations in the system because those points represent x- and y-values that satisfy all the equations in the system. We have even seen that the graphs of quadratic equations (parabolas) can have intersections with the x-axis that indicate the roots or zeros of those equations (which, in turn, correspond to the factors of those equations).

In the next chapter we will discuss the number of solutions to quadratic equations in a slightly different way, but in the final section of this chapter, we want to look at how the number of real solutions to any system of equations can be found by looking at the graphs.

In short, **the number of real solutions to a system of equations is equal to the number of intersections of the graphs of the equations in the system**. If there are more than two equations in the system (more than two lines, parabolas, or any other curves), **all of the graphs must intersect at a common point in order for that point to represent a solution to the system because the x- and y-values of that point satisfy *all* the equations in the system**.

Example 10.6-1

 10.6

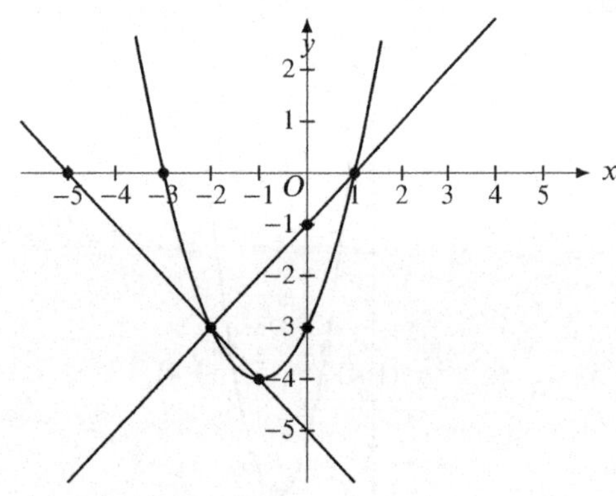

A system of three equations is graphed in the xy-plane above. How many solutions does the system have?

A) None

B) One

C) Two

D) Three

Solution

1. Note that this problem does not ask how many x-intercepts are shown in the picture or how many intersections there are between any of the graphs. In order to be a solution to the system, all three of the graphs have to intersect at the same point. While two graphs intersect at points $(1, 0)$ and $(-1, -4)$, the only point that all three graphs go through is $(-2, -3)$. Therefore, there is only one solution to the system of equations shown in the picture.
2. The answer is B.

Of course, if graphs can be drawn accurately (the xy-plane is provided to you with a scaled grid and the graphs intersect on points where gridlines meet), you can use the graph to determine solutions to the system.

In the following example, it is possible to add a line to the picture in order to determine the solutions, but you must be careful about the scales of the axes if you are going to take this route.

Example 10.6-2

2 10.6

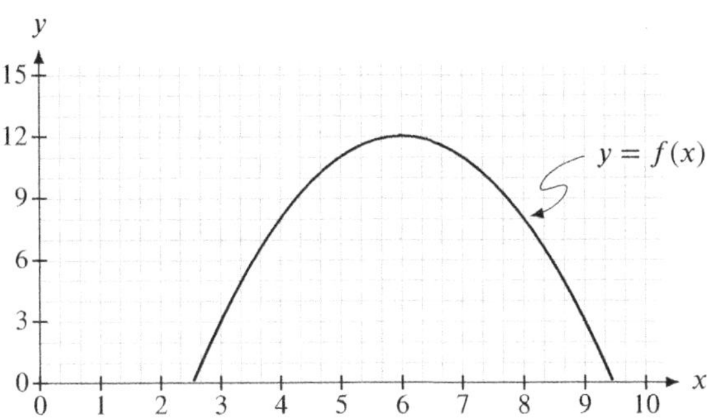

The graph of the function f, defined by $f(x) = -(x-6)^2 + 12$, is shown in the xy-plane above. If the function g (not shown) is defined by $g(x) = -x + 12$, what is one possible value of a such that $f(a) = g(a)$?

Solution 1

The recommended approach here is to be safe and solve the problem with substitution rather than use the graph. Using the graph is technically faster, but there is great risk of doing it incorrectly when taking that route. The axes are scaled differently in the picture you are given, and honestly, you should double check your answer even if you do use the graph and draw the line in.

1. We have a system of equations consisting of a quadratic equation and a linear equation. If we want to find the solution point, we should use substitution.

   We want to know the value of a (which is an x-value) where $f(a) = g(a)$. By substituting a for x, we know that

   $$f(a) = -(a-6)^2 + 12$$

   and that

   $$g(a) = -a + 12$$

   Set $f(a)$ equal to $g(a)$, and substitute their respective expressions.

   $$f(a) = g(a)$$
   $$-(a-6)^2 + 12 = -a + 12$$

2. Expand the expression on the left side of the equation and combine like terms to make a Standard Form quadratic equation.

$$-(a-6)^2+12=-a+12$$

Subtract 12 from both sides of the equation: $-(a-6)^2=-a$

Multiply both sides of the equation by -1: $(a-6)^2=a$

Expand the expression on the left side of the equation: $a^2-12a+36=a$

Subtract a from both sides of the equation: $a^2-13a+36=0$

3. Factor to find the two values of a for which $f(a)=g(a)$. We need to find two numbers that multiply to 36 and add to -13, and those numbers are -4 and -9, so the factors are $(a-4)$ and $(a-9)$.

$$a^2-13a+36=0$$
$$(a-4)(a-9)=0$$
$$a=4,\quad a=9$$

4. The answer is 4 or 9.

Solution 2

Below is an incredibly risky solution method. For one, there is no specific reason to know that the answers will be integers and thus precisely discernible even from a perfectly-drawn line. On what basis could one assume that the solutions lie at intersection points of the grid? Nevertheless, many do try to do this problem using this method, and most fail for the reason outlined below.

In this solution, we will draw in the line $g(x)=-x+12$ and pick out intersection points. This method is faster but many people draw the line incorrectly. If you try to draw the slope of -1 by going diagonally down each square of the grid, you will get a wrong answer because the axes are scaled differently. In the y-direction, each box does represent a change of 1, but in the x-direction, a change of 1 is achieved by moving three boxes over (each tick is 1 apart, but is divided into three equal parts).

1. Since we want to know the values of a for which $f(a)=g(a)$, we can draw the line $g(x)=-x+12$, and find the x-values of the intersection points.
When drawing the line, be careful to slope the line correctly. Based on the grid, a slope of -1 is achieved by moving 1 down as we move 3 boxes to the right.

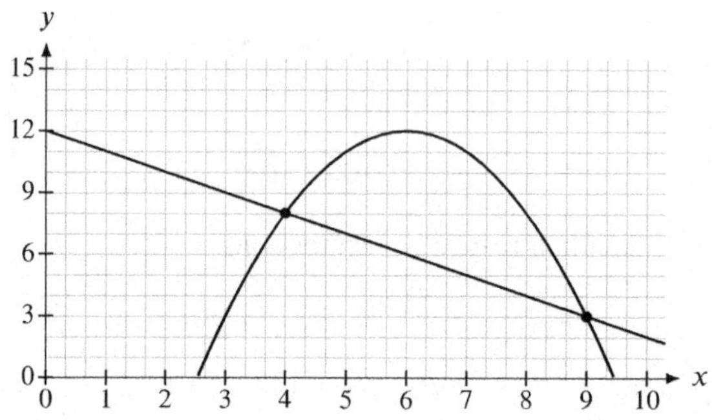

2. The intersections are at the points $(4,8)$ and $(9,3)$, so the values of a (remember a is an x-value) for which $f(a)=g(a)$ are 4 and 9.

3. The answer is 4 or 9.

Notes

Just so you know exactly what most people do incorrectly when trying to solve this problem by the method in Solution 2, we have shown below how people mistakenly believe they are drawing the line $g(x) = -x + 12$ while they are in fact drawing the line $y = -3x + 12$, which intersects the parabola at the point $(3, 3)$. Notice that although the line shows a change of one square at a time, the squares do not represent a 1 to 1 change. This highlights why it is absolutely essential to examine the axes' scaling (and starting values, for that matter) when analyzing a graph.

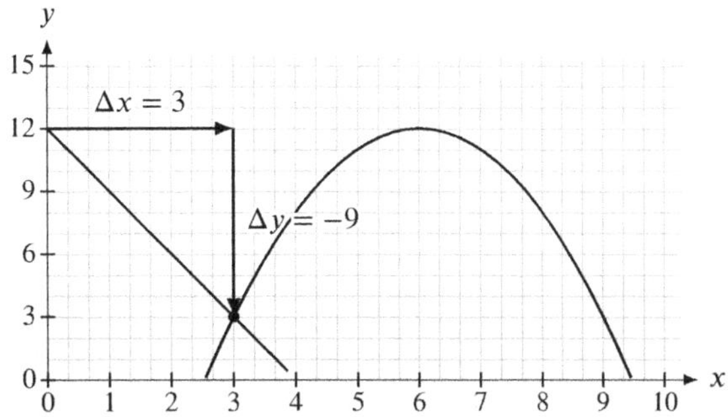

View related real-test problems at 1600.io/p/smtex?topic=10.6

Section 10.6 Practice Problems

1 1600.io 10.6

In the xy-plane, the parabola with the equation $y = (x - 13)^2$ intersects the line with equation $y = 36$ at two points, A and B. What is the length of $\overline{AB}$?

A) $\sqrt{13}$

B) 12

C) 13

D) 23

2 1600.io 10.6

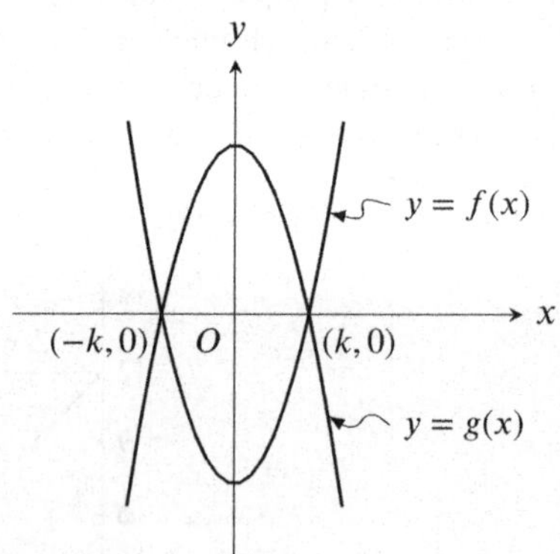

The functions f and g, defined by $f(x) = 9x^2 - 1$ and $g(x) = -9x^2 + 1$, are graphed in the xy-plane above. The graphs of f and g intersect at the points $(k, 0)$ and $(-k, 0)$. What is the value of k ?

A) 3

B) 1

C) $\frac{1}{3}$

D) $\frac{1}{9}$

CHAPTER 10 RECAP

Standard Form

- The Standard Form of a quadratic equation is $y = ax^2 + bx + c$, where a, b, and c are constants.
- For quadratics in Standard Form $y = ax^2 + bx + c$, the value of a (the x^2 coefficient) dictates the direction and elongation of the parabola. High absolute values result in graphs that are stretched vertically. Low absolute values result in flatter graphs. Positive values cause the graph to open upwards. Negative values cause the graph to open downwards.
- Every parabola that represents a function $y = f(x)$ is symmetric about a vertical line through its vertex, which is called the axis of symmetry.
- For a quadratic in Standard Form $y = ax^2 + bx + c$, the x-value of the vertex is equal to $\frac{-b}{2a}$.
- Plug the x-value of the vertex into the Standard Form in order to easily find the y-value of the vertex. This also allows you to construct the Vertex Form of the parabola from the Standard Form.
- To rapidly convert a quadratic equation with an (implied) a-coefficient of 1 from Standard Form to Vertex Form, thus finding the vertex, use the Completing the Square procedure by replacing $x^2 + bx$ with $\left(x + \frac{b}{2}\right)^2 - \left(\frac{b}{2}\right)^2$. If there is a non-1 a-coefficient, replace $ax^2 + bx$ with $a\left(x + \frac{b}{2a}\right)^2 - a\left(\frac{b}{2a}\right)^2$.
- The range of a function is the set of all y-values that can be produced by the function. For parabolas that open upwards (the a coefficient is positive), the range is all y-values greater than or equal to the y-value of the vertex. For parabolas that open downwards (the a coefficient is negative), the range is all y-values less than or equal to the y-value of the vertex.
- For quadratics in Standard Form $y = ax^2 + bx + c$, the value of c (the constant term) is the y-intercept.
- For quadratics in Standard Form $y = ax^2 + bx + c$, the value of b (the x coefficient) is the slope of the tangent line through the y-intercept. The sign of the slope of this tangent line, in conjunction with the sign of the a coefficient, will indicate on which side of the y-axis the vertex lies.

Factored Form

- The Factored Form of a quadratic is $y = a(x + p)(x + q)$, where a, p, and q are constants.
- For quadratics in Factored Form $y = a(x + p)(x + q)$, $-p$ and $-q$ are roots. If $(x - z)$ is a factor of a quadratic, then z is a root of the function and vice versa.
- If $(x - r)$ is a factor and $(x - s)$ is also a factor, then the product of those factors, $(x - r)(x - s)$, is also a factor.
- The x-value of the vertex is exactly halfway between the two root values and can be found by averaging the two roots (add the roots and divide by 2).
- Plug the x-value of the vertex into the Factored Form in order to easily find the y-value of the vertex. This allows you to construct the Vertex Form of the parabola from the Factored Form.
- To convert from Factored Form to Standard Form, expand the terms and recombine them in order of decreasing degree.
- Polynomials will "bounce" off of the x-axis when the exponent of a factor is even; they will go through the x-axis if the exponent of a factor is odd.

Vertex Form

- The Vertex Form of a quadratic is $y = a(x-h)^2 + k$, where a, h, and k are constants.
- For quadratics in Vertex Form $y = a(x-h)^2 + k$, the vertex of the graph is (h, k) and the value of a dictates the direction and elongation of the parabola.
- To convert from Vertex Form to Standard Form, expand the terms and recombine them in order of decreasing degree.

As a final note, the different forms of quadratic equations or functions can tell us different things about the graphs of those equations or functions. The Standard Form of a quadratic shows its y-intercept as a constant. The Factored Form of a quadratic shows its roots as constants. The Vertex Form of a quadratic shows its maximum or minimum value as a constant and shows the coordinates of its vertex as a pair of constants.

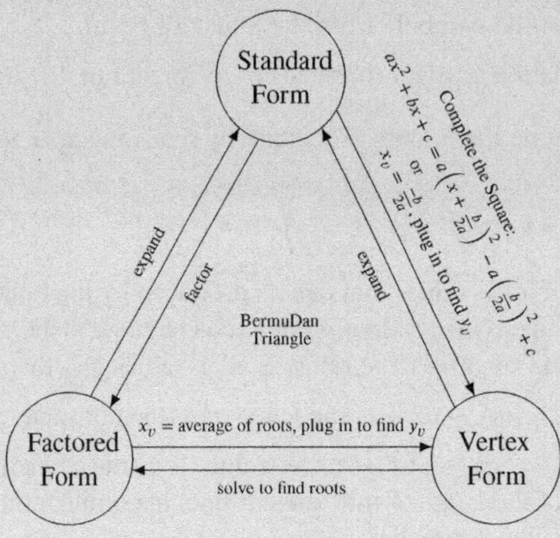

Additional Problems

1 10.4

$$h(x) = -(x-3)(x+3)$$

The function h is defined as shown. For what value of x does the function h reach its maximum value?

A) -3

B) 0

C) 3

D) 9

2 10.4

The graphs in the xy-plane of the following quadratic equations each have x-intercepts of -1 and 3. The graph of which equation has its vertex farthest from the x-axis?

A) $y = -5(x+1)(x-3)$

B) $y = \frac{-1}{4}(x+1)(x-3)$

C) $y = \frac{1}{2}(x+1)(x-3)$

D) $y = 3(x+1)(x-3)$

3 10.3

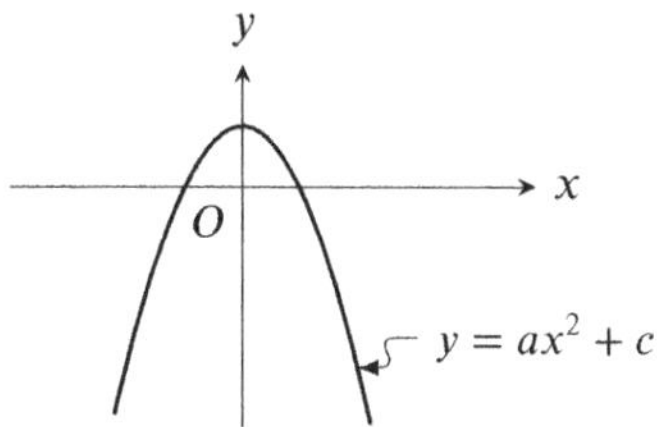

The vertex of the parabola in the xy-plane above is $(0, c)$. Which of the following is true about the parabola with the equation $y = -a(x+b)^2 + c$?

A) The vertex is (b, c) and the graph opens upward.

B) The vertex is (b, c) and the graph opens downward.

C) The vertex is $(-b, c)$ and the graph opens upward.

D) The vertex is $(-b, c)$ and the graph opens downward.

4 10.2

x	$f(x)$
0	2
3	4
6	-2
8	0

The function f is defined by a polynomial. Some values of x and $f(x)$ are shown in the table above. Which of the following must be a factor of $f(x)$?

A) $x-2$

B) $x-3$

C) $x-5$

D) $x-8$

5 1600.io 10.2

$$y = (x - k)(x - h)^2$$

The equation above is graphed in the xy-plane. If h and k are positive constants and $h \neq k$, how many distinct x-intercepts does the graph have?

A) 1

B) 2

C) 3

D) 4

6 1600.io 10.2

Which of the following equivalent forms of the function $f(x) = 9x^2 + 9x - 18$ is the most suitable to indicate the x-coordinates of the x-intercepts of the graph of $y = f(x)$ in the xy-plane?

A) $(3x - 3)(3x + 6)$

B) $3(x - 1)(3x + 6)$

C) $9(x - 1)(x + 2)$

D) $9(x^2 + x - 2)$

7 1600.io 10.3

$$c(t) = -0.27(t - 26.5)^2 + 304.2$$

The function c above models the calorie-burning rate of a certain runner, in calories per day (cal/day), in terms of the running time t, in minutes per day (min/day). What is the meaning of $(26.5, c(26.5))$ in this context?

A) The calorie-burning rate increased by $c(26.5)$ cal/day for every 26.5 min/day increase in running time.

B) The running time increases by $c(26.5)$ min/day for every 26.5 cal/day increase in calorie-burning rate.

C) The calorie-burning rate of 26.5 cal/day results in a running time of $c(26.5)$ min/day.

D) The running time of 26.5 min/day results in a calorie-burning rate of $c(26.5)$ cal/day.

8 1600.io 10.3

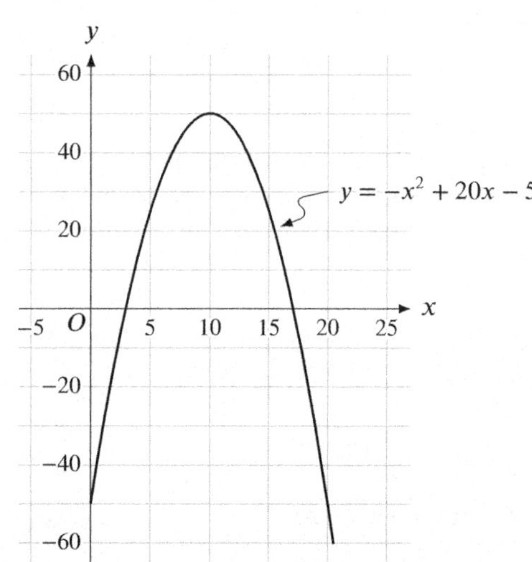

The graph above models the daily profit y, in dollars, that a website expects to make from selling socks for a price of x dollars. Based on the model, what is the maximum daily profit, in dollars? (Disregard the $ sign when writing your answer.)

9 10.2

The polynomial $p^4 - 6p^3 + 5p^2 + 24p - 36$ can be written as $(p^2 - 4)(p - 3)^2$. What are all the roots of the polynomial?

A) 2 and 3

B) 3 and 4

C) -3, -2, and 2

D) -2, 2, and 3

10 10.4

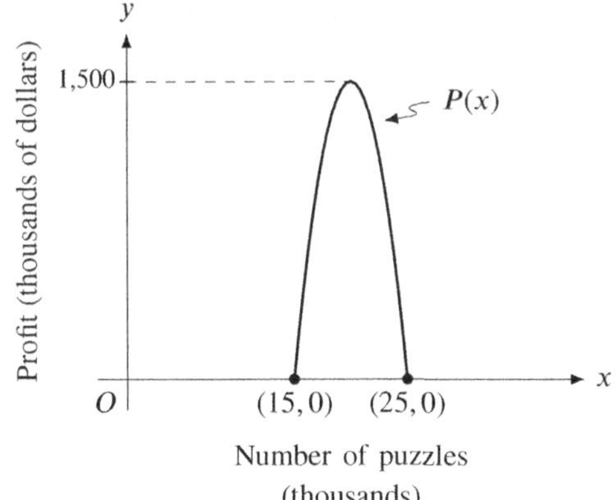

A company produces puzzles and sells them online and in stores. The quadratic function P models the company's monthly profits $P(x)$, in thousands of dollars, when x puzzles, in thousands, are produced and sold. The graph of $P(x)$, where $15 \leq x \leq 25$, is shown in the xy-plane above. How many puzzles must the company produce and sell in order to earn the maximum profit estimated by the model?

A) 15,000

B) 20,000

C) 25,000

D) 1,500,000

11 10.4

$$y = x^2 - 8x + 15$$

The equation above represents a parabola in the xy-plane. Which of the following equivalent forms of the equation displays the x-intercepts of the parabola as constants or coefficients?

A) $y - 15 = x^2 - 8x$

B) $y + 1 = (x - 4)^2$

C) $y = x(x - 8) + 15$

D) $y = (x - 3)(x - 5)$

12 10.6

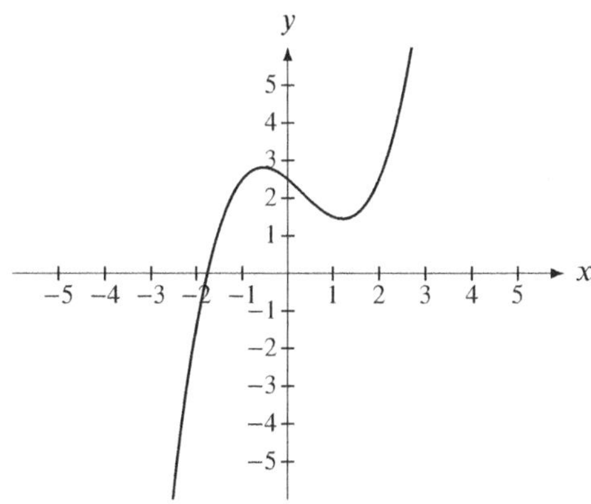

The function $f(x) = \frac{1}{2}x^3 - \frac{1}{2}x^2 - x + \frac{5}{2}$ is graphed in the xy-plane above. If k is a constant such that the equation $f(x) = k$ has three real solutions, which of the following could be the value of k ?

A) -2

B) 0

C) 2

D) 3

13 1600.io 10.3

In the xy-plane, a parabola has vertex $(4, 2)$ and intersects the x-axis at two points. If the equation of the parabola is written in the form $y = -ax^2 + bx + c$, where a, b, and c are constants, which of the following could be a value of c ?

A) -30

B) 2

C) 16

D) 34

14 1600.io 10.2

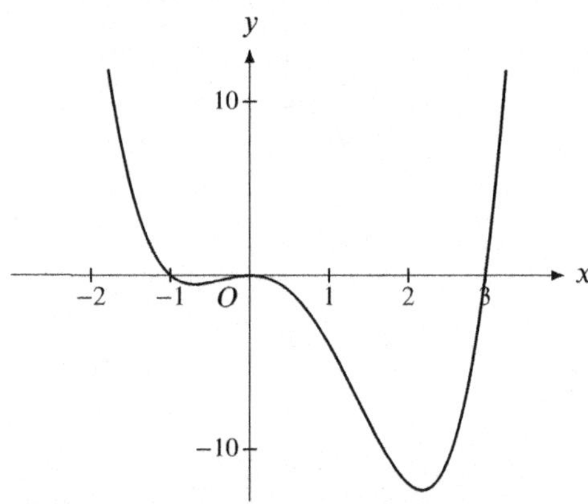

Which of the following could be the equation of the graph above?

A) $y = x(x-1)(x+3)$

B) $y = x^2(x-1)(x+3)$

C) $y = x(x-3)(x+1)$

D) $y = x^2(x-3)(x+1)$

15 1600.io 10.2

If the function f has five distinct zeros, which of the following could represent the complete graph of f in the xy-plane?

A)

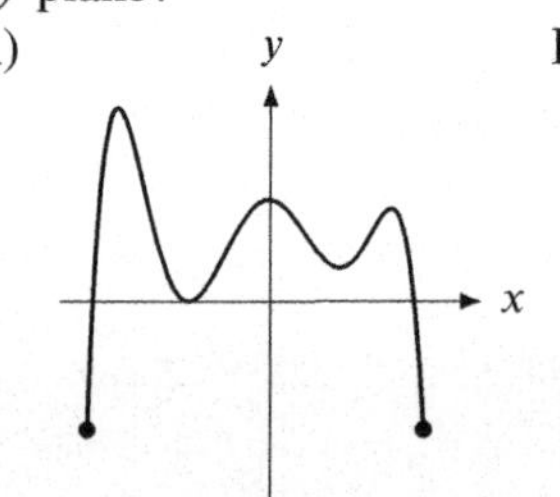

B)

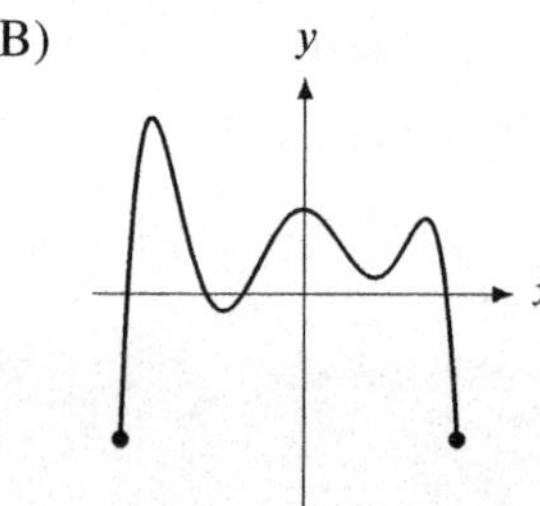

C)

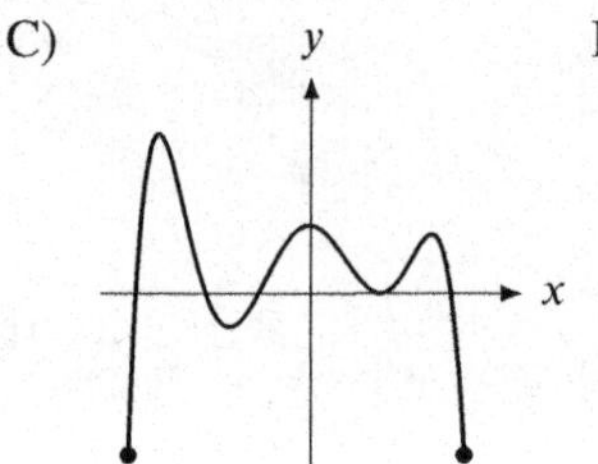

D)

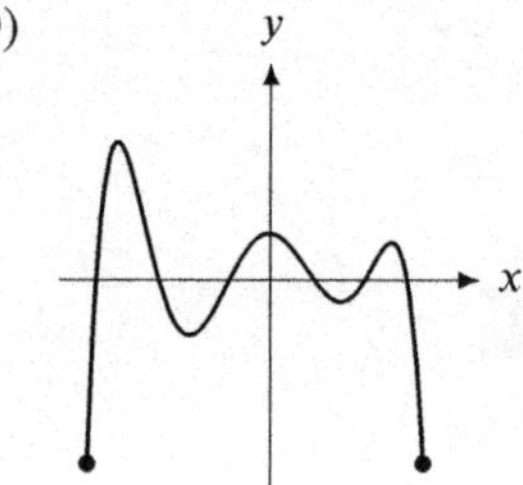

16 1600.io 10.2

x	$p(x)$
−2	0
−1	2
0	4
1	0
2	−3

The table above gives selected values of a polynomial function p. Based on the values in the table, which of the following must be a factor of p ?

A) $(x-4)$

B) $(x+4)$

C) $(x-2)(x+1)$

D) $(x+2)(x-1)$

17 10.2

In the xy-plane, the graph of function f has x-intercepts at -4, -3, and 3. Which of the following could define f ?

A) $f(x) = (x-4)(x-3)(x+3)$

B) $f(x) = (x-4)(x-3)^2$

C) $f(x) = (x-3)(x+3)(x+4)$

D) $f(x) = (x+3)^2(x+4)$

18 10.2

$$f(x) = -200x^2 + 10{,}000x$$

The number of views $f(x)$ that a content creator receives on a video is given by the function f above, where x is the length, in minutes, of the video. The graph of $y = f(x)$ in the xy-plane intersects the x-axis at 0 and a. What does a represent?

A) The number of views when the length of the video is 0 minutes

B) The length, in minutes, of the video that will result in maximum views

C) The length, in minutes, of the video that will result in 0 views

D) The maximum views that the content creator can receive on the video

19 10.2

In the xy-plane, the graph of $y = x^2 + bx + c$, where b and c are constants, has x-intercepts at $x = -5$ and $x = -2$. What is the value of b ?

20 10.2

Parabola D in the xy-plane has equation $x - 2y^2 - 12y - 14 = 0$. Which equation shows the x-intercept(s) of the parabola as constants or coefficients?

A) $x = 2y^2 + 12y + 14$

B) $x = 2(y+3)^2 - 4$

C) $x + 4 = 2(y+3)^2$

D) $y = -\sqrt{\dfrac{x+4}{2}} - 3$

21 1600.io 10.3

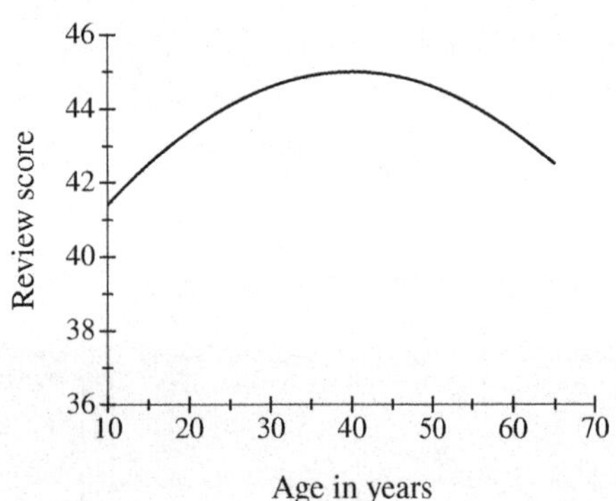

A website received movie reviews from people aged 10 to 65. The graph above shows the quadratic function R, which models their review scores as a function of their age x, in years, Which of the following could define R ?

A) $R(x) = \frac{1}{250}(x - 45)^2 + 40$

B) $R(x) = \frac{1}{250}(x - 40)^2 + 45$

C) $R(x) = -\frac{1}{250}(x - 45)^2 + 40$

D) $R(x) = -\frac{1}{250}(x - 40)^2 + 45$

22 1600.io 10.2

The range of the polynomial function f is the set of real numbers greater than or equal to -3. If the zeros of f are -2 and 4, which of the following could be the graph of $y = f(x)$ in the xy-plane?

A)

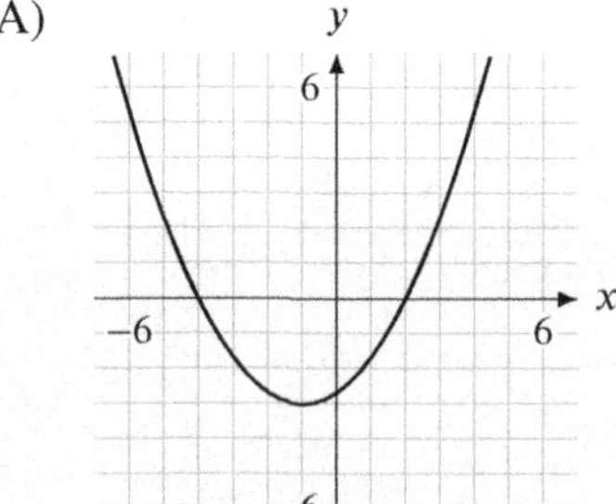

B)

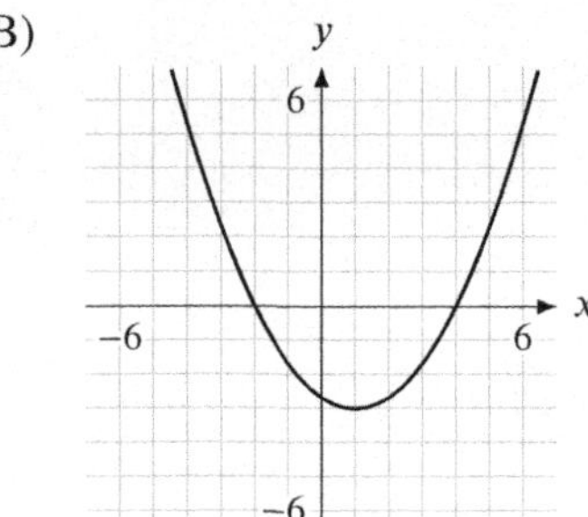

C)

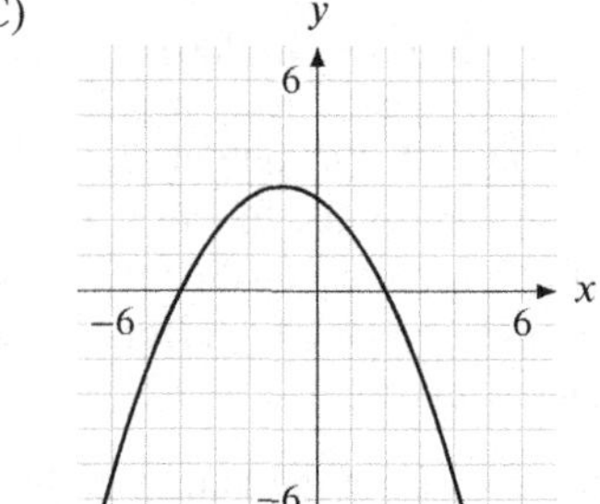

D)

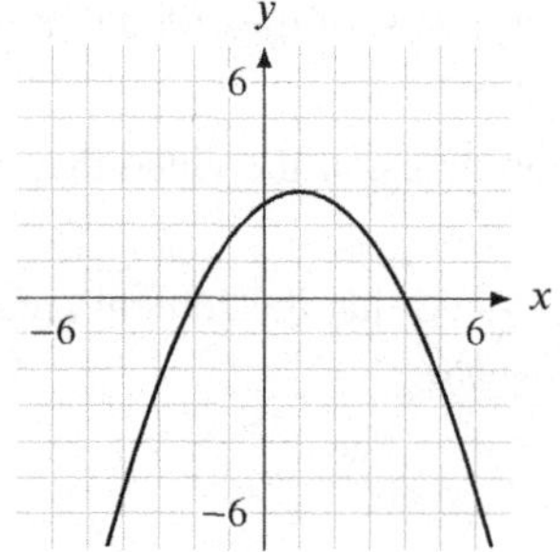

Answer Key

SkillDrill 10.1-1

1. up, left, -6
2. down, left, 1
3. up, right, 5
4. down, 0, -8
5. up, right, -4
6. down, right, -3
7. up, 0, 20
8. down, left, 2

Section 10.1 Practice Problems

1. C
2. B

SkillDrill 10.2-1

1. -2 and 4
2. -5 and -3
3. 1 and 3
4. $\frac{1}{3}$ and $\frac{5}{2}$
5. -24 only
6. -10 and 0
7. 4 only
8. -2 and $\frac{-7}{4}$

Section 10.2 Practice Problems

1. B
2. C
3. A
4. 12

SkillDrill 10.3-1

1. $(1, -3)$, min, -2
2. $(-5, 10)$, max, -15
3. $(-2, 3)$, min, 7
4. $(3, 0)$, min, 9
5. $(1, 1)$, max, -1
6. $(0, 5)$, min, 5
7. $(0, 0)$, max, 0
8. $(2, -5)$, max, -13

SkillDrill 10.3-2

1. $y = x^2 - 2x - 2$
2. $y = -x^2 - 10x - 15$
3. $y = -2x^2 + 4x - 1$
4. $y = x^2 + 5$
5. $x = -1$ and $x = 3$
6. $x = -8$ and $x = -2$
7. $x = -3$ and $x = 5$
8. $x = \pm\sqrt{5}$
9. $x = 1 \pm \sqrt{3}$
10. $x = -5 \pm \sqrt{10}$
11. $x = \frac{-3}{2}$ and $x = \frac{-1}{2}$
12. $x = 6 \pm \sqrt{\frac{3}{5}}$

Section 10.3 Practice Problems

1. A
2. D

SkillDrill 10.4-1

1. $(1, -9)$, $y = (x - 1)^2 - 9$
2. $(-4, -1)$, $y = (x + 4)^2 - 1$
3. $(2, 1)$, $y = -(x - 2)^2 + 1$
4. $(-6, 0)$, $y = (x + 6)^2$
5. $(-5, -50)$, $y = 2(x + 5)^2 - 50$
6. $(4, 0)$, $y = 3(x - 4)^2$
7. $\left(\frac{3}{2}, -4\right)$, $y = 4\left(x - \frac{3}{2}\right)^2 - 4$
8. $\left(\frac{-3}{4}, \frac{1}{2}\right)$, $y = -8\left(x + \frac{3}{4}\right)^2 + \frac{1}{2}$

Section 10.4 Practice Problems

1. C
2. A

SkillDrill 10.5-1

1. $y = (x + 1)^2 - 5$
2. $y = (x - 3)^2 + 11$
3. $y = (x + 5)^2 - 40$
4. $y = (x - 2)^2 - 11$
5. $y = (x - 4)^2 - 13$
6. $y = (x + 10)^2$
7. $y = (x + 7)^2 - 17$
8. $y = x^2 - 10$
9. $y = \left(x + \frac{5}{2}\right)^2 - \frac{29}{4}$
10. $y = \left(x - \frac{3}{2}\right)^2 - \frac{1}{4}$
11. $y = 2(x + 2)^2 + 2$
12. $y = -3(x - 2)^2 + 24$

Section 10.5 Practice Problems

1. C
2. D

Section 10.6 Practice Problems

1. B
2. C

Additional Problems

1. B

2. A

3. C

4. D

5. B

6. C

7. D

8. 50

9. D

10. B

11. D

12. C

13. A

14. D

15. C

16. D

17. C

18. C

19. 7

20. A

21. D

22. B

11 Number of Zeros/Imaginary and Complex Numbers

11.1 Number of Zeros of Quadratics

We've seen in the last few chapters that the zeros (x-intercepts) of a polynomial function correspond to the factors of that polynomial. Focusing on quadratics, we know that factorable quadratic equations can have **two** real factors. For example, the quadratic (written here in Factored Form) $y = (x - 2)(x + 3)$ has two zeros (x-intercepts) at $x = 2$ and $x = -3$, and its graph crosses the x-axis at the points $(2, 0)$ and $(-3, 0)$. We could also say that the equation $(x - 2)(x + 3) = 0$ has two solutions: $x = 2$ and $x = -3$.

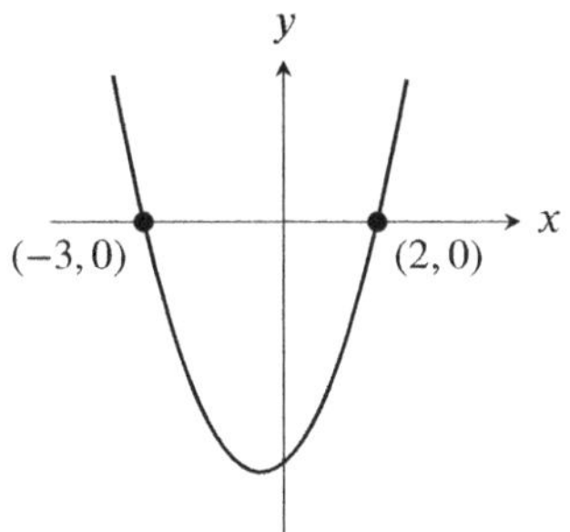

We also have seen quadratics with only **one** factor (of degree 2) that only have a single zero or x-intercept. For example, the quadratic (shown in Vertex Form) $y = -2(x - 2)^2$ has one zero at $x = 2$, and its graph "bounces off" the x-axis at the point $(2, 0)$. Put another way, $-2(x - 2)^2 = 0$ has one solution: $x = 2$.

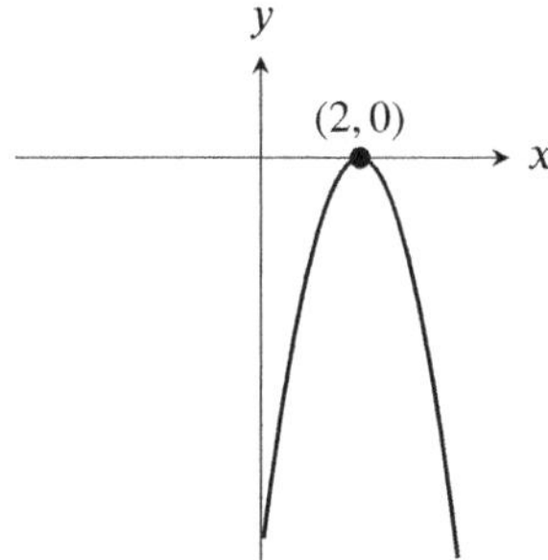

What happens when a quadratic has **no** factors and, when graphed, doesn't even intersect the x-axis? For example, look at the Standard Form quadratic $y = x^2 - 4x + 7$, which never touches the x-axis. That is, there's no value on the x-axis that makes $x^2 - 4x + 7 = 0$ true.

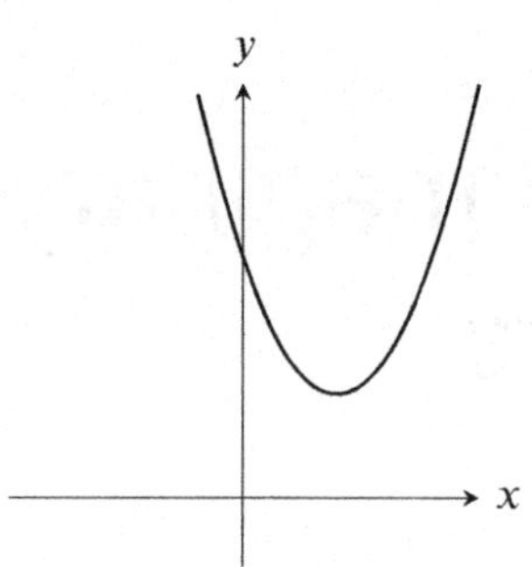

Examining the graph above, it appears that the quadratic function it represents has no zeros in the sense that there are no values on the x-axis for which the y-value will be 0 when the function is evaluated. This means, for example, that try as you might, you won't be able to factor it, because you won't be able to find two numbers whose sum is the b coefficient and whose product is the c coefficient.

But if there are no roots to this function, and we have methods such as Completing the Square and the Quadratic Formula that can find the roots of *any* quadratic function, what happens when we deploy those all-powerful solving tools on an equation that apparently has no solutions? Does the universe collapse to a singularity? Buckle up, because we're about to find out.

Let's attempt to find the roots of the function $f(x) = x^2 - 4x + 7$ using both Completing the Square and the Quadratic Formula.

Completing the Square

$$x^2 - 4x + 7 = 0$$
$$x^2 - 4x = -7$$
$$(x-2)^2 = 4 - 7$$
$$x - 2 = \pm\sqrt{-3}$$
$$x = 2 \pm \sqrt{-3}$$
$$x = 2 + \sqrt{-3}, x = 2 - \sqrt{-3}$$

Quadratic Formula

$$a = 1, b = -4, c = 7$$
$$x = \frac{-(-4)}{2(1)} \pm \frac{\sqrt{(-4)^2 - 4(1)(7)}}{2(1)}$$
$$x = \frac{4}{2} \pm \frac{\sqrt{16-28}}{2}$$
$$x = 2 \pm \frac{\sqrt{-12}}{2}$$
$$x = 2 \pm \frac{\sqrt{4(-3)}}{2}$$
$$x = 2 \pm \frac{2\sqrt{-3}}{2}$$
$$x = 2 \pm \sqrt{-3}$$
$$x = 2 + \sqrt{-3}, x = 2 - \sqrt{-3}$$

Assuming we're all still here, you can see that we've found the zeros, and they have a distinctive form, as they consist of two terms that can't be further combined: a number and **a square root of a negative number**.

We previously explained that the square of a number can't be negative, regardless of the sign of the original number, so the square root of a negative number can't be a real number. And, indeed, that is exactly the label we apply to the types of numbers we've been dealing with up until now: **real numbers**.

A real number is an integer, such as 7 or −13; a fraction made from integers (a rational number), such as $\frac{3}{5}$ or 0.7 (which can be expressed as $\frac{7}{10}$); or an irrational number, such as $\sqrt{2}$ or π. As noted, any real number when squared produces a non-negative result, so that $\sqrt{-3}$ term we got when finding the roots of the quadratic above must not represent a real number. Instead, it represents what is called an **imaginary number. Square roots of negative numbers are imaginary numbers**, and to facilitate referring to and manipulating them, we use a special symbol that represents the square root of −1: we say that

$$\sqrt{-\mathbf{1}} = i$$

where i stands for "imaginary." This is handy because we can then form any negative square root by multiplying i by a real number; for example, here we can write

$$\sqrt{-3} = \sqrt{3(-1)} = \sqrt{3}\sqrt{-1} = \sqrt{3}i$$

Note that by convention, we write the real number first as a coefficient, then the imaginary number next. Sometimes, depending on the value we're working with, we can completely eliminate the square root; for example, if we had $\sqrt{-4}$, we could convert that to

$$\sqrt{4(-1)} = \sqrt{4}\sqrt{-1} = 2i$$

As you can see, we can multiply an imaginary number by a real number to get a term like $\sqrt{3}i$ or $2i$ (and, it follows, the same is true of division). We already know that we can add real numbers together, of course; $5 + 7 = 12$. Similarly, we can add imaginary numbers: $5i + 7i = 12i$. Here, i behaves like a variable or a letter that stands in for a constant. However, we can't add a real number and an imaginary number to get a single term; something like $2 + \sqrt{-3}$ can't be further simplified, as **a real term and an imaginary term can't be combined into a single term through addition or subtraction**; once you've combined all the real terms and all the imaginary terms in an expression, you will end up with one real term and one imaginary term in the general form $a + bi$, where a and b are real constants. This is what resulted from our attempts to solve the example quadratic we're working with, where we got $x = 2 + \sqrt{-3}$ (or $x = 2 + \sqrt{3}i$) and $x = 2 - \sqrt{-3}$ ($x = 2 - \sqrt{3}i$). An expression like this, with one real term added to an imaginary term in the form $a + bi$, is called a **complex number**, so **a quadratic function whose graph never intersects the x-axis has two roots that are complex numbers**. (A minor technicality: real numbers are complex numbers where the coefficient of the imaginary part is 0.)

Let's summarize: A quadratic function can have **two real roots**, and the graph of such a function will intersect the x-axis (which represents real numbers) at two distinct points. A quadratic function can have **one real root** (a double root), and so the graph will touch the x-axis at just one point. Finally, a quadratic function can have **two complex roots**, and its graph won't intersect the real number x-axis at all. (Note that you might hear the phraseology "two imaginary roots" thrown around elsewhere in reference to the last case, but that's not really right; the roots are complex numbers, which can include both a real part and an imaginary part, not just imaginary numbers alone.)

We will discuss more about imaginary and complex numbers later in the chapter. For now, however, let's make use of the Quadratic Formula to explain the logic behind a simple test for finding the number and types of zeros for any quadratic, which is often the fastest route through quadratic problems that ask you about the number of zeros. (We're using the terms "zero" and "root" depending on our mood, but remember that these mean the same thing in this context; we just want you to get used to seeing either term.)

For a quadratic equation in Standard Form, $y = ax^2 + bx + c$, where a, b, and c are constants, the zeros of the equation can be found using the Quadratic Formula.

$$x = \frac{-b}{2a} \pm \frac{\sqrt{\mathbf{b^2 - 4ac}}}{2a}$$

The quadratic formula produces two results, which reflects the fact that there is an expression, $b^2 - 4ac$, under a square root symbol, and both the positive and negative roots must be used. Because only a positive number has different positive and negative real square roots (e.g. $\sqrt{4} = 2$, so $\pm\sqrt{4}$ equals both 2 and -2), and zero has just zero as its one square root ($\pm\sqrt{0}$ is just 0), we can use that $b^2 - 4ac$ expression to figure out whether there will be two real zeros, just one, or none (in which case the two zeros will result from taking the square root of a negative number, and thus they will include an imaginary number term). Because the expression $b^2 - 4ac$ helps us discriminate among these possibilities, we call it **the discriminant**.

The Discriminant

For a quadratic equation in Standard Form, $y = ax^2 + bx + c$, where a, b, and c are constants, the discriminant is the expression $b^2 - 4ac$, which is found in the radical in the Quadratic Formula.

It is simple enough to find the number of solutions to a quadratic equation if you can factor the equation because the number of unique factors is also the number of zeros. However, when a quadratic is not easily factorable or you suspect it doesn't have any real solutions (x-intercepts), the easiest way to tell how many solutions the quadratic has is to make use of the **discriminant**. **The value of the discriminant, $b^2 - 4ac$, will indicate the number and type of zeros of a quadratic equations.**

- **$b^2 - 4ac > 0$: When the value of the discriminant is positive, there are TWO REAL number zeros.**

  Note that the fact that there are two real zeros does *not* mean that those zeros are both integers or that the quadratic would be easily factorable.

- **$b^2 - 4ac = 0$: When the value of the discriminant is equal to 0, there is ONE REAL number zero (a double zero).**

- **$b^2 - 4ac < 0$: When the value of the discriminant is negative, there are NO REAL zeros, but there are TWO COMPLEX NUMBER zeros.**

  The two complex roots are **complex conjugates** of one another (this term will be discussed more in the next section), which means that if $a + bi$ is a root, then $a - bi$ is the other root.

We will look more closely at complex numbers and imaginary solutions momentarily, but for now, we just need to know how to determine the number and type of zeros for quadratic equations (or systems of equations).

Example 11.1-1

1 1600.io 11.1

$$3x^2 - 6x = t$$

In the equation above, t is a constant. If the equation has no real solutions, which of the following could be the value of t ?

A) -4

B) -3

C) 3

D) 4

Solution

1. Subtract t from both sides of the equation to make a quadratic equation in Standard Form.

$$3x^2 - 6x = t$$
$$3x^2 - 6x - t = 0$$

2. We need to find a value of t that causes there to be no real solutions, so we should set the discriminant less than 0. The value of b is -6; the value of a is 3; the value of c is $-t$.

$$b^2 - 4ac < 0$$
$$(-6)^2 - 4(3)(-t) < 0$$
$$36 + 12t < 0$$

3. Subtract 36 from both sides of the inequality.

$$36 + 12t < 0$$
$$12t < -36$$

4. Divide both sides of the inequality by 12 to solve for t.

$$12t < -36$$
$$t < -3$$

5. The value of t must be less than -3, and choice A, -4, is the only choice that is less than -3.

6. The answer is A.

It should be noted that the discriminant is not necessary for every problem in which you are asked about the number of roots or zeros for a quadratic. **The use of the discriminant should be a last resort.**

In general, you should try to find the number of zeros in the following ways:

- If the quadratic is in Standard Form and can be easily factored, then there are two real zeros if the two factors are different; if the two factors are the same (the quadratic expression is a perfect square), there is one real zero.
- If the quadratic is in Standard Form, you can convert it to Vertex Form by Completing the Square. Once it is in Vertex Form, you know the sign of the y-coordinate of the vertex point and whether the quadratic opens up or down and therefore whether (and how many times) it will intersect the x-axis, so you can easily tell the number and type of zeros without the discriminant.
- If the quadratic is in Standard Form, cannot be easily factored, and you're in denial about Completing the Square being awesome, then you can use the discriminant to determine the number of roots (just because you can't factor it doesn't mean it does not have real zeros).
- If the quadratic is in Factored Form with two *different* factors, then it has two real zeros.
- If the quadratic is a perfect square expression (there is one factor squared), then it has one real zero.
- If the quadratic is in Vertex Form, then you can visualize or draw a quick picture that will tell you how many real roots there are. You will know the sign of the y-coordinate of the vertex point and whether the quadratic opens up or down, so the discriminant is unnecessary.

  For example, the quadratic $y = -2(x - 1)^2 + 4$ has its vertex at $(1, 4)$, which is **above** the x-axis, and the parabola **opens downward** because the a-coefficient is -2, so the parabola will intersect the x-axis twice, meaning that there are two real zeros or roots.

All of the same principles apply when working with a system of equations. If you can graph both of the equations easily, then the number of intersections will tell you the number of solutions.

If you use substitution to collapse the system into one quadratic equation, then the number of real zeros of that new equation will tell you the number of solutions to the system. You can use the same procedures described previously for determining the characteristics of the zeros of the collapsed equation.

All of the methods explained above have test problems for which they are well-suited and ones for which they are ill-suited. Luckily, problems involving the number of solutions to a quadratic are not very common, so if you do encounter them on the test, hopefully the rest of your skills are sharp enough that you can afford to spend a little time trying more than one method to verify your findings on these problems.

SkillDrill 11.1-1

Directions: Using any method, determine the number and type of distinct roots for the following quadratics, which are given in Standard, Factored, or Vertex Form (you do not have to find the values of those zeros).

1. $y = (x - 1)^2 - 3$ **2.** $y = x^2 - 5x + 4$ **3.** $y = x^2 - 3x + 4$ **4.** $y = x^2 - 8x + 16$

5. $y = -2(x + 4)(x + 2)$ **6.** $y = -(x + 5)^2 + 10$ **7.** $y = 2(x - 1)^2 + 1$ **8.** $y = x^2 + 5$

9. $y = (x + 6)^2$ **10.** $y = -x^2 - 6x - 9$ **11.** $y = -x^2 - 5x - 8$ **12.** $y = -x^2 + 7x - 12$

Section 11.1 Suggested Problems from Real Tests

View related real-test problems at 1600.io/p/smtex?topic=11.1

Section 11.1 Practice Problems

1 11.1

$$x^2 + bx + 9 = 0$$

In the quadratic equation shown, b is a constant. For what values of b does the equation have only one solution?

A) -3 only

B) -6 only

C) -3 and 3

D) -6 and 6

2 11.1

$$y = 5$$
$$y = ax^2 + b$$

In the system of equations above, a and b are constants. For which of the following values of a and b does the system of equations have exactly two real solutions?

A) $a = -2, b = 4$

B) $a = -2, b = 5$

C) $a = -2, b = 6$

D) $a = 2, b = 5$

11.2 Imaginary and Complex Numbers

We previously explored the idea that a quadratic function might have two complex roots, and we explained that complex numbers consist of a real part and an imaginary part that includes the special imaginary number i, which represents $\sqrt{-1}$. Let's dig into that topic more deeply, as there are problems on the test for which a good working knowledge of imaginary and complex numbers is required.

Imaginary Numbers

There exists an imaginary number called i that is equal to $\sqrt{-1}$.

Because we designate i as the square root of -1, we know that $i^2 = -1$. Let's look at some higher powers of i:

i^3	i^4	i^5
$i^3 = i \cdot i \cdot i$	$i^4 = i \cdot i \cdot i \cdot i$	$i^5 = i \cdot i \cdot i \cdot i \cdot i$
$i^3 = i^2 \cdot i$	$i^4 = i^2 \cdot i^2$	$i^5 = i^4 \cdot i$
$i^3 = -1 \cdot i$	$i^4 = -1(-1)$	$i^5 = 1 \cdot i$
$i^3 = -i$	$i^4 = 1$	$i^5 = i$

You'll notice that $i^5 = i$, or, put more clearly, $i^5 = i^1$; we're back where we started. This indicates that a cycle is beginning again, and therefore there will be a repetition of the four-value sequence shown above as the exponent increases in increments of 1. In fact, $i^6 = i^2$, $i^7 = i^3$, $i^8 = i^4$, and so on...
To summarize:

- $i = \sqrt{-1}$
- $i^2 = -1$
- $i^3 = -i$
- $i^4 = 1$

- $i^5 = \sqrt{-1}$
- $i^6 = -1$
- $i^7 = -i$
- $i^8 = 1$

- $i^9 = \sqrt{-1}$
- $i^{10} = -1$
- $i^{11} = -i$
- $i^{12} = 1$

If asked to evaluate the value of i terms with large exponents, find a multiple of 4 that is close to that exponent (any time i is raised to a power that is a multiple of 4, it will evaluate to 1) and count up or down from there to see which of the four primary powers of i it corresponds to.

For example i^{26} is equal to i^2 (or -1) because 26 is 2 more than 24 (a multiple of 4). Similarly, i^{104} is equal to i^4 (or 1) because 104 is a multiple of 4.

Example 11.2-1

 1600.io 11.2

In the complex number system, what is the value of the expression $13i^4 - 7i^2 + 2$? (Note: $i = \sqrt{-1}$)

Solution

1. Since $i^4 = 1$, replace i^4 with 1. Since $i^2 = -1$, replace i^2 with -1.

$$13i^4 - 7i^2 + 2$$
$$13(1) - 7(-1) + 2$$
$$13 + 7 + 2$$
$$22$$

2. The answer is 22.

To reiterate what we explained earlier, complex numbers consist of a real part and an imaginary part and are written in the form $a + bi$, where a and b are real constants; a is the real part of the complex number, and b is the coefficient of the imaginary part i of the complex number.

Complex numbers can be added to (or subtracted from) each other by simply combining like terms—add the real parts to each other and add the imaginary parts together (treat i like a variable). As previously explained, you can't add a real number and an imaginary number to get a single value.

Example 11.2-2

2 11.2

$$(2 + 6i) - (1 - 3i)$$

In the complex number system, which of the following is equivalent to the expression above? (Note: $i = \sqrt{-1}$)

A) 4

B) $3 + 3i$

C) $1 + 9i$

D) $1 - 9i$

Solution

1. Combine the real terms and combine the imaginary terms. Remember to distribute the negative sign.

$$(2 + 6i) - (1 - 3i)$$
$$2 + 6i - 1 + 3i$$
$$(2 - 1) + (6i + 3i)$$
$$1 + 9i$$

2. The answer is C.

SkillDrill 11.2-1

Directions: Write the complex number expressions in the form $a + bi$.

1. $(2 + 3i) + (3 + 4i)$ **2.** $(4 + i) - (6 + 3i)$ **3.** $i^2 - i$ **4.** $i^3 + 2i$

5. $(5 - 3i) + (8 - 6i)$ **6.** $3i^{12} + 2i^7$ **7.** $4i^6 - 2i^{13}$ **8.** $-3i^4 + 2i^3 - 5i^2 + i$

Going one step further, complex numbers can be multiplied by each other much the same way polynomials are multiplied by each other: multiply each value in one expression by each value in the other expression.

Example 11.2-3

3 11.2

$$(2 + 6i)(1 - 4i) = a + bi$$

In the equation above, a and b are real numbers and $i = \sqrt{-1}$. What is the value of a ?

Solution

1. Multiply the two complex numbers in parentheses to expand the terms. Make sure you write the i^2 term before you attempt to substitute -1 for i^2—many students make a mistake here trying to do too many things at once in their heads. It is too easy to make a mistake with the negative sign.

$$(2+6i)(1-4i) = a+bi$$
$$2(1)+2(-4i)+6i(1)+6i(-4i) = a+bi$$
$$2-8i+6i-24i^2 = a+bi$$
$$2-2i-24i^2 = a+bi$$

2. Since $i^2 = -1$, replace i^2 with -1.

$$2-2i-24(-1) = a+bi$$
$$2-2i+24 = a+bi$$
$$26-2i = a+bi$$

3. By matching corresponding components of the complex numbers on each side of the equation, we can see that $a = 26$.

4. The answer is 26.

Notes

The astute student will notice that because the problem asks only for the value of the real number a in the expression $a+bi$, one could ignore the multiplications that will produce imaginary numbers (that is, where exactly one of the operands contains i) and only perform the multiplications that will produce real values; that's $2(1)$ and $6i(-4i)$, whose sum is $2-24i^2 = 2-(24(-1)) = 26$. You must be very attentive when taking optimized approaches of this sort, but they are valid for the proficient student.

Finally, the last thing you will be tested on involving complex numbers occurs when there is a complex number in the denominator of a fraction. To solve any known problem from previous tests where there is a complex number in the denominator, you will need to find a way to rewrite the fraction so that there are no imaginary numbers in the denominators of any fraction.

We would like to have some operation that will eliminate the imaginary number in the denominator. What can we multiply a complex number by that will result in the imaginary number becoming a real number? Merely multiplying a fraction by $\frac{i}{i}$ won't do it, because then the a term (the real part of the complex number) in the denominator's complex number will become ai (the product of the real part and i will be imaginary), but if we multiply the denominator by the same expression but with the addition (or subtraction) operation negated, we'll get two i terms that will have the same absolute value, but they will be opposite in sign, so they'll cancel out (recall the difference of squares and its factorization).

So, if we have an expression, $a+bi$, we'd multiply it by $a-bi$:

$$(a+bi)(a-bi)$$
$$a^2 - a(bi) + bi(a) - bi(bi)$$
$$a^2 + abi - abi - b^2i^2$$

You'll notice that the two middle terms cancel, leaving:

$$a^2 - b^2i^2$$

We do still have a term with i in it, but because it's i^2, we can replace that with -1, so we no longer have any imaginary numbers, which was our goal:

$$a^2 - \left(b^2\right)(-1)$$

$$a^2 + b^2$$

Note that because both a and b are real constants, we'll be able to calculate a single real value for the denominator when we apply this technique (the numerator is on its own!).

This expression $(a - bi)$ that we can use to eliminate the imaginary number is called the **complex conjugate** of the original complex number.

For example, if we had $\frac{3-8i}{2-4i}$, we could multiply the fraction by the denominator's complex conjugate, which is $2 + 4i$, over itself (so we're just multiplying the fraction by 1) in order to write the value with a real number denominator. Here's the calculation:

$$\frac{3-8i}{2-4i} \cdot \frac{2+4i}{2+4i}$$

$$\frac{(3-8i)(2+4i)}{(2-4i)(2+4i)}$$

$$\frac{3(2)+3(4i)-8i(2)-8i(4i)}{2(2)+2(4i)-4i(2)-4i(4i)}$$

$$\frac{6+12i-16i-32i^2}{4\cancel{+8i}\cancel{-8i}-16i^2}$$

$$\frac{6-4i-32i^2}{4-16i^2}$$

Notice how the two middle terms in the denominator cancel out (exactly like they do with the difference of squares). Replacing i^2 with -1, we get

$$\frac{6-4i-32(-1)}{4-16(-1)}$$

$$\frac{6-4i+32}{4+16}$$

$$\frac{38-4i}{20}$$

Note that the fraction above may be split into two terms (and reduced) in order to match the general complex number form $a + bi$:

$$\frac{38-4i}{20} = \frac{38}{20} - \frac{4i}{20} = \frac{19}{10} - \frac{i}{5}$$

To summarize, **in order to rewrite the fraction so that there are no imaginary numbers in the denominator, you need to multiply both the numerator and denominator by the complex conjugate of the denominator**.

Complex Conjugate

For a complex number $a + bi$, there exists a complex conjugate $a - bi$.

For example, the complex conjugate of $2 - 4i$ is $2 + 4i$, and vice versa.

To reiterate, multiplying by the conjugate of the denominator results in a difference of squares expression where the i terms will cancel out, leaving only a real number in the denominator.

SkillDrill 11.2-2

Directions: Write the complex number expressions in the form $a + bi$. Multiply both the numerator and denominator by the complex conjugate of the denominator. Express any fractions in lowest terms.

1. $\dfrac{2+3i}{3+4i}$ **2.** $\dfrac{4+i}{6-3i}$ **3.** $\dfrac{-2-3i}{-1-4i}$ **4.** $\dfrac{1+i}{2-2i}$

5. $\dfrac{8-4i}{2-i}$ **6.** $\dfrac{5+6i}{6-5i}$ **7.** $\dfrac{3+2i}{3-2i}$ **8.** $\dfrac{10+10i}{6-8i}$

Example 11.2-4

4 1600.io 11.2

Which of the following complex numbers is equivalent to $\dfrac{7+i}{4-3i}$? (Note: $i = \sqrt{-1}$)

A) $\dfrac{7}{4} - \dfrac{1}{3}i$

B) $\dfrac{7}{4} + \dfrac{1}{3}i$

C) $5 + 5i$

D) $1 + i$

Solution

1. Multiply the numerator and denominator by the complex conjugate of the denominator. The denominator is $4 - 3i$, so its conjugate is $4 + 3i$.

$$\frac{7+i}{4-3i}$$

$$\frac{(7+i)(4+3i)}{(4-3i)(4+3i)}$$

2. Multiply the complex numbers in the numerator and denominator. Combine like terms to simplify.

$$\frac{(7+i)(4+3i)}{(4-3i)(4+3i)}$$

$$\frac{7(4)+7(3i)+i(4)+i(3i)}{4(4)+4(3i)-3i(4)-3i(3i)}$$

$$\frac{28+21i+4i+3i^2}{16+12i-12i-9i^2}$$

$$\frac{28+25i+3i^2}{16-9i^2}$$

3. Since $i^2=-1$, replace i^2 with -1.

$$\frac{28+25i+3(-1)}{16-9(-1)}$$

$$\frac{28+25i-3}{16+9}$$

$$\frac{25+25i}{25}$$

4. Factor 25 out of the numerator since both terms are divisible by 25. Since the factor of 25 in the numerator will cancel with the denominator, we will be left with a complex number that has a separate real part and imaginary part.

$$\frac{25+25i}{25}$$

$$\frac{25(1+i)}{25}$$

$$\frac{\cancel{25}(1+i)}{\cancel{25}}$$

$$1+i$$

5. The answer is D.

View related real-test problems at 1600.io/p/smtex?topic=11.2

Section 11.2 Practice Problems

1 1600.io 11.2

Which of the following complex numbers is equal to $(1 + 11i) - (8i^2 - 2i)$, for $i = \sqrt{-1}$?

A) $9 + 13i$

B) $7 + 9i$

C) $-7 - 9i$

D) $-9 - 13i$

2 1600.io 11.2

$$\frac{2 + 4i}{9 - i}$$

If the expression above is rewritten in the form $a + bi$, where a and b are real numbers, what is the value of a ?

A) $\frac{7}{41}$

B) $\frac{2}{9}$

C) $\frac{19}{41}$

D) $\frac{1}{2}$

CHAPTER 11 RECAP

- For quadratics in Standard Form, $y = ax^2 + bx + c$, where a, b, and c are constants, the discriminant, $b^2 - 4ac$, indicates the number of real zeros.
- When the discriminant is positive, there are 2 real zeros or roots.
- When the discriminant is equal to 0, there is one real zero or root.
- When the discriminant is negative, there are no real zeros or roots, but there are 2 complex zeros or roots, and they are the complex conjugates of one another.
- If a Standard Form quadratic is factorable (or is written in Factored Form to begin with), then it has either one (if the quadratic is a perfect square expression) or two real zeros or roots. There is no need to use the discriminant to check for the number of zeros if you can factor the quadratic.
- If a Vertex Form quadratic is given (or you can use Completing the Square to rewrite a Standard Form quadratic in Vertex Form), you can simply visualize or sketch the parabola to determine the number of intersections with the x-axis (these are x-intercepts, which will represent the zeros or roots) because you will know the position of the vertex and whether the parabola opens up or down. Once again, you can forego the use of the discriminant.
- There is an imaginary number i, and $i = \sqrt{-1}$. It follows that $i^2 = -1$, $i^3 = -i$, and $i^4 = 1$; as with all bases, $i^0 = 1$. For powers higher than 4, the pattern repeats for every set of 4. For example, the next four powers of i are as follows:

  $$i^5 = i$$
  $$i^6 = -1$$
  $$i^7 = -i$$
  $$i^8 = 1$$

  If asked to evaluate the value of i terms with large exponents, find a multiple of 4 that is close to that exponent and count up or down from there to see which of the four primary powers of i it corresponds to. For example i^{35} is equal to i^3 because 35 is 3 more than 32 (a multiple of 4). Similarly, i^{73} is equal to i because 73 is 1 more than 72 (a multiple of 4).
- The complex conjugate of a complex number $a + bi$ is $a - bi$.
- If there is a complex number in the denominator of a fraction, multiply the numerator and denominator by the complex conjugate of the denominator.

Additional Problems

1 1600.io 11.1

In the xy-plane, a line that has the equation $y = c$ for some constant c intersects a parabola at exactly one point. If the parabola has the equation $y = -4x^2 + 3x$, what is the value of c ?

2 1600.io 11.1

$$y = x^2 - 2x + 7$$
$$y - 2x - 3 = 0$$

How many solutions are there to the system of equations above?

A) There are exactly 4 solutions.

B) There are exactly 2 solutions.

C) There is exactly 1 solution.

D) There are no solutions.

3 1600.io 11.1

Which of the following equations has a graph in the xy-plane with no x-intercepts?

A) $y = 3x + 2$

B) $y = -4x^2$

C) $y = x^2 + 6x + 10$

D) $y = x^2 - 6x - 7$

4 1600.io 11.1

$$x^2 - ax + 20 = 0$$

In the equation above, a is a constant and $a > 0$. If the equation has two integer solutions, what is a possible value of a ?

5 11.2

$$i^4 + (-i)^4$$

In the complex number system, what is the value of the given expression? (Note: $i = \sqrt{-1}$)

A) -2

B) 0

C) 2

D) $2i$

6 11.1

If $4x^2 + bx + 4 = 0$, where b is a constant, has exactly one solution, what is a possible value of b ?

A) 4

B) 8

C) 16

D) 64

7 11.2

$$(10 - 2i)(4 + 5i) = a + bi$$

In the equation above, a and b are real numbers and $i = \sqrt{-1}$. What is the value of b ?

8 11.2

In the complex number system, what is the value of the expression $3i^4 - 5i^2 + 1$? (Note: $i = \sqrt{-1}$)

9 1600.io 11.1

$$x = 2y + 2$$
$$y = (3x - 2)(x + 4)$$

How many ordered pairs (x, y) satisfy the system of equations shown above?

A) 0

B) 1

C) 2

D) Infinitely many

10 1600.io 11.2

What is the sum of the complex numbers $3 + 7i$ and $1 + 5i$, where $i = \sqrt{-1}$?

A) 16

B) $16i$

C) $3 + 35i$

D) $4 + 12i$

11 1600.io 11.1

$$kx - y = 3$$
$$y = x^2 - k$$

In the system of equations above, k is a constant. When the equations are graphed in the xy-plane, the graphs intersect at exactly two points. Which of the following CANNOT be the value of k ?

A) 2

B) 3

C) 4

D) 5

12 1600.io 11.2

What is the sum of the complex numbers $5 + 3i$ and $7 + 2i^2$? (Note: $i = \sqrt{-1}$)

A) $10 + 3i$

B) $12 - i$

C) $12 + 5i^3$

D) $14 + 3i$

Answer Key

SkillDrill 11.1-1

1. 2 real roots
2. 2 real roots
3. 2 complex roots
4. 1 real root
5. 2 real roots
6. 2 real roots
7. 2 complex roots
8. 2 complex roots
9. 1 real root
10. 1 real root
11. 2 complex roots
12. 2 real roots

Section 11.1 Practice Problems

1. D
2. C

SkillDrill 11.2-1

1. $5 + 7i$
2. $-2 - 2i$
3. $-1 - i$
4. i
5. $13 - 9i$
6. $3 - 2i$
7. $-4 - 2i$
8. $2 - i$

SkillDrill 11.2-2

1. $\frac{18}{25} + \frac{i}{25}$
2. $\frac{7}{15} + \frac{2i}{5}$
3. $\frac{14}{17} - \frac{5i}{17}$
4. $\frac{i}{2}$
5. 4
6. i
7. $\frac{5}{13} + \frac{12i}{13}$
8. $\frac{-1}{5} + \frac{7i}{5}$

Section 11.2 Practice Problems

1. A
2. A

Additional Problems

1. $\frac{9}{16}$, .562, or .563
2. C
3. C
4. 9, 12, or 21
5. C
6. B
7. 42
8. 9
9. C
10. D
11. A
12. A

Made in the USA
Middletown, DE
23 September 2023